Duel of Eagles

Peter Townsend

DUEL
OF
EAGLES

PRESIDIO ★ PRESS

Published in the United States by arrangement with
Cassell Publishers Limited

First published in Great Britain by Weidenfeld & Nicolson 1970
This edition published 1991

Published in the United States by
Presidio Press, 31 Pamaron Way, Novato, Ca 94949
ISBN 0-89141-432-0

Printed in Great Britain by Butler & Tanner Limited,
Frome and London

FOR MARIE-LUCE

CONTENTS

FOREWORD

I am delighted to have been asked by my long-standing friend, Peter Townsend, to write a foreword to this new edition of *Duel of Eagles*. It is many years since I first read it, and it remains for me one of the few books of its kind to offer a balanced, detailed account of the crucial struggle between the German and British air forces up to the end of 1940 as seen through the eyes of the participants on both sides. The author was one of the most successful RAF fighter pilots of the Battle of Britain and *Duel of Eagles* is stamped with the unique authority of first-hand experience. Through it, too, shines something of Peter Townsend's personality, a man who threw himself heart and soul into the demanding challenge of mastering the technique and art required of a top-class operational fighter pilot, but who through it all remained an essentially compassionate and caring person.

One thing I find particularly interesting in the book is its account of how the *Luftwaffe* was clandestinely built up between the wars in Russia. This is just another factor that helps us to understand the extreme lengths to which Hitler went to prepare the ground for the accomplishment of his diabolical dream of conquest and tyranny. I welcome the reprinting of this excellent book for a number of reasons, not least because it serves to remind us that it was, in large part, because of our manifest unpreparedness that Hitler was able to embark upon that dream at all. If any one factor was decisive in giving the free world time to mobilize its resources, this surely was the foresight of the RAF planners in the pre-war years as much as it was the skill and the courage of the pilots and the support services on the ground.

Leonard Cheshire

ILLUSTRATIONS

Heinkel 111 bomber exploding in mid-air (Imperial War Museum)
Lord Trenchard inspecting a RAF unit (Imperial War Museum)
Air Chief Marshal Sir Hugh Dowding (Imperial War Museum)
Adolph Hitler and his senior air commanders (Südd. Verlag, Munich)
Goering with Ernst Udet (Südd. Verlag, Munich)
Heinkel 111 bomber shot down by Peter Townsend (Thomson Newspapers Ltd)
Karl Missy (Karl Missy)
Peter Townsend with his rigger and fitter (Imperial War Museum)
General Hans von Seeckt and General von Blomberg (Ullstein Bilderdienst, Berlin)
Trainee pilots of the *Deutsche Verkehrsflieger Schule* (*Oberst* Johannes Janke)
The town of Lipezk
General Werner Junck with his flight engineer (General Werner Junck)
An aspect of the Battle, as seen by *Punch* (*Punch*)
Heinkel 111 bomber over the London docks (Imperial War Museum)

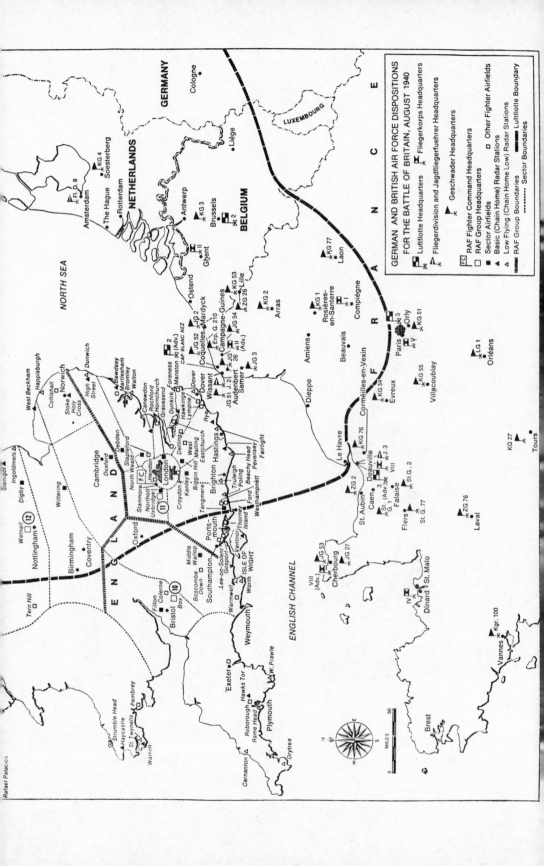

GERMAN AND BRITISH AIR FORCE DISPOSITIONS
FOR THE BATTLE OF BRITAIN, AUGUST 1940

Luftflotte Headquarters
Fliegerkorps Headquarters
Fliegerdivision and Jagdfliegerfuehrer Headquarters
Geschwader Headquarters

RAF Fighter Command Headquarters
RAF Group Headquarters
Sector Airfields   Other Fighter Airfields
Basic (Chain Home) Radar Stations
Low Flying (Chain Home Low) Radar Stations
RAF Group Boundaries   Luftflotte Boundary
                          Sector Boundaries

Rafael Palacios

ACKNOWLEDGMENTS

It is always interesting, if not vital, to see both sides of a question. So when Robert Laffont asked me to write a book on the Battle of Britain I lost no time in going off to Germany to talk to the men who fought against us in 1940. My researches continued in Great Britain and France for over two years. Everywhere I received invaluable help and I can only express here a small token of my gratitude, especially for those personal stories so rich in human interest. I ask to be forgiven for any omissions I may have made.

Robert Wright, Lord Dowding's Boswell, helped me with part of my historical research, gathering for me, with the kind approval of our one time commander-in-chief, many of the latter's personal recollections and extracts from his private notes and correspondence. If, after some months on the job, Robert Wright's researches inspired him to write his own book on Lord Dowding, I can at least find some pleasure in having contributed indirectly to an understanding of history.

Thanks to the kindness of Henry Erlich, of *Look* magazine, who had a remarkably frank interview with Lord Dowding and allowed me to see the transcript, I was greatly enlightened.

Air Chief Marshal Sir Keith Park, my Group Commander in the Battle of Britain, made a warm and full response to my questions and I am grateful to him for the information he gave me, and to Anne Meo and the BBC for the tape-recorded interviews.

I owe a very special debt of gratitude to Richard Collier, author of *Eagle Day*, who saved me an immense amount of labour in allowing me to consult his own notes and documents, including many from the Karlsruhe Collection, translated by Nadia Radowitz.

From the very start of this project I benefited greatly from the friendship and long experience of Mr Louis Jackets, Head of the Air Historical Branch, Ministry of Defence. I deeply appreciate the help he gave me right up to the last, when he and his assistant, Miss A. N. Marks, read the manuscript at record speed for official approval. I am grateful for his permission to consult British and German documents, the property of the Ministry of Defence, and to Mr Gately for helping me to find my way among them.

I acknowledge with thanks the permission of the Ministry of Defence and of the Controller of Her Majesty's Stationery Office to quote from combat reports, operational records, Controllers' Instructions and other official correspondence, and from Lord Dowding's Despatch published in a Supplement to the *London Gazette* of 10 September 1946.

My thanks go to Pamela Colman for contacting many of my comrades who fought in the Battle of Britain and passing on to them my searching questions; I shall not forget how readily they responded. First I must salute Group Captain Tom Gleave for the wealth of information he provided; it went far beyond his personal experiences for, as a senior committee member of the Battle of Britain Association and holding important office in the Ministry of Defence Air Historical Branch, he guided me and put a great amount of official research at my disposal. He also allowed me to use material which went into his own book, *I had a Row with a German*.

There are many others to whom I give my warmest thanks for talking to me of their experiences and for the trouble they took in writing them down for my use: Lord Willoughby de Broke, Air Commodores Alan Deere, Ian MacDougall and John Thompson; Group Captains Douglas Bader, Denys Gillam, James McComb and Norman Ryder; Wing Commanders Mindon Blake, E. 'Gus' Holden, Eric Douglas Jones, Robert Stanford Tuck and Innes Westmacott.

I am sincerely grateful to my friend Michel Nastorg for his poignant story of Dunkirk; to Mrs J. M. Robinson for permission to quote from the diary and letters of her late brother, Bill Millington; to Gérard Ingold for permission to quote from the sensitive book he has written about his late brother Charles, *Un Matin Bien Rempli*; to Leonard Mosley for filling me in further on some passages of his book, *On Borrowed Time*; to Alfred Price for allowing me to consult his personal notes and to use extracts from his book, *German Bombers*; to Peter Breedon for the Saint Mellon's Golf Club Rules, by Major G. L. Edsell; to Miss Wynne Lewis for permission to quote from her unpublished MS, *On the Invasion Doorstep in Sussex*; to Mr Will Barratt for permission to quote from a letter written by his late brother, Arthur Barratt; to the Newcastle *Sunday Sun* and Mr Roy Anderson, Assistant Editor, for the articles in their series, 'The Day of the Eagles'; to Christopher R. Elliott for his article on *Luftwaffe* target documents, published in the *East Anglian Magazine*; to the BBC for Charles Gardner's broadcast on 14 July 1940; to Christopher Doll for allowing me to use extracts from the filmed interview we did together with *Generalfeldmarschall* Milch; to Harry Saltzman, Benjamin Fisz and Spitfire Productions, producers of the film *The Battle of Britain* for allowing me to consult their Chronological Summary and to play with the British and German aircraft used in the filming.

To turn now to my German sources, I am especially grateful to Eduard Neumann, Secretary General of the German Fighter Pilots' Association, and to Frau Neumann for their warm hospitality and the endless trouble they took in putting me in touch with other German fighter pilots, and with Herr Hans Ring, the German fighter pilots' accredited historian. Hans Ring sat up with me to all hours of the night as we consulted his own work, *German Fighter Forces in World War Two*, and his private notes; he also recounted many anecdotes which have been useful to me. As if that were not enough he often acted as interpreter during the lengthy talks I had with ex-*Luftwaffe* pilots.

The record for these Marathon talks was seven and a half hours spent on end with *Hauptmann* Otto Hintze. I am deeply grateful to him for welcoming me so kindly to his home, as well as to the many others who received me with similar kindness and whose tales of the secret base of Lipezk, of *Lufthansa* and the *Luftwaffe* form one of the main themes of my book: *Generalfeldmarschall* Erhard Milch and his son-in-law, *Oberst* Joachim Schlichting; Generals Werner Junck, Carl August von Schoenebeck, Werner Streib, Hannes Trautloft, Dietrich Hrabach, Gebhard Greiling and – the first and the last (as the title of his excellent book goes) General Adolf Galland, whose friendship and help have been precious.

Others to whom I am deeply grateful on the fighter side are Galland's wing-man, General Gustav Rödel, Major Werner Andres and Dr Helmut Rau, who helped me with stories and research; and still others whom I questioned for hours while enjoying their hospitality: *Oberst* Johannes Janke, *Oberst* Claus von Below (Hitler's aide), Major Hans-Heinrich Brustellin, *Hauptmann* Paul Temme and Frau Josef Priller, widow of the redoubtable Major 'Pips' Priller, who lived through the Battle of Britain to be the only *Luftwaffe* pilot, with his wing-man, to attack the invading allied armies on 6 June 1944.

On the bomber side, I owe a very sincere debt of gratitude to *Oberst* Werner Borner and Herr Karl Missy. Thanks to them I have been able to relate how we came to meet in a duel which nearly ended in the death of all of us.

Oberst Robert Kowalewski, President of the German Bombers' Association, put me in touch with a number of bomber pilots. I am grateful to him, and to General Hannes Heise, *Oberst* Werner Kanther, *Oberst*

Joachim Helbig and *Oberst* Hajo Hermann for their invaluable help in constructing my story. I had long and fascinating conversations with *Hauptmann* Rudolf Braun, who survived 500 *Stuka* missions, and with *Oberst* Joachim Poetter; it was through the thought and trouble of 'Bob' Poetter that after 28 years I was able to meet Werner Borner. Finally, I have to thank General Josef Kammhuber for the frank discussion we had in his home about the 'Freiburg Incident', in which his unit, *KG* 51, was involved.

Air Commodore Frank Beaumont, who knew Goering and Udet well since the first war and was air attaché in Prague, Vienna and Budapest during the critical five years before the second war, gave me some invaluable background information on the build-up of German air power. I am grateful to Frau Emmy Goering for inviting me to spend the evening with her in her home and to her daughter Edda for acting as such a sensitive interpreter; both were caught up in a tragedy which they bear today with courage and dignity.

In diverse ways I have received help, for which I am sincerely grateful, from *Generaloberst* Kurt Student, President of the Deutsche Luftwaffen-block; Doctor Jürgen Rohwer, head of the Bibliothek für Zeitgeschichte; Herr Noack and Herr Ziggel, of the Bundesarchiv-Militärarchiv; and Doctor Arenz, of the Militärgeschichtliches Forschungsamt.

Bild Zeitung, of Hamburg, did me a great service in putting me in touch with Karl Missy, as did *Time & Life*, Bad Godesberg, to whose director, Hermann Nickel, and Leny Heinen, I am grateful for finding a splendid collaborator in the person of Alexandra von Buckwald. Her intelligent and painstaking research into German publications and documents was of the greatest help. Elizabeth Leslie, too, with her command of German and her keen flair for detail, did sterling work in helping me interview *Luftwaffe* pilots.

The following books have been of particular help to me: Andrew Boyle's fine study of the greatest of British airmen, *Trenchard*; William Shirer's monumental work, *The Rise and Fall of the Third Reich*; Alan Bullock's *Hitler; A Study in Tyranny*; Willi Frischauer's *Göring*; Winston Churchill's *The Second World War*, Volume II – Their Finest Hour; Telford Taylor's *The Breaking Wave*; Walter Ansel's *Hitler Confronts England*; Ronald Wheatley's *Operation Sea Lion*; Paul Stehlin's *Témoignage pour l'Histoire*; Derek Wood's and Derek Dempster's *The Narrow Margin*; Basil Collier's *The Defence of the United Kingdom*; James Beedle's *History of 43 Squadron*; Cajus Bekker's *Luftwaffe War Diaries* (Angriffshöhe 4000); Richard Collier's *Eagle Day*; Alan Deere's *Nine Lives*; Paul Brickhill's

Reach for the Sky; Larry Forrester's *Fly for your Life*; Hector Bolitho's *Combat Report*; Adolf Galland's *The First and the Last* (*Die Ersten und die Letzen*); Theo Osterkamp's *Avant tout Pilote de Chasse* (*Dürch höhen und Tiefen jagt ein Herz*).

I am indebted to Mr Richard Collier for lending me manuscripts from the Karlsruhe Collection and for putting at my disposal (with the permission of Mr I. Quimby Tobin) the private diary of Pilot Officer Eugene Tobin. I am also grateful to Mr Collier for allowing me to make direct use of eye-witness accounts gathered by him from Mr J. J. Cotterell of the Auxiliary Fire Service, Surrey Docks, London; Corporal Avis Hearn, WAAF, Radar Station, Poling; Constable Ernest Hooper, Catford, South London; Squadron Leader Zdzislaw Krasnodebski, 303 (Polish) Squadron, Northolt; Mr Sid Sharvill and Inspector 'Jock' Thompson, GPO, Tunbridge Wells.

I was very fortunate in being able to count on the moral support and the wide experience of certain friends. Robert Laffont, my publisher in Paris, said at the outset, 'This is going to be our book'; he kept his word. Michael Korda, of Simon and Schuster, after reading the original manuscript, made many wise suggestions which enabled me to improve it considerably. Many helpful comments came, too, from Georges Belmont, of Editions Robert Laffont; I am profoundly grateful to them both for their advice and encouragement. I owe a further debt to Georges who, with Hortense Chabrier, rendered my English so vividly and faithfully into French and attended to the endless details involved in transforming my manuscript into a book. It was always a pleasure to work with them.

Heide Herzog rendered me invaluable service in translating pages and pages of German texts and I am grateful to her for the impressions of Berlin during the first RAF raids. Françoise Claude also gave me valuable help in translating German documents; and Olga Robertson had the courage to type 700 pages of manuscript.

During the seven months I spent writing them, my wife lived with a phantom husband who showed up only at meals and crept into bed in the small hours of the morning. She showed rare courage in seeing me through to the last line.

Prologue
3 February 1940

'Standby, standby, standby . . .' The steady voice of the girl duty operator at Danby Beacon Radar Station on the Yorkshire coast, was heard two hundred miles away by another girl at Fighter Command Headquarters.

At that moment, 9.03 a.m. on 3 February 1940, Heinkel 111 No. 3232 of the 'Lion' *Kampfgeschwader* 26 was approaching the English coast. 'Hostile 2 now at thirty-five miles, Charlie 2710. Height one thousand,' said the quiet voice from Danby Beacon. Fighter Command flashed the information to 13 Group Headquarters at Newcastle.

A few miles up the coast, at Royal Air Force Acklington, the telephone rang in 43 Squadron Pilots' room. 'Blue section scramble,' and a few minutes later three Hurricane fighters rose into the chilly morning air.

I was in the lead, Folkes and Hallowes following close in my wake. 'Vector 180, Bandit off Whitby, Angels one.' We raced south at full throttle, a few feet above the waves, to have the best chance of seeing the enemy first.

'*Achtung, Jäger!*' Suddenly Peter Leushake, the Heinkel's observer, saw three fighters curving up steeply from below. The words were hardly past his lips when bullets ripped into the Heinkel and killed him. At the same instant, in the lower gun position, Johann Meyer, the flight engineer, was badly wounded. Only *Unteroffizier* Karl Missy, in the top rear gun position, remained to defend the stricken aircraft. He aimed carefully and fired at the leading Hurricane. His single MG15 machine-gun was a feeble answer to the eight ·303 Brownings of the British fighter, which was firing again. Missy never moved from his swivel seat at the gun position. He knew the fighter's second volley had hit him, but how badly he could not tell.

Hermann Wilms, the pilot, pulled the Heinkel up into the cloudlayer just above, but the speed dropped off sharply until the bomber sagged in his hands and he knew the engines were hit. It was a mile or two to the coast, but somehow Wilms made it, gliding low over Whitby Town.

At that moment the Castle Park bus had just stopped on the Parade, and a woman who got off had the fright of her life when she saw the Heinkel loom just overhead, so low that she caught sight of Wilms through the cabin window and the black swastika on the Heinkel's tail. To her and to hundreds who were now watching with her the swastika meant one thing only: a Nazi. This was one of Hitler's bombers and it had brought the war to Whitby.

Unteroffizier Missy was in a serious condition when I visited him in Whitby hospital next day. I brought him a tin of Players cigarettes, small compensation for what I had done to him and his comrades. I was sorry for him, not for my actions. Afterwards I often thought of the mute, pathetic look he gave me and the way he clasped my hand, but never that I should see him again.

Twenty-eight years later in Rheydt, Missy opened the door for me of the home where he was born and where he now lives. In the hours that followed he told me how he came to join the *Luftwaffe* and to be in Heinkel 3232 that day.

We and a few hundred others on both the German and British sides were of the second generation of airmen, born when the aeroplane, too, was in its infancy. My story tells how some of us came to fight each other to the death over England in the summer of 1940.

Missy's Heinkel made the news next day. 'It was the first enemy plane to crash on English soil in this war, the RAF's previous success having been in Scotland,' announced the Whitby *Gazette* with a nice touch of north-country pride.

On 3 February 1940 a tall, straight man with a voice of thunder was celebrating his birthday. In his own service – and no one more than he could call it his own, for he had built it – everybody called him 'Boom'. Marshal of the RAF, Lord Trenchard, was sixty-seven that day. It was a trivial, but perhaps not entirely irrelevant coincidence. . . .

Part One

THE
FLEDGLING
YEARS

Chapter 1

On 18 May 1918, General Trenchard had arrived at Nancy, France, to take command of a small fleet of bombers – about one hundred in all. His mission was to pay back in kind the bombs which the Germans had been raining down on England during the last three years. The very next night forty-three Gotha bombers of the Imperial German Air Service set out for London. Six crashed, one in Kent at Harrietsham. Although the British did not know it at the time, that Gotha was to be the last German plane to crash on English soil until Missy's Heinkel slid to a standstill outside Bannial Flat Farm on 3 February 1940 . . .

Kaiser William himself had given the green light for the German air offensive against England in January 1915. He had strong popular support. Full of enthusiasm for the graceful, gigantic Zeppelin airships, the German people and press were at one with the German High Command in believing that the Zeppelins would break the will of the English: they had visions of London in flames. Under cover of darkness, these giant dirigible airships roamed at will, scattering their bombs over south-east England and the fringes of London. At first they caused negligible damage and killed relatively few people, but they were a nuisance, and the public indignation they provoked made the British government uneasy. Then on the night of 8 September 1915, *Kapitänleutnant* Heinrich Mathy, the commander of naval Zeppelin L13, cruised majestically and unimpeded over London to drop half a ton of bombs into its heart. The toll in property and lives was heavy. That night Germany took the first significant step towards a new kind of warfare: strategic bombing. The objective of Mathy's mission was of course ostensibly military: but as most targets were situated in residential areas, defenceless citizens of all ages and both sexes were bound to be killed.

Strategic bombing or, more realistically, total air warfare, is a German invention, though in their turn the English later directed it against Germany. Both sides soon realized that if indiscriminate slaughter of civilians from the air had a desirable effect on the enemy's morale then civilians were as natural a strategic target as munitions factories. If civilian morale was the easiest target to hit, it was also the hardest to destroy. The sole redeeming feature of this barbarous new form of warfare was to be that it fired the courage of ordinary people.

Trenchard had been appointed General Officer Commanding the Royal Flying Corps (the British Army air service) on 19 August 1915. The new C-in-C had the stature, the heart, and the voice of a giant. His aide-de-camp, Maurice Baring, wrote of him at this time that he was 'tall, straight as a ramrod, covering the ground quickly with huge strides and forcing his shorter aide to move in a quaint kind of turkey-trot at his side, trying to keep up with him.'

The task of Trenchard's squadrons was to give support, protection, and reconnaissance for the army battling in the Flanders fields below, and to those squadrons he gave all his immense and aggressive energy. He spared neither himself nor his squadron commanders in their struggle to wrest from the Germans permanent command of the air.

Anyone not for Trenchard was against him. In July 1915, a month before he relinquished command of the First Wing to take up his new post, he received a complaint from the commanding officer of No. 16 Squadron that a batch of wrong sized propellers had just been delivered. Trenchard was infuriated by the young officer's 'pernickety primness'. 'You'll fit those propellers, and I want no argument. That's an order,' he boomed at the squadron commander, Major Hugh Dowding. Dowding risked his own neck making the first test flight, which proved the propellers unfit. Dowding thought this incident typical of Trenchard's 'technical stupidity'; Trenchard thought it revealed Dowding's 'self-righteous stubbornness'.

While Trenchard built up his squadrons in France, the German Zeppelins continued to bomb an almost defenceless England. The new year was hardly in when nine Zeppelins attacked the Midlands and killed fifty-nine civilians. This time the public clamoured loudly for something to be done about the hopelessly inadequate home air defences. Yet the death-roll mounted. In April 1916 naval Zeppelins reached as far north as Scotland, where eighty-four more civilians were killed.

But to Trenchard, far away at St Omer, the deaths of a few hundred civilians and the destruction of a million pounds' worth of property were of less concern than the bitter, relentless war his pilots were waging against the Fokker *Eindeckers* of Major Stempel's *Kampfeinzitzercommandos* and

6

the airmen led by Max Immelmann and Oswald Boelcke – among whom was an unknown young lieutenant, Manfred von Richthofen.

In June 1916 Trenchard's advance headquarters were in the little village of Fienvillers, near Doullens in the Somme department. The Headquarters Wing possessed four squadrons. Its wing commander, Hugh Dowding, was now a twenty-four-year-old lieutenant-colonel. His natural reserve and somewhat solemn countenance had earned him the nickname 'Stuffy'. Few realized that his forbidding exterior, his 'pernickety primness' as Trenchard had called it, concealed an unexpected depth of feeling.

In the House of Commons critical voices were raised against Trenchard for accepting heavy losses among his pilots in France while German Zeppelins cruised unscathed in the English skies. 'I see they have been talking in the House as if I was afraid of being shot at and . . . that I never go over the lines,' he wrote to General Henderson. 'I hope you'll ask these political people whether they're prepared to come as my passenger.' Trenchard in fact felt deeply about the losses of his airmen but seldom betrayed the sadness it caused him. His deepest conviction was that in this new three-dimensional form of warfare it was impossible to survive simply by remaining on the defensive. The only way to defeat the enemy in the air was to attack. In any event, Trenchard, like every other commander, had little time to spare from the urgent and intensive preparations for yet another 'great offensive' – the first battle of the Somme.

At 4.45 a.m. on 1 July, the British infantry went over the top into a murderous storm of gunfire. Eight hours later, fifty thousand of them were dead. Such bloody slaughter was absent from the air war – still a highly individual form of combat – but proportionately, the toll of life was as high. What Trenchard wrote at the end of the first week of the Somme offensive sounds incongruous: 'I have lost eight machines in low bombing. I am afraid the pilots are getting a bit rattled . . .' Dowding however puts it more prosaically: 'The Germans could attack our small patrols in greatly superior numbers and [our] casualty rate was about 100% a month.'

If the fury of the land battle died down towards the end of August, there was no let-up in the air fighting. The violent air fighting steadily thinned out the British flyers' ranks. But by September 1916 Trenchard and his airmen, through sheer, dogged aggressiveness, had swept the German *Staffeln* from the French skies. The achievement of air supremacy over the Western Front was, however, to be short-lived and continually challenged. Germany's air power was symbolized by the rising star of a single, charismatic flyer. On 23 November Manfred von Richthofen, of the *Boelcke Jasta*, claimed his eleventh victim. The new year was hardly in when he added four more British airmen to his score, and on 17 January 1917 he was awarded the coveted blue enamel cross of the *Ordre Pour le Mérite*, Germany's highest military decoration.

That day, led by Major Sholto Douglas, 43 Squadron of the Royal Flying Corps, left Northolt near London for Treizenne in France. For reasons that Lieutenant Harold Ward, Sholto Douglas's observer, described as 'lousy weather, engines conking out and just getting lost', it was a full week before 43 arrived at its destination. By that time Richthofen had left the *Boelcke Jasta* to take command of *Jasta* 11. He came into his own at a time when German and British airmen were clawing each other out of the sky with unrelenting fury. 'Nearly every day,' wrote Sholto Douglas, 'somebody was wounded or missing.' Within three months of their arrival there were only six survivors from 43 Squadron's original strength of thirty-two officers.

Opposite 43 was *Jasta* 11. B Flight Commander Captain Harold Balfour wrote, 'We were up against Richthofen's Circus ... we would watch these gaily painted Albatrosses gambolling around each other ... looping and rolling and spinning, just like puppies playing with each other.' On the approach of 43 Squadron's Sopwith 'Pups' the German fighters would draw off up-sun and come swooping down. 'Beware of the Hun in the sun.'

On 4 March 1917 Richthofen pounced on one of 43 Squadron's aircraft whose pilot was obviously new to the deadly game of aerial combat. At first he did not notice that he was under fire, let alone attacked by Germany's most famous ace. Then he turned violently and a wing broke away. Richthofen noted with disappointment that 'only the Lewis guns Nos. 17500 and 20024 were recoverable', for he was an ardent souvenir collector as well as a killer, and adorned his study with relics of his victims' aircraft.

43 Squadron again fell foul of the Red Knight on 2 April. Richthofen's first burst of machine-gun fire mortally wounded Sergeant Dunn, the gunner in Lieutenant Warren's aircraft, and his second attack reduced the aircraft practically to scrap. But it continued to glide down out of the fight as Richthofen came in again. Warren was miraculously untouched by the bullets which ripped through his shoes and shirtsleeves. At last he managed to crashland, and as he helped Dunn the German ace attacked for the last time. Richthofen claimed 'he had been hit by several shots ... from the enemy machine as he flew over it.' In fact the brave Warren's preoccupation with his dying gunner precluded anything of the kind.

Harold Balfour says the men of 43 Squadron soon found the best way to protect themselves was to 'go round and round in a circle . . . each chasing the next machine in front . . . then edge slowly towards the lines.' (Twenty-three years later when I was B Flight commander in 43 Squadron, it was the Messerschmitt 110's which had to go into a 'defensive circle' as we dived on them in our fighters.) If the British fighters left the circle they were in for trouble. Balfour noted the consequences of this error. 'The wings were shot off a machine in front of me and one of my best young pilots, a South African named Rimer, and his observer, were pitched out into space . . . I watched Rimer's bright leather coat as his body fell . . . I could follow it for thousands of feet.'

Though a pack-type parachute was in use in the USA as early as 1912 the airmen of 1917 fought without parachutes. The subject of parachutes was mentioned among the members of the Advisory Committee on Aeronautics in 1917. Mr J.L.Nayler, then Assistant Secretary, well recalls that one of the members (it was possibly O'Gorman of the Royal Aircraft Factory) said that General Trenchard would not have pilots equipped with parachutes as he did not want them to desert their aircraft, just as a naval captain was expected not to abandon his ship. 'Bloody murder,' was Sholto Douglas's comment, on hearing this.

One of the mysteries about Trenchard was that his pilots worshipped him as much as he did them. Harold Balfour remembers, 'Trenchard came to the squadron just when our losses were at their worst . . . and told us to stick it, and that we should have to continue to suffer casualties but that at all costs we must maintain a moral ascendancy by keeping at our daily task of offensive patrols . . .'

The major effort of the Royal Flying Corps was directed against the German squadrons in Flanders and France, but to the discomfort of the *Luftschiffsabteilung*'s Zeppelins some steps had been taken to strengthen England's home air defences. In the early hours of 3 September Lieutenants Leefe Robinson and Fred Sowrey of 39 Squadron were on patrol when Robinson sighted Zeppelin SL11. His deadly shooting transformed the wooden-framed airship into a blazing funeral pyre in which the sixteen brave men of its crew perished. Turning night into day, it plunged like a fiery comet into the ground near Cuffley, Middlesex.

It was the turn of Fred Sowrey on the night of 23 September, when eleven Zeppelins headed for England. One of them, L32, was over Dungeness at 1.00 a.m., hit by AA fire and held in the dazzling searchlight beams. At 1.10 a.m. Sowrey dived on L32, and in the words of a pilot patrolling nearby, 'hosed it with a stream of fire'. Fred Sowrey wrote in his combat report, 'I could distinctly see the propellers revolving. The first two drums of ammunition had no effect, but the third caused . . . fire in several places. I watched the burning aircraft strike the ground . . .' Luckily for him he could neither see nor hear the last moments of the men he had immolated in an inferno clearly visible to the crew of a British submarine in the Straits of Dover sixty miles away.

On the night of 1 October 1916 *Kapitänleutnant* Mathy, who had opened the new age of strategic bombing just over a year before, died in the flames of Zeppelin L31, shot down by Second Lieutenant Tempest, who described the Zeppelin's end: 'I noticed her begin to go red inside like an enormous Chinese lantern. She came roaring down on to me. I nose-dived with the Zeppelin tearing after me, roaring like a furnace.'

Dismayed but undeterred by the Zeppelins' failure to reduce London to ashes, the German High Command redoubled their efforts. On 28 November Lieutenants Brandt and Ilges flew over Victoria station in broad daylight and dropped six bombs.

By May 1917 the plans of the German High Command for a new air offensive were ready, this time using heavy bomber aircraft. On 25 May twenty-one Gotha bombers crossed the English coast, but on that occasion the weather saved London – as it would do on many occasions in the future. In a futile gesture which killed several British citizens without advancing the war the Gothas dropped their bombs over Kent. They then returned unmolested, save for the loss of one machine, to their base at Ghent. After another unsuccessful attempt to reach London, *Hauptmann* Brandenburg, leader of the *England Geschwader*, at last realized his dream. From two miles up above London at 11.35 on 13 June he was able to report that 'the Thames bridges, the railway stations, the City, even the Bank of England could be recognized . . . Our aircraft dropped their bombs without any hurry or trouble . . .' It needed about seven tons of them to kill 162 Londoners and injure 426. A single British aircraft attempted to intercept them, but flying on unperturbed in diamond formation, the Gothas killed its observer with their return fire.

This attack brought from the British public a roar of rage and indignation. The Government reacted at once. They sent for Trenchard. The chief of the Royal Flying Corps presented himself before the War Cabinet on 20 June 1917.

There was nothing original in the defensive air strategy that Trenchard proposed to the Cabinet. It was modelled on the defensive strategy that England had practised since the attempted invasion of the Armada in the sixteenth century: first, capture the Belgian coast where the enemy is based. Defensive patrols by fighters would be necessary, just as were naval patrols, but with no early warning system a prohibitive number of men and machines would be needed to maintain the continuous standing patrols which alone could provide a reliable means of defence. Trenchard firmly insisted that the best form of defence lay in attacking from the air the enemy's bases, machines and hangars. Finally, he stated with a cold, detached logic that, 'Reprisals on open towns are repugnant to British ideas, but we may have to adopt them. It would be worse than useless to do so unless . . . they will be carried through to the end . . . Unless we are determined to go one better than the Germans, it will be infinitely better not to attempt reprisals at all.'

The Prime Minister, David Lloyd George, insisted angrily that 'We must bomb Mannheim at once.' But Trenchard refused. For want of bases close enough the raid would be a dismal failure, and he was in any case against the kind of sensational revenge that the Prime Minister wanted. 'Then you must send us two crack fighter squadrons from France to defend London,' said Lloyd George. Within a few days 56 and 66 Squadrons stood at readiness at their bases in Essex. But Trenchard went on record against the move. 'By bombing raids against London and England,' he declared, '[the enemy] have tried, trusting to their effect on public opinion . . . to make us dislocate our flying forces in the field.'

After two weeks of uneventful patrolling 56 and 66 Squadrons returned to France. Within a few hours the Gothas were back over London. On 7 July 1917 the members and staff of the Air Board crowded on to the balconies of the Hotel Cecil (their headquarters in the Strand), craning their necks to watch twenty-two Gothas three miles up in a clear sky begin their run-in over the city in perfect formation. Making short shrift of the defending fighters, they dropped ten tons of bombs, taking two hundred and fifty civilian casualties.

This new assault so outraged the public, press and politicians alike that the Chief of the Imperial General Staff wrote, 'One would have thought the whole world was coming to an end.' Lloyd George, deeply shaken, insisted once more on bombing Mannheim. Trenchard replied from France, 'We must stop the bombing of London, but the only way to do it is to knock out completely the German aviation here . . . There is no doubt that we ought to do bombing and directly you can get me de Havilland 4s I will . . . start the bombing of Mannheim.'

Two days after the raid General Robertson expressed the growing weight of opinion: 'I am inclined to think that we need a separate air service, but that would mean a big business . . .' Lloyd George too, had arrived at this conclusion. Jan Christiaan Smuts, the South African general and statesman, was to inquire into the matter.

By August 1917 Smuts had produced two reports documenting the lamentable state of England's air defences and his suggestions as to how they could best be remedied. With the wisdom and vision of a prophet he wrote, 'The day may not be far off when aerial operations with their . . . destruction of industrial and populace centres on a vast scale . . . may become the principal operations of war . . .' Irrelevant as this seemed at the time, the logic of Smuts's proposal to amalgamate the military and naval air services under one separate air ministry appealed to the harassed Prime Minister. Trenchard, fearing that it would fatally weaken the air forces under his control in France, was at first one of the many who opposed it.

While the great men were deliberating, the German air force struck once more. On 24 September a minor air raid on London led the Westminster *Gazette* to state that the Prime Minister had hurriedly left the capital to avoid the bombs. The statement was untrue and would have serious consequences for the newspaper's owner and the President of the Air Board, Lord Cowdray, as well as for the air force which was then in a state of gestation.

From 27–30 September German Zeppelins and Gothas raided London in earnest. On the first day of October General Robertson wired to France, 'Cabinet desires immediate action against . . . German objectives . . . Send Trenchard over at once . . .' Next day in London the War Cabinet were again hanging on Trenchard's words. 'The airfield at Ochey, near Nancy, is ready,' he told them. 'Send me the aircraft and within a week I will strike back at Germany.'

He kept his word. On 17 October half a dozen de Havilland bombers took off on the first British long-range raid against Germany. The Burbach iron foundry near Saarbrücken was hit in broad daylight. Then the giant Handley Page bombers of the Royal Naval Air Service joined the de Havillands of the Royal Flying Corps. It was now the turn of defenceless German citizens to be killed from the air.

On 15 November the table at No. 10 Downing Street was set for two: Lloyd George was lunching in private with Lord Northcliffe, owner of the *The Times* and the *Daily Mail*. 'I would sooner go for a sunny evening stroll . . . with a grasshopper as try and work with Lord Northcliffe,' the Prime Minister had once said. Yet now he was offering him the post of

First Air Minister. Lloyd George had his reasons. Lord Cowdray had for the past eleven months been the successful President of the Air Board. Although the Prime Minister had exacted damages and apologies for the Westminster *Gazette*'s defamatory article of 25 September, he was determined to avoid rewarding Cowdray with the new position. Well before the luncheon was over, Lloyd George felt sure that he had his man in Northcliffe.

But a disconcerting telephone call from Max Beaverbrook that evening warned him of the worst. Next morning Lloyd George read in *The Times* an open letter addressed to him by Northcliffe. After explaining that he must decline the post of Air Minister, Northcliffe ended: 'I can do better work if I maintain my independence and am not gagged by a loyalty I do not feel to . . . your administration' – which he described as wobbling and unworthy of the people of Britain.

The first candidate for Air Minister having turned on him, Lloyd George turned to the second, Northcliffe's younger brother Lord Rothermere, who accepted. On 29 November the Air Force Bill received the Royal Assent. It only remained to find a Chief of Air Staff.

The scene of this shameful drama then moved to Rothermere's private suite in the Ritz Hotel in London, where Trenchard had been summoned without warning from France on 16 December. It was the first time he had met Rothermere, and he did not like him. The new Air Minister wanted him as Chief of the Air Staff, but his motive made Trenchard turn the offer down flat. 'My brother and I are going to start a press campaign against Haig [the C-in-C of the British Army in France] . . .' he told him. Rothermere's aim, which had the tacit support of Lloyd George, was to use Trenchard in his role as head of the new air force to oppose the demands of the army in France for air support – in other words, to destroy everything Trenchard's airmen had won in the last sixteen months.

In Trenchard's own words, 'I warned them that I would not fight against the army and navy during the war, but the arguments got hotter and more unpleasant.' When they ended at 3.30 a.m. the following morning, Trenchard was exhausted. The two brothers had worn him down and he finally agreed to become Chief of the Air Staff, believing that by accepting he could best serve and protect the Royal Flying Corps and the Naval Air Service, though he knew that 'I should have to fight Rothermere and Northcliffe from the day I took the job.'

Within hours of parting that day at the Ritz, the Air Minister and his Chief of Air Staff crossed swords. Rothermere wrote saying the War

Cabinet was uneasy about preparations for the long range bombing offensive against Germany. Trenchard retorted, 'I am uneasy about other people being uneasy about ... the preparations for the long range bombing. I am responsible for it ... but if they cannot trust me then I cannot see the object in your asking me to come as Chief of Air Staff.' Meanwhile, under the command of Major Cyril Newall, preparations were going ahead with the willing help of the French at Nancy.

Hotel Cecil, in the Strand, was in the beginning of 1918 headquarters for the Air Board (which in a few weeks was to become the Air Council). In the words of that keen observer of air matters, C.G.Grey, it was 'one of those grim mid-Victorian edifices which was full of gilt mouldings and aspidistras. The atmosphere was enough to kill any enterprise that any of its inmates ever had.' Someone nicknamed it Bolo House, after a Frenchman who had been shot for spying. Grey said that the name 'tickled our curiously warped English sense of humour' and that Bolo House was so named because everybody in it was 'either actively interfering with the progress of the war, or doing nothing to help ...'

It was in this grim environment that the friction between Trenchard and Rothermere steadily increased. At the end of January Trenchard managed to steal a couple of days to visit in France with his old chief, Haig. He opened his heart to him, and Haig wrote in his diary for 26 January, 'General Trenchard came to dinner. He could think and talk nothing else but the rascally ways of politicians and newspaper men.' And again, 'Lord Rothermere ... is quite ignorant of the needs or working of the air service ...' On 11 February Trenchard wrote, 'The great curse of this place is that there are too many officers doing different jobs...' In fact of the 207 officers in Bolo House only twenty-nine were pilots. A few days later the harassed Chief of Air Staff wrote, 'My worries at home are increasing ... I come up against snags every day in making this air service.'

The biggest snag was Lord Rothermere. On 18 March matters between the two men came to a head. Incensed by the 'failures and shortcomings and delays of the past' Trenchard wrote to Rothermere, 'I am your adviser on these matters ... if you have not sufficient confidence in me even to tell me what is happening ... in my own department I consider ... the situation ... an impossible one.' Replying, Rothermere pretended there was never any question about Trenchard's position.

'You are Chief of Staff and are my principal, not sole, adviser . . . it is always open to the political heads of any departments to confer . . . with whomsoever they please without consultation with their Chiefs of Staff . . .

Before noon the next day Trenchard's letter of resignation reached Rothermere's office, shortly followed by Trenchard himself. Rothermere pleaded with him to stay: he himself was shortly to resign. Would Trenchard postpone his resignation until then? To his own cost, Trenchard agreed.

In France, less than forty-eight hours after this cold exchange between the two men, a million Germans were sweeping forward in the mist on to the British positions. The British were quickly overrun and retired behind the Somme. Trenchard remembers Rothermere telling him during that bleak week-end of 22–24 March, 'No more reinforcements for Haig. Get back as much of the Air as you can from France for the defence of England, whatever the army do.' Trenchard gathered that he wanted to leave the army to its fate, but he spoke so excitedly that it was difficult to understand exactly what he meant. Trenchard suggested to Rothermere that he should go to the country and rest for a few days (apart from the pressure of events, Rothermere was deeply stricken by the death in action of his two sons). Then he rushed all available aircrews over to France, with a letter to air C-in-C Salmond saying, 'You are splendid . . .' Indeed, Salmond reported next day that his aircraft 'were so thick over the ground that I fear some collisions occurred, but this has to be put up with.' And from Nancy, Newall's bombers were at last thrusting deep into Germany.

On 1 April 1918 King George V, unaware of what had been going on behind the scenes, sent a telegram to Rothermere. 'Today the Royal Air Force, of which you are Minister in charge, comes into existence as the third arm of the defence of the Empire . . . I congratulate you on its birth and I trust it may enjoy a vigorous and successful life . . .' Thus the Royal Air Force was born – an unwanted foundling. Its Chief of Staff had already submitted his resignation and its Minister was about to leave. Trenchard was unable to work up any enthusiasm for the celebrations. He thought the date perversely chosen and the event only too appropriate. To relieve his sunken spirits he visited the bomber squadrons at Nancy on 5 April. The formidable morale of Newall and his aircrews immediately revived him. 'We are giving them hell in the air,' they all told him, and he felt proud.

On 13 April Rothermere formally accepted Trenchard's resignation. For posterity he recorded, 'In getting rid of Trenchard I flatter myself that I did a great thing for the Air Force. With his dull and unimaginative mind and his attitude of *je sais tout* he would within twelve months have brought death and damnation to the Air Force.'

Trenchard was in his office that day when Major-General Frederick Sykes knocked at the door. 'Lord Rothermere has sent me,' said the new Chief of Air Staff. Till that moment Trenchard had no inkling of his successor. Sykes was the last person in the world he wished to see take his place as he neither liked nor trusted him. 'Is there anything you wish to know?' he asked Sykes. 'No, nothing, thank you.' Trenchard gathered up his papers and left the room.

Sir Henry Wilson, Sykes's opposite number at the War Office (the Chief of the Imperial General Staff) was also a new incumbent. Sykes had served under him in 1917 and had found it had 'invariably been a great pleasure. He was always original, versatile and resourceful.' Sykes's view was by no means universal. Wilson has been variously described as garrulous and scheming, a scandal-monger with an objectionable and arrogant manner, and a tiresome and unpleasant character. At least he did not lack the first quality of a soldier, courage. Four years later he stood sword in hand and faced the Irish gunman who murdered him. Until then, he would prove to be a thorn in Trenchard's side.

On 25 April it was clear that at least one of the inmates of Bolo House would no longer be 'actively interfering with the progress of the war.' That morning numbers of RAF officers were leaning out of the windows waving newspapers and cheering. One of the many passers-by who stopped to watch in the Strand below shouted, 'What's up? A victory in France?' 'No,' came the reply, 'a victory at home. Rothermere's resigned.' Others more in the know thought it more probable he had been told to go.

Trenchard read the news in his bachelor flat in Berkeley Square the next morning. In the post came a note from his friend Sir Godfrey Paine, chief of Personnel – 'I am feeling years younger and see daylight again.' And he added a word of encouragement to Trenchard, whose resignation had caused widespread despondency in the RAF, 'Sit tight my friend.' He counselled patience until the new Air Minister took office.

On 6 May the new Minister, Sir William Weir, offered Trenchard the choice of four posts. The one which attracted him most was command of the Independent Bomber Force in France. But Trenchard hesitated. Then on 8 May while he sat reading in Green Park, two senior naval officers strolled by. They were discussing him. From behind his newspaper Trenchard heard one of them say, 'It's an outrage . . . a man who threw his hand in at the height of the battle . . . I'd have him shot.' As soon as they were out of sight Trenchard rose and strode back to his flat. He wrote to Weir, 'I will accept command of the long distance bombing force . . . and do my best to make it a success.'

On the Western Front, in the fierce duels which raged daily in the air, the British fighter pilots were steadily proving their supremacy over a brave and determined foe.

On 5 April, Major Sholto Douglas, now commanding 84 Squadron, led them in to land in the pretty countryside north of Amiens at their new base at Bertangles. Fighter squadrons 48 and 209 were already there. A remarkable career had brought the tall, slim commander of 48 Squadron all the way from New Zealand to Bertangles. His name was Keith Park and he had joined the New Zealand Artillery in 1914 as a gunner – in his own words, 'the lowest form of artillery man'. Sailing from the Antipodes in December he fought his way through the disastrous Dardanelles campaign and the murderous battles of the Somme, eventually arriving in England on a stretcher. There his wounds ruled him as permanently unfit. But as he 'heartily disapproved of a cushy job in England', he 'wangled' a transfer to the RFC ground staff. At this juncture his medical papers were lost. So he did another 'wangle', this time into a pilots' flying course. He was then still an out-patient of Woolwich Hospital and permanently unfit for active service. Six months later he joined 48 Squadron as a pilot and after only eight months he was making a fine name for himself as its commanding officer.*

One of the flight commanders in the other squadron at Bertangles, 209, was Captain Roy Brown, a Canadian. He had been in the Royal Naval Air Service before it joined hands with the Royal Flying Corps to form the RAF. A veteran of many combats, Roy Brown appeared to Sholto

---

*That 'wangle' of Keith Park's must have set an all-time record, but the day would come when he would help me to bring off another quite extraordinary one. But for it I should never have fought in the Battle of Britain.

Douglas as a sick and a tired man – not too sick, as it turned out, to fight the combat of his life.

Against the British fighters were ranged a dozen or more German *Jagdstaffeln* (*Jasta*), but the most dreaded of all were the four which formed *Jagdgeschwader* I, Richthofen's Circus. Only a few weeks earlier Richthofen had taken a trip down to Le Cateau (near Cambrai) to talk to Ernst Udet, the commander of *Jasta* 37. A brilliant, if somewhat reckless pilot, Udet needed little persuasion to accept Richthofen's invitation to join the Circus. Udet had then won twenty victories. Two days before Douglas arrived at Bertangles, Richthofen had shot down his seventy-eighth allied aircraft. But this ghastly death-roll was haunting him. Of the months during the Somme battle he had said, 'During the whole of my life I have not found a happier hunting ground.' The happy hunting ground had now become a grisly Valhalla, haunted by the spectres of his charred and mutilated young victims. 'The last ten I shot down burned,' he said one day with feeling. It was inevitable that with such visions in his mind even the most hardened killer would begin to lose his grip.

'When it gets too hot for you, get to hell out of it.' These were the unmistakable orders of Captain Roy Brown to Lieutenant W.R.May, an inexperienced young fellow-Canadian in his flight. And that is exactly what young May did when, at ten thousand feet over the Somme valley on 21 April, a red Fokker triplane was on his tail. Twisting and turning in a headlong dive, he came out a few feet above the river heading with all he had for the allied lines. But the Fokker was still there, firing all the time. Its pilot was so intent on killing the young Canadian that he never bothered to look behind him. Had he done so he would have seen a British Sopwith trailing him. Behind its twin Vickers guns Captain Brown held a firm bead on the Fokker. As they skimmed over the Australian lines a hail of rifle and machine-gun fire came up at the German. At that moment Brown opened fire. He saw the German pilot fall forward. Then the triplane faltered and fell heavily like a wounded bird to make an awkward landing. Australian soldiers were soon on the scene. They lifted Manfred von Richthofen from the cockpit stone dead. A single bullet had pierced his heart.

His body was duly laid out in one of 84 Squadron's hangars; British airmen (among them Sholto Douglas) went to pay their homage. 'It was a curious experience,' he said, 'after all we had heard about him, to see him lying there.'

Only the day before, Richthofen had shot down his eightieth allied aircraft. Many were two-seaters, so well over a hundred allied airmen had fallen victim to his shooting. The single-handed killing of that number of men – the bereaving at the touch of a button, of so many mothers, wives and lovers gave Richthofen the incongruous qualities of supreme hero and public executioner. Manfred von Richthofen's exploits were acclaimed and his death mourned by the German nation and the brave company of British airmen among whom he would have found his next victims. The afternoon following his death his body was reverently borne by six RAF officers to Bertangles cemetery and there laid to rest – for the time being.

In May 1918 a British pilot, his aircraft shot to pieces, managed to pull off a forced landing at a German airfield. He was brought before the commander of the *Jagdgruppe*, a short man with ruddy cheeks and strong blue eyes. Unabashed, the pilot asked his German captor if he could fly the aircraft which had just shot him down. To his astonishment the German agreed. But his parting words were, 'Don't try any tricks – you have only ten minutes' fuel.'

The German commander was Erhard Milch. Milch had wanted to be a fighter pilot since 1915, but they made him an observer in a reconnaissance squadron. When he made that sporting gesture to the British pilot he remembered the time when one of his own pilots was shot down east of St Omer, at Cassel, by an aircraft of 5 Squadron, RFC. Next day the British had sent a message, 'Send over pilot's uniform and effects 1 p.m. tomorrow. Safe passage.' At the appointed time a German aircraft had dropped the clothes by parachute.

In Milch's words, 'Chivalry is only possible between our two peoples. They are close to each other . . . I was born in the real old Saxon country where some of our words are the same as in English.' Milch was alleged to be of Jewish origin, though this did not worry him or anyone else at the time.

Between him and Major Trafford Leigh-Mallory, the commander of No. 8 Reconnaissance Squadron there was a certain resemblance – short stature and solid build, pink cheeks and a forceful, dynamic manner. Both were industrious, ambitious men. But if Milch's intelligence was as sharp as a knife, Leigh-Mallory's was more of the steam-hammer variety.

Both were originally reconnaissance men who ended up commanding fighters – although Leigh-Mallory's turn would come years later and lead to his falling out badly with Keith Park, now commanding 48 Fighter Squadron at Bertangles.

A new squadron had arrived at Bertangles to join Park's 48 and Douglas's 84. The new boys were 85 Squadron, led by Major Billy Bishop. 'Bish', a Canadian (and one of the top-scoring fighter pilots) had gathered around him a thoroughly cosmopolitan crowd which included New Zealanders, Australians, Canadians, and a South African (not to mention an assortment of Scots, Irish, and Englishmen and finally – four Americans. They set the pace, and a hot one it was too. One of them, Elliot Springs, would write the story of 85 during those times in one of the best and liveliest of all books about flying, *War Birds*.)

Springs and his friends Larry Callahan, Mac Grider, and Jake Stanley were trained on Maurice Farman Shorthorns. Springs called the Shorthorn 'an awful looking bus . . . They say you test the rigging by putting a bird between the two wings. If the bird gets out there's a wire gone somewhere.'

85 Squadron's departure from Hounslow early in May was in Springs' words 'a scream'. Before the assembled crowd of wives, sweethearts and senior officers Billy Bishop 'told us that Lympne would be our first stop, and to be sure and take a good look at the wind sock and to land squarely into wind. But he didn't call it a sock. He called it by the name we always call it . . . when there are no ladies or gentlemen present. He turned red and the ladies lowered their parasols.'

The arrival of 85 Squadron at Bertangles was the occasion for a binge. One of 84 Squadron's flights was entirely American and its commanding officer, Sholto Douglas, had known Billy Bishop for some time. But, says Sholto, 'the drinking . . . was not nearly so strenuous . . . as Springs leads one to believe, hilarious though the effect is in the book . . . we had discovered in the beginning that we could not indulge in heavy drinking and fighting in the air at the same time. We were all for it in the right place and at the right time; but if we had been at the bottle as constantly as Springs makes out we would have been in our graves very quickly.'

Elliott Springs had the true fighter pilot's disdain for rank or class. One day south of Courtrai six Germans got stuck on his tail and he dived away so steeply that the fabric came adrift from his top wing. Shaking like a leaf Springs landed back at Bertangles and promptly taxied straight into his commanding officer's aircraft. Bish 'was all set to ball him out'. So Springs walked calmly up to him and ran his finger across the major's imposing row of medals, which included a Victoria Cross. 'You see these medals?' asked Springs. 'Well, I just want to tell you that you're welcome to them.' Then he stumped off to the bar.

At the end of May Billy Bishop handed over 85 Squadron to Major Mick Mannock and returned to England. During those days at Bertangles Sholto Douglas thought that Bishop seemed to live 'in a rather brittle, hard world of his own'. It would be years before Sholto Douglas would see him again and then 'he seemed to have become more likeable and companionable'. That is just how we found him the day he came back to visit 85 Squadron twenty-two years later, when I was its commanding officer.

Chapter 2

The Germans had sown the wind; now they would reap the whirlwind. It was nearly a year since Trenchard had warned the War Cabinet that reprisals would be useless unless the British were prepared to undertake heavier attacks than the Germans. Now the time had come when they were in a position to do so. Weir (the Air Minister), who believed that the Germans were 'susceptible to bloodiness', actually wrote to Trenchard, 'I would very much like it if you could start up a really big fire in one of the German towns.' Then he advised Trenchard, '. . . I would not be too exacting as regards accuracy in bombing railway stations in the middle of towns . . .'

But Trenchard was too professional to be tempted away from his strategic aim by the pure 'bloodiness' envisaged by Weir. His purpose was, first and foremost, to hit war factories.

Trenchard, however, had no illusions about the sufferings that his 'strategic' bombing would cause the German civilians. To Weir he replied, 'I do not think you need be anxious about our degree of accuracy when bombing stations in the middle of towns. The accuracy is not great at present, and all the pilots drop their eggs well in the middle of the town generally.' A Rhinelander who lived 'well in the middle of the town' wrote, 'My eyes won't keep open while I'm writing. In the night we took refuge in the cellar twice and again this morning. One feels as if one were no longer a human being . . . This is no longer war, but murder.'

Having failed to subdue England by bombing, the German Air Force now very sensibly concentrated its energies on more profitable targets. One was the airfield at Bertangles. One night Keith Park gave a movie show in one of 48 Squadron's hangars. Nigger Horn brought his two Americans, Larry Callahan and Elliott Springs; Sholto brought Alex Matthews, an American from his squadron. The show was in full swing

22

when five German night bombers arrived overhead. The whistle of bombs startled the audience. Sholto, in the front row, immediately dived under the piano, while the others flattened themselves in the gangways. The orderly officer rushed in and called for the Fire Party, but was greeted by a rude ribald shout from the audience and the deafening explosion of a near miss, followed by several more. The audience now rose as one man and bolted for the exits. Several hangars were ablaze and by their light the German airmen were machine-gunning the running figures. Alex Matthews and several others were killed. 48 Squadron lost ten Bristol Fighters, and five hangars were burnt out. As an exercise in tactical bombing the attack was a resounding success. Here, with what was officially described as 'an inconsiderable number of bombs', the Germans had scored more heavily against the allied war machine than in any one of their strategic raids on London.

With the death of Alex Matthews that night, the two Americans of 85 Squadron lost a good friend. Springs and Callahan were getting hardened to war. 'I have learnt many things, especially that discretion is the better part of valour,' wrote Springs. 'When there are two Huns above you and your immediate vicinity is full of lead, well, my boy, it's time to go home. Never mind trying to shoot down any of them . . . try again tomorrow.'

Skill in air fighting is no use unless luck, and plenty of it, is also on your side. Major Mick Mannock, 85 Squadron's new commander, nursed and cherished his young pilots – and it was this that killed him. He was emotional and highly strung. At the very start of his career he had said: 'That's the way they're going to get me – flames, and finish.' He always carried a revolver in the air 'to finish myself off as soon as I see the first sign of flames.' Despite a faulty left eye, he could pick out distant objects like a hawk. A cunning tactician, one of his schemes was to act as a decoy, with Larry Callahan as his wing man. Larry admired him for many reasons. For one, 'he was not a headhunter', like Richthofen, whose score Mannock nearly equalled. 'He would always be the low man . . . and I knew it because I was with him. When a bunch of Huns came along he would goad them into attacking him while the rest of the boys were in the distance, waiting . . . Mannock was such a hell of a fighter and such a good shot that he could afford to get himself into the worst position and still shoot his way out.'

Nobody will ever know whether Mick Mannock drew his revolver on himself. Donald Inglis, a young New Zealander, was with him at the time low over the enemy lines, when he suddenly saw flames spurting from Mannock's machine. Then it dived headlong into the ground and was soon burnt out. It was the fate he had always dreaded.

The pace was telling on everyone except, apparently, Callahan. Springs noticed that 'nobody in the squadron can get a glass to his mouth with one hand after one of these decoy patrols except Cal, and he's got no nerves – he's made of cheese . . .'

As Elliott Springs wrote of himself: 'I'm all shot to pieces. I only hope I can stick it. I don't want to quit. My nerves are all gone and I can't stop. It's not the fear of death . . . I'm still not afraid to die. It's this eternal flinching from it that's . . . made a coward out of me. Few men live to know what real fear is.'

Before his death Manfred von Richthofen had scrawled in pencil on a sheet of paper, 'Should I fail to return *Leutnant* Reinhard shall take over the leadership of the *Geschwader*.' Two months later, on 18 June, Reinhard and the commander of *Jasta* 27, Hermann Goering, met in Berlin at the Adlershof airfield, where they were to test a new fighter. It was Goering's turn first. The aircraft behaved perfectly. Then Reinhard climbed into the cockpit and was off. Some minutes later the people watching on the ground were horrified to see the aircraft's wings collapse. With Reinhard still in the cockpit it plummeted straight into the ground. The Circus was once again without a leader and Goering, much upset, returned to *Jasta* 27. Three weeks passed. Then on 8 July *Leutnant* Karl Bodenschatz, Adjutant of *Geschwader* I, assembled the pilots and read them a message from the High Command. 'Order No. 178,654 of 8 July 1918: *Oberleutnant* Hermann Goering has been appointed Commander of *Geschwader* I.' To the pilots the news was a surprise – whatever his talents as a fighter pilot, Goering was an outsider. At Bagneux airfield, he took command of the most renowned of all *Geschwaders*. Its aircraft were painted in every hue, and he lost no time in devising his own colour scheme, having his trim little Fokker D. VII daubed in mauve and yellow. His garish taste was already showing. A month later he went on leave.

Before Goering left, the French and American armies were beginning to thrust forward in the southern sectors of the line. Then on 8 August at 4.20 a.m. the British armies (spearheaded by Australians and Canadians) moved forward in thick fog from Amiens, taking the Germans completely by surprise. That day the German High Command realized the war was lost. By 9.00 a.m. the fog had lifted and RAF squadrons roared into the air to support and protect the army. On the German side the Circus was thrown into the thick of the fighting, moving up and down the line to reinforce the weak points. Both 85 Squadron and Sholto Douglas's 84 had several mix-ups with the multi-coloured Fokkers. Lothar von Richthofen, Manfred's brother, led the Circus in Goering's absence. But a few days later he was wounded and Ernst Udet took over until Goering returned at the end of August. It must have pained him somewhat to find 'Udlinger' in charge of his Circus. There was already little love lost between the two men.

The German airmen fought bravely. Goering, in H. A. Jones's view, 'was possibly gifted with a temperament more offensive than his predecessor', Manfred von Richthofen. Sholto Douglas, on the other hand, thought Goering's lack of caution led to the Richthofen *Geschwaders'* being decimated. Their losses were so great that they had to join forces with a *Jagdgruppe* under Robert Ritter von Greim, and Bruno Loerzer's *Jagdgeschwader* 3. Valiantly as they fought, this hotch-potch of units was overpowered by the array of squadrons put into the air by the RAF and the French, who were now stiffened by the American air force. Goering's despair was apparent in his report to the High Command of 1 September. 'The enemy aeroplanes are strongly armed and operate very well in close formation, even when attacked by several German single-seaters.'

On 5 November the Circus fought its last action. Then the weather clamped down and they were grounded until the ceasefire came on 11 November. That day a German pilot chalked on the pilots' room blackboard, '*Im Krieg geboren, im Krieg gestorben*' (born in the war, died in the war). It was a fitting lament for the German air force.

A few days earlier, Goering had already let the pilots of *Geschwader* I know that the end was near. On 11 November he received an order to hand over his aircraft to an American unit. He ignored it and wrote an order himself, 'Take-off at dawn tomorrow, 12 November. Destination Darmstadt.' The following day the Circus brought to Darmstadt airfield all the colours of the rainbow. But a most terrible humiliation awaited them. They were immediately grounded by a force of revolutionaries who had seized the airfield. Goering, livid and dismayed at this treatment of the nation's heroes, threatened his captors with an immediate low-level machine-gun attack by the rest of the Circus if they did not free his aircraft. They did. It was the French who eventually caught up with Goering a few days later at Aschaffenberg, where he agreed to surrender his aircraft. But that day the pilots of *Geschwader* I purposely made the worst landings of their lives. Goering's last act of defiance was to destroy the aircraft of the Circus.

News of the German surrender reached Corporal Adolf Hitler in the hospital at Pasewalk. He took it badly. 'Everything went black before my eyes as I staggered back to my ward and buried my aching head between the blankets and the pillow . . . the following days were terrible to bear and the nights still worse . . . During these nights my hatred increased, hatred for the originators of this dastardly crime.'

Mick Mannock was killed on the 26 July 1918. Around this time I would often sit with my brothers on the compact, sweet-smelling turf above the high cliffs of Trebarwith, Cornwall. Who could have told me that one day I would inherit command of Mick Mannock's and Billy Bishop's squadron? Or, like Elliott Springs, feel the real fear that so few men ever know? Not yet four years old, I feared nothing—except the sea which stretched out from the foot of the cliffs until it reached the sky beyond. It was the enormity of the sea which terrified me. With my eyes and ears I recorded the rhythm and the thunder of its immense, relentless motion, as the waves rolled in, unfolded, and spread themselves across the yellow sand of the cove below, or dashed themselves headlong against the red granite cliffs. It was this ceaseless, effortless attrition that made the sea so august and frightening. Later, when I realized it was in my blood (as it is in the blood of every Englishman), it dawned on me that the sea provided us with a solid wall of defence and that the obstinate resistance of our island to its ceaseless battering somehow became implanted in the English character.

To the small boy that I was the sky seemed much more friendly and genial. Unlike the sea, it was changing and ethereal. And if you had the wings you could range not only far and wide but upwards – to heaven, to the sun. Unlike the gloomy, invisible depths of the sea, the air was full of enchantment. I was too young to have any cogent thoughts on the subject, but as I sat on the cliffs at Trebarwith and watched the sea-birds wheeling in the void below I wondered what kind of magic it was that held them up. I suppose I had been shown aeroplanes in pictures, but it never occurred to me that they could fly. That kind of magic worked only with the birds. Then one afternoon a noise brought me running bare-footed from the house. Nobody took any notice of the object in the sky so I called out at the top of my voice, 'Quick, quick, an aeroplane.' That afternoon a seed was planted. In time it would germinate.

The second generation of airmen were of a tender age when on 11 November 1918 the Germans begged the Allies to stop the war they themselves had started four years earlier. Norman Ryder came into the world six days after me in India, where I was born. Bob Tuck was born as thousands of his countrymen were dying in the carnage of the first day of the Somme battle. In Westphalia Paul Temme became the tenth child of his father in November, as winter brought an end to the frightful slaughter. The father prayed that his son would never have to go to war. At Grevenbruck in Westphalia, Werner Borner was a pupil more enterprising than the rest. Karl Missy was just beginning at the *Volksschule* at Rheydt in the Rhineland. Whoever would have said that those two boys who walked every morning to the *Volksschule* at Grevenbruck and Rheydt were on their way to a machine-gun battle with the child who sat on the cliff-top at Trebarwith looking down at the threatening sea?

Part Two

THE
DAWN
OF
PEACE

Chapter 3

'Make up your mind whether you would like the War Office or the Admiralty. You can take the Air with you in either case. I'm not going to keep it as a separate department,' the Prime Minister Lloyd George told Winston Churchill early in the January of 1919. Churchill took over as Minister for War and Air on 15 January.

Trenchard had just arrived at Southampton to deal with the mutinous soldiers and sailors who had seized the docks. A man of Trenchard's iron authority was needed to retrieve the very ugly situation. Group Captain Smyth Piggot greeted Trenchard warmly on his arrival at the South Western Hotel, but he immediately noticed that the great man he had known in RFC days was no longer accompanied by a large number of staff officers. 'Once he was all-powerful,' said Smyth Piggot, 'now he had nothing. The hotel was packed with hordes of junior officers and . . . the noise was dreadful. There . . . sat this old eagle among a squealing flock of parakeets.' Smyth Piggot had always associated Trenchard with a fleet of cars, typing pools and everything else he wanted. Now he was shocked to see him 'deprived of everything. As far as I could make out,' concluded Smyth Piggot, 'he was finished.'

A few weeks later, in early February, Trenchard was at breakfast with Smyth Piggot and Maurice Baring, his aide since he took command of the RFC in France in 1915. A telegram was brought to Trenchard, and Smyth Piggot noticed how annoyed he looked as he read it. The telegram instructed him to return to London forthwith and to report to the Minister for War and Air on 'urgent air force business'. Trenchard was puzzled. What could this mean?

He left for London immediately and called on Churchill at the War Office. The two men chatted for some moments and Churchill complimented Trenchard on his masterly handling of the Southampton riots. Then he turned to the RAF. 'As far as its remaining independent is concerned,' said the Minister for War and Air, 'my mind is open.' Thereupon

Trenchard gave the Minister some of his own mind. During his spell as commander of the independent bombing force, he felt the utter joy of a personal command free from the fetters and intrigues of government. He had forgotten the interference of Bolo House and the gnawing responsibilities for the infant RAF which he had transferred to Sykes. The RAF must remain independent. Trenchard reacted violently because of the Minister's lukewarm feelings for the RAF for which he, Trenchard, was prepared to give his soul. There could be no other solution. 'Then how would you like to come back as Chief of the Air Staff?' asked Churchill. 'Impossible,' retorted Trenchard, 'you already have one.' 'Oh, you can leave Sykes to me,' Churchill reassured him. 'Civil Aviation is going to be under the Air Ministry. We'll call Sykes Controller of Civil Aviation and console him with a GBE.'

It revolted Trenchard to think that once again he was on the verge of becoming a pawn on the political chessboard. Memories of Rothermere came crowding back. Churchill guessed his doubts. 'There will be no one against you in the Cabinet,' he reassured him. 'Think it over – and meanwhile I'd like you to put down on paper your ideas on how to reorganize the Air Ministry and let me have them.'

Back in his flat that evening Trenchard went to work. He wrote only eight hundred words, arranged in seven paragraphs on a sheet and a half of foolscap paper. Then he posted the document to Churchill. Nothing happened for a week. Then Trenchard once more received a summons to Churchill's office. 'I like your ideas,' the Minister told him. 'You must come back, and I won't hear any refusal.' On 15 February 1919 Trenchard became, for the second time in less than a year, Chief of the Air Staff. Within two weeks he lay prostrate in bed with Spanish flu. Pneumonia had already set in and there was little hope that he would recover.

Churchill's predecessor as Air Minister, Sir William Weir, was (in his own words) 'horrified and scandalized' at Lloyd George's indifference to the fate of the Royal Air Force. But (according to Sir Maurice Hankey who as War Cabinet Secretary 'had practically lived with Lloyd George') the Prime Minister was so immersed in the details of the Peace Conference due in June, that he could think of nothing else – least of all the RAF, the dissolution of which was for him a foregone conclusion.

The Allied Powers first met in January 1919 to discuss the best means of punishing Germany. Lloyd George spoke his mind on the subject in a memorandum dated 25 March 1919: 'It must be a settlement which will contain in itself no provocation for future war. You may strip Germany of her colonies, reduce her armaments to a mere police force and her navy to that of a fifth rate power. All the same, in the end, if she feels that she has been unjustly treated in the Peace of 1919 she will find means of exacting retribution from her conquerors.'

But as the months of negotiation rolled on towards June the mood apparently changed. In the opinion of William McElwee, 'Lloyd George approached the business of a peace treaty as he would have approached a tricky contract or a political deal. So long as he kept within the letter of the law and satisfied his client the general principles could go hang ... He brought to the task, in a very high degree, the cleverness of a Welsh solicitor, but not the wisdom of a responsible statesman.'

As far as the victorious allies were concerned German air power was dead. It called only for burial, and Article 198 of the Treaty was meant to see to that. It prohibited military aviation in Germany. Submarines were also forbidden, but Germany was allowed to maintain an army – the *Reichswehr* – of one hundred thousand men. In vain did Friedrich Ebert, President of the new Weimar Republic, plead for leniency. Clemenceau would not hear of it. On 16 June he demanded that the German Government accept the terms – within five days. There was nothing else to do. On 28 June when the Allied delegates met in the Hall of Mirrors at Versailles for the final signature, they hoped to end all wars.

Their views were not shared by their vanquished foes. Ten years later, when Adolf Galland would start learning to glide, he would feel the 'atmosphere of national frustration. The man who could one day throw off these fetters was assured of the fullest support from the enthusiastic aviators ... of Germany's youth.' The man existed.

In 1919 he had just got a new job in Munich. Adolf Hitler's gift for politics had found recognition in his appointment as a *Bildungsoffizier*, whose role it was to instruct the troops on the insidious dangers of socialist, pacifist and democratic ideas. For the moment, it was the ideal job. Meanwhile another man of a very different kind was beginning to think up schemes to save Germany from the crushing humiliation of the Versailles Treaty. As a member of the German peace delegation he had first-hand knowledge of allied vengeance. His name was General Hans von Seeckt and he would see to it that in neither letter nor spirit would Germany carry out the disarmament clauses of the Treaty.

Young Tom Gleave had been crazy about aeroplanes since 1911, when he was only three. It was the little Blériot monoplane which flew over his home in Walton, Liverpool, that started it. Incidentally the pilot, Mr Melly, was hauled up before the authorities and accused of flying over Liverpool. Happily, he was acquitted of the crime. Other aircraft from across the Mersey would fly low over Tom's home and Tom, like the piper's son, would run after them when they appeared to be gliding down to land – nearly always to find as he panted up to the field that they had taken off again.

As the peace conference delegates were getting down to their negotiations in early 1919, Tom's uncle was appointed aircraft disposal officer of the airfield at Aintree, better known for Becher's Brook just over the hedge. 'I used to trek out there with the faithful family hound,' Tom said. There was not much flying going on, but one pilot seemed busier than the rest. Tom later found out his name was Alan Cobham, whose trail-blazing flights during the next decade would win him renown as one of the greatest aerial pioneers. But what struck Tom most at Aintree were the rows of aircraft fuselages laid out in the open with their wings stacked alongside. In the aircraft factory more rows of fuselages were stacked on their noses. What puzzled Tom was that while two plywood flying boats were being built in the factory – he believed for the Spanish Air Force – scores of other aircraft were being heaped on to a huge bonfire in the corner of the airfield, and brand new Sunbeam Arab engines were being sold as scrap. What sacrilege, thought young Tom! And so thought many others. For this was the inglorious fate reserved for most of the twenty-two thousand aircraft possessed by the RAF when the war ended in 1918. Fire and the scrap dealers reduced the ninety-six RAF squadrons in France at the Armistice to twenty-three in May 1919. And only ten of these were operational, the rest having no ground crews to service them.

Trenchard had survived the illness which, to less robust constitutions, would have proved fatal. In May 1919 he was back at the Air Ministry. The first shock he got was to learn that scores of his best officers had been demobilized. Even Salmond, his successor as RAF commander in France, was on the point of quitting. Trenchard remonstrated, 'I was offered a job ... worth four times what I am getting now ... and two other fine jobs. I declined ... directly I accepted this. Unless I am kicked out I intend to see it through at whatever pecuniary loss to myself and in spite of a very hard, difficult and not too pleasant task ...' This was too much for Salmond, who changed his mind.

Trenchard was overjoyed. He needed men like Salmond for now he felt that, although the RAF's immense material strength was going up in smoke before his eyes, its existence as a separate, independent service was a fact. This was thanks largely to Winston Churchill who, despite Lloyd George's sentence of death on the RAF, had granted a stay of execution. Trenchard was working day and night to create a future for the condemned service. He wrote to Salmond, 'I feel certain you will agree that I must not give way ... Never again shall we have the opportunity ...'

Meeting with members of the Army Council in July he had a chance to measure the hostility of its chief, Wilson. The subject under discussion was the RAF's new ranks. Wilson sneered at Trenchard: 'So you want to bring disrepute to the rank of Field Marshal by inventing "Marshal of the Air"?' But Trenchard was a jump ahead of the soldier, himself a Field Marshal. 'You should have thought of that before,' he boomed, 'the word marshal already exists in several contexts.' And he quoted them, ending with provost-marshal, court-martial and Marshall & Snelgrove, the big London store. To Wilson's discomfort, no one laughed louder than Churchill. But when Trenchard discussed the subject a few days later with the King at Buckingham Palace, George V remarked, 'Don't you think Marshal of the Air is poaching a bit on the preserves of the Almighty? Why not simply Marshal of the Royal Air Force?' And thus the matter was settled.

In March 1919 Parliament had voted £66,000,000 for the Air. But most of this was to meet the cost of liquidating the RAF. 'I was left with nothing but two heaps of rubble,' said Trenchard, 'one of bricks and mortar, the other of men.' Trenchard told his Minister that he would need only £25,000,000 to build up a new service from these 'heaps of rubble.'

If Churchill was pleased by Trenchard's modest needs, Trenchard now began to feel far from happy about his Minister's unswerving support. Churchill had lately been carried away by the forlorn cause of the White Russians against the Bolsheviks. The millions he was squandering on the force of twenty thousand British troops dispatched to fight the Bolsheviks were alarming the Prime Minister and the Cabinet. Lloyd George thought that his Minister for War and Air 'had Bolshevism on the brain'. Churchill came under a cloud and his Cabinet colleagues began to refer to him as 'that wild man'.

This was bad for Trenchard. There was nothing the Cabinet was more touchy about than money. Lloyd George had just invented a way to curb the spending of the three services: it was called the Ten Year Rule, and it assumed that the country would not become involved in a war for the next ten years. It could be extended year by year as the government thought fit. Standing last in the queue the RAF would obviously be the first to suffer. Meanwhile, if Churchill was overspending as Minister for War, he would have to cut his expenditure as Minister for Air. And running a separate air service was not the best way to accomplish this.

Trenchard had to 'live and work in a barrage of criticism'. He said, 'I was continually being pressed by the high-ups that the army and navy should train my people to be "officers and gentlemen" . . . I could also use their medical, dental, engineering, clerical, scientific and spiritual facilities. It would save untold money.' After 'a little cogitation' it seemed to him that there were two ways open. One was to give in to the pressure of the government and the older services. But as he saw it, this would be to misuse the air force, which he foresaw as the key to home defence. The other way was to defy the other services and build foundations – if precious little else, for the moment – which would be hard to destroy.

Fortunately for England, Trenchard set his heart on the latter course. In doing so he took a step which would ensure the existence two decades later of an air force whose skill-at-arms, weapons and fighting spirit were equal to their historic task. Had Trenchard given in (then or later), science, technique, training, tradition, would have remained with those whose minds were earthbound. Soldiers and sailors could never have devised a weapon as efficient as Fighter Command, any more than airmen could have successfully tackled the problems and hazards peculiar to fleets and armies. War in the air as much as at sea or on land called for experienced professionals.

But as Trenchard made this momentous decision he felt that Churchill, who had been so helpful, was cutting the ground from under his feet. Trenchard noted 'his tendency to wobble when attacked' – very unlike the Churchill of 1940 – and that he was in danger of being swayed by the arguments of the admirals and generals. Trenchard decided on a show-down with his Minister. On 11 September he strode unannounced into Churchill's office. In a few minutes the two men were engaged in a shouting match which echoed down the staid corridors of the War Office. When calm was eventually restored Churchill said thoughtfully, 'You said something just now about the absurdity of trained airmen becoming chauffeurs for the army and navy. It's a good argument. I'd like you to develop it, and everything else you have told me, on paper.'

Seven months had passed since Trenchard's page and a half of notes which had provoked Churchill's remark, 'I like your ideas.' Once again he got down to his 'homework' and by late that night had knocked out a rough and ready draft. He summed up in the following words: 'I think the consensus of expert opinion would be that the power of the air will be an increasing power in years to come ... It seems to me there are two alternatives. (1) To use the air simply as a means of conveyance, captained by chauffeurs, weighted by the navy and army personnel, to carry out reconnaissance ... drop bombs ... or observe for the artillery. (2) To make an air service which will really encourage and develop airmanship, or better still, the air spirit ... and to make it a force that will profoundly alter the strategy of the future ...' Churchill echoed his words when he presented Trenchard's detailed plans to the Cabinet, 'If we are not to ... lose that predominance which we have won at such cost during the last five years, we must create a real service, not necessarily large, but highly efficient.'

A new figure now loomed on the horizon – Admiral Beatty, hero of Jutland and archetype of the bulldog breed of British sailor. In the Admiral's wake steamed a flotilla of other naval personages (including Trenchard's brother-in-law, Admiral Roger Keyes) all determined to cut the naval air service off from the RAF and steer it back to the Fleet. Beatty at first moved ahead cautiously and for obvious reasons. In 1917 he had supported the fusion of the naval air arm in a separate service. But soon he put his helm hard over until it brought him onto a collision course with Trenchard. Trenchard fired a warning shot in a letter he wrote him on 22 November. He spoke of the future of the RAF and his plans for two branches of the new service which would be trained to work with the navy and army. But the main part of the RAF, he stressed, 'will be an Independent Air Force'. Trenchard asked for a period of quiet, and freedom from criticism.

Meanwhile Beatty had taken on board the Army chief, Wilson. He was a passenger, but could make himself a nuisance. Beatty's hostility was based on the decision that Trenchard should control all aircraft, including naval aircraft. It was a slight to the Senior Service. Wilson's sprang from a personal and bitter prejudice against Trenchard and all other men who flew. What Trenchard longed for was 'an official ring where I can face Wilson and Beatty as an equal. If they intend to destroy me they'd have to do so under Queensberry rules.' Beatty, the principal adversary, continued to stand off. So Trenchard decided to close with him.

It was a crisp, bright winter's day at the beginning of the second week of December 1919, and the sun slanted into the First Sea Lord's room at the Admiralty. As Trenchard entered Beatty was seated squarely at his desk. Behind him Wilson leaned on the mantelpiece, the monocle screwed into his eye giving a more than usual cynical look to his wrinkled face. He was there merely to enjoy the admiral's broadsides against Trenchard.

Trenchard sensed the hostile atmosphere. To make it worse, he was sure that neither Beatty nor Wilson believed in his doctrine that the 'air was one and indivisible'. This as he had already written to Beatty was the core of Trenchard's argument for keeping control of all squadrons, including those working with the army and navy. But Beatty would have none of it – the naval squadrons had to belong to the navy.

As the discussion warmed Trenchard began to pace the room. Wilson remained motionless, his arms still draped on the mantelpiece and only echoing 'hear, hear' to the admiral's each point. Beatty was showing signs of impatience. He had to shade his eyes against the sunlight to watch the pacing Trenchard. Then he got up irritably and began to stride to and fro in the opposite directions. Neither he nor Trenchard would give an inch. But suddenly Trenchard said, 'If you and Wilson are determined to oppose me I cannot stop you. All I ask is a sporting chance – give me twelve months to get started.' Beatty seemed to think this fair enough. 'All right,' he replied, 'I'll leave you alone for a year.' No 'hear, hear' came from Wilson this time. There was no question for him of playing ball with Trenchard.

Back at Adastral House, the Air Ministry's new headquarters in Kingsway, Trenchard's 'English merchants' had been fashioning his original draft memorandum into a White Paper for all those who were interested to read it. According to one of his later 'English merchants', John Slessor,* Trenchard 'was very inarticulate – his mind always worked quicker than his tongue; he was almost physically incapable of expressing his thoughts on paper – his handwriting had to be seen to be believed, his dictating was a nightmare to his stenographers . . .' He never gave anyone the impression of being 'an intellectual type of officer'. The secret of Trenchard's success was 'a flair, an instinct, for getting at the really essential core of the problem'.

Churchill presented the Trenchard Memorandum to Parliament on 11 December, a few days after Trenchard's meeting with Beatty and Wilson. It encountered a tepid reception. Reflecting the public mood, MPs were apathetic. The press, especially the newspapers of Rothermere and Northcliffe, were more outspoken but less enthusiastic. Only a few realized that the Memorandum was one of the most remarkable statements of military policy ever written.

* Today, Marshal of the RAF, Sir John Slessor.

No one had ever before set out to write the statutes of a fighting service. The Army and Navy had been moulded through centuries of British history. But following a few brief and hasty discussions, the RAF had been created by Act of Parliament. Almost everything but the Act itself had been dumped on the bonfire or the scrap heap.

The Memorandum was the work of a prophet and a professional. Independence was to be the basic principle of the new RAF. Trenchard envisaged in one stroke its fundamental needs: technical experts for research and the development of aeronautical science; training colleges for officers and technical apprentices. The officers' cadet colleges would provide permanently commissioned officers to form roughly one-third of the strength while the remaining two-thirds would be 'short-service' officers with a five-year commission. This would build up a reserve at minimum cost. An Auxiliary Air Force of 'week-end flyers' would provide a permanently active backing to the regular squadrons. A part of the RAF would be specially trained to work with the Navy, another part with the Army. To ensure the quality of the air service, training was to have first priority. Officers must learn to be more than mere 'air-chauffeurs'; mechanics must become masters in their trade.

The Memorandum laid down so exactly the needs and functions of the new service that fifteen years later (practically unchanged in form) it would provide the basis of the RAF's immense expansion schemes. It would become, too, the model for most of the air forces of the world. Finally, it would mould the lives of thousands like myself who stood on the brink of the new air age.

One of those upon whom fell the shadow not only of the Memorandum, but of its author, was Group Captain Hugh Dowding, now at Kenley, near London, commanding No. 1 Training Group. He evidently was still on Trenchard's black list, for despite his flying and administrative talents, no offer had yet come to him of a permanent commission. It looked as if he might have to return to the artillery.

In the preface to his Memorandum, Trenchard compared the RAF to the prophet Jonah's gourd. 'The necessities of war created it in a night, but the economics of peace have to a large extent caused it to wither in a day . . .' The message had the same ring as another, chalked on the pilots' room blackboard of Goering's *Geschwader*: Born in the war, died in the war. The only difference was that the once-victorious RAF had not quite died. But it had been reduced practically to the level of its vanquished foe.

And this was not the only thing that the two had in common. If only in the mind of General von Seeckt, Chief of the *Reichswehr*, the revival of the German Air Force, like that of the RAF, was imminent.

Carl August von Schoenebeck and the pilots of his *Staffel* 33 had been dumbfounded to hear of the German surrender on 11 November 1918. As for handing over their Fokker D VII's *Staffel-Kapitän* von Schoenebeck, like Hermann Goering, would not hear of it. As soon as the weather cleared he led his *Staffel* off from the airfield near Brussels and set course for Doberitz, Berlin.

Schoenebeck and his comrades still felt they had plenty of fight left in them, so they joined the *Freikorps* and went off to fight the Bolsheviks on the Baltic front. In the summer of 1919 Carl was with *Staffel* 424 at Altautz, in Curland. One day without warning a party of British officers arrived from Riga. They announced curtly that they were from the Allied Control Commission. 'To hell with these meddlesome Englishmen,' thought Schoenebeck and his friends, and while the Control Commission men were nosing round the *Staffel*'s aircraft and hangars the Germans took the opportunity to 'fix' their cars. When they refused to start, the Germans obligingly offered their own. It was a good exchange, as the English cars were much better.

For Werner Junck the war ended in Silesia. The disbanding of his own fighter *Staffel* took place without incident, and he went off on Christmas leave. Like Schoenebeck he felt quite ready to go on fighting, so when trouble broke out with the Reds in Upper Silesia he leaped at the chance of forming a fighter *Staffel* there. The machines (Siemens SSWD 3s) belonged to the *Reichswehr Fliegerhorst* at Brieg, but to avoid the attentions of the Control Commission it was decided to operate from a field near the frontier. Every evening towards dusk, Werner Junck flew a machine to the field. His mechanics, waiting in the bushes for him to land, rushed out and hurriedly wheeled the aircraft into a shed belonging to a sugar factory. After a dozen trips like this the *Staffel* was ready for action. But local gossip soon reached the ears of the Control Commission. Junck had to pack up his outlaw fighter *Staffel*, which was ignominiously transformed into the 8th Motorized Infantry Battalion.

The Control Commission failed in a difficult task. This was partly through its own fault, but mainly because the Germans had not the slightest intention of sticking to the letter, much less the spirit, of the Versailles Treaty. This was joy to Carl Schoenebeck and Junck and a host of young German fliers who felt bitterly resentful at having their wings clipped.

Schoenebeck was hit in the foot by Bolshevik anti-aircraft while ground-strafing in November of 1919. Repatriated to the Fatherland for treatment, he found that no hospital would take him – he had been deprived of his nationality as a penalty for soldiering against the Reds. So he stayed with friends until the wound healed. Then he went to Freiburg and joined the *Reichswehr*.

The Treaty of Versailles had liquidated the Imperial Army and its Grand General Staff, prohibiting the revival of both. Only a rump, the one hundred thousand man *Reichswehr* was left to Germany. Despite the Treaty General von Seeckt, its Chief, managed to surround himself with fifty-five generals and 670 staff officers. Three hundred more worked in the massive grey building of the *Reichswehrministerium* in Bendlerstrasse in Berlin.

The general's own regiment was the *Badische Leib Grenadiere*, and it was Schoenebeck's privilege to join it for he and the other officers worshipped von Seeckt. He was a man of few words. But when he did speak it was only to talk sound good sense in sparing terms and leavened with humour. In appearance 'the Sphinx', as they called him, was the ideal German general, tall, slim and straight, an elegant figure in his perfectly tailored uniform. The clipped moustache (which helped to conceal a cynical droop of the left side of the mouth) and the monocle added the final touches to his appearance as a member of the German officer corps. Only his hands belied his martial aspect: they were not at all the hands of a soldier, but long, slender and artistic.

One day early in 1920 General von Seeckt visited the 8th Motorized Infantry Battalion and told them, 'It is useless to go on fighting the Russians. This is not the time for Germany to fight. We have years of preparation before us. Then Germany's hour will come.' Werner Junck was deeply impressed by the General's talk. 'Then the champagne flowed and we felt von Seeckt was right. He was a marvellous man, the best officer we ever had.' With the dreadful blow to German arms still rankling there was no *Reichswehr* officer who did not on meeting von Seeckt feel reassured by his compelling authority and his silent resolve to retrieve the honour – and the lost territories – of the Fatherland.

So Werner Junck returned to his own regiment, the 18th Infantry. He and the other ex-air force pilots of the *Reichswehr* were a rather special breed of soldier, 'as if we were branded like thoroughbred Trakehner horses,' Junck put it. However, his regimental commander soon disillusioned him. 'You and your beautiful pilots,' he laughed, 'all that's over now.' But this was not what the Chief of the *Reichswehr* was thinking.

A month before he was appointed to the post, General von Seeckt summoned his chiefs and senior staff and warmed their hearts by denouncing the Allied demand for the surrender of the Kaiser and other 'war criminals' – mostly senior generals in the now defunct Imperial Army. If the German Government bowed to the demand, said von Seeckt, the *Reichswehr* would take up arms again and retire fighting until it joined up with the Russian army. It would then turn, liquidate Poland, and march back westwards against the French and British. The three main objectives in von Seeckt's thinking were, first, the removal of Poland from the map; next, co-operation with the Russians. The general was no communist sympathizer, but he respected their fighting qualities and was determined to attain with their help his third and most cherished ambition, the revival of the German military machine.

Unlike Wilson, his British opposite number – and although a soldier – von Seeckt was very much alive to the possibilities of the air and lost no time in creating a secret air section in the *Reichswehrministerium*. One hundred and eighty ex-air force officers were judiciously planted throughout the ranks of the *Reichswehr* and others from the army itself were attached to the air section. Among these were Albert Kesselring from the artillery, Hans-Juergen Stumpff, and Hugo Sperrle, who had served as an air observer. In 1940 they would command the three *Luftflotten* in the attack on England.

Goering meanwhile had his hands full at Stockholm, where he managed to combine the pleasures of courting the beautiful Carin, the wife of Nils Kantzow, with the less inspiring duties of Flight Chief of a Swedish air company, *Svenska Lufttrafik*.

Chapter 4

'The disintegration of nations ... will be accomplished directly ... by aerial forces ...' So wrote the Italian General Giulio Douhet in his book *The Command of the Air*, published in 1921. His outrageous views shocked and offended people in his own country and abroad. The old guard, soldiers, sailors and civilians alike, dismissed his writings as ridiculous. Even experts in air circles thought that he was going a bit too far. Like Trenchard, Douhet was a prophet before his time, but his views did not go unheeded in Germany. Hans von Seeckt, it is true, had little to say about the air, nothing about Douhet. But there was nothing extraordinary in the fact that the Sphinx, who seldom said much anyway, should remain silent about military aviation. The less said about it the better.

Douhet's horrific visions of annihilation from the air did not permeate to the British fighting services, let alone the British public. Slessor wrote: 'All we early RAF officers were alleged to sit up every night learning the works of General Douhet by heart. We may have had this book in the Staff College library, but I never saw it.' The British, after all, had their own air prophet – and Trenchard was now about to out-do Douhet himself.

His publicly expressed opinion that 'we may yet see governments living in dug-outs and holding cabinet meetings in the bowels of the earth' might be passed off as a good-natured joke from this 'air-crank', as he well knew most people thought him. But an official paper which followed in March 1921 dropped like a bomb on the angry and indignant Board of Admiralty. In the prevailing mood of government parsimony, Trenchard cleverly based his argument on economic considerations. He proposed quite simply that the RAF should take over the Navy's ancient role as Britain's main defence. Battleships and aircraft-carriers were, according to Trenchard, 'expensive and vulnerable'. Weight for weight a bomb was more powerful than a shell and could be carried further. Even if the effect of air attack on capital ships had yet to be proved no one could deny that for the cost of one capital ship several bomber and torpedo squadrons could be provided instead.

Trenchard hit at the orthodox thinking of the older services. New ideas and imagination were needed in defence strategy. The main threat to Britain in the future would come 'not from a landing on these islands, but from repeated incursions on a large scale by hostile aircraft . . . Unless we can put up an adequate defence we must be prepared for a dislocation of national life . . . unthought of in the past . . . The army and navy cannot materially assist us to face this attack . . . Responsibility should be assumed by the Air Ministry . . .'

This heretical but cogent argument pleased Churchill immensely, and in reply to it Beatty and Wilson chorused loudly with the same old tune – 'Give us back our own air arm.' Secretly debated by the Committee of Imperial Defence, the rival claims resulted in deadlock. So the Government asked its elder statesman, Arthur Balfour, to arbitrate. He listened to the contestants for two months, then asked the question, 'Are there, or are there not, military operations . . . in which the main burden of responsibility is thrown on the air force . . . The air force claim that there are; and it seems to me that their claim must be allowed.'

Dealing with defence against air attacks, Balfour observed, 'Here we have a military operation which not only can be carried out independently by the air force, but which cannot be carried out by anything else . . . There is a tendency . . . to minimize . . . the military effect . . . of air raids . . . on a very great scale . . . There is a picture drawn of Great Britain with its capital in ruins and the Admiralty and War Office carrying on . . . undismayed in . . . some disused coal-mine. Even such a catastrophe (it is claimed) would not force a decision . . .' With studied gravity he continued, '. . . As a matter of history, peace has usually been arranged long before the worsted party was reduced to so pitiable a condition; and while . . . the General Staffs of the army and navy heroically carrying out their functions at the bottom of a coal-pit might . . . be less disastrous than it seems . . . the enemy aeroplanes wandering at will over the country could carry out their work of destruction, however numerous and however heroic might be the armies and navies of the country they are reducing to ruin . . .'

One sultry day in August the telephone rang in Trenchard's office. It was Guest, the Air Minister, to tell him of Balfour's decision. Before he had finished Trenchard pressed all the bells on his desk and in a few moments he was confronted with his entire staff. 'We've won,' he boomed at them, elated. Next day he read in his own copy of Balfour's findings, 'The conclusion that I draw is that the air force must be autonomous . . . Against air raids the army and navy must play a secondary role . . .'

Trenchard had won the first round on points. But he had to re-enter the ring for the next one sooner than he expected – and with a different referee. This time it was Sir Eric Geddes. Accused on all sides of extravagance, the Government asked Geddes to show them how to cut their spending down to a minimum. The fighting services were at the top of the Geddes list and the RAF was first to be called to the witness stand.

Trenchard was afraid of what Geddes's economic 'axe' might do to the RAF, that 'plant of deeper root' he had been tending so carefully throughout the storms of the last eighteen months. It might be cut down, or trampled under foot by the older services, or both. His fears were quickly justified. Wilson asked the War Office to circulate a minute which told Geddes that the Air Ministry was the place to look for cuts. But Trenchard was ready for this kind of sabotage. 'I shall wholeheartedly welcome any proposal for . . . searching examination . . . provided [it] includes the army . . . I am confident that . . . the air arm is our cheapest form of defence and that, if only we . . . move with the times and leave the ruts of obsolete dogmatism the . . . transfer to the Air Ministry of certain functions . . . vested in the War Office . . . will make for substantial economies.'

It was good shooting. And Geddes was impressed with the help he got from the Air Ministry, where Trenchard had ordered that the minutest details were to be revealed. But, shrewd and intelligent as he was, the inquisitor did not know one end of an aeroplane from another. Trenchard took great pains to 'educate Geddes without upsetting him'.

By October the admirals began to launch their torpedoes. Admiral Chatfield of the Admiralty wrote to the new Deputy Chief of Naval Staff, Admiral Roger Keyes, 'We have at last started to attack the Air Ministry, but only indirectly through the Geddes Committee.' It happened that Keyes was Trenchard's brother-in-law and family relations, particularly among the ladies, cooled as the firing in the air-naval battle grew more intense.

It was then that Churchill, the gleam of battle in his eye, came in with a decisive blast as the acknowledged expert in defence. 'We are sure,' he wrote, 'that if . . . war on a great scale broke out again, the Power which had made the most intensive study of aerial warfare would start with an enormous initial advantage . . . We contend that the British policy is to develop . . . the air as an art, an arm and a service . . . To keep this new arm, with its measureless possibilities in perpetual thraldom to the army or navy . . . will be to rob it of its most important developments . . . we think that the growth of the Independent Air Force will . . . take place largely at the expense of the two older services . . . there should be substantial savings in expense.'

This only sharpened Geddes's zeal as he turned to probe the accounts of the army and navy. Wilson now descended to a new low in trying to distract Geddes's attention. On 18 November he attended a regimental memorial service at Amiens. On French soil, and in those solemn surroundings, he chose to insult the RAF in a speech calling it a movement 'for killing women and children'. Trenchard read the speech which made headlines the next day in all the papers. Then in a letter to Wilson he expressed his anger and disgust: 'It is impossible for me to sit still under these perpetual attacks – inspired . . . and led by you . . .' Next, he wrote to the Cabinet protesting against Wilson's 'implacable animosity against this service . . .' And he added, 'It is not the right place in this letter to argue as to the humanity of the air as compared with the army, though I am prepared to do so . . . if necessary.' He sounded a cry of alarm as he ended – '. . . disastrous consequences are bound to ensue if the . . . head of one fighting service is . . . free to state to the world at large his dissent from . . . another. Rightly or wrongly the Government have established an air service . . . How much easier our task . . . would be if the older services had always said, "How can we help you?" instead of . . . "How can we destroy you?" '

Then it was the admiral's turn to take to print. On 5 January 1922 the *Pall Mall Gazette* blared, 'Chaos in the Air Force.' The writer had it straight from a serving officer. While other papers took up the cry Trenchard had the leak swiftly traced to an ex-naval pilot now serving with the RAF. Without hesitation he confronted his brother-in-law Keyes, demanding an explanation for this clumsy attempt to turn public opinion against the RAF. Keyes admitted to having received certain confidential documents from the misguided pilot, but upon hearing that he was up for court-martial had hastily burnt them. He did not wish to get mixed up in the affair. As if to redress matters he sent Trenchard the Admiralty's latest memorandum to the Cabinet. In it Beatty and Keyes had done their best to sabotage the findings of Geddes.

Attacks from the naval contingent of MPs continued against the RAF and were echoed and amplified in the press. Then in February 1922 just as the Geddes report was due for publication, a rumour spread through

Whitehall that Lloyd George had decided once and for all to put the RAF out of business. A few days later the Report appeared. Geddes's conclusion on the RAF was, 'Economies ... ought to result in the older arms from the advent of the air force ... not only the substitution of aircraft for certain other arms of the older services ... but a revolution in ... carrying out certain operations.' The referee had once again blown the whistle for the RAF. But only the Cabinet could confirm or reject his decision.

Rumours of the RAF's imminent demise were now so frequent that Trenchard feared the Cabinet would be blackmailed into proving them correct. He knew that only one man could save the young service and that man, Churchill, rose magnificently to the occasion. On 11 March he informed Lloyd George and Austen Chamberlain, the Privy Seal, that he for one as a member of the Cabinet refused to be blackmailed into opposing the RAF. Why did they not do something to curb the rumours? Did they not realize that the RAF had been created by an Act of Parliament and only by repeal of that Act could the service be abolished? It was certainly not in the Cabinet's power to decide the issue. Chamberlain ought to have made this clear in public and put an end to the evil gossip so harmful to the junior service.

Fortunately, the Prime Minister and the Lord Privy Seal were of the same mind. On 16 March in the Commons Austen Chamberlain dwelt at length on the air problem in his quiet and impeccable manner. The Government's conclusion, he said, was that 'it would be a retrograde step ... to abolish the Air Ministry and to reabsorb the air service into the Admiralty or War Office.' 'Sailors and soldiers,' he had said, 'could not be expected to pursue its development as an independent service.' Then in almost the same words as Balfour he pronounced the Government's verdict: 'First, the air force must be autonomous ... ; second, against air raids the army and navy must play a secondary role.'

In the cut-and-thrust of the debate which followed this stunning public announcement, John Moore-Brabazon (Parliamentary Private Secretary to the Air Minister and a veteran airman) jibed irreverently at the dismayed partisans of the older services. Their rumour-mongering was a national disgrace. One would have understood had it been motivated by 'very old generals wearing the medals of Crécy and Agincourt'. But no, it was the Royal Navy, 'the spoilt darling of this nation for a hundred years', whose professional pride was ruffled by the encroachment of air power on its preserves. 'If the Channel had dried up,' he taunted, '... the defence of England would have passed to the army. But a larger miracle

C

has happened. The air has been conquered and consequently . . . the navy cannot be responsible for the defence of these islands.'

As the debate reached its climax on 21 March and again on 23 March, readers of *The Times* were shocked to find out what this meant in hard fact. *The Times* revealed that of the 185 squadrons possessed by the RAF in 1918 there now remained but twenty-eight. Only seven of these were in England and a paltry three were allotted to home defence. France at that moment had 126 squadrons. For the Air Ministry this was not news, but said the author of *The Times* articles, Brigadier-General Groves, 'the country as a whole was staggered when the facts about this great betrayal were published . . .' The *Observer*, he said, spoke of every shade of opinion in the British press in condemning it as the 'Supreme Blunder since the Armistice'.

Groves was more than generous in allowing that the British press was so scandalized. A section of that press itself was guilty. Since 1919 the press had not ceased to pillory the RAF and open columns to the older services to bully and generally kick it and its chief around. The RAF was mocked as 'The Royal Ground Force', accused of waste, inefficiency and even of atrocities. Said Groves (no friend of Trenchard's) 'the British people were in no way responsible for this demolition of their air defences. Had it been referred to them . . . they would not have allowed it.' But Samuel Hoare, who would soon be guiding the RAF's destiny, deplored the fact that '. . . any stick came in handy to the popular press for belabouring the unwanted child'. Now, at all events, the Commons debate and *The Times* had momentarily alerted public opinion. In the heat of the moment Colonel Wedgwood, the Labour party's defence spokesman, detected a change in outlook: '. . . There will be more people who realize that the navy is not our front line defence, but the air service is.'

While during February and March 1922 the Geddes Committee and the House of Commons were weighing the RAF's fate, the Germans were secretly negotiating with the Russians. The world first knew about the Treaty of Rapallo on the day following its signature, 16 April 1922. The thinking of the *Reichswehr*'s commander, Hans von Seeckt, had borne fruit. Anyone could see by the treaty terms that Germany and Russia had decided to co-operate in the political and economic spheres. But not a word was mentioned about another arrangement the two powers had made in a secret clause. In return for German technical knowledge the Russians agreed to put three bases at their disposal. One was the gas-warfare school at Saratov, the second the tank-training centre at Kazan;

the third and most valuable for both countries was the air base two hundred miles south-east of Moscow at Lipezk. From then on a steady stream of aircraft, engines, ammunition, spares and technical staff would be smuggled into Russia by sea via Stettin and Leningrad. A rail journey brought them to Lipezk. Here the Germans established their future air force. Here it was nurtured in secret, years before it came to be baptized '*Luftwaffe*'.

Barely two weeks after the Germans had so cunningly outflanked the Allies at Rapallo the Allies themselves followed up with a gesture which considerably helped the Germans' clandestine plans. It was also untimely for the British. As early as 1920 Trenchard had informed those staunch pillars of the British aircraft industry – Sopwith, de Havilland, Handley Page and Fairey – that in its emaciated condition, the RAF could not give them enough orders to keep them in business. 'Look for foreign markets, or take to toy-making,' Trenchard advised them. The British aircraft industry was steadily withering away when, on 3 May 1922, the Allies saw fit to relax the Versailles veto on Germany's right to construct civil aircraft. It was a move which saved those giants of the German aviation industry – Junkers, Dornier and Heinkel who, with the help of Sweden, Switzerland, Turkey and Italy (herself a party to the treaty), had defied the ban and set up shop abroad. Now they could get back into business in the Fatherland. Heinkel was even invited by the *Reichswehr* to build a reconnaissance plane, the He. 17, then two trainers, the He. 18 and He. 21. They managed to avoid the Control Commission's notice by keeping their designs within the specifications for sports planes. Albatros and Arado started up again, and even Ernst Udet, who had been earning his living as a stunt pilot, formed a small company (*Udet Flugzeugbau*), near Munich. Not far away at Augsburg a young aircraft designer opened another works. His name was Willy Messerschmitt.

As a change from soldiering, Carl von Schoenebeck was thrilled to get back to flying, even if only as a pilot of one of those gliders which soared like eagles above the Wasserkuppe, in the Rohn. Carl was a great friend of Ernst Udet, and 'Udlinger' asked him to fly one of the products of the *Udet Flugzeugbau* in a contest at Kissingen – a peaceful resort which one day would resound with the scream of aircraft from the Stuka School. The only problem was that Schoenebeck was not one of the small quota of pilots allowed by Versailles to fly powered aircraft. But when the day came he taxied Udet's plane to the starting line. 'Unfortunately I won,' he said, 'and after landing had to taxi in front of an admiring crowd which included the judges and the press, who immediately saw it was not Udet at the controls.' Of course it was in the papers next day and everyone asked, 'Who is this Schoenebeck who flies without a licence?' So he hurried off to the *Luftreederei* at Magdeburg, the only authorized flying school in Germany, and got himself a licence – duly antedated. The situation was thus saved, and the Air Control Commission once more hoodwinked.

Werner Junck lived at Magdeburg. He was a member of the *Luftreederei* and spent every leave flying there . . .

As the dust from the Geddes Report and the service debates was settling, spring was casting its vivid mantle over an England more aware that ever before of its aerial impotence. The summer months rolled by and, when the chilly autumn winds were tearing the last leaves from the trees, Lloyd George resigned. A general election returned Bonar Law as the new incumbent at 10 Downing Street. He had picked his colleagues beforehand; to Samuel Hoare he offered the Air Ministry. But he cautioned, 'Before you reply I must warn you that the post may be abolished in a few weeks . . .' The Prime Minister made no bones about his intention to liquidate the RAF as quickly as possible. Samuel Hoare differed once more with Groves. 'Bonar Law's attitude . . . represented the main weight of public opinion.' His opinion was that 'if there had been a referendum in 1922 . . . the answer would have been, "Two fighting services are quite enough . . . let us get rid of the third and divide it between them." '

Though it seemed that the Air Ministry had no future, Hoare gladly accepted it. After his first talk with Trenchard he felt no regrets. 'I listened enthralled,' he said. 'I suddenly realized that I might . . . have come to the Air Ministry not to wind up, as Bonar Law had suggested, but to help . . . create a peacetime air force as an independent service in no way inferior to the army or navy . . .' Such inspired optimism was sorely needed at the moment, for on 25 November Bonar Law presided over a full meeting of the Committee of Imperial Defence and coolly informed it of his firm intention to exterminate the RAF. Hoare, who was present, trembled. Trenchard, whom he informed next day, was aghast at the Prime Minister's blind foolhardiness in casting away the one weapon capable of defending Britain in a future war.

Within only a few days of Bonar Law's death sentence for the RAF, destiny beckoned to the future chief of the German air force. One grey

Sunday morning in November Hermann Goering, a genial vagabond supported by the modest fortune of Carin, now his wife, attended a mass meeting on the Königsplatz in Munich. It was held to protest against the Allies' demand for the extradition of Germany's 'war criminals' who, to the ardent, romantic Goering, were heroes and the true defenders of Germany. 'I went . . . as a spectator,' said Goering, 'I had heard (Hitler's) name once before and wanted to hear what he had to say.' Clad in a dirty raincoat Hitler confided angrily to a group of friends 'I am not going to speak to these lame bourgeois pirates.' Goering heard only this, but this was the kind of talk which pleased the reckless ex-fighter ace.

Two days after the Konigsplatz meeting Goering attended one of Hitler's own meetings and heard him say, 'Germany must be strong again.' Hitler's message was simple. 'Our motto shall be: if you will not be a German, I will bash your skull in. For we are convinced we cannot succeed without a struggle.' Goering warmed to this strange, violent individual. The next day he went to see him; the ex-corporal of the 16th Bavarian Reserve Infantry was flattered by this attention from the one-time *Kommandeur* of the famous Richthofen *Geschwader*. Moreover Hermann Goering was just the man he wanted to lead his Brownshirts and knock some discipline into them. Hitler offered Goering the job and Goering jumped at it. He shook Hitler's hand and told him fervently, 'I unite my fate with yours . . . I dedicate myself to you . . .' On the wings of Hitler's own fate Goering would be borne upwards from commander of the infant *Sturmabteilung* to leader of the most powerful air force on earth.

Within a few days of that decisive handshake on 25 November, Bonar Law presided over the meeting of the Committee of Imperial Defence. One question, he told them, had to be decided: not if, but *how* the RAF could best be liquidated. He wanted to abolish it at one blow by decree. Hoare admitted it was 'very nervously' that he asked for an impartial inquiry. Balfour, whose own inquiry only three months ago had concluded in favour of the RAF, weighed in with Hoare. Perhaps it was this that made the Prime Minister reflect and finally entrust a sub-committee under Lord Salisbury with the study of more constitutional methods of dismantling the RAF.

The fate of the German air force's future adversary was again in the balance. It was still on the cards that his Lordship might save Goering a great deal of trouble.

Not all the cards were against the RAF. A chubby, bespectacled Scot, Robert Watson-Watt – working, ironically for the navy 'in pursuit of thunderstorms' – picked up one which looked interesting. It was on the evening following the electoral victory of Bonar Law, to whom the RAF was such anathema. Watson-Witt 'listened to [a report] about a new cathode ray oscillograph which . . . American colleagues had developed. There were only two of these tubes in the country. I returned to Aldershot with one; the other was soon to go to Dr E. V. Appelton at . . . Cambridge.'

Despite Watson-Watt's excitement there was nothing new in the cathode ray idea. A German professor, Ferdinand Braun, had invented it in 1897 when Goering was still playing with his tin soldiers. Another German, Christian Hulsmeyer, had long ago hit on a use for the magic tube. British Patent No. 13170 dated 22 September 1904 had officially recognized his 'hertzian-wave Projecting and Receiving Apparatus . . . to give warning of the presence of a metallic body such as a Ship or a Train . . .' Since then scientists in America, Germany, Britain and even Japan had been exploring the fantastic realm of electro-magnetic waves. The Germans and the British both held the same card. Everything would depend on how they played it.

By the beginning of 1923 the state of Germany's economy was so disastrous that she asked for a halt in the payment of reparations to the Allies. Her pleas left the French President Poincaré unmoved. On 11 January 1923 he sent the French army forward to occupy the Ruhr, an unwarranted act which would plunge Germany further into ruin and unite the country as never before against her avenging neighbour. The vigorous protests of the British Government did not in the least deter the French, safe in the knowledge that their 126 air squadrons were a threat which the seven home-based squadrons of the RAF could hardly allay.

The latest committee, that of Lord Salisbury, was making little progress when Admiral Beatty gave a sharp blast on his foghorn. On 20 February he called at No. 10 Downing Street and informed the Prime Minister that unless the Government handed back to the navy its own air arm he would resign and carry on the fight in Parliament.

Samuel Hoare passed the dramatic news on to Trenchard the next day. He spent the morning with him drafting plans for the imminent battle.

He was then summoned to 10 Downing Street where the Prime Minister told him to settle the matter directly with Beatty. On 22 February Hoare received Beatty alone at the Air Ministry and the First Sea Lord 'pressed his case quite pleasantly, but in its extreme form.' But when Hoare suggested the decision should be postponed, Beatty became tough. 'I've waited year after year and can wait no longer. I insist on the issue being joined at once.'

Next day Beatty and Trenchard confronted each other in the presence of their respective ministers. Beatty's threat of resignation still stood, so Trenchard told him, 'Two can play at that game.' Later that day Trenchard was sent for by the Prime Minister, now thoroughly upset not only by Beatty's threat to quit, but by Trenchard's as well. 'I made no threat,' Trenchard told him. 'But I won't stay a moment longer if the RAF is carved up to suit Beatty.'

Considering that within the last three months, the RAF's right to exist had been recognized first by Balfour then by Geddes and finally by Austen Chamberlain's statement to the Commons, Trenchard felt that Bonar Law was giving in to blackmail by Beatty in ordering yet another inquiry, this time by the Committee of Imperial Defence. The inquiry was to be in two parts: Lord Salisbury would examine the wider issue of the RAF's role in national defence; Balfour would try to settle the apparently irreconcilable views of the navy and RAF. Each side would be heard separately both in the main ring and the smaller one. As Andrew Boyle has put it, the air inquiry of 1923 became 'an uninterrupted duel between the two chief protagonists, Beatty and Trenchard, with their rival staffs as seconds in the background ... and the tribunal ... keeping one eye on the rules and the other on the score'.

It was accepted for the sake of the argument that France was the potential enemy. There was certainly no question – as far as the inquiry or anyone else knew – of Germany qualifying for the role then or ever again. The fact that she eventually did, made no difference to the validity of Trenchard's argument: in a war with France Britain's survival would depend on keeping command of the air at home. 'In a democratic country like ours ... war cannot be continued unless the bulk of the people support it. If the people are subject to sufficient bombing they will compel the Government to sue for peace.'

There were two ways of defending Britain from air attack. One was to sit on the defensive and wait for the enemy bombers to arrive with their deadly loads – but it was impossible to predict when, where, and at what height they would approach and the only hope of catching them would be to maintain standing patrols. But this would require a prohibitive number of fighter aircraft and pilots, and even then would not provide complete protection. The alternative was to exploit the principle that 'Attack is the best form of defence' – the strategy Trenchard favoured. Apart from technical considerations it was much more akin to his nature. He had proved during the war, though at great cost, the efficacy of hitting out hard when threatened. 'It is on the bomber offensive that we must rely for defence. It is on the destruction of enemy industries and, above all, on the lowering of morale of enemy nationals caused by bombing that ultimate victory rests . . .' Trenchard did not hedge. With brutal frankness and realism he stated the object of strategic bombing and made it clear that if another war came civilians were in for a bad time.

Bonar Law became so ill that he had to resign as Prime Minister. The two most likely candidates for the succession were Lord Curzon and Stanley Baldwin. Curzon's chances seemed by far the strongest, not least to Curzon himself. This worried Trenchard. Curzon disliked the RAF and did not believe in it as a defender of Britain. If he became Prime Minister he might well send the RAF to the wall without further ado. But fate intervened in the strangest way. A memorandum on the relative merits of the two suppliants, which was far from flattering to Curzon, was laid before the King. A true constitutional monarch, His Majesty, assuming that the document was the work of his retiring Prime Minister, acted on its advice. He sent for Baldwin and asked him to accept the premiership. Only later did it come to light that the memorandum was not the work of Bonar Law at all, but of an assistant with a poor opinion of Curzon. But Baldwin was in, and Trenchard breathed more freely.

The inquiry reopened and the two giants were once more at grips. Beatty stuck to his theme of a separate naval air arm. Did not the letters patent of the Lords Commissioners of the Admiralty make the Admiralty solely responsible for the fighting efficiency of the Fleet? Without control of the fleet air arm that principle was destroyed. Trenchard thought this irrelevant. 'The Naval Staff,' he said, 'refuse to recognize that the extension of warfare to the air has introduced a new and permanent complication in the problem of national defence. If at some future date the British Empire is compelled to fight in the air for its existence . . . it is vital that our air forces should be reared on a single policy and trained on a single system, imbued with a single doctrine . . .'

It was a winning argument, but before it could sink in Balfour, the committee chairman, retired to bed at his home in Norfolk, a victim of phlebitis. The inquiry forged ahead without him and reached the conclusion that on the navy's side, '. . . the existing conflict of opinion is to a great extent the resultant of psychological elements of pride of service, prestige and loyal service conviction.' The RAF provided a common service to the Army and Navy in an element strange to them both. 'Are we justified,' the committee asked, 'in breaking up an existing common service merely on psychological claims?' No, they decided, and threw out the Admiralty claim for a separate service.

But still languishing in bed, the chairman refused to endorse his committee's verdict. It was unbelievable to him that arrogance and service jealousy could send the Navy into tantrums over the RAF. There must be a deeper reason and it had to be found. With that he lay back on the pillows while his committee put to sea aboard the aircraft carriers HMS *Eagle* and HMS *Argus* to try and discover the reason. What struck them all were the good working relations between the two services. They returned to Balfour's sick room more convinced than ever that the problem turned on the *amour propre*, not of the senior service as a whole, but of its admirals. Balfour admitted he was mistaken; the original verdict could stand: no separate air arm for the Navy.

Conveyed to the Admiralty on 21 July, the findings had the effect of a direct hit. Beatty and the entire Board of Admiralty threatened to resign if the results were accepted by the Government. 'Well, let them. It would be good riddance," was Trenchards' comment. And there was at least one admiral who agreed with him – Lord Fisher, the toughest old sea-dog of the lot. 'The approaching aircraft development knocks out the fleet,' he blasted, 'makes invasion practicable, cancels our being an island, transforms the atmosphere into a battleground for the future. There is only one thing to do to the ostriches who are spending . . . millions on what is as useful for the next war as bows and arrows. Sack the lot.'

On 26 July Baldwin gladdened the hearts of RAF supporters by proclaiming in the Commons: 'In addition to meeting essential air-power requirements of the Navy, Army, India and overseas commitments, British air-power must include a home defence force . . . to protect us against air attack by the strongest air force within striking distance of this country . . . In the first instance the home defence force should consist of fifty-two squadrons to be created with as little delay as possible.'

Then he retired to the peace of Chequers for the weekend of 27–29 July and pondered over the admirals' dudgeon. The newspapers speculated noisily. It was clear that Baldwin faced a major crisis and, what was worse, press and public (who were largely cheering for the Navy) had wind of it. Would Baldwin give in to the heckling and yield to Beatty? Many thought so.

But Baldwin was made of sterner stuff. To the chagrin of navy supporters he declared on 2 August that the Cabinet had decided in favour of the Air Ministry. He gave reasons for an independent air service. Firstly, '. . . the air service, although it must have intimate relations with the other armed forces . . . differs . . . essentially from both. On the other hand aircraft, whether flying above the sea or elsewhere, are governed [by] . . . the same principles.'

Secondly, '. . . the whole science of air power is in . . . rapid development. . . . Experience . . . whether on sea or on shore is vital to success.'

Thirdly, '. . . shore-based aircraft and the air force of the fleet may be called upon to act together . . . Efficiency therefore prescribes common knowledge, common training, common material provisions and a common service. Economy points . . . against the duplication of training schools and aerodromes and building plant . . . For these reasons the conclusion . . . that there should be a single air service must be . . . accepted . . .'

Fighting for their lives against heavy odds, Trenchard and the RAF had come through the last round victorious. The key principle that 'the air is one and indivisible', which he had expounded that crisp, sunny morning in December 1919 as he paced to and fro in Beatty's office, had at last triumphed. It would be the cornerstone of his future building.

While Trenchard was battling for the survival of his air force, the Germans were conspiring for the future of theirs. Parliament closed for the summer recess. As Trenchard left for the Highlands and Baldwin for the waters of Aix-les-Bains, German and Russian delegates were putting the finishing touches to the agreement concerning German use of the airfield at Lipezk – itself a watering place which had once enjoyed the patronage of Czar Peter the Great.

The news would have cheered Hitler, had he known. He had met General von Seeckt face to face back in March in Munich and had demanded violent action both against the French and against the German Government who had tolerated their occupation of the Ruhr. Little did Hitler know that von Seeckt had other, more subtle plans to settle accounts with Germany's vanquishers. The general remained unmoved by Hitler's tirade, and left him with the words, 'You and I, Herr Hitler, have nothing more to say to each other.' Hitler went off to continue preaching his unvarying theme, '. . . If a people is to become free it needs pride and will-power, defiance and hate, hate and once again hate.' His fulminations alarmed the government. In November Chancellor Stresemann, fearing a putsch, summoned his Cabinet. Anxiously he asked von Seeckt, 'Will the *Reichswehr* stick to us, General?' 'The *Reichswehr*, Herr *Reichskanzler*, will stick to me,' was the icy reply.

It was 8 November 1923. Everyone well known in Munich politics and society attended the meeting in the Burgerbraukeller that evening. Reich Commissar von Kahr had been speaking for twenty minutes when suddenly Hermann Goering burst in at the head of a group of armed SA troopers. During the uproar Hitler leaped on a table, revolver in hand, and let off a shot into the ceiling. Bellowing 'the National Revolution has begun . . .' he warned the terrified audience that the hall was surrounded by six hundred more SA. Then, leaving Goering to keep the crowd quiet, he retired to an adjoining room to negotiate with von Kahr and the other speakers.

The next day with the veteran hero General Ludendorf and other Nazi leaders and sympathizers, Hitler and Goering linked arms in a protest march through Munich. Goering wore a heavy leather overcoat with the collar turned back to reveal the *Pour le Mérite* round his neck. On his head he wore a steel helmet, embellished with a white swastika. But to no avail. When at half past midday the column reached the narrow Residenzstrasse the police opened fire and Goering received a vicious wound in the thigh.

Frau Ballin, wife of a Jewish merchant, and her sister rescued the wounded SA leader and dressed his wound. After dark he was smuggled to the clinic of his friend Professor Ach for expert treatment. Meanwhile a warrant was out for his arrest, but some nights later Carin managed to get him, dressed in a night shirt and fur coat, across the frontier into Austria and temporary safety. Meanwhile the Bavarian police arrested Hitler.

In the hospital at Innsbruck Goering received two shots of morphine a day to quell his pain, but still he suffered so terribly that he bit the pillow to stifle his cries. Very slowly he got better and was able to leave the hospital on crutches to spend Christmas at the Tiroler Hof Hotel, whose Nazi owner had provided a free room. Goering and Carin were now penniless exiles. Only food parcels from her family in Sweden saved them.

By February 1924 the wound had healed and Goering began to launch out into a series of violent speeches in the Nazi cause. Indignant, the Austrian Government ordered him to quit the country. Swearing that if he returned it would be in triumph, he accepted asylum in Italy.

As the Goerings settled into a back-street hotel in Rome in the April of 1924, Adolf Hitler began an eight-month prison sentence in Landsberg jail, west of Munich. Soon he would start dictating the first chapters of *Mein Kampf* to his friend Rudolf Hess. His was an easy, comfortable life compared to that of the Goerings. Despite the Goerings' social contacts, an audience with Mussolini, and the visits of Carin to Germany to seek help, they were soon penniless. In May they trekked sadly back to take refuge in Sweden. Now a drug-addict on the verge of insanity Goering entered Langbro public asylum. There was no question of his finding a new job in civil aviation. But far away on the banks of the Voronezh river south of Moscow the air force he would one day command was at this very moment being launched on its clandestine career.

Chapter 5

A building and equipment programme had started some months before, but it was soon obvious that the original budget of two million marks was not going to be enough to finish the air base at Lipezk. More had to be found and the French army occupying the Ruhr provided the pretext. Von Seeckt had said, 'If the French won't leave we must drive them out.' He appealed to Ruhr industrialists for money to buy arms, and it was forthcoming – apparently not from the industrialists' own pockets, but by expropriating ten million marks from the Ruhr workers relief fund. Intended to provide for the overworked and underpaid who were toiling for Germany's economic recovery, this sum was diverted to cover the purchase of one hundred D13 fighter aircraft from that loyal Dutchman Anthony Fokker, and the provision of hangars and buildings at Lipezk for the embryo German air force. Ironically, the Fokker D13s which the Germans bought were powered by British engines – the sturdy Napier Lion. Presumably the Napier Company felt it was not their business to inquire about the final destination of the engines they delivered to Fokker, who had them mounted in his D13s and shipped direct from Holland to Leningrad. It was a clever arrangement.

Werner Junck had arranged his retirement from the *Reichswehr* in May 1923. Through a friend he got an offer from an airline company in Colombia, South America. In Berlin he pleaded with his friend Major Wilburg at the *Reichswehrministerium*, 'I've got the chance to fly again. Nothing else interests me, so please fix my discharge.' 'Impossible,' replied Wilburg, 'the regulations only allow discharge on grounds of physical or mental deficiency.' 'Well I am physically deficient,' argued Junck, 'I was wounded three times. And if I go on much longer in the army I shall certainly qualify on mental grounds.' They argued for hours, but Junck got his discharge and took the next boat to South America. He stayed in

Colombia until 1924, when the airline went bankrupt. Then he returned to his home in Magdeburg, to become an instructor at the *Luftreederei*.

Carl von Schoenebeck was eating his heart out in the *Reichswehr*. Flying gliders every now and then was all very well, but he longed to hold a throttle lever again and feel the incomparable thrill of powered flight. Then in 1924 he was suddenly sent off to Lipezk to test the Fokker D13 fighter. He was wild with enthusiasm. And soon after this came an order from the Ministry sending him to the Dornier Company in South America, which was now becoming a kind of El Dorado for German aviators hungry for the flying experience denied to them in their own country.

There was a grotesque contrast at this stage between German military aviation – it was as yet only the embryo of an air service – and the RAF. If the young RAF was an unwanted child, German military aviation was simply illegitimate. It had been conceived in the darkest secrecy and the most extreme precautions were being taken to conceal its existence. Its old eagles were banned from the air, and it had no leader. Its eventual leader would not be found among those reluctant soldiers like Albert Kesselring and Walther Wever, who had been forcibly abducted from their regiments to serve underground in the secret Air Section of the *Reichswehrministerium*. Goering was far away at Stockholm, past caring about the air and aeroplanes. But for the moment Von Seeckt saw to it that the needs of German military aviation were provided for with generosity and enthusiasm.

The RAF, on the other hand, had had an uncommonly tough struggle for existence. It had groped doggedly through an almost impenetrable cloud of constitutional and parliamentary procedure, trying to make its voice heard above the carping protests of its elder sisters and their friends, who had often tried to do it in. But by the beginning of 1925 it stood sure of itself under the firm hand of Trenchard.

On the first day of 1925 a new Command, the Air Defence of Great Britain, was formed under the direction of Air Chief Marshal Sir John Salmond. The bomber was still the main weapon of defence, its role being to counter-attack the attacker and neutralize him by destroying his air bases and factories and by demoralizing his citizens. The bomber force of the Air Defence of Great Britain consisted of the Central and Wessex Bombing Areas. A thousand years had passed since the great King Alfred had reigned over the Kingdom of Wessex and repulsed the

Viking invaders. Central and Wessex Bombing Areas aspired to an equally heroic role. Unfortunately their aircraft, equipment and bombing technique were more appropriate to the Wessex of Alfred's day.

It was the same with the fighters whose organization, Fighting Area, at least had a more heroic ring to its name. What Fighting Area lacked in strength – only one fighter aircraft was then produced for three bombers – it made up for in the colourful character of its pilots and the peculiar style of their dress. Their rakish 'Fighting Area caps', the top buttons of their tunics invariably undone, marked out the 'fighter boys' as a special breed who never took themselves too seriously or tried to persuade anyone else to do so.

But Trenchard did not believe in fighters for defence. Even if he had known about those two cathode ray tubes, of which Watson-Watt had appropriated one and Dr E. V. Appleton the other, there was no reason for him to see the connection between them and fighter defence. All the same Appleton was getting warm. He had been able to measure the ionosphere by 'bouncing' radio-magnetic waves off its upper limit. The invention of 'radar' was in the making.

But Trenchard was adamant about fighters. In a speech at Cambridge in April 1925 he said, 'The airplane is the most offensive weapon that has ever been invented. It is a shockingly bad weapon of defence ...' He believed whole-heartedly in strategic bombing as a deterrent and as the best means of defence. 'Although it is necessary to have some defence to keep up the morale of your own people, it is infinitely more necessary to lower the morale of the people against you by *attacking* them ...' But the Chief of Air Staff was not at heart the brutal, ruthless killer he may have seemed. In the same speech he said, 'If I had the casting vote I would say "Abolish the air". It is an infinitely more harmful weapon than any other ...' No one knew better than he what he was talking about.

The Air Defence of Great Britain was not going to be left entirely to the 'regulars'. Trenchard hit on the idea of backing them with a permanent active force of auxiliaries. The army had its Territorials, why not the RAF? For once the Cabinet did not demur. The low price of the scheme made it attractive. Citizens of London, Glasgow and Edinburgh were enthusiastic. The problem was to seed the long list of volunteers. By October each of the three cities had formed their own squadron while the County of London made the number up to four. Some of the finest war-time pilots leaped at the chance to serve again, although some found the conditions somewhat changed. The Commander of the City of Edinburgh Squadron complained to Trenchard, 'I can't make head or tail of these new regulations,' to which the Chief of Air Staff simply replied, 'You're running your own show. If you don't like the regulations, re-write them.' It was in this spirit that private citizens during the week became, during the weekend, flyers as intrepid and skilful as any and with a degree of *insouciance* frowned upon by the regulars.

The German civilians who travelled to Lipezk were quite a different sort. Many of them were not civilians at all, but officers of the *Reichswehr* masquerading in civilian clothes. They travelled in small groups by boat from Stettin to Leningrad under assumed names with forged passports. Once on Russian soil the Soviet travel agency, *Intourist*, passed them on by rail to Lipezk. There they found themselves members of the 'Fourth Squadron, Red Air Force'. To provide a realistic touch a few old Red Air Force planes were dispersed around the field. It was guarded by Russian soldiers and no strangers were allowed within the precincts. The basic flying personnel who arrived at Lipezk in 1924, consisted of sixty German pilots and instructors. The 'open season' extended from May to September and during it the number of flying personnel rose to about a hundred.

The Russians supplied basic building materials, but all other supplies down to the last nut and bolt were shipped out of Stettin to Leningrad, then by rail to Lipezk. The movement of this contraband material was handled by a spurious Soviet company, the Society for Promotion of Industrial Enterprise. When range permitted, aircraft were flown non-stop to Lipezk. Otherwise – as with the Fokker fighters – they were shipped in crates through Leningrad. Equipment such as bombs, likely to attract unwelcome curosity, was smuggled across the Baltic in small boats manned by German naval officers, plying on apparently innocent business to various Russian ports. There were few fatal accidents at Lipezk, but when grim necessity demanded bodies were shipped back to Stettin in cases labelled 'Engine Parts'.

One day early in 1925 Werner Junck was called to the *Reichswehrministerium* in Berlin, where he was informed that he had been selected as Chief Flying Instructor of the secret Russian project. Later he learned that Udet's name had also come up, but his career as a film star had weighed against him. Shortly afterwards Junck sailed from Stettin – this time on a mission which would pay a considerably bigger dividend than the abortive Colombian adventure. Disembarking at Leningrad he noticed at once that the Russians all wore caps. His small group of Germans seemed the only ones in hats. South of Moscow the train stopped at a small junction where the party changed for Lipezk. A porter came straight up to Junck and said, 'You are a German – I can tell by your hat. I was a prisoner in Germany and I like your country.' This genial welcome immediately earned him the appointment as official travel agent for visiting Germans. His technique was simple. He would accost anyone wearing a hat and lisp in his ear, 'You are for Lipezk? Come with me.'

At the same time Carl von Schoenebeck travelled to Lipezk. He and a man named Borman were the only two staff instructors under Junck. The *Reichswehr* officers had left their uniform behind in Germany. Here they were just 'civilian employees'. Although on Government service, their time in Russia did not count for a pension. However there was some consolation in that they were well paid, for their quarters were far from palatial. The furniture was knocked up from old Fokker crates.

For the time being they had to turn their backs on the Fatherland. Direct correspondence was impossible and letters were forwarded by way of a Berlin cover address and the Embassy in Moscow. Junck's ageing father had no inkling that his son was in Russia. Despite these comparatively minor privations, the three instructors were allowed off the camp. For the pupils it was like living in a monastery. They met the Russian air force people only at the Casino. Carl did not particularly take to them, but they got along all right with the airmen. The Germans one day challenged the Russians to a mock air combat and flew rings round them. Then they swapped aircraft – the Russians had some rickety old De Havillands and Martinsydes said Junck, which made a noise like piano wires. In spite of this the Germans outmanoeuvred their Russian opponents who thereafter showed them great respect.

Divested as they were of their military trappings, Junck and his companions found their prowess as pilots was a strong advantage with the Russian ladies. But Major Hugo Sperrle was not so lucky when he took a week off from the Ministry in Berlin to attend exercises at Lipezk. He had flown for the army during the war, but as an observer. Ignorant of this a lady asked him, 'Tell me, Major, do you fly or merely shoot a gun in self-defence'? On hearing it was the latter her interest cooled. You had to be a pilot to make a hit with the ladies of Lipezk. They wrote off the portly Sperrle as 'only an observer'.

Experimental aircraft of all shapes and sizes arrived at Lipezk for testing under military conditions – from the Junkers factory at Fili, near Moscow; from Dorniers in Switzerland, from Rohrbach in Copenhagen and even from the Heinkel factory at Rostock in Germany. There was no problem in shipping or flying them in from foreign based factories. As for Heinkels, Werner Junck's opinion was that the Allied Control Commission simply closed their eyes.

The first batch of pupils at Lipezk were mostly ex-wartime pilots, some of them highly decorated, who came for a refresher course. But they did not stand up well to the strenuous flying conditions, so Werner Junck wrote to the Ministry in Berlin suggesting that they should recruit younger pilots, like those he had been instructing at Magdeburg. The Ministry hesitated – they were worried about the pupils graduating straight from the sixty m.p.h. sports aircraft direct to the one hundred and fifty m.p.h. military machines at Lipezk. Junck reassured them, and when autumn came and the weather put an end to flying for six months, he and Carl von Schoenebeck returned to Germany where they selected at leisure a dozen young pilots from the authorized flying clubs like Magdeburg and from the *Deutsche Verkehrflieger Schule* (Commercial Pilots' School) then at Stettin. Those first twelve pilots became instructors for the *Reichswehr* officers who were soon to arrive at Lipezk in droves. And those *Reichswehr* officers would form the vanguard of the future *Luftwaffe*.

Erhard Milch, who had once lent his own aircraft to an English prisoner-pilot, had been with Junkers since 1920. He went quite often to Russia – not to Lipezk, but to the firm's factory at Fili, near Moscow. Milch's career as a pilot had not been particularly distinguished, but since being with Junkers he had developed into a brilliant organizer, though he harboured a trace of contempt for the professional flying men he had out-classed. In his eyes Lipezk seemed an irrelevant nonsense. 'It was a child's toy and gave us no great benefit. None of the people there later achieved high seniority. It was a simple playground – nice for those who were there.'

Milch failed to see that there in exile on the banks of the Voronezh German military aviation was being revived. At least 120 outstanding fighter pilots and another 450 flying personnel, including reconnaissance and dive-bomber pilots, were trained at Lipezk. They would form the hard core of Hitler's *Luftwaffe*.

But the benefits were not all one-sided. Red pilots were attached to

Lipezk for flying courses. And their technical ground staff benefited enormously from round-the-year instruction given by German technicians. The engineers of the Soviet Technical Institute (*Zagi*) worked closely with the Germans in the development and testing of German aircraft at Lipezk and had access to their plans and designs. In some ways it proved a difficult collaboration. The Soviet pilots had a long way to go to match the expertise of the Germans. 'You cannot put primitive people in complicated machines,' one Red Air Force officer explained.

Forbidden to construct military aircraft in Germany, the German aircraft industry used the immunity of Lipezk to develop highly efficient prototypes of all-metal fighters, bombers and reconnaissance aircraft. They would be ready for mass production years before the other European Powers had even designed theirs.

The K48, first dive-bomber from Milch's old firm of Junkers and forerunner of the *Stuka*, would undergo its flight trials at Lipezk. And Erhard Milch himself would one day become the formidable architect of the new *Luftwaffe*.

Meanwhile Manfred von Richthofen had once more captured the attention of his countrymen. On 20 November 1925 bells tolled and flags were at half-mast throughout Germany. The Red Knight, its immortal hero, had returned at last to the Fatherland from his modest resting place in a French war cemetery. His coffin, upon which reposed his *Uhlan* officer's sword, lay in state for two days in the chilly gloom of the *Gedankneskirche* in Potsdam. Thousands came to pay their homage. The impressive funeral on 20 November brought thousands more to line the streets and to watch as the splendid cortège passed to the leaden beat of the Dead March, on its way to the *Invaliden* Cemetery. A team of shining black horses drew the gun-carriage, which was flanked by members of the *Ordre Pour le Mérite*. Among them was Udet, one-time ace of the Red Knight's renowned *Geschwader*. Immediately behind walked Richthofen's mother with President *Generalfeldmarschall* Paul von Hindenburg at her side. Following them came high officers of state and of the *Reichswehr*, and many old eagles of *Geschwader* I.

Of the thousands who watched none knew that one day the *Richthofen Geschwader* would patrol again. And how many of those silent watchers noticed the absence of the *Geschwader*'s last commander? Hermann Goering was still in the Langbro public asylum in Sweden. His craving for drugs was slowly diminishing under treatment.

'Better a Zero than a Nero,' said Hindenburg's enemies when he became President in April 1925. Von Seeckt and the *Reichswehr* willingly gave the old *Generalfeldmarschall* their allegiance and the President in turn gave his blessing to their policies – above all to the secret liaison with Russia. At the same time the Germans sat down at Locarno with France, England, Belgium, Italy, Poland and Czechoslovakia to talk about peace, brotherhood and disarmament. A year later they would join the League of Nations.

For Winston Churchill, now Chancellor of the Exchequer, the peace doves cooing at Locarno provided a welcome pretext for cuts in the fighting services' spending. In October 1925 he warned that the RAF must brake expansion and – true to time-honoured British methods – two committees were formed to review military spending. One, under Lord Colwyn, would audit the accounts; the other, under the direction of Churchill and his friend Lord Birkenhead, would study measures for scaling down the fifty-two squadron Home Defence programme.

This double inquiry was the signal for Beatty to go full steam ahead. Under covering fire from the army, the bulldog sailor turned in for his last and most determined attack against the RAF. As Trenchard said later to Baldwin, everything had been done to ensure that 'the need for economy should not become a peg on which the older services could hang a fresh demand for our abolition . . .' He had asked Churchill to try and avoid further controversy, but he was told that it was impossible – the Admiralty and the War Office had chosen to reopen the issue 'on the pretext alike of efficiency and economy'.

Trenchard begged Churchill 'to look at the service which has been formed and is fast growing up . . . Wherever you go, whether it is in a Punch and Judy show or in Grand Opera, in the highest circles or the lowest, you will hear the opinion that the air force do better than anyone else. Yet because a few people . . . state to you that they can save £4 or £5 millions by taking over the air service . . . you think we have made a mistake.' Churchill replied that he was under considerable pressure from the Treasury and hoped that Trenchard would understand. Trenchard was not consoled and redoubled his efforts to defend the RAF against the combined attacks of the Navy and Army. Then came the day in December when he could write, 'I've had the toughest fight . . . for a long time over this matter and have gained my finest victory . . .'

To the unitiated, air disarmament seemed to offer an easy way of economizing. Trenchard was asked for, and gave, his professional advice. In typically forthright terms he replied: 'Only by total abolition of all aircraft, civil and military, can air disarmament be rendered effective', the main reason being that 'commercial aircraft ... can be very readily adapted for use in war ... If all civil flying were to cease, an effective stage in the possible limitation of air armaments would have been reached.'

This was not the kind of talk that appealed to the board of *Lufthansa*, the German national airline founded on 6 January 1926. One of its directors was a tall, lean man with narrow eyes, Konrad Adenauer. But the man who would make it the leading airline in Europe was Erhard Milch, its new Managing Director.

His tremendous dynamism set *Lufthansa* on the way to success – after one year its one hundred and twenty aircraft had flown four million miles to destinations as far-flung as Peking, Moscow and Rio de Janeiro. Navigational aids for blind and night flying were developed and standardized both in Germany and abroad. The RAF soon adopted the blind-approach system invented by a *Lufthansa* pilot. Milch had secret ties with the *Reichswehr* through Captain Ernst Brandenburg, the former Zeppelin ace. General von Seeckt himself had got him his job. Just as *Lufthansa*'s aircraft could be rapidly converted to military use, so its aircrew training programme was conceived with an eye to military needs.

In March of 1926, as Milch was rising to fame, Goering strode out of Langbro public asylum near Stockholm, finally cured of his drug addiction. His doctor saw in him an hysteric, with marked inconsistencies of character. He was sensitive, yet thick-skinned; violent, yet dominated by anxiety; capable of great courage when driven by despair, yet lacking in real valour; in summary, a weak character given to self-display in order to conceal his lack of moral courage. But once out of Langbro asylum he pulled himself together and set off along the road which led back to Germany and to Erhard Milch. First he would have to serve this astute and ambitious airline director; later he would become his tyrannical master.

At this juncture Germany's secret operations with Russia came under the scrutiny of the foreign press. *The Times* was first to suggest that there might be a secret military protocol attached to the Russo-German Treaty. Lipezk had been going for two years, not to speak of the two other secret bases, Kazan, the tank training centre, and Saratov, the gas warfare school. Nothing daunted, Chancellor Stresemann stated that 'there is talk of . . . secret agreements between Germany and the Soviet Union. That has been denied often enough already . . . If one respects such insinuations today I can no longer believe them to be well-intentioned.'

Not long afterwards von Seeckt made a *faux pas* in permitting the eldest son of the Crown Prince to participate in the *Reichswehr*'s annual manoeuvres. A political storm engineered by the sinister, intriguing General Kurt von Schleicher forced President Hindenburg to dismiss the ablest of his generals. But the plans von Seeckt had so sedulously laid for Germany's military revival would in time be accomplished beyond his wildest imaginings by the generation of Germans now coming forward.

Karl Missy was one of this generation. He left the *Volksschule* in 1926 at the age of fourteen. Having helped his father after school hours, he already had a feeling for the plumbing business. Then the old man sent him as apprentice to a friend, master-plumber Albert Koellges. Both men were artisans, city fathers and esteemed by the people of Rheydt. Karl wanted to become like his father, a *Meister* and a city father. He got off to a bad start. One day old Koellges sent him up on the roof to fix something. As Karl reached for a tool he slipped and fell, only just saving himself from crashing to the ground. It was the nearest he had so far come to flying, and he did not enjoy it, especially as old Koellges boxed his ears for his error.

While Karl Missy was performing his antics on the roof in Rheydt I was at Wychwood Preparatory School in the pinewoods behind Bournemouth. It was a redbrick Victorian building with towers and weathercocks on top. A drive curved uphill to the front door outside which the headmaster's dark blue sports Bentley was often parked.

One of my best friends was Mr Longley, the school carpenter. Through him I became alive to the grain and the scent of pine and oak and the stench of his little black glue-pot which he heated on the fire. Mr Longley had been a sailor and he taught me to make model sailing boats. Under his expert eye I spent hours shaping the hull and sewing and rigging the sails. I was enchanted with my boats as they sailed across the local pond, heeling gracefully to the wind. Then one day my father took me to an air meeting at Bournemouth. As the aircraft tore low overhead banking vertically, I could see the pilots huddled behind their windscreens with their scarves streaming in the wind. It thrilled me, and from that day hulls and sails gave way to wings and fuselages. One of the pilots who banked steeper and lower than most was my future Commander-in-Chief, Sholto Douglas.

When Missy left the *Volksschule* I was at Wychwood in the top form, along with Anthony Hughes, a boy with a big dark head full of brains. Hughes was a major frustration in my life for I very rarely beat him for first place, and worse, the headmaster favoured him while taking unfair advantage of my sensitivity. But one day I gave him a surprise. As he taunted me playfully in front of the rest of the class I stood up and blurted out, 'You're a bloody fool and I can't stick you.'

An ancient engraving in our red history book showed the Armada sailing up the Channel in 1588. At each corner a fat cherub puffed furiously and the legend ran, 'He blew and they were scattered'. So with a bit of help from Sir Francis Drake it was mostly God who repelled the Spaniards. Somewhere else in the book was another quotation. We could never remember who uttered it or when, but it stuck – 'This England never did nor ever shall bow at the proud foot of a conqueror.' With Nelson's splendid Trafalgar signal thrown in for good measure we were, at the age of twelve, mentally equipped to resist all attempts to subdue our island. But the Reverend Batley had added a final touch to remind us of our heritage. He divided the seventy pupils into four sections, Celts, Saxons, Danes and Normans. I was a Norman, with a friendly contempt for my less sophisticated tribal brothers.

Such were the subtle ways in which our patriotism was kindled. Karl Missy was treated, of course, to a similarly strong patriotic line at the *Volksschule*. They too learnt to love and to serve their Fatherland.

Chapter 6

One day early in 1926 the little town of Westport in New Zealand's South Island was bathed in sunshine. Three small brothers were engrossed in a game of marbles when a strange sound came to their ears. As it drew nearer they suddenly jerked their heads up to fasten their eyes on something they had never seen. A small biplane droned overhead. Then it glided down to land on the firm, sandy beach. Forgetting their marbles, the boys ran towards the spot. The last to arrive was the smallest of the three, an eight-year-old named Alan Deere. With his brothers he sat down and gazed for hours, fascinated, at the little machine which had come down from the sky. Then they were allowed to look in the cockpit. Al touched the 'joy-stick'. For months his only dream was to fly in a machine like that. But no more aircraft came to Westport, and Al's flying fever died down.

Flight Lieutenant Cyril Burge was Personal Assistant to the Chief of the Air Staff, Boom Trenchard. He was also Douglas Bader's uncle. During the summer of 1927 Bader had nearly died of rheumatic fever. The fact that his heart had been affected did not deter him from writing to his uncle at Christmas to ask about entering the Royal Air Force College at Cranwell. Bader's mother disapproved. She disliked flying, and it would cost more than she could afford to send her son to Cranwell. But Bader's ardour was not so easily damped. In the Spring of 1928 he took the exams in Burlington House, that grim building off Bond Street in London. He arrived at Cranwell in September 1928, and a month later his instructor climbed out of an Avro 504 Trainer and said, 'All right off you go. Don't bend it.' At that moment Douglas Bader took off on a flying career without equal in the annals of flying.

Johannes Janke had an uncle too, an Admiral in the *Kriegsmarine*. One day in 1927 just after Johannes had taken his *Arbitua*, the Admiral startled him.

70

'You must learn to fly, my boy,' he said gruffly, 'it's the best thing a young man can do. I will use my influence to get you in to the DVS.'*
He was as good as his word. In 1927 Johannes joined the DVS, which had just moved from Stettin to Schleissheim, near Munich. But Johannes's father owned a large estate near Stralsund in Pomerania and hated losing his son, who he had hoped would take over from him. Moreover he thought flying dangerous.

His initial training over, Janke moved in 1928 to Warnemunde seaplane station on the Baltic. Werner Junck was test pilot for Heinkel close by at Rostock. There a new fighter, the He. 38, was being developed under the noses of the unprotesting Air Commission. With a 750 h.p. BMW engine it had a top speed of 186 m.p.h. – faster than the RAF's fighter, the Bristol Bulldog. Watching enviously as the little German fighter manoeuvred overhead, Janke vowed that one day he would escape from the lumbering civil aircraft he was now flying and get on to fighters. How, he did not quite know, for he seemed destined to fly aircraft which got heavier and heavier. After the seaplanes at Warnemunde he went on to Brunswick to fly three-engined Rohrbach Rolands before gaining his *Flugkapitän*'s licence and being assigned to *Lufthansa*'s Munich-Madrid service.

Working in Berlin as the agent for *Lufthansa* was an ex-patient of the Langbro Public Asylum. Hermann Goering got the job in 1927 when, taking advantage of a public amnesty declared by President Hindenburg, he returned to the capital. Goering was determined to mend his ways and make money. Leaving Carin in Sweden for the time being, he took a small flat in Berchtesgadenstrasse and fixed himself up as a representative for BMW and Tornblad parachutes. As agent for *Lufthansa* he struck up a close relationship with Erhard Milch.

Upon hearing that Hitler was on one of his rare visits to the capital Goering dropped in at the Sanssouci Hotel, where the Fuehrer always stayed. Far from rejoicing at finding his brave SA leader again after all these years, Hitler received him coolly. Hitler had gathered others around him – like Heinrich Himmler, who now ran his newly formed personal bodyguard, the *Schutz Staffel* (SS), and Josef Goebbels, whose keen intelligence and fiery oratory fitted him as the Party's *Gauleiter* for Berlin. However, Hitler needed men who could help him financially. Goering, whose business was beginning to flourish and whose contacts

* *Deutsche Verkehrsflieger Schüle* (German Civil Airline Pilots' School).

were increasing rapidly, soon persuaded Hitler that he was the right man. Hitler agreed to support him as party candidate for the *Reichstag*.

Carin then joined Goering, and they moved into a bigger flat in Gaisbergstrasse. Milch came there often and rallied to Goering's aid in the election campaign. On 20 May 1928 Hermann Goering was one of twelve Nazi deputies chosen to represent the eight hundred thousand who had voted for the Party. Goebbels was another. Then *Lufthansa* ran into financial trouble and the Board decided to turn its accounts over to Milch. All he could say was, 'I admire your courage. I have never read a balance sheet in my life.' He immediately set to work reorganizing the airline from top to bottom, and the first man he turned to was Goering. As the new deputy began to plead the cause of *Lufthansa* in the *Reichstag*, so also did he begin to overhaul its managing director on the long climb to the summit of power.

The Nazis were on the move. In November 1928 the streets were full of SA chanting '*Deutschland erwache!*' (Germany awake!) under the incitement of Goebbels, then Party Director of Propaganda.

When some months later one of the SA toughs (Horst Wessel) was killed in a street brawl, Goebbels was quick to take advantage. He made a martyr out of Wessel and the *Horst Wessel Lied* was in future chanted by the street mobs.

Meanwhile the Goerings had moved into a fashionable flat in the Badenschestrasse. Erhard Milch was still a frequent visitor. One day Goering confided to him, 'When the Party gets into power we shall create a new Air Force.'

Foundations for the future air force were going steadily ahead at far off Lipezk when in 1928 they were badly shaken. Two German aircraft collided over Lipezk and the pilot of one, *Rittmeister* von Hammlinger, was killed. With the usual discretion his body was shipped back to Stettin. As the ship with von Hammlinger's body aboard entered Stettin Harbour his young widow, who was expecting a baby, was overhead in a chartered aircraft. Somehow she wrenched the door open and jumped out.

There were headlines in the German press. They revealed the existence of Lipezk and spoke of the secret conspiracy between the Germans and the Russians. In *Die Weltbuhne* Carl von Ossietzky, later to win the Nobel Prize while in a concentration camp, openly accused the Government of complicity. But the Government once again denied all knowledge. Von Hammlinger, they said, was a retired captain and no concern of theirs.

Johannes Janke, who had never forgotten the Heinkel fighter he had seen at Rostock, one day burst out to his uncle, 'I can't stick flying those lousy old passenger crates any longer.' Once again the old sailor rose to the occasion. Not only did he arrange for Johannes to go to Lipezk – he actually escorted him there, in May 1929.

At Lipezk, Janke realized his dream. He flew fighters at last – the same Heinkel 38 he had admired at Rostock.

Schoenebeck, now Commandant, saw that in view of his exceptional flying experience Johannes was allowed special privileges. He was allowed to go wild-fowling within a hundred miles of the base and drive around in a little Chevrolet truck. Even the other pilots found ways of stretching their limited freedom. They made false passes covered with homemade 'official' stamps. They were never questioned by the Russian guards, who could not read.

Hans-Heinrich Brustellin came from a family of Silesian land-owners. He was at school in Stettin in 1927 and used to watch the aircraft from the DVS. But aeroplanes did not interest him. He wanted to go into the cavalry. When he applied in 1929 Germany was in the throes of an economic breakdown and jobs were scarce. Of three thousand applicants for the services, three hundred were accepted. During the 'aptitude test' they were asked 'Do you want to fly?' When Hans-Heinrich replied 'yes' he was told, 'Don't breathe a word about flying.' He didn't, and on 4 April 1929 he arrived at the DVS at Schleissheim. By May 1930 he was on his way to Lipezk.

As a pupil-pilot, Brustellin found the life at Lipezk tough. The food was bad but the mess was reasonably comfortable. The officers were nick-named *Altmarker* and the pupils *Jungmarker*, after the *Markers*, inhabitants of the Mark (Germany's contested eastern frontier zone). At Lipezk *Altmarkers* and *Jungmarkers* lived separately, but all were united in a secret bond to defend the Fatherland.

Even for the *Jungmarkers*, the Lipezk of Brustellin's time was not all work and no play. Sometimes they would stroll in the Kurgarten with girls who had a maddening habit of disappearing the moment they felt they were being spied on. Sometimes they would take them down to the river to swim – and the *Altmarker* would fly over and drop notes such as '*Schont Eure Nerven, Jungs*' (Take it easy, boys), and other ribaldry.

Bad as the food was, the Russians fared worse. This gave rise to a problem. The mechanics were all Russians, and the German pilots had strict orders to ensure that there was one holding each wing tip of their Fokker D13s while taxiing. The Soviet Commandant, a martinet, immediately sent for any pilot who taxied so fast that the wing-tip men had to run. But when the German pilots landed just before midday the Russian mechanics implored the pilots to go faster, or they would arrive at the cookhouse late and get nothing to eat. It was a delicate situation. Eager to get their men to the cookhouse in time, the Germans were frequently reprimanded.

While a few privileged German airmen were flying powered aircraft at Lipezk, thousands of less fortunate but equally passionate enthusiasts were limited by the Versailles Treaty to gliding. They felt angry and frustrated at this ruling, which one of them described as 'A most arbitrary expression of arrogance on the part of the victors.' His name was Adolf Galland, and in 1928 the fast-growing glider movement reached his home town of Westerhold (in Westphalia) where the nearby Gelsenkirchen Club established a camp. The sight of the gliders being catapulted into the air from a nearby hill, the Borkenberge, gave young Adolf the longing to fly and his father allowed him to go off to Gelsenkirchen twice a week to attend the Club's theoretical courses. The short-term result was that Galland failed his school exams. However, 'with the help of God and my schoolmates', he managed in the future to keep abreast of his studies without having to sacrifice his weekends at the Borkenberge. So far he and the other youngsters could only watch with longing eyes and work like slaves, dragging the gliders back to the hill-top after each take-off. But the great day came at last in 1929 when at the glider's controls seventeen-year-old Galland felt himself being shot into the air like an arrow from a bowstring. He nearly smashed the glider on that first landing but quickly improved and was awarded an A Licence badge – a white gull on a blue background.

Another young enthusiast soon to come to the Borkenberge was Werner Borner. After leaving school he enlisted in the 18th Infantry Regiment in the May of 1929. 'I longed to fly,' he said, 'but the Versailles Treaty made it impossible. So I joined the army.' Some months later Borner was transferred to his father's old unit, the 5th Battalion of the 18th Infantry Regiment at Munster. Borkenberge was not far away and with his craze for flying Borner joined the glider club. He and his friends, all in their late teens, built their own glider, a Zoegling. The day came when Borner, like Galland, won his A Licence and the white gull badge on the blue background. But almost more important were the congratulations he received from a First War ace who had always encouraged him, his friend and hero *Hauptmann* Heldmann. Borner was happy at being a glider pilot, but he still longed to pilot a powered aircraft.

Meanwhile he became a good infantryman and his prowess with the 98 rifle and the 08/15 machine-gun won him a special prize. Borner's deadly aim was one day going to prove fateful to me.

In the summer of 1929 I was too young to pilot either a glider or an aeroplane. But like Galland and Borner, I did manage to get off the ground. I was a schoolboy of fourteen and a half. The year before I had gone to Haileybury, wearing like every other 'new Guv'nor' a blue suit and bowler hat. Perhaps it was because he had been gassed in World War I that my housemaster, Leslie Ashcroft, was such an air fanatic. He had many friends in air circles.

During the summer term I missed more than one catch at cricket watching the Siskins from North Weald gambolling overhead. No doubt one of them was piloted by Sholto Douglas, then Station Commander at North Weald. It was he who had thrilled the crowd – and me – at Bournemouth air races.

One day three Siskins landed on one of the playing fields. It was the first time I had felt – and smelt – an aeroplane, and the effect was intoxicating. But better was to come. That summer I went to OTC camp at Tidworth. Ashcroft arranged for three of us (out of a hundred) to fly, and I was one. The aircraft was a Bristol Fighter, veteran biplane of World War I. I was attached in the observer's cockpit by the 'monkey-tail'. Crouching behind the broad shoulders of the pilot, Flight Lieutenant Guy Charles, I soared into the air. The rain stung my cheeks, and the cold, clean rush of the slipstream was so clean and fresh and exhilarating that it cut the air right out of my lungs. Green fields and woods and rows of ripening corn slipped away beneath us as we rose up into another world, and the features of the world we had left grew small and unimportant. Yet what amazed me was that for all our speed, the aeroplane seemed to be supported motionless in space by an invisible hand. I looked out along the wings and back at the tail. Nothing moved, but the great blast of air from the Rolls-Royce Eagle gave a feeling of mighty power.

That day I decided I would be a pilot.

No thought of flying had yet entered Karl Missy's head. When his three years as apprentice-plumber ended he joined his father who then became ill, so that Missy began to take over the business. It was a hard time in Germany. The one and a half million unemployed in September 1929 soared to three million in 1930. With hardly any new building there was little doing in the plumbing trade. But Missy was never without work. Small businesses like his managed to keep going on sub-contracts from big firms. Missy and Son specialized in the assembly of spinning machines imported from England – a country that Missy would unexpectedly visit some ten years from then.

Up in Lancashire where some of those machines were made, Tom Gleave had never lost his longing to fly since the days just after the First War when he ran to see flimsy little aeroplanes which landed near his home.

In 1927 a few enthusiasts (including Tom) had held a meeting in Liverpool Town Hall, with Sir Frederick Marquis in the chair. Thus the Liverpool and Merseyside Flying Club came into being; Tom became a founder-member. In 1929 he began flying in earnest and gained his A Licence.

Tom's family were in the tanning business. In 1930 he sailed to Canada to work for a tanning company near Toronto. But at home in the evening he began to build an aeroplane. It was never destined to fly, for the Wall Street crash hit Canada in 1930 and Tom sailed back to Liverpool, leaving the bits and pieces behind.

Back in England, he applied for a five-year 'Short Service' Commission in the RAF. That autumn he joined the RAF Flying Training School at Sealand, and learnt to fly all over again.

Tom found that flying had its dangers. But most accidents give pilots something to laugh about. One day the grass airfield at Sealand was partially flooded and flags marked the take-off lane. There were a number of 'foreign gentlemen', as Tom called them, on the course. One of them taxied out for his first solo while the usual crowd gathered to watch. Opening the throttle he mistook the flags and sped forward straight into the flooded area. As the tail of his Bristol Fighter rose higher and higher, its propeller churned the shallow lake into a gigantic moving waterspout. The Brisfit stood on its nose, then flopped onto its back. For a moment all was still and silent, save for the fire-tender and ambulance which raced to the spot. Before they could release the unfortunate pilot hanging upside down on his straps, he released himself and fell head first with a large splash into the water. He had obviously pulled everything he could lay hands on, for a moment later his parachute billowed out across the water, filled with wind, and dragged the pilot from his unfortunate predicament.

Tom became a fighter pilot at Sealand. Because of this he would one day suffer the most horrible physical torture – but never would he regret having quit the tanning business.

The Warwickshire Hounds got a new Master in 1929 in the person of John Verney, twentieth Baron Willoughby de Broke. John Willoughby's regiment, the 17/21 Lancers, was then at Hounslow Barracks and some of his brother officers were learning to fly at Heston, close by. One of them, Ronald Cooke, used to fly to Sywell, thirty miles from John's home, to spend his two months' leave hunting with the Warwickshire.

Though not yet a pilot, John Willoughby had always wanted to fly since his enthusiasm had been fired by Louis Blériot's crossing of the Channel in 1909. At Eton he used to read flying magazines and textbooks and his room was papered with aeroplane pictures. In a shed in the corner of a meadow near Eton an 'amazing little man', E.J.Benton, was constructing an aeroplane and John used to run over on half holidays to help.

The day arrived for the first test flight. Not only had Benton's machine never flown, but neither had Benton. He proposed to learn by trial and error. The take-off was successful, but not knowing how to turn, Benton landed straight ahead and fetched up in a ditch. John watched sadly as the bits of his machine were driven back in a farm cart.

While with the 17th Lancers in France in World War I, John Willoughby tried unsuccessfully to get transferred to the RFC. Then he lost touch with flying until he became Master of the Warwickshire and his friend Ronald Cooke took him up, 'and that clinched matters'. 'Pedlar' Palmer, instructor at Sywell, had a new pupil. One day Pedlar, who weighed seventeen stone, was giving an aerobatic display. The seat collapsed under the strain and, according to John, 'he had to land with no support for his posterior'.

In the spring of 1929, shortly after receiving his A Licence, John Willoughby was watching when 'a most beautiful red monoplane with a silver nose' hopped into Sywell. It was a German Klemm. John fell in love with it and bought it. Not long after, he set out on a grand tour of Europe – Le Touquet, Brussels, Stuttgart, Vienna, Budapest, Prague,

Berlin, Amsterdam and home. It whetted his appetite for further ventures of this sort.

In 1929 no airplane so advanced in design as the little Klemm Swallow existed in England. The penury which the First Lord of the Treasury had enforced on the RAF obliged it to make do with wooden biplanes of First-War vintage like the Bristol Fighter in which I had flown at Old Sarum. Lack of orders prevented development in the aircraft industry. The RAF fell back to fifth place among the world's air forces. In March 1929 J.L.Garvin wrote in *The Observer*, 'We are relatively weaker than we ever were . . . since the Norman Conquest . . . we are the nation in the whole world most vulnerable to air power.'

Trenchard came in for criticism but with Churchill's hand so firmly on the budget there was little he could do. And pursuing its dreams of unarmed peace the nation was in no mood to support a powerful air force. If Trenchard could do nothing about the weakness of Britain's air defences, he understood better than anyone the menace to Britain of attack from the air.

On the verge of retirement in December 1929 he uttered this prophetic warning: 'There can be no question . . . that this form of warfare will be used. There may be many who, realizing that [it] will extend to the whole community the horrors and sufferings hitherto confined to the battlefield, would urge that the air offensive should be restricted to the zone of the opposing armed forces. If this restriction were feasible I should be the last to quarrel with it, but it is not feasible. We ourselves are particularly vulnerable to this form of attack . . . our enemies will exploit their advantage over us in this respect.'

But his words were to go unheeded by his countrymen. They thought it preposterous, almost indecent, to conjure up such horrors when high-minded men were striving to realize the shining dream of world peace.

Adolf Hitler never entertained any illusions on the subject. At a meeting of the Party leaders in Munich in September 1928 he had spoken of the 'pitiable belief in possibilities . . . such as the belief in reconciliation, understanding, world peace . . . we destroy these ideas. There is only one right in the world and that right is one's own strength.'

And now Hitler was at last on the road to power. The depression and unemployment which had begun in 1929 brought hardship and discontent among the workers, despair and ruin to the *bourgeoisie*. A saviour was needed. Adolf Hitler seemed to many to be their man.

The economic depression naturally caused repercussions in the German aircraft industry. Ernst Udet went into liquidation in 1929 and was bought out by the *Bayerische Flugzeugwerke* of Augsburg. 'Udlinger' then went back to stunt flying. Late in 1930 he went to the Sudan to film wild animals from the air. Then one day Udet and his cameraman failed to return.

Luckily for him one of his ex-enemies of Circus days (Sholto Douglas), was now at RAF Headquarters, Khartoum. Sholto immediately dispatched three aircraft of 47 Squadron to look for Udet. Campbell Black found him, but it was Sholto's aircraft which landed mechanics who repaired Udet's aircraft. A day later he was back in Khartoum staying with Sholto.

The two old eagles talked of the old times when they fought each other on the Western Front. Thanking Sholto for his rescue, Udet said, 'I never thought I would live to see the day when I was actually glad to see RAF roundels flying above me.' So Udet was saved by the RAF to fight against them later.

Willy Messerschmitt was a more astute businessman than Udet. He merged his company with the *Bayerische Flugzeugwerke* and stayed in business. The giants – Junkers, Dornier and Heinkel – survived.

On 21 October Dornier's DoX flying boat staggered into the air with 169 people aboard. Nothing like it existed and in my study at Haileybury, poring over the magazine *The Aeroplane*, I gazed in wonder at this flying monster which was dragged into the air by a row of twelve air-cooled Bristol Jupiter engines, built in Germany by Siemens. Cooling problems led to their being replaced later by watercooled Curtiss engines. The Junkers factory turned out two more giants, type G38. Double-deckers, they carried thirty-four passengers and the proud names *Deutschland* and *General Feld Marschall von Hindenburg*. Heinkel continued to produce conventional biplanes, but they also had some remarkable things in the making. The German aircraft industry was ready for Hitler.

Yet power eluded him despite his Party's prodigious increase in strength. 'Through Hindenburg to power' was Hitler's slogan. But the ex-corporal stood little chance with the *Generalfeldmarschall*. Goering would see him. The old soldier could not refuse an audience to the holder of the *Pour le Mérite*.

Goering went to work. He visited the President at his palace at Neudeck. Then he went again. Things were shaping well with the President when Carin became desperately ill and asked Hermann to take her back to Sweden. Although at any moment he expected a summons from the President to bring Hitler to see him, it was even more vital to Goering that he should accompany his dying wife to her home and family.

Back in Stockholm he waited anxiously at her bedside. Then on 14 October 1931 a telegram from Berlin announced that Hindenburg would receive Hitler. Goering took leave of his beloved Carin for the last time. On the 16 October Hitler and Goering were received by the President. At that moment Carin was unconscious. At 4.00 a.m. on 17 October she died.

Goering never went back to the flat in the Badenschestrasse. Instead he took a bachelor flat in Kaiserdamm. There he gathered his old flying comrades around him – Milch, Bruno Loerzer and Udet. Sometimes Karl Bodenschatz, one time adjutant of the *Richthofen Geschwader*, would look in and they would spend hours talking of the good old times – and of the future.

Despite those cheerful evenings Goering was a lonely man. Then one Saturday evening in March of 1932, after a political meeting in Weimar, he went to the theatre. The play was *Minna von Barnhelm*, the leading lady Emmy Sonneman.

On 31 January 1932 the country went to the polls and returned two hundred and thirty-two Nazi deputies to the *Reichstag*, of which Goering was now elected President. 'We're in the saddle now!' exclaimed the exultant Goering. As he settled into his new office for the first time his eye lit upon the official writing paper with its letter-heading '*Der Praesident des Reichstags*'. He took a sheet, writing on it in a bold hand, '*Ich Liebe Dich. H.*' and had it sent forthwith to Frau Sonneman.

One of the sentries who stood on guard in front of the presidential palace would one day make a determined attempt to kill me. He was *Obergrenadier* Werner Borner, whose battalion regiment in the 5/18 Infantry had done so well that they were transferred to guard duties in Berlin. Werner had now joined the élite of German soldiery. 'It was not easy,' said the *Obergrenadier*, 'standing there at attention for two hours at a time, while the tourists stared at you.'

The sentries only saluted officers. Deputy Goering merely raised his hat as he passed as did Herr Meissner, the Secretary of State, who called every morning. For the President the whole guard turned out. Hindenburg, calm but severe, would inspect them. At night the guard patrolled inside the palace grounds. The *Generalfeldmarschall* never drew the curtains and Werner and the other soldiers would watch irreverently as he went to bed.

One day when Werner was on guard at Kruppstrasse he saw Adolf Hitler arrive at the Moabit prison to attend court. Hitler's Nazis were constantly clashing with the communists in street brawls and the guards sometimes had to intervene. In those days Werner Borner had to fight against Hitler; soon he would be fighting for him. Already, on 6 June 1931, he had made his first flight in a powered aircraft. 'It was sensational. Those 15 minutes made me long more than ever to fly.'

In the autumn of 1931 the British had reason to feel proud of their air force. A Supermarine S6B of the RAF High Speed Flight had won the Schneider Cup race for the third time. The coveted Trophy was forever in the keeping of the British. It was a dramatic event. In spite of two earlier consecutive wins the Government had refused eight months earlier to finance the High Speed Flight. Lady Houston, disgusted, patriotically came to the rescue with £100,000. The Rolls-Royce R engine was boosted to give 2,300 h.p. for a few minutes. The Italians could not compete with this prodigious output and withdrew. Then the French challenger, Bernard-Hispano, crashed six weeks before the race. On 13 September 1931 Flight Lieutenant Boothman completed the course alone at a speed of 340 m.p.h. Two weeks later with a Rolls-Royce R engine giving 2,530 h.p., Flight Lieutenant Stainforth created a world record of 407 m.p.h.

Trenchard was criticized as a spendthrift. But Reginald Mitchell, Supermarine's designer, would bring out a fighter three years later which bore an uncanny resemblance to the S6B. It was given the name Spitfire and its Merlin engine was developed from the phenomenal Rolls-Royce R. Lady Houston's £100,000 investment would pay a big dividend.

I doubt whether any English schoolboy had my luck that Autumn. Ashcroft took me to Martlesham Experimental Station where I saw the latest RAF types. But the event of the day was the S6B at Felixstowe. I sat in the cockpit of the sleek blue Schneider Trophy winner, little dreaming that one day I would come back to Martlesham and Felixstowe under rather more dramatic conditions.

The Air Ministry were so excited by the RAF's Schneider that they suggested a large budget for further contests. But Air Vice Marshal Dowding (the Air Member for Supply and Development) vigorously opposed the idea, and urged spending the money on making more and better fighters. The Air Ministry agreed.

The RAF's Fighters in 1931 were the Hawker Fury and the Bristol Bulldog. Both were biplanes, ideal for aerobatics, but slow. Despite Versailles the Germans could out-pace the Bulldog with their Heinkel 38. Douglas Bader's Squadron (No. 23) had just been re-equipped with Bulldogs. Before this they had Gloster Gamecocks and in these nippy little machines they gave a superb display of formation aerobatics at Hendon. Bader was one of the team of three. *The Times,* which called it the 'event of the day' said there were 175,000 spectators. I was one. Ashcroft gave me special leave and I craned my neck marvelling at the formation areobatics of Harry Day, George Stevenson and Douglas Bader. That was the Gamecock's swan-song. The Bulldogs then replaced them in 23 Squadron. They handled differently, with a tendency to drop out of a roll.

On 14 December 1931 Douglas Bader flew to Woodley airfield, near Reading. After lunch someone said, 'I bet you won't roll at nought feet.' Bader did, and the graceful little Bulldog ended up in a shapeless ball of twisted metal. After hovering at death's door Bader lost both legs. At Cranwell he remembered the Commandant had admonished him, 'The RAF needs men, not schoolboys.' Now he was neither, and the RAF would not need him anymore.

One of the 175,000 spectators at Hendon was Erhard Milch. 'I learnt a lot from the Hendon displays,' he admitted. One thing he learnt from one of the Bristol Company's technical staff, was the theory of fuel injection for engines. 'My English then was very bad, but he explained everything so kindly that I understood. We had nothing of the kind in Germany at the time.' In the early thirties German engine development lagged badly. But by 1940 the fuel injection system in the engines of German fighters would give them an important advantage. The British had not followed the matter up.

Another device fitted to the Messerschmitt fighters in 1940 was the wing-slot. Invented by the British Company Handley Page, it was fitted to many British biplanes to improve their slow-flying characteristics. But the Air Ministry was sceptical when Handley Page wanted to adapt it to a monoplane. In any case no suitable monoplane existed in England at the time so Handley Page, who were friendly with Heinkel, asked to see one of theirs – the He. 64. Werner Junck, Heinkels' chief test pilot, demonstrated the He. 64 at Radlett in November 1932 and got the order. The wing-slot worked perfectly in the He. 64, as it would do later on Messerschmitt's fighters.

A far more remarkable product had just come out of Ernst Heinkel's workshop. With a top speed of 234 m.p.h. the new He. 70 was faster than the Fury, the RAF's front-line fighter. Heinkel's chief designers, Walther and Siegfried Gunther, designed it to a *Lufthansa* specification for a 'fast mail plane'. In reality it was an experimental military two-seater. From it was developed another 'High-speed airliner' for *Lufthansa* – the Heinkel 111. Werner Junck flew it for the first time on 2 December 1932. In time it would become well known in Britain – not as an airliner but as a bomber, like the one in which Karl Missy was to crash near Whitby.

Lufthansa could afford to pick the cream of the passionately air-minded German youth. In 1932 there were four thousand candidates for the *Deutsche Verkehrsflieger Schüle* at Brunswick. Adolf Galland was one of only twenty chosen. 3,980 were rejected into a labour market which at that time had six million unemployed. Those bitterly frustrated would-be pilots were all ready for the creed of National Socialism which was sweeping through the country. As Galland said, 'The flame of unselfish enthusiasm burnt bright and pure in us boys.' The thousands of young members of Germany's gliding clubs were not flying for any material gain, but for sheer love. 'From this idealism,' said Adolf Galland, 'National Socialism drew its strength.' The first German aero clubs were brought into the Party 'full of enthusiasm, of their own free will, solely because the cause appeared to them good and just.' Their day would soon come.

Idealism was all very well, but the first thing was to find a job – where six million others had failed. This was the problem facing Hannes Trautloft in 1931 when he was nineteen. He was just one more of the thousands of German boys who longed to fly. He had watched the gliders soaring over the Wasserkuppe and at school in Schloss Bieberstein had joined an enthusiastic group which made its own glider.

Each boy managed a two-second hop – a meagre reward for his labours, but at least he had 'flown'. After a few landings the glider was *kaput* and a new one was built from the surviving parts. Trautloft's home was at Ettersberg, a tiny village in the Thuringian Forest, where his father was *Frostmeister* in the forestry service. From him Hannes learnt all the hunter's lore and cunning. He grew up a fine athlete, tall and powerful.

Trautloft decided to try for the *Reichswehr* and wrote to the Colonel of the 15th Regiment at Kassel, undeterred by the fact that three hundred other applicants were applying for the two available vacancies.

A physical test was held on the regimental parade ground and the Colonel turned out to watch the candidates hurling a dummy stick grenade. Trautloft made a gigantic throw, which landed his grenade in a puddle in front of the Colonel, splashing his immaculate uniform from head to foot. 'What's that man's name?' bellowed the Colonel and when led before him Trautloft was surprised to be invited to lunch in the mess. Shortly afterwards the Colonel informed him that he could join the regiment in a year's time. But he also wrote to the *Reichswehrsministerium* saying, 'Trautloft would make a good pilot' – it was in this way that likely young men found their way into the 'black' *Luftwaffe*. Sure enough the Ministry soon wrote to him, 'Report to the DVS at Schleissheim.' He did not need to be told twice.

There were thirty pilots on the Schleissheim course. A year later ten, including Trautloft, made the secret trip to Lipezk.

Hannes Trautloft's schoolboy glider had catapulted him into a flying career. While he was training at Lipezk in the summer of 1932 Paul Temme and his schoolmates were building their own glider. They had a job finding a shed in the local town of Lippstadt big enough to take the fuselage and one wing. It was a crude affair, which they called the *Schadelspalter* ('the skull-splitter'), but it would give them the thrill they longed for – a few seconds of flight.

First they had to clear a strip in the woods, working after school hours. Temme was used to roughing it. He was a member of the 'Quick-born', a Catholic youth group, and often went off for days on expeditions in the wood round Lippstadt. He thought it all marvellous, the camaraderie, the open air and the tough jobs they were often given. But clearing that strip was the devil's own job. It was their own idea but when the authorities, heard of it, they were given every encouragement. No wonder, for the one hundred by three hundred yard strip would one day be enlarged to become a *Luftwaffe* base. At last the strip was ready and the catapult flights began.

Paul was the tenth child of a father who did not take kindly to his boy's dreams of flying. One day he took Paul off into the woods near the gliding strip where he kept his beloved bees. Suddenly, with a swish a glider was on top of them and they dived headlong into a ditch. 'So you still want to be a pilot?' asked the old man. With his exams still ahead Paul Temme was left to dream of the day.

The clandestine base at Lipezk had been going for nine years and Hannes Trautloft's course would be the last. The treaty terms were due to expire, but that was of no importance. New and startling developments were in store for the 'black' *Luftwaffe*.

Meanwhile Trautloft was drafted into the army on leaving Lipezk. His unit was a *Jager* Battalion at Magdeburg. During manoeuvres his Commanding Officer always warned, 'If aircraft appear pretend they are the real thing and take cover.' This made Trautloft smile. His CO had no idea that he was an experienced fighter pilot.

Wherever they were posted, graduates of the Lipezk Fighter School were in jobs which gave no clue to their qualifications as fighter pilots. Johannes lanke had joined the *Reklame Staffel* whose pilots spent their time in their little Albatross F86s, innocently trailing streamers advertising various products.

Hans-Heinrich Brustellin had joined the 2nd *Reiter* Regiment. A fully qualified fighter pilot, he now became a trooper, strapping horses and being cursed by the Troop Sergeant. He was sworn to secrecy about his Lipezk training.

After a year with the Regiment he went on leave to the DVS at Brunswick, where he did a refresher course. It was wonderful to be away from the regiment and among airmen again. But after four glorious weeks of flying he returned for another year to the army, this time to the Infantry School at Dresden. He only lived for his next 'leave' which consisted of another four weeks' refresher course in September 1932. Then he went on to the cavalry school at Hanover. He was there on 30 January 1933, the day Hitler became Chancellor of the Third Reich. The only change as far as Brustellin was concerned was to replace the gold-red-black cap-button of the Weimar Republic with the white-red-black cockade of the old Imperial Army.

Part Three

GATHERING STRENGTH

Chapter 7

In Berlin the birth of a new Germany was celebrated with wild rejoicing. In the streets *Deutschland über Alles* mingled with the *Horst Wessel Lied*. The two symbolized the fusion of the old and the new Germany. In the evening a massive torchlight procession filed past the new Chancellor in the Wilhelmstrasse. Goering was at Hitler's side in SA uniform, addressing the immense throng, 'My German comrades . . . the thirtieth of January 1933 will enter German history as the day on which the nation, after fourteen years of torture, need and shame has found its way back to itself . . . The future will bring everything for which the Fuehrer and his movement . . . have fought . . . in spite of all reverses and disappointments . . .'

Goering spoke as much for himself as for the nation. His own days of torture, need, and shame were now behind. Goering had proved his courage and chivalry as a fighter pilot, his devotion as a husband; then drugs and poverty had reduced him to shame and robbed him of his health. But tenacity and ambition had enabled him to climb from the dark depths of exile and despair to a dizzy pinnacle of power.

Goering turned without delay to the task of creating an air force. His goal was to create an air force powerful enough to play the decisive role in a European war. It was to be autonomous – the exclusive domain of its master. It was to draw its inspiration from the writings of General Douhet, the protagonist of total air warfare, of whom Goering was an ardent disciple.

Goering created the legend that he had created the *Luftwaffe*. This was not the whole truth. Under von Seeckt's enlightened guidance and with Russian help the *Reichswehrministerium* had created the basis for the *Luftwaffe*, both in human and technical material during German military aviation's ten-year secret exile at Lipezk. The Ministry also worked on the theories of air warfare and Douhet's theories had not escaped them either. Besides, Goering had at his elbow a man whose brilliant grasp of the technical and administrative side of flying put Goering in the shade: Erhard Milch.

According to Ernst Heinkel, Goering chose Milch because 'he possessed great capabilities and unbounded personal ambition and a ruthless energy'. Goering badly needed Milch, who was loth to leave *Lufthansa* now that it was Europe's leading airline. Apart from that, it would mean a sharp drop in his salary. But Hitler sent for Milch and said to him, 'I claim your scabbard,' meaning that Milch was honour bound to accept the post of Goering's deputy. 'Hitler took a man's soul from him,' Milch said, 'he was amazingly quick at grasping technical details. He knew much more than Goering.' Yet Hitler trusted Goering and always left air matters entirely to him.

If a hard core of flying and technical personnel had been created by Lipezk and *Lufthansa* there was an almost total lack of professional airmen fitted for high command. This was the crisis von Seeckt had foreseen. The reluctant soldiers he had drafted into the *Reichswehrministerium*'s secret Air Section were now ready for the top jobs: Walther Wever became Chief of Operations: Albert Kesselring took over supply and organization: Hans Juergen Stumpff ran Personnel. Ex-observer Hugo Sperrle – the one of whom the girls of Lipezk had made fun – and the young Hans Jeschonnek, were both on their way up. Goering would have preferred to fill the post with his own friends – Bruno Loerzer was given the *Luftsportsverband*, the Flying Clubs Association – but, luckily for the *Luftwaffe*, the War Minister Werner von Blomberg and Erhard Milch selected the best available men from the army. But none of these officers, except Jeschonnek, had ever piloted an airplane. They were courageous enough to learn, considering their advanced age and slower reflexes.

Kesselring found Goering a hard task master, generous enough with praise but always demanding more. Goering took a very dim view when Kesselring spoke his mind, which was often.

Goering's private life became more pleasant. He had been seeing more of Emmy lately and one bright summer's day he took her for a walk through the Schorfheide, a pretty stretch of woods and moorland just north of Berlin. Suddenly he stopped before an old Imperial hunting lodge in a large glade between two lakes. He decided this was where he would build his home, and – in spite of Emmy – the last resting place of his beloved Carin. For the sake of appearances he also had a small house built close to the Berghof in Bavaria, and named it *Adolf Hitler Hoehe*. But he was never really a part of Hitler's *Tafelrunde*, the Fuehrer's cronies.

The Aviation Commission became a Ministry in April 1933, with

Goering as its Air Minister and Milch as Secretary of State. Goering had kept up with Mussolini since the days of his stay in Rome, when he had first met *Il Duce* to announce that he had 'found a marvellous place to train my pilots – Italy'. He summoned seventy pilots to meet him at the Air Ministry, among them Brustellin, who had emerged from the Hanover Cavalry School, and Adolf Galland who, as a civilian pilot, was somewhat unexpectedly on an advanced aerobatic course at Schleissheim. Galland was amazed at Goering's girth, but fired by the enthusiasm of '*Der Dicke*' (Fatty). Goering told them, 'The time has come to throw off the chains of Versailles. Now that the secret training in Russia is over, Mussolini will help out for the time being with the training of our fighter pilots. But in order to avoid complications you will go to Italy under the strictest secrecy.'

Hans-Heinrich Brustellin, of the IInd *Reiter* Regiment was transferred to the non-existent *Luftwaffe* on 16 June, a few days before leaving. With Adolf Galland and others of the DVS he appeared at the beginning of July on the Brenner frontier as a Tyrolean recruit, a comic disguise maintained until they reached the base at Grottaglie. There they were transformed into Italian airmen. But the course was a fiasco for the good reason that Goering had overlooked the fact that the Germans were already well-trained pilots – better, as it turned out, than their Italian instructors. In autumn 1933 Brustellin was sent to Schleissheim Fighter School as an instructor, but in civilian clothes. Galland returned to the Brunswick DVS, then resumed his normal duties with *Lufthansa* on the Stuttgart–Barcelona run.

Early in 1934 came another summons from the Air Ministry, where Galland joined a large group who were asked, 'Do you want to be taken on the active list?' It meant a considerable drop in pay, but hardly a man hesitated. On 15 February 1935 Galland and his comrades marched through the gates of the Grenadier Barracks at Dresden to start three months of drill.

When in April Galland received from Goering orders which would start him off on his career as Germany's most famous ace, Douglas Bader received other orders which ended his. He had learned to walk again, on two metal legs, and was bravely trying to hold down a ground job at Duxford Fighter Station. One day the Adjutant handed him a letter and Bader read: 'Flying Officer D.R.S. Bader: The Air Council regrets ... he can no longer be employed in the General Duties Branch of the RAF ...

and therefore that this officer revert to the retired list on the grounds of ill-health.'

A few days later Douglas Bader left Duxford for good – as he thought – and became a civilian.

As Galland put it 'Things were simmering in the German retort' in 1933. The initiated could already detect the beginnings of the new *Luftwaffe*. But good care was taken to present an innocent front to people able to influence public opinion abroad, such as the twenty-five members of both Houses of Parliament who went on a flying tour of Germany during the Whitsuntide of 1933.

Lord Willoughby de Broke was one of the ten private aircraft owners who piloted their own planes. Landing at Düsseldorf, they were hospitably welcomed by hordes of brown-shirted Nazis. Throughout the trip their German hosts took pains to explain that rearmament, especially in the air, was out of the question. It was unfortunate that Versailles restricted aircraft construction so terribly – hence the tremendous popularity of gliding, the innocent sport of itself an indication of Germany's desire for disarmament. Their hosts often escorted them in their own 'sports' aircraft, apologizing for their slowness. They did not mention the Heinkel 70, which a month later would set several international speed records, or Willy Messerschmitt's astonishing little Me. 108 'Taifun'. From Me. 108 to Me. 109 would be a short step.

The party visited the giant Junkers' works at Dessau, which appeared virtually deserted with a few old fuselages lying about. Fortunately none of the visitors knew about the works near Moscow at Fili, or the K48 dive-bomber made there and tested at Lipezk.

Goering himself was present at the magnificent dinner given by the *Aero Klub von Deutschland*, wearing a black uniform with a 'comparatively modest amount of medals'. John Willoughby shook hands with him and noticed the 'cold and calculating look' in his eyes.

At dinner Lord Willoughby was well placed opposite Udet. They got on famously, Udet drawing an excellent caricature which Willoughby stuck in his scrap-book.

A more serious assignment awaited the brilliant flying star of the *'White Hell of Pitz Palu'*. Goering did not mean to lose Udet to Hollywood but had a more serious role in mind for the glamorous stunt pilot . . .

The parliamentarians were not altogether taken in by the innocent façade, but they could not see behind it. Yet Goering personally let a young English student, Innes Westmacott, into the secret. Innes was twenty when in April 1933 he stayed with a family in Hamburg to learn German before going up to Cambridge. Innes met families who were strongly anti-Nazi, and he became friendly with many Jews. Young as he was, everything he learned convinced him that one day there would be a war. With his hosts' son, a naval cadet, and other young naval officers he went to a local air display. They were all in uniform, with swords, and Innes was told that they were to meet an important Nazi. The display ended with a rousing display of aerobatics by a 'sports-plane'. 'With guns and a bigger engine – what a wonderful fighter!' thought Innes.

A portly individual then addressed them. Suddenly he spotted Innes. 'Who is that? Does he speak German?' he asked, and was told, 'No, he's a young English student,' but Innes understood well enough. He shook Innes's hand and Innes told him in English that he was going into the army. 'Congratulations,' said the great man. Then he returned to his theme: 'The aircraft you have seen today are nothing compared with what you will see in a year or two when Germany will be strong again in the air.'

The speaker was Hermann Goering.

Innes would never become a soldier. But as a fighter pilot he would one day help to defend England against Goering's Air Force.

Goering had created an auxiliary police force including fifteen thousand of the SS, or *Schutz Staffel*. They were Hitler's answer to the SA, a disorderly rabble of brown-shirted street thugs whose cruel violence had helped to carry him to power, and now, under the obese homosexual Ernst Rohm, were a thorn in his side.

Under Himmler, their sinister chief, the SS were later forged into a weapon of terror. But when Karl Missy applied to join, they were a *corps d'élite*, hand-picked and sworn to absolute obedience. Missy had the right qualifications – his professional status, his father's standing in the community and, of course, his pure Aryan descent. Though too old for the *Hitler Jugend*, he had to do a spell with them first. When he became a member of the SS Missy had the satisfaction of knowing that he was among the chosen few of German youth. He still stuck to the plumbing business, being called out in emergency to help the state police.

While Missy had taken to the black uniform of the SS, I had donned the blue of the RAF.

My first attempt to enter the RAF College at Cranwell ended in failure. As scrum-half in the school XV, I collected a knock on the head which temporarily ruined my chances. But more disconcerting were the results of the written examination and the all-important interview before three benevolent air officers – I passed fifth with a cadetship, only to be informed that it would not count. When medically fit I should have to re-sit the written examination.

This I did in the summer of 1933 and to my utter surprise this time passed fourth. That kick on the head would land me seven years later in the Battle of Britain. Without it my career would have taken a different course.

On 15 September 1933 Flight Lieutenant Poyntz Roberts, my energetic ruddy-cheeked instructor whose sincerity and enthusiasm more than out-weighed his imaginative vituperations, climbed up on the wing of the Avro Tutor, patted me on the shoulder and said, 'Off you go.'

That day my dreams were realized. I had longed to emulate those pilots who sped low overhead in the Bournemouth Races, their scarves streaming, the intrepid fighter pilots who rolled and looped their Siskins, the aces of the High-Speed Flight streaking through the air in their Schneider Cup Supermarines. Now at least I had one thing in common with them. I had flown alone.

I was eighteen. In the vigorous air of Lincolnshire two years of hard and varied training lay ahead: drill, aeronautical science, English history, literature, the strenuous pursuit of sport – and our graduation from the gentle Tutor trainers to the serious art of flying a fighting aircraft.

James McComb felt no longing whatsoever to fly. All he knew after four years' footslogging in the Stowe OTC, was that he would never be an infantryman. He nearly joined the Tyne Electrical Engineers – 'A searchlight and a case of beer on a lorry' was how he described it. Then a friend told him, 'In the Auxiliary Air Force they even give you a cushion to sit on.' That decided it. He would apply to join 607 County of Durham Auxiliary Squadron.

When Hitler became Chancellor, McComb was twenty-four and read-ing for his Solicitor's Finals. It was obvious, thought James, that there must be a war. His 'Victorian type' mother would have approved of his join-ing the Navy, or even the Army – but the Air Force? 'Who are these wild motor-bike type young men who seem rather mad and not too well-mannered?' she asked. But as McComb explained, 'The old girl would never have stopped a son doing what he wished, provided only it was for God, King and Country.' So he began his training in September 1933 at Usworth. From the very first he had no doubts, 'even if it did scare the hell out of me'.

On 27 September Udet was in Buffalo, New York. The star pilot, who could pick up a handkerchief on the ground with his wing-tip, saw something that thrilled even him – a Curtiss Hawk dive-bomber, the famous 'Hell-diver'. He had *carte blanche* from Goering to buy two. 'We'll pay,' said the Reich Minister for Air, 'with private funds, of course.'

But for all his brilliance at flying Udet failed to convince Milch and Kesselring, or the staff officers who watched his masterly demonstration at the Rechlin Experimental Airfields. Udet refused to give up and by the end of 1933 he had Junkers working on the *Stuka*★ dive-bomber which one day would strike terror into soldiers and civilians alike throughout Europe.

Heinkel, Dornier, Junkers, Messerschmitt and Arado spent 1933 tooling up and expanding. Three great engineering firms – the Henschel Locomotive Works, the Gotha Rolling-Stock Factory and Bloehm and Voss, the ship builders, branched out into the aircraft industry. These and many smaller firms were the backbone of Milch's aircraft production programme launched on 1 January 1934. His target was four thousand aircraft by the end of 1935. His impulsive chief was screaming for the five-year programme to be completed in twelve months. Far wiser than Goering, Milch wanted to plan on a long-term basis for a long-range strategic air force. If he had had his way . . . But he did not. So Goering's Air Force, redoubtable enough though it became, was less so than it might have been when it came to attack England.

The Arado company at Warnemunde saw the 'black' *Luftwaffe* through its early years with the Ar. 64 and Ar. 65 fighters. The development of the excellent Arado fighters was in the experienced hands of Carl von Schoenebeck, their chief test pilot since he left Lipezk in 1930. A better

---

★*Stuka-Sturtzkampflieger* or 'Dive-attack aircraft'. Although a generic term, it is usually applied to the Junkers Ju. 87.

fighter was needed for the future – and by now it was clear to Germany's aircraft industry that there was a future despite certain problems.

One of these was the lag in engine development. Here British engines helped the Germans over a difficult period, Napiers (unwittingly) with power plants for the Fokker D13 at Lipezk: and Bristol, whose licence was held by Siemens. Then came the turn of Rolls-Royce. The improved Arado fighter (Ar. 67) was experimentally fitted with a Rolls-Royce Kestrel, the power plant of the RAF's crack Fury Interceptor squadrons. The Ar. 67 gave birth to the Ar. 68, which, with the Heinkel 51, would equip the *Luftwaffe*'s fighter units until 1937, when the Messerschmitt 109 would appear on the scene. Its prototype was powered by a Rolls-Royce engine.

The Heinkel 111 bomber which Werner Junck had flown for the first time in December 1932 began life as a 'fast mail plane'. Another 'fast mail plane', the Do. 17, had just been produced by Dornier. (It was the type in which Werner Borner would one day shoot me down into the North Sea.) Both these 'civil' aircraft were turned down by *Lufthansa*. But this did not deter the airline's ex-managing director, now Deputy Air Minister Milch, from ordering both in vast quantities and with certain simple modifications, as high-speed bombers for the *Luftwaffe*.

The exchange of machines worked both ways. If the *Stuka* and the Me. 109 both flew with Rolls-Royce engines, the Merlin engine was first-flown in a German aeroplane purchased from Heinkel.

The Germans were now familiar with the Kestrel engine but they had not yet heard of the Merlin, nearly twice as powerful and still on the secret list. The Heinkel 70 Blitz, beautifully streamlined with shapely elliptical wings, would make a perfect flying test-bed for it. The Blitz was far faster than the RAF's biplane fighters – or, for that matter, anything else then available in England.

So it was that Heinkel unwittingly assisted in perfecting the famous Merlin, the power plant of the Spitfires and Hurricanes, of the Whitleys, Mosquitoes – and Lancasters – the instruments of Germany's defeat . . .

With the Government behind it, the aircraft industry was gathering momentum. The Government gave a loose rein to the illegal craze of so many young Germans – flying. Although Hajo Hermann was a law student he longed to fly. But to get into the 'black' *Luftwaffe* one had to go round by the back door. So Hajo went through a 'camouflaged' organization called the *Landespolizei*. He became an infantryman, impatient but hopeful. His chance came one scorching summer's day when he was on manoeuvres near Berlin at Doberitz. As he lay sweating in a ditch, in his clammy field-grey uniform and steel helmet, his face darkened with lamp-black, he cursed the heat and the hardships of a foot-soldier. Then a miracle happened. A portly General rode up on a horse. He looked down at Private Hermann and seemed to read his thoughts. 'Why don't you go in for flying?' asked the horseman, whom the President himself had only recently promoted to General. He was Hermann Goering. Private Hermann needed no further encouragement. First he needed his parents' permission. His father did not demur. Hajo did not ask his mother. He merely forged her signature.

Rudolf Braun was an engineering student at Augsburg, the town north-west of Munich famous for the *Bayerische Motor Werke*. He had many friends at the works. One day he was strolling by a lake near Augsburg when an aircraft landed in a nearby field. He silently admired this winged marvel which had glided down out of the sky. Then suddenly, 'It struck me (*Eriss Mich*),' he said, 'I must fly.'

Like Hajo Hermann he knocked at the back door and on 6 April 1934 he was drafted to the *Panzers* for six months' drill. By October he would start his flying training at the DVS, the Civilian Airline Pilots' Training School – the name now had little meaning – at Schleissheim, Munich.

The thought of flying had never struck Otto Hintze. His ambition was to join the *Pioneers*. Just after Rudolf Braun had left Augsburg for the *Panzers*, Hintze applied for admission to the Sappers' Depot there. He was dismayed to be told, 'Sorry, my boy, you're too late. The lists are closed.' As an afterthought the recruiting Sergeant added, 'How about trying the *Luftsportsverband*? They might take you on as a pilot.'

Since Joachim Poetter's father was a General, it was not unnatural for him to have joined the 1st Prussian Artillery. But a 'feeling for the third dimension' had never left him since one day in 1918 when a little aircraft had landed on his uncle's estate in Silesia. At Königsberg, on the Baltic, he saw a lot of the *Reklame Staffel* and the Flying Club people and longed to emulate them. But with millions of unemployed and the provision of the Versailles Treaty only allowing thirty pilots a year, a General's son was better off in a good regiment.

One day in 1933 the young officers of the Juterborg Artillery School, south of Berlin, were summoned to a secret meeting and asked if 'anyone wanted to be a pilot?' Sixty per cent applied, Poetter among them. He was accepted but he had trouble persuading his Regimental Commander, who complained, 'We breast-feed you youngsters, then you leave us.'

When in February 1934 Poetter came to the Civil Airline Pilots' Training School (DVS) at Cottbus he of course left his uniform behind him and wore civilian clothes. But *Leutnant* Poetter was assured that he would be treated like an officer.

At the end of June 1934 *Obergrenadier* Werner Borner returned his uniform to store and was all set to leave the army for the *Luftwaffe*. He then received an urgent order to draw his uniform again and to report to his unit. He only knew why a few days later when the story of the 'Night of The Long Knives' was public knowledge – and even then Borner did not know the extent of the blood-bath ordered by Hitler.

Neither did Galland. 'The Roehm incident aroused little excitement,' he said, adding, 'it was of little interest to us.'

While the 'black' *Luftwaffe* was advancing steadily under cover, the RAF also had its eye on the future. The man behind the RAF's technical development since 1930 was the Air Member for Supply and Research, Air Vice Marshal Dowding. In 1934 his department was split in two. Dowding took charge of the Research and Development. The other department, Supply and Organization, fell to Newall with whom Trenchard had replaced Dowding in 1916 as Commander of his Headquarters Wing.

Dowding could call on the best talent of the RAF's technical branches. Captain F. W. Hill of the Armament Experimental Establishment, Martlesham, was in Dowding's words 'just the sort of chap who would get a new idea five years before anybody else.' On Thursday 19 July Captain Hill told a meeting of armament specialists at the Air Ministry, 'It would need eight machine guns firing one thousand rounds a minute to destroy a bomber in two seconds' – the time a fighter pilot could normally keep a bomber in his sight. Air Marshal Brook Popham, 'one of the old school', as Dowding called him, objected. 'Eight guns is going a bit too far.' He disapproved also of closed cockpits.

Reginald Mitchell (designer of Supermarine's Schneider winner) and Sydney Camm (the Hawker Company's chief designer) were working on a four-gun monoplane fighter. Then this specification was scrapped and the designers received a new one (F 5/34) for an eight-gun fighter with retractable undercarriage and closed cockpit.

That Thursday, 19 July 1934, the British Government made a long overdue announcement: it intended to expand the RAF by forty-one squadrons. Many would be equipped with Mitchell's and Camm's new eight-gun fighters.

Chapter 8

'The Night of The Long Knives' was a far cry from the third day of the Test Match at Old Trafford, Lancashire. It was that day, 23 July, while England only had eyes for the cricket scores, that the House of Lords debated the Government's RAF expansion programme.

'What is the object of this sensational increase?' demanded one noble Lord. 'Where is the imminent danger?'

Another protested, 'What is the reason? . . . If it is Germany it is only right to point out that Germany is the one power in Europe which has unconditionally offered to abolish air warfare.'

In Germany there were no doubts about the value of air warfare. A few days after the debate, Hans-Heinrich Brustellin received orders to proceed to Doberitz, near Berlin. There he would join the *Reklame Staffel Mitteldeutschland des Deutschen Luftsportverbandes* – the central-German Publicity Unit of the German Flying Clubs. The name looked innocent enough, but shortly it would be changed for the more romantic one of *Jagdgeschwader Richthofen*.

Nor was there any suggestion of abolishing air warfare, in the activities of *Obergrenadier* Werner Borner, who had finally obtained his discharge from the army and joined the Air Observers' Training School at Prenzlau. Werner now wore civilian clothes with a uniform cap and he and his comrades were told to spread the story that they belonged to an aerial crop-spraying outfit. In fact a unit called the *Versuchsanstalt für Schadlingsbekampfung* – the Agricultural Pest Control Unit – *did* exist. It would soon become the *Luftwaffe*'s first bomber *Geschwader*.

As yet conditions at the Observers' School were rudimentary. On gunnery exercises Werner flew without oxygen at eighteen thousand feet, in the open rear cockpit of a sturdy Heinkel 45 biplane. Most observers collapsed from the exertion of handling the gun. They flew in a Ju. 52 for navigation and bombing exercises. The type still carried each week hundreds of satisfied *Lufthansa* passengers. Borner's 'adapted' version had an externally fitted bomb-sight. He had to crane his neck out into the slipstream to use it. But the trainees made progress and one day Goering and Milch flew down to inspect them, Goering in a luxurious Ju. 52 bearing the proud name of Manfred von Richthofen. To the pupils the very sight of that name was inspiring.

On 30 July it was the turn of the House of Commons to debate the RAF's expansion programme. The Opposition held that it was ' . . . neither necessitated by any new commitment, nor calculated to add to the security of the Nation.' Mr Baldwin, for the Government, replied that in spite of eight years of disarmament negotiations France, Italy, Belgium, the United States and Russia had all increased their forces. Of Germany he could say that there was the greatest interest in aviation. There was a spirit abroad, he said, which 'if it became powerful enough might mean the end of all that we . . . believe makes our life worth living'.

Then came the statement which made everyone sit up: ' . . . Since the days of the air our old frontiers are gone. When you think of the defences of England you no longer think of the chalk cliffs of Dover; you think of the Rhine. That is where our frontier lies.'

Winston Churchill, now MP for Epping, weighed in. Britain was extraordinarily vulnerable to attack, 'with our enormous Metropolis here, the greatest target in the world, a kind of tremendous fat cow . . . tied up to attract the beasts of prey.' Churchill, who as head of the Treasury in the twenties had cut back the RAF's 52 squadron home defence scheme, had now changed his mind. Germany was the specific danger, he said. He had obtained from 'private sources' some 'broad facts'. In violation of the Versailles Treaty Germany already possessed a military air force nearly two-thirds as strong as the RAF's Home Defence Force. At the end of 1935 it would nearly equal it and by 1936 it would be stronger – even if the proposed RAF expansion scheme were approved. In civil aircraft convertible to military uses, in trained pilots and glider pilots, Germany already far surpassed Britain.

In fact, he had the full story – but it only incited the Opposition to jeer, 'Mediaeval Baron!' and, 'He's holding the reins of the Apocalypse.' Mr Attlee recalled that it was Baldwin who had said, 'The bomber will always get through.' Thus said Attlee, 'The only defence is in offence, which means that you have to kill more women and children more quickly than the enemy if you want to save yourselves.'

Three days later, on 2 August, the senior officers of the 'black' *Luftwaffe* were summoned to the grand hall of the Air Ministry. There, in the subdued voice of an actor in a tragedy Goering told them that Hindenburg was dead. He drew his sword and called on them to swear the new oath. Milch stepped forward first and put his hand on the sword while an aide read the oath and every man raised his hand and repeated it. They all swore allegiance to the person of Adolf Hitler.

In August 1934 the RAF's air exercises showed up the weakness of the 'early warning' system. It depended on the eyes and the ears of the Observer Corps. The earliest they could plot hostile aircraft was when they came in sight or within earshot. The warning was too short for the defending fighters – even when the 'hostiles' were Vickers Virginia bombers cruising at seventy-five m.p.h. and at seven thousand feet.

The Chandler-Adcock system of radio direction-finding had made promising progress. It enabled the defending fighters to be 'fixed', 'plotted' and controlled from the ground. But of course the system depended on regular transmissions from the fighters. A hostile bomber would not be so obliging and a scientific system of detection had yet to be discovered.

In June 1934 – when I was learning to be a fighter pilot and Werner Borner was training at the Observers' School – Mr A. P. Rowe, of the Air Ministry Directorate of Scientific Research, was searching for a clue to the process which six years later would enable me to find Borner's bomber among thick clouds miles out over the North Sea.

Rowe searched diligently among thousands of files. Then he wrote a dramatic report to his chief, H. E. Wimperis: 'Unless science finds some new method of assisting air defence, any war within ten years will be lost.'

Unknown to Wimperis and Rowe, Dr Rudolf Kuhnold, head of the German Naval Signals Research, had been working for some time on a radio-magnetic under-water detection apparatus. Then, completely ignorant of the machine for which twenty-nine years earlier his fellow countryman Hulsmeyer had been granted British Patent No. 13170, Kuhnold extended his detection experiments to surface objects. Their principle was identical to Hulsmeyer's.

The Gema Company was formed to further the work. In October 1934 Kuhnold gave a demonstration at Pelzerhaken, near Lübeck. As fascinated spectators watched the 'blip' of the battleship *Hesse* in a cathode tube a little seaplane happened to fly over leaving a clearly visible 'trace' on the tube. 'There,' exclaimed the delighted Kuhnold, 'the apparatus will even detect aircraft.' The Gema Company was awarded a development grant of seventy thousand marks (£11,500).

But neither Kuhnold nor the Air Ministry knew that British Post Office Report No. 233 had already noted, in June 1932, that aircraft interfered with radio signals and re-radiated them. The Report was signed Robert Watson-Watt. It was he who had received one of two American cathode ray tubes at Farnborough in 1922. It was to the genial, bespectacled Scot that Wimperis then turned. He asked him to find as quickly as possible the answer to the problem of aircraft detection – even death-rays were not to be excluded.

At the Air Ministry the scientific survey of air defence was entrusted to a committee headed by H. T. Tizard. At its first meeting in January 1935 Watson-Watt reported that death-rays were out, but that he had ideas for detection. The experiment that Dr Appleton had made with that second cathode ray tube on the height of the ionosphere provided the principal, and Post Office Report No. 233 the proof, that aircraft reflected radio signals. A cathode ray tube would perform the necessary magic to show the distance and height of the target.

Dr Watson-Watt so impressed the Tizard Committee with his report 'Detection and Location of Aircraft by Radio Methods', submitted on 12 February 1935, that they suggested an immediate grant of £10,000 for development – £1,500 less than the Gema Company received. But the Air Member for Research and Development, who in 1931 had protested that Air Ministry money should be spent on fighters rather than racing aircraft now objected again: 'Let us first see if the system works,' said Air Vice Marshal Dowding. So a demonstration was arranged for 26 February.

When Galland's army training ended in October 1934 he went to the Schleissheim DVS, the Civil Airline Pilots' Training School which Brustellin had recently left for the *Reklame Staffel* (the 'publicity' unit). Galland was again ostensibly a civilian, even when the Civil Airline Pilots' Training School was transformed into the first Fighter Pilots' School. He wore 'an odd kind of uniform', the number of eagles embroidered on the lapel indicating – to those in the secret – the 'civilian's' military rank.

Hannes Trautloft, then an instructor at Schleissheim, was any day expecting confirmation of his commission as an officer in the *Luftwaffe*. But Rudolf Braun, then a pupil pilot at Schleissheim, had every intention of becoming an airline pilot, so it never occurred to him to apply for a commission.

One day in February Air Minister Goering visited Schleissheim, dressed in civilian clothes and a long leather cape. With him came *Rittmeister* Bolle, in a grey-blue uniform with collar and tie which no one had ever seen before.

The pupils and instructors of the Fighter School heard Goering say, 'We are going to build a new air force, and you will be the first officers.' *Rittmeister* Bolle then stepped forward. 'This will be your new uniform,' Goering announced. The collar and tie – unlike the high-collared tunic of the German army – earned the aviators the nickname 'Mufti' soldiers.

A few days later, on 26 February, Hitler received Goering and the War Minister Blomberg at the Chancellery, in order to put his signature to the decree that Goering laid before him, establishing the *Reichsluftwaffe* as the third armed force.

Late in the afternoon of that same day another historic scene was being enacted in a caravan which had been towed by a Morris car to a field near the lofty Daventry transmitter masts. Overhead a Heyford Bomber cruised up and down, its bored pilot and crew unaware of the drama it was causing in the caravan below. There were gathered Dr Watson-Watt, his assistant Mr Wilkins and Mr Rowe, who had started it all with his search among the Air Ministry files. The driver of the Morris, Mr Dyer, was of course invited inside. The four men listened to the approaching bomber, their eyes glued to the luminous screen of what in fact was a crude television set. The green spot in the middle grew larger, then diminished as the sound of the bomber faded in the distance. Robert Watson-Watt beamed at the others. He had found the instrument which would be vital to the defeat of the *Luftwaffe*, which was that day celebrating its birth.

While the pilot of the Heyford Bomber 'stooged' up and down, I was airborne in a dual-control Bulldog Fighter at Cranwell. Flying Officer McKenna was in the cockpit behind. The dual Bulldog was a bastard in every sense, with the single-seater's graceful upswept wings and a fuselage elongated to take a cockpit for the instructor. It could also be a bastard in a spin. Spinning was forbidden under eight thousand feet, where I found myself that afternoon with McKenna. 'OK, spin her to the left.' Over we went and down. One turn, two, three. 'Bring her out,' McKenna called down the Gosport speaking-tube. But as often happened the spin became flat and the aircraft refused to answer. We were down to five thousand feet when McKenna yelled, 'I've got her!' and I could feel his vigorous movements of rudder stick and throttle. Still we spun, and McKenna, his voice now urgent, called 'Get ready to bale out!' Praying I should not have to jump I pulled the release pin of my Sutton fighting-harness. Then, with a final burst of engine, the little bastard straightened out. 'Phew,' I heard McKenna say, 'now climb up and we'll do another.'

I was learning to be a fighter pilot.

Chapter 9

After 26 February 1935 events in Germany moved fast. The decree signed that day became effective on 1 March, when the officers, NCOs and airmen of the new service swore allegiance to Hitler. A week later Hitler publicly ordered the *Luftwaffe* to give the usual military salute. The secret was out. It only remained for Goering to confirm it.

This he did on 10 March to Ward Price of the *Daily Mail*. 'The objective ...', Goering told him, 'is not the creation of an offensive weapon threatening other nations, but rather a ... military aviation strong enough to repulse attacks on Germany.' Goering added that Germany demanded equality in the air. 'A new German Air Force has stepped onto the scene of world politics.' Events would soon confirm his boast.

Two months later the Commander-in-Chief of the *Luftwaffe* was already in a more bellicose mood. 'I intend to create a *Luftwaffe* which, if the hour should strike, will burst upon the foe like an avenging host. The enemy must feel he has lost everything before he has started fighting.'

On 13 March Paul Temme was lying on the sofa at home, reading, when suddenly a friend burst in. 'Have you heard?' he cried excitedly, 'Hitler's just announced *Wehrfreiheit* [military freedom]. Germany's going to re-arm.' Temme leapt up. It was like shaking off the chains.

He had been waiting for this moment since January when his headmaster had gathered the senior boys together and discreetly suggested the *Luftwaffe* as a career. Each received a leaflet marked 'Private', and was sent to an address in Berlin for an interview. Then came a medical examination followed by a psychological test at Münster. So all those preliminaries were not for nothing. He was overjoyed.

The next day, 14 March, another decree was published: 'The *Reichsluftwaffe* is created as a new military service ... in it shines brightly the name of ... von Richthofen and his Fighter *Geschwader*.

'The last *Geschwader* commander, *General der Flieger* Goering has kept his spirit of combat and victory as a holy legacy . . . Owing to his initiative a first Fighter *Geschwader* has been created. The Fighter *Geschwader* will from now on be called *Jagdgeschwader Richthofen*.' The *Reklame Staffel* had received its new name.

Goebbels, the Minister for Propaganda, was next to speak. On 16 March he announced to the world a new law 'for the re-creation of National Defence Forces'. Hitler, he said, had decided to tear up the parts of the Versailles Treaty concerning the German Armed Forces. The next day (Sunday) there was, according to William Shirer, 'a day of rejoicing . . . in Germany. The shackles of Versailles, symbol of Germany's defeat and humiliation, had been torn off.'

The following Sunday, 24 March, the British Foreign Minister, Sir John Simon, accompanied by Anthony Eden, came to talk to Hitler. They were met by 'a warlike guard of the SS whose commander . . . delivered a message to the Foreign Secretary, who looked unhappily down his nose'. William Strang of the Foreign Office found Hitler's mood changed. 'His manner was abrupt, verging on the truculent . . . his gestures betrayed ill-concealed exasperation.'

Simon asked Hitler bluntly, 'What is the strength of the German air force?' Hitler hesitated, then replied, 'We have reached parity with Britain.'

It was a lie, but it caused consternation in the British government which decided on a further RAF expansion scheme.

Overnight, Brustellin's 'publicity' unit had become *Jagdgeschwader* 132. Hans-Heinrich was on leave at Winkelmoosalm when he received a telegram addressed to '*Oberleutnant* H-H Brustellin' which said, 'Congratulations on your promotion.'

He returned to duty at Doberitz, a model air base with buildings among the pinewoods. 'A tremendous social life started.' said Brustellin – 'There was a distinguished visitor every day.' One of them was Hitler, who to Brustellin looked far from distinguished. His visit in April was the most depressing event Brustellin could remember. The Fuehrer seemed ill at ease. His movements were clumsy, his manner *gauche*. He held himself badly, with rounded back and hunched, sloping shoulders. He did not know what to say to the officers who stood around him but only stirred more and more sugar into his tea. When Brustellin talked to Hitler he was struck above all by his pale, watery eyes.

The next day in Berlin Brustellin met a friend, himself no partisan of Hitler. He looked surprised and asked, 'What's the matter? You look as if you'd seen a ghost.'

'Hitler was in the mess yesterday,' explained Hans-Heinrich.

'And you did not shoot him? Why not?' asked his friend.

Another visitor was the new Chief of Air Staff, General Walther Wever. 'He radiated enthusiasm,' said Brustellin. 'He was so carried away by his own enthusiasm that he made people laugh' – for Generals Wever and Kesselring (Chief of Administration) both well advanced in their forties, were now learning to fly.

Galland was also in the first group of the *JG Richthofen*. Now he could wear the uniform which *Rittmeister* von Bolle had modelled at Schleissheim. A second group (II/JG 2) was soon formed and Galland found himself under the command of an 'old eagle' of World War I, Major Theo Osterkamp.

Another member of *JG Richthofen* was Johannes Janke. But when *JG Richthofen* threw off a new unit, JG 134 (*JG Horst Wessel*), Janke went with it as *Staffel Kapitän*. Some thought it unfortunate that Richthofen's glorious name should be associated with that of Horst Wessel.

'Uncle Theo' Osterkamp had consulted Werner Junck, still with Heinkel at Warnemunde, about joining the *Luftwaffe*. Over a bottle of Burgundy they discussed the pros and cons. Junck had already been reproached by Goering for not having returned to the service. Junck told him, 'My job is here, testing for Heinkels. If I join they'll make me a bomber pilot. I have no wish to work at night.' Osterkamp agreed – he felt that he too would be more useful where he was, commanding the Seaplane base at Norderney.

Then Milch stepped in. He told Osterkamp, 'You owe it to the young fighter pilots,' so Osterkamp joined. So did Junck. They sacrificed a monthly salary of two thousand five hundred marks for a lieutenant's pay of three hundred and sixty marks.

It was the same with Carl von Schoenebeck, except that Colonel Stumpff, Chief of Personnel, did the persuading. Carl agreed – he really had no choice – to leave his job as Arado's test pilot. But he made a good bargain. Stumpff agreed that he could take command of the Rechlin Experimental Establishment. The old eagles were coming back to roost. But first they had three months' pack drill and manoeuvres at Doberitz. Many did not survive the course.

Udet held out for a long time against Goering's pleas. He loved the carefree life of a stunt pilot. Discipline of any kind irked him and he detested office work. Only his passionate belief in the *Stuka* dive-bomber led him to succumb to Goering's offer of a commission as Colonel and the title of Inspector of Fighters and *Stukas*. Goering told him, 'In that post you will have a much better chance of getting the Air Staff to accept your ideas.' So Udet at last joined the *Luftwaffe*.

Now that the *Luftwaffe* was 'official', Werner Borner had a proper uniform at last. In January 1935 he had arrived in plain clothes at the Army Radio School at Halle. In spite of having left the army six months earlier he was immediately issued a field-grey uniform. When chosen to carry the standard of an old Prussian regiment, he goose-stepped proudly through the market square of Halle.

A trained radio operator, he reported to the *Fliegergruppe* at Merseberg, east of Berlin. His commanding officer was Graf von Lückner, nephew of the famous 'sea devil', whom the graf called the black sheep of the family. Things were pretty rough at Merseberg. There were hangars, but no living quarters. Werner slept with ten comrades in a disused pigsty. But he did not care; he lived only for flying, and 'there on the tarmac, our wonderful machines, Ju. 52s and Do. 23s, stood waiting'. There was a splendid spirit, too, among the other crewmen and the pilots and officers. Then one day he was allowed to sit in the second pilot's seat and take the controls. He had always dreamed of this, and it made him very happy.

One day Goering came to open the Hermann Goering stadium. He wore brown riding boots with spurs, a brown jacket and an odd-looking hat with an eagle feather in it. He looked quite ridiculous, but people only smiled and said 'That's our Hermann', as he talked to everyone like a friend.

The flight training school at Kitzing-am-Main was working overtime. One of its more enthusiastic pupils was Hajo Hermann. His instructor, *Feldwebel* Hetzel, only increased Hermann's enthusiasm by his low–flying antics.

On 12 August Hermann spent a day off in the Steiger Wald. He missed the last bus back and had to walk twenty miles, arriving at 7.00 a.m. on

13 August. Three hours later he made his first solo flight in a Heinkel 172 Cadet, but lost himself after chasing a pheasant – as Hetzel had often done. Hajo was grounded for three days.

One of the best pupils at Kitzing was Otto Hintze. When he left in December 1935 after a nine months' course he had one hundred and fifty-seven flying hours to his credit.

At the end of two years' training at the RAF College, Cranwell, I had exactly the same total. And during the previous six months I had been growing more and more impatient to join a squadron. I was one of three Under-Officers in the running for the Sword of Honour, but my interest fell off badly as I grew more restless. One day the Assistant Commandant, Air Commodore Philip Babington, asked me to tea. Casting round among my friends I was dismayed to find none of them were invited.

During that solo tea-party Philip Babington gave me a serious lecture. He told me very quietly that I was a disappointment to him and the training staff. 'Your trouble is that you are a rebel,' he told me, 'and you are too much inclined to head off on your own.'

I had joined the RAF to fly. The relatively short time spent in the air compared with the hours spent in studying became irksome. We all felt the same, but some hid their feelings better. I lived only for the moment when I should settle into the cockpit of one of the graceful little Bulldog fighters. The pilot sat in line with the trailing edge of the top wing, so that he felt the wings were his. It was supreme joy to fly away from the earth and forget its binding influences.

At the end of July 1935 I said goodbye to the RAF College and to Bulldogs. At least as far as flying was concerned I had redeemed myself in Philip Babington's eyes. He wrote in my flying log book, 'No faults [he was over-generous]. He needs encouragement.' As a pilot I was rated 'above average' which meant little with only one hundred and fifty odd hours in my log book. Experience, as in all things – but especially in flying – was the best school.

I always looked on Tangmere, where I joined No. 1 Fighter Squadron in August, as an outsize grass meadow. They had not yet cut the hay through which our wheels swished pleasantly as we landed. The hay crop that year was good and when they had carted it a flock of sheep were put in to graze the airfield. Sheep and aeroplanes not being made for one another, we – and they – had our anxious moments. Then autumn came and with it an abundant crop of mushrooms.

With their gently curving roofs, wooden beams and uprights, the hangars at Tangmere gave an old-world feeling to this peaceful place. They had been built by German prisoners in World War I – after some twenty years of useful life they would be demolished by German airmen in World War II.

On the Sussex Downs to the north a windmill served us as a vital landmark in this pastoral scene. Even our squadron call-signs had a birdlike ring. Waxwing was 1 Squadron's; our sister-squadron 43's was Woodpecker, and Woodcock was the ground station.

The slim silver Hawker Furies that we flew were a pure delight – swifter and more powerful with their Rolls-Royce Kestrel engines than the Bulldog, yet more docile. Someone once said that the RAF of those days was the best flying club in the world. Life in 1 Squadron at Tangmere gave me exactly that feeling.

The role of the Interceptor Squadrons with their rapid climb was to attack the enemy as far forward from the target as possible. How, no one could say. Without a scientific means of 'plotting' and following the enemy and the fighter from the ground, accurately controlled interception was ruled out. We knew of the Adcock-Chandler direction-finding system for plotting the fighter, but it was not installed at Tangmere. What we did not know was that on 12 May, about ten weeks before I joined 1 Squadron, the first 'Ionosphere' Research Station had been opened in great secrecy at Orfordness, in Suffolk. There Mr Wilkins and Dr Bowen were making experiments which would provide the longed-for 'eyes' of the fighter defence. By September 1935 they could already 'see' an aircraft fifty-eight miles from the coast. On this basis, interception, and above all 'forward interception' well ahead of the target would at least be feasible.

Since the beginning of the year the chief designers, Sydney Camm (of Hawkers) and Reginald Mitchell (of Supermarine) had both been working on the new fighter specification F 5/34. One day during the summer Mitchell saw the Heinkel 70 Blitz belonging to Rolls-Royce at Martlesham. Its clean lines and shapely, elliptical wings impressed him deeply.

He went back to work on his single-seater fighter, F 5/40. But meanwhile Camm had beaten him to it with his version of the specification

E

F 5/40. His Merlin-engined Hawker Fighter, registered number K.5083, took off on its first flight on 6 November 1935.

Two new German aircraft also made their first flights that autumn. One was Messerschmitt's fighter, the Me. 109. The other was Udet's brainchild, the Ju. 87 dive-bomber. But the Jumo engines intended for the Me. 109 and Ju. 87 were not ready. Instead, cleanly cowled in the nose of each German aircraft was an engine made in Britain – the famous Rolls-Royce Kestrel of our Hawker Furies. If the Heinkel 70 were doing the British a service as test-bed for the new Merlin, the British were repaying in kind.

In October 1935 Mussolini threw his armies against Abyssinia. The British Government was alarmed – and we felt the effect at Tangmere. 1 Squadron lost half a dozen of its pilots and Furies for reinforcement of Middle-East units. Three more aircraft were chocked up ready for dispatch.

Despite the Abyssinian crisis there was little doing at Tangmere. In November I went for a week to Catfoss Armament Training Camp on the Yorkshire coast. I spent most of my twenty-first birthday in front of a smoky stove at Catfoss waiting for the chilly November mist to clear. It would have been hard to find a bleaker outpost of Britain's Empire. But there were days when I fired my guns – two Vickers mounted in the cockpit and firing through the propeller. A small bag of tools was conveniently attached near the dashboard for clearing stoppages.

Back at Tangmere again we shivered under the icy blast of a bitter winter. I felt restless again. I regularly badgered Philip Babington, now director of postings. In January 1936 the eagerly awaited telegram came at last: 'Posted to 36 Torpedo Bomber Squadron Singapore.' This was more than I had bargained for, but I was delighted. We reached Singapore four weeks later. The first thing we learned was that the night before our arrival three of our Squadron had been lost on exercises over the sea.

A factor, almost a presence, in our lives were our aircrafts' Bristol Pegasus engines – upon which our lives depended. They never failed us. Sometimes a plug would blow, but the 'Peggy' would always get home, puffing like a steam engine. The aircraft they dragged through the sky on the end of an enormous wooden propeller was the Vickers Vildebeeste –

the name was well chosen, for it was no beauty. But fighter pilot as I was, I became fond of the Vildebeeste, and half a dozen of my friends from Fighting Area agreed. It had character. And we fighter boys always took care to give a Fighting Area polish to our handling of these unlovely, square-winged torpedo bombers.

Chapter 10

The immense new Air Ministry Building in Berlin's Leipzigerstrasse was completed early in 1936. In this magnificent modern building most of the basic ideas of the *Luftwaffe* were conceived and developed. Inside it impressive mural decorations depicted the history of German aviation from balloons to bombers. Its vast and grandiose Hall of Honour was used for special ceremonial occasions. Everything about the German Air Ministry was calculated to impress the visitor and instill in him awe and enthusiasm for the *Luftwaffe*.

Within these lavish surroundings Goering occupied an office of vast proportions. One of his visitors in February 1936 was *Capitaine Aviateur* Paul Stehlin, the newly arrived French Assistant Air Attaché. Stehlin, who would come to know Goering well, became an intimate witness of the history of the next three and a half years.

On entering Goering's office Stehlin saw him at his desk – but so far off that he looked like an actor alone on the stage. Goering's greeting was cordial and Stehlin noticed that, obese and flabby as he was, Goering's face was handsome with well-chiselled features, a high intelligent forehead and clear penetrating eyes – hard, disturbing and pitiless. The twenty-eight-year-old *Capitaine* summed up Goering: 'Already obese [he] was in some ways notorious for his love of uniforms . . . of his own design . . . of decorations and jewellery – a ridiculous figure with his greed for the things of this world, a crook. But to the end he was a man of courage.'

Boasting about the strength of his air force Goering declared in February 1936: 'If Germany and England stand together there is no combination of powers in the whole world can oppose us.'

By the spring of 1936 the first of Germany's new military aircraft were rolling off the assembly lines. The Heinkel 111 and Dornier 17 bombers, the Ju. 87 dive-bomber and the Me. 109 fighter – types without a rival in any other country. Three prototypes of the four-engined Dornier 19 bomber were made but it was fated never to see service with the *Luftwaffe*.

The *Luftwaffe's* expansion was impressive, but the RAF was not standing still. Within a few days of Goering's boast, a new RAF Expansion Scheme F was approved. Its target was a home-based air force of 1,736 machines by 1939.

Lord Swinton, the new Air Minister who fired the expansion with his drive and imagination, introduced the 'shadow factory' scheme which enlisted, among others, the five leading motor-car manufacturers in a sub-contract for four thousand Bristol engines. Then Rolls-Royce and Bristol built their own shadow factories. Another was entrusted to Vickers.

Meanwhile the Vickers Supermarine Fighter prototype was ready. On 5 March 1936, four months after the Hawker Hurricane prototype's first flight, the Spitfire prototype K.5054 taxied out at Eastleigh Airfield.

Bob Tuck had joined the RAF with a Short Service Commission at about the same time as Caesar Hull, a lively, husky-voiced South African. Caesar would fly Hurricanes. Like me he would become a Flight Commander in 43 Squadron, of A Flight. Two weeks later Bob Tuck arrived at Grantham Flying Training School where his instructor was A.P.S. Wills, a brilliant teacher. But he could not teach Bob Tuck to fly, for he was a backward pupil. Tuck had visions of a 'bowler hat', but he would turn out to be one of the best and bravest pilots in Fighter Command.

Gus Holden arrived at Grantham a few months after Bob Tuck had left to join 65 Fighter Squadron. For two weeks he had been 'drilled, grilled and generally brow-beaten by our soulless Flight Sergeant'. One nervous and confused recruit saluted with the left hand, making even the Flight Sergeant laugh. 'This was the first indication we had that he was human,' said Gus.

At Grantham he thought that 'the sweetest noise in the world to young men anxious to become fully-fledged pilots was the sound of the Rolls-Royce Kestrel engines of the Hawker Harts and Furies'. Gus did well at Grantham, which earned him a posting to a crack Fighter Squadron, No. 56 at North Weald. It was they who had thrilled me stunting their Siskins when I was a schoolboy at Haileybury. Now they had Gauntlet biplanes.

Norman Ryder, who had returned from India as a boy of ten, went to school in England and on a cold autumn day in 1931 joined the Royal Fusiliers at Hounslow Barracks. The surroundings were dour and austere. Not a drop of hot water, no creature comforts. The barrack room furniture consisted of two wooden forms, a trestle table and about twenty iron pull-out beds. The only heat came from a dismal little fire grate which was lit after duty. It was doused an hour before lights out to let it cool off so that the unfortunate fellow whose duty it was could clean it out and paint the fire bricks and the chimney with white Blanco – using his shaving brush to perform this worthless mission.

'We paraded,' said Norman, 'we fell out, we paraded again. We wore canvas overall suits as working uniform which we scrubbed nightly for the next day's dawn parade, sleeping on them to dry them. We even gargled by numbers to fend off a 'flu epidemic, dressed in impeccable straight lines either side of an open drain.'

In 1934 Norman left the army, 'disillusioned with the petty, futile and stagnant life in a foot regiment'. To clear his ideas he became a mathematics master at Tredennick School, in the suburbs of Worcester.

One night he was working late in the common room which was unimaginatively furnished with a large table, a well-worn settee and two armchairs. Norman's friend Bill, the classics master, was sitting in one of them reading the *Daily Telegraph*. Suddenly he read out an advertisement, 'Join the RAF with a Short Service Commission.' The two then started a discussion which changed the course of Norman's life. War, they agreed, was inevitable and it was obviously better to be trained for it in time. The army was out, the navy was attractive but they disliked the prospect of being on a frigate in icy seas . . . No, it had to be the RAF – Norman was determined to fight in a clean collar.

Within a few months Acting Pilot Officer Norman Ryder had begun his flying training at Thornaby, in Yorkshire. Graded 'exceptional' as a pilot he joined 41 Fighter Squadron at Catterick, Yorkshire.

Of the 'old eagles' who survived the pack drill at Doberitz, 'Uncle Theo' Osterkamp was one. He did have a close shave while on parade, sword drawn and mounted on a splendid horse. Returning the sword to its scabbard he missed and jabbed his horse. Osterkamp was found later wandering in a nearby forest.

He felt more at home as *Staffel Kapitän* in the II *Gruppe Jagdgeschwader* 2 (*JG Richthofen*), stationed south of Berlin at Juterbog. Carl von Schoenebeck commanded another *Staffel*. When one of his aircraft was wrecked in a crash they managed to drag out the pilot, his face badly smashed. It was Adolf Galland, who survived his severe head injuries.

On 7 March 1936 Osterkamp led his *Staffel* into the air before dawn. Having reached their patrol line, he tore open the sealed orders handed to him before take-off. He read, 'The Fuehrer has decided to occupy the Rhineland. II Group/*JG* 2 proceed to Werl. Thereafter patrol north of Moselle, cover troops entering Rhineland.'

Back in Berlin the French and British Ambassadors were informed that Germany had renounced the Locarno Treaty, previously binding all three and five other nations to guarantee peace and mutual protection. Soon after, German troops were reported across the Rhine.

It would have been the end of Hitler if the French Army under General Gamelin had resisted. They probably would have done so with the help of Britain. But Britain was unwilling to go further than acting as mediator. So Gamelin, whose forces far outnumbered the Germans, did not bar their way. Hitler himself said that 'the forty-eight hours after the march into the Rhineland were the most nerve-racking of my life. If the French had then marched . . . we would have had to withdraw with our tails between our legs . . .'

The *Luftwaffe* was as stretched as the German Army. Osterkamp briefed his pilots: 'We must show ourselves everywhere to give the impression we have a strong fighter force. If the other side interferes, we attack.' He did not say how. His Heinkel 51s had no guns.

Hajo Hermann had just joined *Kampfgeschwader* 4, which was equipped with the 'milatarized' Ju. 52 Airliners. *KG* 4 was briefed to be ready to fly to Paris.

The IIIrd Group of *JG* 134 (*Horst Wessel* – formed only a week or so before the Rhineland occupation) moved to Lippstadt, now an airfield enlarged from the glider strip cleared by Paul Temme and his young friends in 1932. Johannes Janke was now *Staffel Kapitän* of *Staffel* 8. He knew no better than Osterkamp what to do if attacked. His *Staffel*'s aircraft had full ammunition tanks – but no guns!

Meanwhile the Schleissheim Fighter School had been disbanded. Hannes Trautloft and the other instructors were transferred to the IIIrd Group/*JG* 134. Even the flying school at Kitzing-am-Main, where Otto Hintze and Hajo Hermann were trained, closed down and sent its instructors to the Rhineland. Their aircraft (Arado 65s and Heinkel 51s) had guns but they were not synchronized.

To 'encourage the population' Osterkamp did a few loops over Aachen. He led his boys down low over Cologne, skimming the cathedral spires.

III Group/*JG* 134 roared low over Cologne too, Janke leading *Staffel* 8, Claus von Belöw (soon to be Hitler's adjutant) *Staffel* 7. Hannes Trautloft said, 'It was a great moment.'

And so it was. But not only for the pilots. Below them the Rhinelanders waved, feverishly excited by the antics and the apparently unlimited numbers of their new *Luftwaffe*, which with a few unarmed aircraft, had pulled off a daring and highly successful bluff.

Still in the plumbing business and an auxiliary in the SS at Rheydt, Karl Missy was not far from this excitement. Lately he had become interested in joining a *Flak* regiment. It seemed to him the most heroic way of defending one's country – the last ditch stand against hordes of assaulting aircraft. Not that Missy really believed Germany would be attacked. Even stronger than his ambition to defend the Fatherland was his technical interest in *Flak*.

In the spring of 1936 Missy had a serious quarrel with his father, and the old man boxed his ears. Karl told him he was through. 'I'm going away to join the army,' he said, 'you can find someone else to help run the business.' He put in for the *Flak*. In a few months he was told that there was no vacancy in *Flak*, and was instead accepted for the 7th Infantry Regiment.

So Missy left the SS and his home. Still angry at his father he departed early one morning for the station. To his surprise his father was there. His eyes full of tears, the old man embraced his son affectionately. Then he boarded the train and set off to the 7th Infantry Depot in far away Silesia.

Werner Borner hardly noticed the Rhineland occupation. He was too busy on a blind-flying course at Berlin-Rangstorf. *Hauptmann* Bauer, who ran it, was Hitler's personal pilot. He commanded the communications flight, whose aircraft were used for training. Borner flew in them all. Hitler's had the most austere interior. Himmler's was painted in the black and silver of the SS. A brown band encircled that of the SA Chief of Staff, Viktor Lutze. Goering, not surprisingly, had two aircraft. Luxuriously fitted and painted in red, silver and black stripes, they were as colourful as the aircraft he had flown in the Richthofen Circus.

The *Luftwaffe* Chief of Staff, General Walther Wever, liked to pilot himself. Osterkamp worried about the General. He had learnt to fly only the year before at the age of forty-three and was as happy as a child at having his 'wings'. But Osterkamp realized that the Chief of Staff's flying knowledge was negligible. He respectfully offered him a few tips, insisting on the importance of being shown the 'taps' – the knobs and instruments – of a new aircraft.

On 3 June 1936 General Wever took off from Dresden in a Heinkel 70 Blitz. All went well until he was airborne. Then the onlookers saw the aircraft plunge sideways into the ground. Wever was killed instantly. It was found that the aileron locking device was not released. Had Wever tested the movement of the controls before take-off – an elementary precaution – he would have known the ailerons were locked. Nor had he learnt the 'taps'. In the cockpit was a red button which unlocked the ailerons.

His death was a serious loss to the *Luftwaffe*. Wever was a strong believer in the four-engined strategic bomber, heavily protected and capable of reaching from German bases as far as Scotland with a large load of bombs. Two prototypes (the Dornier 19 and the Junkers 89) were nearly ready when he was killed.

At this time specifications were only just out for Britain's Lancaster, Halifax and Stirling four-engined bombers. Germany had the lead. Had she maintained it she would have had a four-engined bomber force for the Battle of Britain, but with Wever's death the project was dropped. His successor, Kesselring, told Goering 'You can either have three four-engined bombers or four twin-engined.' Goering decided on the twins, brushing protests aside with the unanswerable argument that 'the Fuehrer is not interested in how big our bombers are but in how many we have'.

Following General Wever's death a new bomber unit at Nordhausen (*KG 253*) took his name. One of those who proudly wore the 'General Wever *KG 253*' badge issued to aircrews was a radio-operator, Werner Borner.

Enthusiasm was lacking for the four-engined bomber, but thanks to Udet the dive-bomber was beginning to cause a furore in *Luftwaffe* circles. At Rechlin Experimental Establishment a year earlier, Johannes Janke had done the first dive test on the Henschel 123 *Stuka*. On his first attempt he dived from fifteen thousand feet, scattering his bombs half a mile off in the forest. The Commandant (Colonel Student) told him dryly, 'If you go on like that Goering will have you shot for killing his deer.' Janke also tested the Ju. 87. It was slow and heavy, but in the dive it handled much better than any other type.

When in February 1936 Janke left Rechlin to join the *Jagdgeschwader* Richthofen at Doberitz Rudolf Braun had made a fateful decision at Schleissheim. Pilots were being asked to volunteer for *Stuka* units. It was a hazardous occupation, they were told. They could have all the fun they wanted with the girls – but marriage was forbidden. Braun joined the *Stuka Geschwader* (*Immelmann St.* G 1) at Schwerin, between Hamburg and the Baltic Coast. It was equipped with Ar. 65s and He. 50s. Part of *St.* G 1 became *St.* G 168 and *Unteroffizier* Braun moved with it to nearby Lübeck. There for the first time he flew the Ju. 87 *Stuka*.

The *Stuka* pilots soon realized that diving was not the problem it was thought to be – it was more like 'level flight downwards'. The fear that haunted designers and pilots alike was structural failure: the first *Stukas* had no dive-brakes and were not especially strengthened. The big problem was pulling out of the dive, when centrifugal force could be as much as 6 G – which meant that the weight of a twelve stone pilot became seventy-two stone, that of his five ton aircraft, thirty tons. Sometimes the wings were torn off – Braun lost some good friends that way.

In the old machines without dive-brakes bombs were released at two thousand five hundred feet in a seventy degrees dive, with the pull-out height at nine hundred feet. But in the Ju. 87 with its dive-brakes, bombs were released at fifteen hundred feet in a 275 m.p.h., eighty degrees, nearly vertical dive. The pull out height was three hundred feet. The efficient reflector bomb-sight could be adjusted for wind-speed and direction, release height and dive-angle – the steeper the better.

There were few who were not infected by Udet's '*Stuka* madness'. Milch was a notable exception. He had demonstrated his faith in the twin-engined level bomber by ordering a high performance aircraft from Junkers the year before. Their designers, Evers and Garner (the latter an American), went to work. Between them they produced a 'wonder bomber', the Ju. 88. Even then Udet insisted on air brakes, as he did also for the Heinkel 111 and Dornier 17 – so that they could dive-bomb.

For months these three bombers and the Messerschmitt 109 Fighter were put through their paces at Rechlin, the Experimental base near the Baltic where Carl von Schoenebeck arrived as Commandant in autumn 1936. He tested them all. Two or three Me. 109s dived straight into the ground. Carl nearly did too, until he noticed the tail-trim wheel creeping towards the nose-heavy position. That was the cause of the fatal accidents.

The Ju. 88 was easily the best of three excellent bombers. Strengthening the He. 111 and Do. 17 for dive bombing turned two excellent machines into a couple of heavy old crates.

At Rechlin on 27 June all eyes turned to the Ju. 87 and He. 118 true dive-bombers. The competition intended between them nearly cost Udet his life. He mishandled the He. 118 and it crashed. The Ju. 87 thus became the *Luftwaffe's Stuka* dive-bomber.

Dive-bombing was supposed to be one of the roles of our Vildebeeste. The Vildebeeste however was no hell-diver, and a long-winded notice in the cockpit explained why. At a cruising speed of one hundred m.p.h. one had leisure for reading – and the notice said, 'This aircraft is not to be flown at a speed in excess of 140 m.p.h.' Even if you slowed up till the Handley Page wing-tip slots flopped out of the top wing, your sight – a nut which happened to protrude conveniently from the top of one of the rocker-boxes on the cylinder head – was barely on the target before the whistling and vibration in the wires and structure announced that you were approaching the fatal speed limit. Beyond it you were likely to continue your dive without a tail plane.

Like the Vildebeeste, life in Singapore proceeded at a gentle pace. We reported at the hangars at 7.30 a.m. and knocked off for the day at 1.30 p.m. In the afternoon we slept, or sailed. I mostly sailed in the small boat I shared with a friend, Ted Thornewill, like me a fighter pilot by training and inclination. All of us revelled in our happy hunting grounds, the air and sea around us.

Foreign ships were always putting into Singapore and we often went aboard. Our preference was for the German liners – they had the best beer, straight from Dortmund and Munich.

One day the German training cruiser *Emden* dropped anchor. The Tanglin Club invited the ship's officers for golf and tennis. That evening there was a party and the band played *Deutschland über Alles.* Many of them thrust their arms out in the Nazi salute and we thought they looked rather funny.

The *Emden* sent a soccer team to the air base and we beat them by a narrow margin. Afterwards songs were sung in the mess and glasses raised to the toast, 'Germany and England will beat the world.' Which was exactly what Goering had said in February.

Above all we lived for flying. In its unhurried way the Vildebeeste was a good torpedo-bomber. The most serious limitations were in the torpedoes. We were told that they were bought at a cut price from the Navy at the end of World War I and therefore were nearly as old as we were. You had to 'put them in' at a hundred m.p.h. from twenty-four feet. Less, and the splash would hit your tail plane with an alarming thump; more, and the 'tin fish' would leap out of the water like a scotch salmon – a lovely sight, but not one which earned us the congratulations of our CO. He himself leapt with rage one day on learning that Miller had inadvertently pressed the button at eight thousand feet over the middle of Singapore Harbour, causing consternation below.

We liked our CO, Peter Davies. Tall and massive, he was indulgent with us and a man we would follow anywhere. He led us over the jungle and out over the sea. If we had confidence in our Pegasus engines, we had confidence in him too. Together, they always brought us home.

Night torpedo attacks miles from the coast were the most 'dicey' of our exercises. In the glimmering light of flares we dived to twenty-four feet – more or less – above the sea. We carried no radio and, unable to communicate between aircraft and aircraft or with base, we followed our leader's navigation lights. He carried a radio , with a long trailing aerial.

One day I had a strange experience which made me aware of fate, or providence or what you will.

The officers' mess at Seletar air base was a long, airy building of two wings which looked out across the grass airfield some two hundred yards beyond. I kept my car at the back, near my room. One afternoon I was changing a tyre – it was the right rear one – when something made me leave the job to fetch a cloth. I walked to my room ten yards away and during the few seconds I was there heard an aeroplane fly over the mess on its way to land.

A few seconds later I was back at the car. The right rear wing where I had been working was deeply gashed and on the ground lay a dozen heavy lead beads, the kind which were attached to the end of a trailing aerial. During the minute or so that I had been away the aeroplane had come in to land at seventy m.p.h. with its aerial trailing. I was never a fatalist, but the more I flew the more certain I became of some will beyond our own.

Some more than others are receptive to such things. One was Dowding, now Air Marshal. He was nevertheless a stern realist and a clear thinker.

For more than ten years all functions of air defence had been joined at the Air Defence of Great Britain Headquarters. By 1936 it had become what Dowding called a 'ponderous system'. The Bomber and Fighter Forces were under one Commander-in-Chief who had too much to do, including the impossible task of reconciling the competitive need of the two forces. ADGB was now broken down into specialized commands: Bomber, Fighter, Coastal and Training.

Of the past ten years Dowding had spent nine at the Air Ministry, which he left for one year to command Fighting Area. He knew every problem of training, research, development and, of course, air defence. From the start he was behind the development of radar and the eight-gun fighter. He had a perfect grasp of air defence problems and had always differed with Trenchard's policy of putting emphasis on the Bomber Force. The principle favoured by Trenchard was 'attack is better than defence' but, as Dowding said, 'he seemed to have forgotten that "security of the base" is an essential prerequisite.' Dowding was the natural choice as first Commander-in-Chief of the new Fighter Command.

Taking over his new headquarters on 14 July 1936, at Bentley Priory, Stanmore, just north of London, he found 'there were some lamentable deficiencies to be made good' – not that he was criticizing his predecessor 'whose task had been well-nigh impossible'.

Fighter Command started as a destitute child. 'The most crying need,' Dowding found, 'was for Operations Rooms at all Commands and Stations with tables on which courses of all aircraft, hostile and friendly could be tracked ... There was absolutely no establishment for the manning of any Operations Room. In the silly little exercises which were sometimes held in the long evenings of summer the [Unit] Commander himself acted as Controller and his staff ... and had to man the Operations Room ... These duties would have to be carried out twenty-four hours per day ...

'Next, there had never been any attempt ... to represent our own bombers leaving and returning to the country. Everything on the table was assumed to be hostile.' (The Air Staff sometimes even refused to provide 'friendly bombers' in exercises.)

The Observer Corps were all volunteers who trained in the evening after working hours. There was no mobilization scheme and no authority for paying them.

One of the most serious needs was for all-weather runways. There were none. During the coming winter Kenley airfield was to be out of use for three weeks. But the Air Staff objected to runways – a specially seconded Army Officer had devised an airfield camouflage scheme. Runways, he said, would spoil the camouflage.

Dowding's long battle with the Air Staff was just beginning.

On 17 July, three days after Dowding arrived at HQ Fighter Command, civil war broke out in Spain. On the night of 22 July Hitler was at the theatre in Bayreuth when the local Nazi leader handed him a letter from General Franco.

Hitler immediately consulted Goering who urged him to support Franco, first to combat Communism and second 'to test my young *Luftwaffe*'.

That night Hitler decided to send help to Franco. Once again numbers of the *Luftwaffe* were to depart on a long journey, as usual, in civilian clothes.

Hannes Trautloft was one of the first to leave. Within a week of Hitler's decision at Bayreuth Trautloft was in Seville, one of six fighter pilots sent with Heinkel 51s to train Franco's pilots. Twenty Ju. 52s were also sent to operate with the 'Hisma Airline Company'. No one noticed that they were militarized Ju. 52s, bomber transports which by September had transported fourteen thousand Moroccan troops to Spain.

Within a short time Spanish fighter pilots had crashed three He. 51s. Berlin then agreed that the Germans should fly the other three. Trautloft gained their first victory. 'Three Breguets bombed our lines,' he said, 'dropping bombs by hand.' He shot down one. 'It was a copy-book attack.'

On Friday 13 August he achieved the honour of being the first German shot down. He had attacked a Potez which flew on. Then suddenly it began to smoke and the crew baled out. At that moment he was hit – a Dewoitine had crept up behind him. Hanging on the end of his parachute Trautloft felt rather an idiot – he was wearing an open shirt, shorts, and tennis shoes, and the Dewoitine was attacking again. Finally he fell on a farmhouse, crashing backwards against the wall. He came immediately under fire from both sides.

After dark he crawled to a nearby olive grove only to find himself surrounded by eighty soldiers who regarded his tennis costume with some suspicion. A swarthy sergeant stuck a pistol in his stomach and punched him on the mouth. Trautloft then reached for his passport, but this earned him another punch. Having noticed the sergeant's red and yellow badge, his last hope was to mutter through bruised lips the only Spanish he knew, '*Viva Franco*'. At that, the sergeant threw his arms round Trautloft and kissed him.

At the Air Ministry in Berlin the preparations for the departure of the Condor Legion for Spain were giving Kesselring, the Chief of Staff, endless troubles. In November 1936 the SS *Usaramo* sailed from Hamburg on a 'Strength Through Joy' cruise – but the 370 eager young men aboard, dressed in sports clothes, were *Luftwaffe* aircrew bound for Seville. Hajo Hermann was among them. Recently arrived in *KG* 253, Werner Borner's unit, Hajo had baulked his CO landing one day at Nordhausen. All the CO said to Hajo was, 'I'm sending you to Spain.'

As the Condor Legion headed in civilian clothes for the Iberian Peninsula, No. 36 Torpedo-Bomber Squadron set course for the north-west frontier of India. At dawn on 6 November we left in a 'Balbo'* of twelve aircraft. Cruising at one hundred m.p.h., five days' hard flying brought us across Burma and India to within sight of the Himalayas. Their lofty peaks emerged faintly from the distant haze, a pinkish white, as we drew near to our destination of Risalpur.

The trickiest landing was at Victoria Point, a small grass airfield in southern Burma where we arrived after a four hours' flight from the flower-scented island of Penang. Since he was strapped into the open cockpit ahead of the Vildebeeste's wings, a pilot's facilities for relieving himself were limited, if not practically non-existent. Shorty Ayres had invented an ingenious 'Modification P 1', as he called it, with several feet of Gosport speaking-tube.

My own method was less elaborate. I merely passed a note to my fitter in the cockpit just behind, Leading Aircraftsman Roberts, saying, 'Please open hatch.' This was beneath my cockpit on the floor of the bomb-aimer's position which was now crammed with equipment. A few minutes later Roberts tapped me on the shoulder and handed me a little piece of white paper fluttering in the slipstream, on which was written, 'Sorry cannot open hatch. Please mind my hat' – a small pith sun-helmet with a narrow rim, especially designed for aircrew. Roberts wore his only on the ground, for the 'Bombay Bowler' had a snag to it: if you raised your head above the windscreen the slipstream would catch the rim and nearly break your neck. I preferred to risk sunstroke in a cloth helmet.

*A flying formation named after the Italian general and pilot.

Meanwhile, sunbathing in the spacious rear cockpit which we called the bath, Flight Sergeant Spinks was blissfully unaware of the little drama going on up front.

At Victoria Point we refuelled with two-gallon tins, sitting on the top wing and pouring the petrol through a chamois leather. The coolie helping me dropped an empty can which holed the fabric of the lower wing. The repair was no problem for the imperturbable Flight Sergeant Spinks. In a few moments he had arrived with a curved surgeon's needle and thread, and sewed up the rent, sticking a patch on top.

We stayed a week at Risalpur and flew up the Khyber Pass, landing at a little fortress garrisoned by the Indian Army. The return flight to Singapore was more leisurely and took us via a string of new airfields along the Burma coast and on to Bangkok.

By then I was in trouble. I lived for flying but in some mysterious way it made me ill. I broke out in sores and my feet swelled so much that I had to fly without shoes. Back in Singapore the doctor said, 'You must stop flying and go home.' I was very unhappy. But my spirits rose again when on reaching England I was posted back to Fighter Command – and better still, to Tangmere, and this time, 43 Squadron.

The C-in-C of Fighter Command was 'an unpopular little boy' at Winchester College because, in his own words, 'he was too cheeky'. Stuffy Dowding said of himself, 'Since I was a child I have never accepted ideas purely because they were orthodox, and consequently I frequently found myself in opposition to generally accepted views.'

This was the philosophy behind his energetic and farsighted efforts to build an efficient air defence. His requirements were enormous – in men, aircraft, ground equipment, buildings and telecommunications – which included radar, then still in its infancy. Everything had to be done and time was against him. Dowding was not a man for half measures. He was resolved to get what he needed to make the 'base' – Britain – safe and secure. On one occasion a senior officer propounded to him at length, as if they were sacred words of truth, the Trenchard doctrine, 'attack is better than defence'. Stuffy disagreed vigorously: 'It's a shibboleth, a play on words with just enough truth, but not enough to make it a clear case. Why must it be accepted without question? Only because you think that you are going to do so much damage that the enemy will be smashed right at the outset. And how are you going to do that?' Fiercely he insisted that, 'the one thing vital before going over to the offensive is security of the base. That overrides all considerations.' His unshakeable belief in the principle and his obstinate insistence that all his demands should be met, did not endear him to all his brother officers. 'Always remember,' he would say later, 'that my name stank on the Air Staff.' In February 1937 the bad odour was beginning to spread. As time went on Dowding was to become more and more aware that certain of the Air Staff were trying to get rid of him.

Dowding was at the start of a hard and lonely fight against orthodoxy and obstructionism. The first blow was about to fall. Before he left the Air Ministry Dowding had been given to understand by Sir Edward Ellington that he would succeed the latter as Chief of Air Staff. He was apparently unaware that in June 1935, a year before he left the Air Ministry, Trenchard was talking freely about the RAF's expansion to Newall, who was then 'being groomed as CAS'.

When Dowding had been at Fighter Command for nearly seven months he received the first news of this in the form of a handwritten letter from the Chief of Air Staff. It was dated 3 February – the year (1937) was omitted – and it said, 'The Secretary of State [Lord Swinton] has asked me to let you know, in advance of the official announcement, that he has decided that Newall will succeed me as CAS . . .' No reason was given, and Dowding had no idea what lay behind the change.

His reaction was natural. 'This came as somewhat of a blow to me since it is always an attractive prospect to reach the top of the tree.' Trenchard's choice had taken Dowding's place in France and had then passed him in the home straight: Newall was junior to Dowding. It was indeed a blow, but later Dowding would see in it the hand of Providence.

Dowding wrote to Ellington next day, with a very modest request: 'I trust I may be permitted to continue to serve until I have completed a year in my present rank.' Referring to views he had expressed earlier to Ellington he said, 'I did this at a time when I had reason to believe I should be your successor . . . In the altered circumstances I would ask you to disregard my papers . . .'

On 8 February Ellington replied in his own handwriting. He informed Dowding that the Chief of Air Staff was appointed personally by the Secretary of State, who was not bound to consult the retiring CAS. Ellington did not say whether Swinton had consulted him, only that it was Swinton's choice and his alone.

Regarding Dowding's retirement Ellington reassured him that he would normally serve until the age of sixty, that is, until April 1942. He added, 'I hope you will continue to serve for two or three years.' As to

Dowding's views, 'I do not see why you should not . . . put forward your views . . .'

The very next day Dowding did so. After expressing his 'contemptuous pity for superseded officers who complained . . .' and affirming, 'I have no intention of joining their ranks,' he came to the point. 'It seems to me in the highest degree undesirable that it should be possible for a civilian Minister to select the future head of one of the fighting services without seeking the advice of its existing Chief.' Then there was the 'attitude of the new CAS to be considered. He might find it embarrassing if anyone senior to himself . . . stay on in the Service for some years.' For Dowding was indeed senior to Newall.

Again Ellington wrote back in his own hand, '. . . the selection by Secretaries of State of Chiefs of Staff is . . . of long standing . . . This was the . . . case when I was selected. I only mentioned this . . . because . . . you wrote . . . as if it was my decision who was to succeed me.'

So Ellington, who since indicating him as his successor had signified no change of his own mind to Dowding, had apparently been overruled by Swinton. Trenchard was 'talking freely' to Newall when Swinton became Air Minister. Did Trenchard sway Swinton? He gives no hint. Only in his last letter did Ellington add, 'I hope you will decide to stay on . . . I know Newall will wish it.'

Chapter 11

The year 1937 was above all one of visits between the Royal Air Force and the *Luftwaffe*. The natural curiosity of visitors on both sides to know all was matched by the determination of the hosts not to show all. Air Vice Marshal Courtney, Director of Operations and Intelligence, started the ball rolling at the end of January 1937. The *Luftwaffe* showed him several of their units and he toured factories, including Heinkel's at Rostock.

The Heinkel 111 high-speed airliner built for *Lufthansa* had been demonstrated in public at Berlin-Templehof for the first time exactly a year earlier. But its ingenious designers, Walther and Siegfried Gunther, had included in its design the basic requirements of a bomber. At the time of Courtney's January visit, the Heinkel 111 was rolling off the mass production lines. Rejected by *Lufthansa*, the 'high-speed airliner' versions were put to excellent use by Colonel von Rohwehl and the special unit he commanded at Berlin-Staaken. They made 'civil air route proving flights' over Britain – collecting invaluable target data. Meanwhile, the military machines were being delivered to the Condor Legion in Spain.

In the middle of Seville airfield lay a wrecked aircraft. On the tarmac, a tall man with an intense and almost frightening look in his eyes confronted Hannes Trautloft. 'I am von Richthofen,' said the man, who was dressed in civilian clothes. It was Wolfram, Manfred's young cousin. 'We have two Me. 109s,' he went on. 'One is there,' and he pointed to the wreck in the middle of the airfield. 'The other you must fly. It is a world beater.'

There was nobody to show Trautloft the 'taps' so he asked the mechanic. Considering that this was Hannes's first flight in an aircraft with closed cockpit and retractable undercarriage, which swung viciously on take-off, he did not do too badly.

On his return from Spain at the end of February 1937, Trautloft was summoned to the Fuehrer's presence. After the easy life in Spain he made a special effort to smarten up. He was waiting in an ante-room at the Chancellery when an aide entered. He sniffed and addressed Hannes, 'Your hair oil stinks to heaven.' – it was a product of Spain – 'You can't possibly see the Fuehrer like that.' So Trautloft had to go and wash his hair.

His interview was for ten minutes, but he stayed an hour. Hitler spoke slowly and calmly – he surprised Trautloft, who had only heard him bawling on the radio. He had a hundred things to tell Hitler, but the Fuehrer seemed to know everything already. Trautloft told him, 'They need Me. 109s in Spain,' and Hitler said something would be done.

The newly arrived Heinkel 111s of the Condor Legion were in action on Monday 26 April. The target was a vital road bridge at Guernica. The market-place was crowded when at 4.30 p.m. Heinkel 51 fighters suddenly dived, machine-gunning. The plaza was quickly strewn with the dead and the dying, particularly women and children, and those who made for the open fields were mown down. Then came the first wave of He. 111 bombers which released their loads of high explosives. They were followed by a second wave which dropped incendiaries – by then the air displaced by the He.s had come rushing back to fan the fires.

Adolf Galland was that day on the high seas *en route* to Spain. The version he heard on arrival was that after the attack the German bombers 'found the bridge untouched, but the local village badly damaged'. The 'local village' was Guernica. Another version gave the number of dead as sixteen hundred men, women and children. Yet another said, 'In the form of its execution and the scale of the destruction . . . the raid on Guernica is unparalleled in military history . . .'

It would not remain so for long. Against Warsaw, Rotterdam, London and a host of British cities, and later, Hamburg, Berlin, Dresden and the rest, Guernica was but a modest beginning. But that Monday 26 April the Germans had re-invented the total air warfare which they were the first to employ against Britain in World War I.

Even Galland, on reaching Spain in May 1937, found that Guernica 'caused great depression among the members of the Legion'. The whole attack, as he said, 'had to be regarded as a failure since one of our first principles was to destroy the enemy ruthlessly but, if possible, to spare the civilians'.

Goering was less naïve. 'Guernica had been a testing-ground for the *Luftwaffe* . . . We had nowhere else to try out our machines,' he said.

He had realized what Trenchard had seen fifteen years before Guernica: 'It is in the destruction of enemy industries and, above all, on the lowering of morale of enemy nationals caused by bombing, that ultimate victory rests.' Trenchard and the RAF faced the grim, revolting facts – which is why they would in the end beat the German air force at the terrible game the Germans themselves had started.

It was the Germans' turn to visit England, and the Coronation of King George VI served as the pretext for a long-cherished ambition of Goering's. He felt he would be well received in London. Miss Ellen Wilkinson MP did not. 'Can we have a guarantee,' she asked the Under Secretary of State for Foreign Affairs, Lord Cranborne, 'that this country will not be insulted by the presence of General Goering?'

Hitler sent instead the War Minister, General von Blomberg. But Goering was not to be done out of his London trip. On 11 May his Junkers 52 landed at Croydon Airport with the gatecrasher on board. Thanks to Scotland Yard, he was then driven unobtrusively to the German Embassy.

Even Emmy was unaware of Goering's escapade. She never thought for a moment that the Ambassador, Joachim von Ribbentrop, would stand for the visit to London. 'Arrogant, vain, humourless and spiteful,' Alan Bullock calls Ribbentrop. *Capitaine Aviateur* Paul Stehlin thought him 'insolent and self-opinionated'. It was unlikely that Ribbentrop would take kindly to being eclipsed by so celebrated a person as Goering, not to speak of the attitude of the British Press. Ribbentrop spent an hour trying to convince Goering that he was likely to be booed if he so much as showed his face in London.

Next morning a disgruntled and furious Goering was winging his way back to Berlin.

On 1 July Goering was Trenchard's host at Berlin and welcomed him warmly as a fellow airman. It was rare to see Goering so respectful. 'You are well known in Germany,' he told Trenchard, 'and I have a high regard for the air force you have created.'

That afternoon Trenchard inspected air raid shelters and the civil defence organization. But in the evening he saw the other side of German air preparations – and of Goering.

At the banquet in Trenchard's honour at the Charlottenburg Palace the wine flowed and Goering, in a white uniform festooned with medals, warmed to his subject. 'It will be a pity if our two nations ever have to fight,' he told Trenchard. 'Your airmen are very good. It's a pity they haven't the machines we have.'

After dinner the one hundred guests went outside to watch a spectacular firework display. Then came an unearthly din. Trenchard commented that 'someone seemed to switch on an amplification of a modern artillery barrage mixed with the whine of . . . dive-bombers . . . dropping their loads'. Goering beamed at his guest. 'That's German might for you. I see you trembled. One day German might will make the whole world tremble.'

Trenchard flew into a rage. 'You must be off your head,' he boomed. 'You said you hoped we wouldn't have to fight each other. I hope so too, for your sake. I warn you Goering, don't underestimate the RAF.'

Trenchard made an excuse and left. He never saw Goering again.

'He's vulgar and coarse and brutal,' he later said of Goering, 'but he's a great man.'

The RAF invited Udet, Junck and Schoenebeck to the Hendon Air Display in July. They were a strong team: Udet, Head of Technical Development; Junck, Director of the Experimental Section and Schoenebeck, Commandant of the Rechlin Experimental Station – the three most experienced pilots in Germany. Each flew a Me. 109 Taifun to London. What they saw at the air display confirmed their opinion of the RAF. Junck thought 'The British, unlike the French, have the makings of a fine air force with excellent equipment, especially on the engine side.'

After an enjoyable weekend at the Master of Sempill's country place they were due to return to Germany on Monday. Bad visibility grounded the airlines that morning, but the three crack pilots showed what the *Luftwaffe* was made of – they flew off into the mist to keep a dinner date in Hanover.

Except for the British everyone in the aviation world was at Zurich during the last week in July for the International Flying Meeting. Hannes Trautloft had heard that the British would be the strongest competitors but they never turned up. He led the *Kette* (three aircraft) of Me. 109s which won the speed race.

The Me. 109 astonished everyone by its remarkable qualities of speed and climb, which were superior to those of the Hurricane (the first of which would only reach No. 111 Squadron in December, five months hence). The faster Spitfire was lagging further behind. RAF Fighter Squadrons would only get them a year after Zurich. It was as well that the British hid their hand. Especially as the Dornier 17 Bomber, which stole the show, proved itself over fifty m.p.h. faster than the elegant but outmoded Furies which were then flying in 43 Squadron at Tangmere.

After the stormy scene between Goering and Trenchard three months passed. Then on 17 October General Milch flew to Croydon with Generals Stumpff and Udet. On 18 October the Germans were received by the Air Minister, Swinton ('a very nice man', said Milch) and Air Chief Marshal Newall, by then Chief of Air Staff, of whom Milch thought, 'not a great man'.

It was in the Cadet College and technical schools, in the Squadron pilots' rooms that Milch found most to admire. 'I could find no difference between your boys and ours – the same quality, the same spirit. Both the German and British fighter pilots had that same light-heartedness and bantering talk. They were really brothers by nature.' But one difference struck Milch. 'England had the training resources of her Empire and I wondered what would happen if war came. In the *Luftwaffe* we had no experienced leaders.'

Milch did not know that plans for the Empire Training Scheme were at that moment held up. Australia and New Zealand had readily responded but the Canadian Premier, Mackenzie King, stubbornly refused. Later Canada's help would be immense – but too late to help England in 1940.

Quick-witted and inquisitive, Milch provided one or two anxious moments for the RAF. He visited Hornchurch Fighter Airfield, where he met Dowding and the pilots of 65 Squadron. Their Gladiator biplanes had just been fitted with the latest in gun-sights – the optical 'reflector sight' with range indication. The Station Commander, Group Captain 'Bunty' Frew, had warned the pilots, 'If the Germans ask about the sight, keep mum.'

Milch stopped opposite a Gladiator. 'May I see the cockpit?' he asked the pilot. It was Bob Tuck. Milch poked his head into the cockpit. 'How do you work the gun-sight?' he asked and Bob replied smartly, 'I'm sorry General, it's so new I've not yet found out.'

He then heard the Air Vice Marshal say, 'Let me explain, General.' Bob's hair stood on end while Milch inspected the gun-sight, noting that it compared favourably with the German reflector sight. No doubt he remembered the Bristol engineer at Hendon who had told him some years before about the fuel injection pump.

Air Vice Marshal Gossage, commanding 11 Group, was at the luncheon given for Milch at Fighter Command and he told John Willoughby de Broke who – in his own fashion – told me, 'While the VIPs were warming their back-sides in front of the ante-room fire over drinks General Milch suddenly addressed the assembly in a loud voice, "Now gentlemen, let us all be frank! How are you getting on with your experiments in the radio detection of aircraft approaching your shores?"

'Several of the VIPs nearly had a fit and more than one glass was dropped to the floor with a crash. Red in the face with confusion, the host tried to laugh the matter off. "Come, gentlemen!" said Milch, "there is no need to be so cagey about it. We've known for some time that you were developing a system of radio location. So are we, and we think we are a jump ahead of you." '

Milch was over-optimistic. It was true that the German Freya Radar Set had caused a sensation at the German manoeuvres at Swinemunde in the autumn of 1937, when it plotted an aircraft sixty miles away. Already on order for the *Kriegsmarine* and the *Luftwaffe*, delivery was due to begin shortly.

But the RAF were just ahead. Milch did not know that during the August air exercises 'hostile' bombers were being 'plotted' by three radar stations: Bawdsey in Suffolk, Canewdon in Essex and Dover in Kent. The system (called CH – Chain Home) was far from complete, but it was the basis of what would become the key element in Britain's air defences. The Filter Room, an all-important adjunct which checked and analysed plots before passing them to Fighter Command Operations Room, was installed at Bawdsey. Results were encouraging: formations of six or more aircraft were 'plotted' at ranges of one hundred miles at ten thousand feet and more.

But a chain of twenty-one stations was needed and it would take two years to complete. Watson-Watt was frantic at the delays and red tape and told Churchill so one day over a cup of tea at the House of Commons. A few days after the air exercises the Treasury had approved the twenty-one station scheme. A current of urgency began to galvanize the air defence preparations. The manufacture of the sets went ahead in complete secrecy.

Meanwhile at Bawdsey, the first radar training school was turning out
women operators. Watson-Watt had noticed how quickly the girl typists
at Bawdsey had adapted themselves in the early days, but when he suggested women operators the Air Ministry objected. Women might be
emotionally unstable under fire. Fortunately the Air Ministry relented.
Many of these girls later became heroines.

'Deeply impressed' by his visit, Milch hastened back to Berlin on 25
October to report to his Commander-in-Chief. But Goering was not
interested. For some time trouble had been brewing between the two top
men of the *Luftwaffe*. It was rooted in Goering's jealousy – 'a bad German
characteristic', Milch admitted. Since the Rhineland occupation in 1936
Milch's name became more and more coupled with Goering's as the
Luftwaffe's guiding force – much to Goering's displeasure.

Milch was a tireless worker and, according to his chief of staff Kesselring,
managed the Air Ministry practically singlehanded. Goering, said
Kesselring, only worked when he had to, but then it was with passionate
drive. Otherwise he left it to Milch, the organizing brain, and Udet, the
technical genius. Bruno Loerzer, Goering's old friend, acted as go-
between. The fortunes of the *Luftwaffe* were in the hands of this trio.

So Goering began clamping down on Milch. For months he refused to
see him. He withdrew the air staff, personnel and technical departments
from Milch's iron control. In mid-1937 the Chief of Air Staff, Kesselring,
quarrelled with Milch. Kesselring was pushed out and his friend, General
Stumpff, became Chief instead. And Goering put in Udet as Director
of the Technical Department. 'A nice boy,' was what Milch thought of
Udet, 'very good for bringing young pilots together over a few drinks.'
Milch was astonished when Goering made Udet technical chief. 'He had
no idea of organization or production,' said Milch. This did not worry
Goering. He knew that there was no love lost between Milch and Udet,
and Udet's presence would effectively put a spanner in Milch's wheels –
which is exactly what Goering wanted.

Milch now told Goering, 'It's time I went. Apparently I have not done
my job properly and I should like to go back to *Lufthansa*.' 'On the
contrary,' replied Goering, 'you have done your job too well. Everyone
thinks you are the head of the *Luftwaffe*.'

Goering conveniently forgot how Milch had helped him when he had
fallen on hard times. Now that he was Milch's boss he still needed his
help. 'I will not let you resign,' he told Milch, 'and don't go and pretend

you're ill. If you want to commit suicide, go ahead. Otherwise you'll stay where you are.' So Milch was kicked upstairs as Inspector General. It was not the last service that Goering would perform for the RAF.

Unable to see Goering, Milch had for some time been going directly to Hitler. On his return from England the Fuehrer summoned Milch. 'Come round and tell me about your visit,' he said, 'and never mind about Goering.' Milch told Hitler that the British planes were old and slow, but new production was coming on fast. The British were more businessmen than soldiers, but they had leaders – and that was where the *Luftwaffe* was weak. Milch recounted how at dinner one evening he sat next to Churchill. 'If only you would take the engines out of your aircraft and stick to gliding, we would feel happier,' said Churchill. 'We should be only too pleased to do so,' replied Milch, 'if the Royal Navy would return to sailboats.' Hitler thought this an excellent joke.

Milch confided to Hitler that because of Ribbentrop German interests were suffering in England. Milch thought another man should be sent to London to bring about an understanding with the British in accordance with the Fuehrer's wishes. 'You must rest assured,' said Hitler, 'that I shall always rely on England and try to co-operate with the English.'

I myself paid a brief visit to Germany, my first, in September 1937 on my way home from leave in Denmark. A uniform entered the train compartment soon after Warnemunde and the ticket collector inside it flapped his hand backwards and said rather wearily, 'Heil Hitler'. Everyone in Germany seemed to be wearing uniforms. A crowd of young *Luftwaffe* men were on the train, all of them with the *Dolch* – a short sword – dangling from their waists.

The only people I noticed in Germany wearing civilian clothes were a young couple. They caught my eye because on entering a restaurant they stopped and with outstretched arm gave the Nazi salute. My twenty-four hours in Germany only confirmed my childhood dread of the Germans.

Could Karl Missy have been among those young *Luftwaffe* men on the train? It is not impossible, for he was then at Lüneberg, not far away. While serving with the 7th Infantry Regiment Missy still harboured the idea of joining the *Flak*. Then came six weeks of manoeuvres. 'I could see the *Flak* at work,' he explained, 'and realized it was not the super-human machinery I thought it was, but that the aircraft they were trying to shoot down were themselves a far greater technical achievement.' He developed a new and burning ambition to fly. In the regiment he had been a simple soldier, a small, impersonal cog in a vast machine. He wanted to be something more individual, to be in control of his own machine or apparatus. The individualism which makes all airmen was beginning to grow in Karl Missy.

During the manoeuvres he had a chance to inspect some aircraft on the ground, even to climb in the cockpit. All at once he became enthusiastic. He wanted to be a pilot, but men with a technical background like his were wanted for aircrew. His mind was made up. He sent in his application and on 1 October 1937 Missy was transferred to the *Luftwaffe* – an event which, barely two years later, would have grievous consequences for him.

He changed from his drab field-grey to the handsome blue uniform of the *Luftwaffe*, with collar and tie. Then he was posted to *KG 26* at Lüneberg.

As British children were building bonfires and parading their guys, Hitler was closeted in the Reich Chancellery with five of his war chieftains and advisers on foreign affairs. It was 5 November 1937. Those present were the War Minister, von Blomberg, the Foreign Minister, von Neurath, and the three Commanders-in-Chief: General von Fritsch, Admiral Raeder and *General Der Flieger* Goering. A sixth person was Hitler's military aide, Colonel Friedrich Hossbach. The talk, which Hossbach recorded for posterity, was of *Lebensraum* and war.

The Fuehrer first reminded them that the aim of German policy was to 'preserve the racial community and to enlarge it. It was therefore a question of living-space (*Lebensraum*).' Germany's future security depended on living-space which was to be found not overseas but in Europe – and then only at the risk of war. 'The attacker always comes up against a possessor,' said Hitler.

By Europe Hitler meant Eastern Europe He had no territorial ambitions in the already overcrowded west. From the time he wrote *Mein Kampf* in 1925, Hitler's policy never changed: German expansion must be eastwards. But, he told the meeting, Germany's problem could only be solved by means of force.

In his calculations Hitler saw Russia, the intended victim, as one problem. The other more basic one was to deal with Germany's 'hate-inspired' antagonists, France and Britain – this three days after he had told

Milch, 'I shall always rely on England and try to co-operate with the English.' All three of these problems would have to be dealt with one way or another.

The question was, when? Germany would reach the peak of her power in 1943–45. Hitler was determined to resolve Germany's problem by then. 'It is while the rest of the world is preparing its defences that one must take the offensive. One thing is certain, we can wait no longer.'

The first victims in Germany's march eastwards would be Austria and Czechoslovakia. Their conquest would ensure Germany's eastern flanks, increase her economic resources – and add twelve divisions to the German army.

Hitler believed that Britain and France had probably written off the Czechs. France in any case would hardly oppose Germany without British support. If Germany's western defences were held in strength it would suffice to deter the Allies.

Of the men who listened to Hitler, Goering alone approved. Enthusiastically, he suggested pulling out of Spain. Admiral Raeder was silent. Only Neurath, Blomberg and Fritsch objected. Within three months they would be sacked.

Hitler, an opportunist but prudent and determined, would wait his moment – which was nearer than he expected. But that day, 5 November, he was decided on changing the fate of Europe, and of millions of men and women.

Chapter 12

My own fate meanwhile had been decided in a most displeasing manner, by some official who got it into his head that because I had done fourteen months in a far-away torpedo squadron I had become the property of Coastal Command. I was dragged off protesting from 43 Fighter Squadron and its Furies, and sent to the School of Air Navigation at Manston in Kent on a four months' course. If I had known that within three years the *Luftwaffe* would pound Manston to dust I would have cheered.

The transfer from fighters to coastal reconnaissance made me feel suicidal. I had joined the RAF because I loved flying. I was by birth and breeding a fighter pilot. In 1 and 43 Squadrons, even in 36 skimming over the water and the jungle in my venerable Vildebeeste – I had found all the joy I ever expected of flying. No thought of war marred it.

But those twenty-four hours in Germany had set me thinking seriously about war. It was a grim, depressing prospect, not in the least heroic. There was some of that feeling in the crowded mess at Manston. Things had changed since I first went to Tangmere, when I felt I belonged to the best flying club in the world. Singapore gave the same feeling. We flew and it made us happy. Being young we did not ask for more. When I returned to Tangmere there were new faces and an inescapable feeling that the good days were gone. But I was among fighter pilots – Caesar Hull, John Simpson, Fred Rosier and the rest – whose language was my own and whose company I enjoyed. At Manston only one man helped me out of my depression, Larry Skey, a lanky Canadian from Toronto. We were detailed as co-navigators on the course.

Between fits of depression I quickly found that Larry was a good friend who enjoyed a laugh. The biggest one we had was after a search exercise far out over the grey North Sea. We successfully found our ship and flashed its position in code back to base. Unfortunately we slipped up in the coding. We had reported the ship high and dry in the neighbourhood of a small village in the middle of Norfolk.

On 5 November 1937 I was circling over the North Sea as navigator in an Avro Anson, wondering how on earth I could ever get back to fighters. Larry encouraged me by saying that he thought I could fix anything.

The Manston course ended at last. I felt rather shamed by what was written on my 'diploma', because it belied my whole attitude to the course. 'Has taken a keen interest in the work ... with experience should become a very sound navigator/observer.' I thought that was the last straw. But worse was to come. A new Coastal Squadron had recently formed at Tangmere and I was sent to it. My new commanding officer and I instantly shared a profound dislike of one another, and I had the chagrin of seeing my friends in 1 and 43 revelling in their Furies – completely outmoded, but always a delight to fly.

At that moment I providentially became ill again. It was the one chance of deliverance, but I could never have 'fixed' things without the sympathy of two people. The first was Doc Moynahan, a charming rebel Irishman who told me to write in to the medical authorities. My letter was a simple one. It said that flying as a passenger or second pilot in a twin-engined aeroplane made me ill and I was ill enough to prove it. If steps were not taken to put me back on single-seaters I should resign my commission.

The station commander understood too. He had been a fighter pilot all his life. His name was Keith Park. He was a close friend of 'Ginger' Bowhill, Coastal Command C-in-C. Other than that I do not know what magic he used, but with a touch of his wand I was changed from a 'very sound navigator/observer' back into a fighter pilot. Within a short time I had rejoined 43 Squadron – this time to stay.

On 10 March my career in the Coastal Command Squadron ended a week after it began. Germany's rape of Austria was only hours away. During the night of 10 March Hitler issued his orders – 'If other measures prove unsuccessful I intend to invade Austria with armed forces ...' When we went to bed in the small hours of 11 March, German Panzers were moving up to the Austrian frontier.

The possibility of British intervention had not been overlooked by the *Luftwaffe* Chief of Air Staff, General Stumpff. On 18 February he had asked General Helmuth Felmy (commanding *Luftflotte* 2) to prepare an operational plan for air attack on Britain. At present none existed – then, only twenty years after the last German bombs had fallen on Britain, a 'case' arose again for attacking her from the air. Its code name was

Fall Blau (Case Blue). But nothing more was heard of it for the time being.

At 2.45 p.m. on 11 October the *Luftwaffe*'s C-in-C had his hands much too full to think about air attacks on Britain. He had taken the Austrian operation very much as his own personal affair and was on the telephone to Vienna. At 5.30 p.m. he was still shouting over the line at his man in Vienna, the Minister of the Interior, Seyss Inquart.

Goering had arranged a big party that evening at the *Haus der Flieger*, and was still on the line to Vienna when the first guests arrived. They and a thousand others waited over an hour for him. As the State Opera Ballet danced, Goering scribbled a note to the British Ambassador, Henderson. 'I should like to talk to you . . .'

Henderson saw Goering in his room and delivered a 'protest in the strongest terms', which had absolutely no effect. Goering then summoned the Czech Minister, Dr Mastney. 'I give you my word of honour that Czechoslovakia has nothing to fear from the Reich.'

Capitaine Aviateur Paul Stehlin missed the party. An accident had put him in hospital, where Goering's sister and sister-in-law visited him regularly. On 9 March Stehlin was able to inform his ambassador that the German army would cross the Austrian frontier on 12 March. It did, and shortly after lunch that day Hitler himself was driving through the cheering crowds in Linz. When next day a proclamation was read to him, 'Austria is now a province of the German Reich . . .' tears ran down his cheeks. Austria had disappeared from the map. That night the Gestapo went to work. In Vienna alone they would arrest seventy-six thousand people.

Hans-Heinrich Brustellin also went to Linz – not that he had any more love for the place than for Hitler. His unit (I *JG* 51) flew in to cover the army's and the Fuehrer's advance. Its IIIrd *Staffel* had just got its Me. 109s. The other two stuck to their He. 51s until the *Anschluss* was over. *JG* 51 then moved on to Vienna-Aspern. Hans-Heinrich said they were greeted like liberators. Veteran officers of the Austro-Hungarian Imperial Army, wearing their old uniforms, were among the thousands who streamed out to the airport to welcome the *Luftwaffe*. Meanwhile those who preferred independence were being arrested in thousands by the Gestapo.

Rudolf Braun's unit (I *Stuka Geschwader* 168) was moved to Graz. Between flights they had aircraft recognition lectures regularly and Rudolf got the impression that the RAF were about equal in numbers and quality to the *Luftwaffe*. Now in IV *JG* 253 at Düsseldorf, Otto Hintze also found himself for the first time studying aircraft recognition. He did not think that if ever they met, the Hawker Fury with its neat silhouette would be much of a match for *JG* 253's Messerschmitt 109s. But for the present the unit was at readiness, guns loaded, to defend the Ruhr against possible raids by Allied bombers.

Had war broken out there is no doubt that the Do. 17 bombers of Joachim Poetter's unit (*KG* 51) would have been the first to be involved. Since 1937 they had been at Memmingen, only a stone's throw from the Austrian frontier.

Poetter's idea was that the eidelweiss, the little flower which grows in the Alps so close to Memmingen, should be the *Geschwader*'s emblem. The *Anschluss* caused little excitement in *KG* 51. They flew over the Alps to Vienna to impress the Austrians. It was a small effort for such a big result.

Hajo Hermann had spent a whole year in Spain before getting back to *KG* 4 at Nordhausen. During the Austrian crisis their diesel-engined Ju. 86s were 'bombed up' and like Otto Hintze's fighter unit, they were ready to strike in the west. Even if Felmy's operational plan, *Fall Blau*, had not yet materialized the *Luftwaffe* did not overlook the possibility of an attack by England and France.

Werner Borner had left Nordhausen with a new bomber unit (*KG* 153) for Liegnitz, in the east. They too had Ju. 86s. Bombing and air-firing practice was stepped up and they were ready for action.

It was as well that the 'conflict' Hitler dreaded did not occur. For the diesel engines of the Ju. 86 were extremely unreliable. Aircraft from Borner's unit made forced landings all over Germany. Werner would never forget the smell of the engines as they started up, with clouds of milk-white smoke – it was the same smell as when his mother baked potato-cakes. The difference was that the aircraft seldom burned.

Borner saw one which did. One of the best mechanics had just had words with the *Hauptfeldwebel* (flight sergeant). He left his office swearing. 'I'll put that bloody Ju. on his desk for him,' they heard him say. He climbed into a Ju. 86 which had just refuelled, and started up. Shouting to the radio operator to get out, he opened up the throttles. Hardly airborne, the aircraft hit a pole and caught fire. They saw the demented mechanic on the roof and heard him yell, 'Long live my friends and the Fatherland.' Then he jumped into the flames and perished.

Like Werner Borner before him, Karl Missy passed through the Halle Radio School. He was there when the Austrian crisis broke. A *Luftnacht-richten Einheit* was formed and Karl went with it by train to Breslau, north of the Czechoslovakian border. It was purely a security measure, Missy was informed. No one thought there would be war. Early in April he was back at Halle.

Ein Volk, Ein Reich, Ein Fuehrer, shouted the fifteen thousand Germans who demonstrated on 27 March 1938 in Saaz, in the Sudetenland, Czechoslovakia's northern frontier province. Echoed by three million Sudetens their slogan was to be the pretext for Hitler's next move – the destruction of the young Czechoslovak state. *Fall Groen* (Case Green) was the code name for the operation.

By now the *Luftwaffe* was ready to carry out Hitler's intentions against Germany's neighbours. On 1 August 1938 it possessed 2,930 aircraft, of which just over half were serviceable. Of these, 690 were bombers and dive-bombers and 450 were fighters. *Capitaine Aviateur* Stehlin had ascertained from sources close to Goering himself that half the bomber force was deployed against Czechoslovakia. This left less than 350 bombers to operate against France and England. On the other hand, most of the fighter force was stationed in the west. It was only wise to take pre-cautions, but Hitler assured Goering that a war against England would be utterly impossible. And as long as Goering was himself convinced of the RAF's inferiority he could afford to pour his contempt upon it.

Meanwhile the Commander-in-Chief could not afford to take any chances with the RAF. To the Chief of *Abteilung 5*, the *Luftwaffe's* Intelligence Section, Major Josef Schmid (better known as Beppo) gave orders to carry out a target survey of Britain. A committee was formed with Schmid in the chair and Milch, Udet and Hans Jeschonnek, deputy Chief of Air Staff who had recommended Schmid to Goering. Unfortunately for the *Luftwaffe*, Schmid was not the ideal choice. He was not a pilot, he could speak no English, he had never been out of Germany and he was only a Major. His opposite number in the RAF was an Air Commodore, the equivalent of a Brigadier. Hard things were said about Schmid: 'One of the most disastrous men in the *Luftwaffe* general staff . . . with a boxer's face, without wit or culture. An alcoholic, he started his career with factually false, optimistically exaggerated opinions . . .' The *Luftwaffe* was to suffer from this 'unqualified man in a key position'.

Milch, Schmid's senior committee-man, said of him, 'In all this underwater shooting he was one of the key men. But the information he provided – it was dreadful. He made a report on Sylt and I thought, "Never have I read such rot." But Goering said, "You know nothing about it." ' Goering always had the last word.

Milch had instigated target research on British industry as long ago as 1933. He asked Herr Voegeler, director of a steel factory, to recommend a standard work on British industry. He then ordered three copies from the London publisher. They cost seventy marks each and contained everything which was of interest to the German target researcher. Milch had shown the book to *Oberst* Walther Wever who exclaimed anxiously, 'I hope there are no books like this in Germany.' Once again Milch had found the English helpful – the book formed the basis of the target-committee's report, '*Studie Blau*'. *Studie Blau* would provide the basic information for most of the *Luftwaffe*'s attacks on England.

During two years as Commander-in-Chief of Fighter Command, Dowding had made immense progress in repairing its 'lamentable deficiencies' and welding into a united air defence system its diverse elements – men, women, aircraft, airfields, radar, Observer Corps, anti-aircraft batteries and balloons. All were knit together by an elaborate and complex system of radio and telephonic communications.

But time was against him and, more insidious than time, the interference and obstructionism of the Air Ministry. His relationship with the Air Ministry, so vital in perfecting the air defences of Britain, lapsed into a series of acrimonious conflicts which would continue until the end of his career.

Many believed he could have settled at least some of these disagreements by discussing them personally with the Air Staff. Even Dowding admitted it was perhaps a just criticism. 'It is probably a defect in my character,' he said, 'but I have found that a stage . . . can be reached where more harm than good is done by verbal discussions.'

He was senior to everyone at the Air Ministry concerned with his work at Fighter Command. Very naturally he felt that 'it was not pleasant to have one's recommendations turned down by somebody who had quite recently been one's direct subordinate'. Dowding was not to be fobbed off with anything that failed to meet with his own carefully conceived plans. 'It would have been easy to remain on good terms with the Air Staff if one had accepted every ruling.'

He complained continually that without any consultation with him or his staff the Air Staff took decisions vitally affecting his command. While willing to forgive oversights on the part of busy people, he begged the Air Ministry to ensure that he was consulted in matters affecting Fighter Command. But incidents occurred which convinced him that his exclusion from policy decisions was deliberate. Once, he submitted a paper on inland radar coverage. A number of the radar stations vital to his plans were struck out and 'the mutilated remainder' forwarded without further reference to him to the Committee of Imperial Defence.

Again, he found out by chance that the Home Defence Committee was planning, without reference to him, an emergency Fighter Command Operations Room. Quite naturally he offered certain suggestions, only to be informed that the plans were settled and could not be changed. The Commander-in-Chief was denied a say in the planning of his own Operations Room.

Periodically, however, Dowding was invited to Air Ministry conferences to discuss equipment. At one of these he asked for bullet-proof windscreens for his Hurricane and Spitfire fighters. 'To my astonishment,' he related, 'the whole table dissolved in gusts of laughter as though I had asked for something grotesquely impossible.'

Without flinching he told them, 'If Chicago gangsters can have bullet-proof glass in their cars I can see no reason why my pilots should not have the same.' The chief gain, he said later, was 'the confidence engendered when flying into a stream of bullets from the rear turret of an enemy bomber. I had no idea how many lives were saved'.

My own life would be one.

The embryonic air defence system had scraped through its first serious test, the air exercises of the summer of 1937. But Fighter Command's biplane fighters were often too slow to catch the new Blenheim bombers. Since then, three squadrons had been re-equipped with Hurricanes and the radar chain – the fighters' 'eyes' – had been increased from three to five stations. The air exercises set for 5–7 August would be the vital test of Dowding's immense efforts, the hoped-for reward of his 'forceful, cogent and entirely outspoken protests' to the Air Ministry.

On the first morning of the exercises Dowding received a letter from the Permanent Under Secretary of the Air Ministry. It was dated 4 August 1938 and said, 'I am commanded by the Air Council to inform you that ... they will be unable to offer you any further employment in the Royal Air Force after the end of June 1939.' The Air Ministry had

Duel of Eagles

already decided on Dowding's successor, the Air Vice Marshal, Christopher Courtney. The RAF was justified in congratulating itself on the results of the air exercises. Results were promising, and on the assumption that the Germans would maintain daily raids of two hundred aircraft it was estimated that ten per cent could be destroyed.

Another basic assumption was that the raids would approach from the east and north-east, from bases inside Germany.

On 17 August General Vuillemin, Chief of Staff of the French *Armée de l'Air*, arrived in Berlin, invited by Goering for a week's visit. From the first cheer which greeted the General in the *Unter den Linden* he was convinced that the Germans had nothing but the friendliest feelings towards France – precisely the effect the Germans wanted to give. The weakness of the French Air Force was no secret to the Germans, but they knew it could still intervene directly in an attack on France's ally, Czechoslovakia.

General Vuillemin visited Döberitz, and Paul Temme was among the young pilots of the *Jagdgeschwader Richthofen* who stood rigidly to attention as the General reviewed them.

After the fly past in impeccable formation, Temme met the General and his staff in the comfortable, well-furnished mess. *JG Richthofen* was out to impress the French Chief of Staff. Temme and his comrades felt sure of themselves. The *Luftwaffe* was an élite force, the *Jagdgeschwader Richthofen* a crack unit. That day it showed itself worthy of its illustrious name, as it did of its one-time *Kommandeur*. Hermann Goering showed an almost brutal pride in his old unit. Their youth, their spirit and their flying skill astonished Vuillemin as much as the excellence of their equipment.

The tour continued with visits to the Messerschmitt factory at Leipzig and Augsburg, where the Me. 109 and Me. 110 – the two best fighters of their class in the world – were rolling off the lines. Even the good beer offered to the guest and the lovely Bavarian maidens, about whose charm, *Capitaine* Stehlin remarked, the Chief of the French Air Staff seemed particularly sensitive. Even the genial company of Ernst Udet could not alleviate the glum feelings of the Frenchmen when they compared the German air industry with their own, the oldest in the world and until recently the foremost, but now lagging badly in design, quality and output.

At the Tactical Experimental Centre at Barth, General Vuillemin and General d'Astier de la Vigerie, who accompanied him, watched spellbound for three hours while the *Luftwaffe's* bombers and dive-bombers manoeuvred with incredible skill and effect against moving ground targets. After lunch they were shown the library which contained works by military experts of many countries, among them some by Colonel Charles de Gaulle. *Capitaine* Stehlin was shocked to find that none of General Vuillemin's staff had heard of the Colonel, already an eminent authority on armoured warfare.

On leaving Berlin the French Chief of Air Staff called aside *Capitaine* Stehlin and his chief, General de Geffrier. He was shocked and disturbed, he told them, by all he had seen and heard. To the Ambassador, François-Poncet, he expressed the fear that if it came to a show-down with the *Luftwaffe* the French air force would be *hors de combat* in a fortnight. A month later he would repeat the same views to the French Premier Daladier, as he left for the Munich conference.

The day that Vuillemin flew back from Berlin to Paris, the *Luftwaffe* Chief of Staff, General Hans-Juergen Stumpff, sent another request – urgent this time, with the *Sudetenland* crisis blowing up – to the *Luftflotte* I commander, General Felmy, to prepare plans for an air campaign against England.

Hitler was then at Kiel for the naval manoeuvres. He received the Hungarian dictator Horthy aboard his ship the *Patria*. Hitler told Horthy that if he wanted to take advantage of the Czech invasion he had better rally quickly to Hitler's side. 'Those who want to take part in the meal must first help in the cooking,' said Hitler.

No one landing at Dinard for the International Air Rally at the end of August dreamed that a month later France and Germany would be on the verge of war. That was the opinion of Werner Borner, who was chosen as radio operator in one of the Messerschmitt 108 Taifuns. It was a wonderful chance to see France. At Dinard a great reception awaited the visitors, who were welcomed by the Air Minister, Guy La Chambre, and by General Vuillemin.

To Borner it was obvious that the French Chief of Staff – just back from his visit to Germany – was out to make the bravest show possible. But the ex-*Wachtsoldat* of the Presidential Guard was not impressed by the march past. The German airmen climbed into a Morane fighter and a new Potez bomber. Both machines looked good – in spite of the wooden broom-handles mounted in place of machine-guns.

Then came the flying display – a mock attack on Dinard with air raid alarms and smoke bombs. 'Is this the French air force?' Borner and his comrades asked. 'We could not believe our eyes. The hotch-potch of land and sea aircraft looked as if they were left over from the First World War.'

By mid-September, shortly before the Munich Conference, we were busy getting 43 Squadron at Tangmere ready for war. We worked every night in the hangar with the ground crews, belting ammunition and (in our view an act of vandalism) daubing our silver Furies in brown and green camouflage war paint. By dawn on 28 September, the day of the Conference, we were ready for battle, but with what woefully inadequate weapons! A Fury in perfect trim might reach 210 m.p.h. The weight and skin friction of its warpaint slowed it by several miles per hour. The modest fire-power of our twin Vickers guns was academic – for enemy bomber diagrams in the pilots' room left us all too painfully aware that we should never even catch the Heinkel 111 and the Dornier 17, which did well over two hundred and fifty m.p.h.

We might even have found something to laugh at in the lamentable shortcomings of our equipment, but the atmosphere was too heavy with anxiety and depression for that. The older officers who had already seen one war sat round with their heads in their hands repeating the fervent hope that they would never see another. Only Caesar longed to have a 'crack at the Huns'.

Perhaps because 54 Squadron at Hornchurch had Gladiators with four guns and a top speed of 245 m.p.h. they were more enthusiastic. Al Deere, the New Zealander who had now realized his youthful ambition to fly, dreamed already of great air battles. But Norman Ryder, in 41 Squadron at Catterick, which had Super-Furies a little faster than ours, thought they would have made a 'pitiful show'. What we all agreed on was that our biplane fighters, so wonderfully light and nimble to fly, belonged to a bygone age of aerial combat.

The *Luftwaffe* General Staff did not share our doubts. In an OKL memorandum dated 25 August 1938 it was pointed out that in the event of

British intervention the *Luftwaffe* would be unable to achieve an effective blockade, since it would be needed to support the Army in Czechoslovakia and perhaps to attack France. While Chamberlain was pleading with Hitler at Godesberg on 22 September, the Chief of Staff, Stumpff, was studying Felmy's plans for air warfare against England.

They did not make good reading. Felmy pointed out that, operating from German bases, the range and bomb load of *Luftwaffe* bombers would not enable them to achieve decisive results against England. In Felmy's opinion the Royal Navy was the most important target, but their ships would probably be moved out of range. Air force targets would have to be limited to RAF airfields and air factories around London and in south-east England. In a subsidiary paper on *Fall Groen* which envisaged France and then England aiding Czechoslovakia in a war against Germany, it was stated that the *Luftwaffe* was in no state to launch a strategic bombing attack on England. Its role could not be extended beyond the tactical support of the German army.

The deputy Chief of Air Staff, Hans Jeschonnek, returned Felmy's memorandum to its author, observing that it made the *Luftwaffe* look ridiculous. 'It is as good as slapping Goering in the face. He wants you to know that if he combined all the *Geschwader* in an attack it would darken the sky over London.' Goering himself noted sourly, 'I have not asked for a memorandum which weighs the possibilities of success or points out our weaknesses. These I know best myself . . .' Henceforth Felmy would be under a cloud.

Edouard Daladier was profoundly influenced by Vuillemin's warning that the French air force was weak and might be rapidly put out of action by the *Luftwaffe*. However sincere his intentions to help Czechoslovakia, the menace of the *Luftwaffe* held him back.

Goering's personal staff officer and confidant, Carl von Bodenschatz, had in fact privately informed Stehlin just as the Conference was ending that 'the *Luftwaffe*'s attack, which normally would have been launched today, would have been shattering. We had stationed two thousand aircraft around the Czech frontier . . . The crews had studied their targets on large-scale maps . . . This shattering air attack would have consisted of low-flying Heinkels and Dorniers . . . We knew that our losses might amount to fifty per cent . . . but we were certain that all targets would have been destroyed . . . The losses anyway could have been made up without delay from our ample reserves . . .'

The motives and actions of Chamberlain were different from those of Daladier. The Air Minister, Kingsley Wood, was one of his closest friends in the Cabinet and he left Chamberlain in no doubt about Britain's pitifully inadequate air defences. The Air Minister had been telling Ministers and Opposition leaders that Germany could spare fifteen hundred bombers to attack Britain and that the country must reckon on half a million casualties in three weeks.

This pessimistic picture made a deep impression on Government and Opposition leaders alike. But it was based on a false assumption. The Air Staff estimate of *Luftwaffe* bomber figures was well under fifteen hundred. In fact the *Luftwaffe* strength on 1 August was a total of 1,670 serviceable machines. Of these, only 582 were long-range bombers. Chamberlain knew that the Air Minister's figures were exaggerated, but he did not reveal this to the Cabinet.

Cowed by the apparently fearful strength of the *Luftwaffe*'s bomber fleet, the Cabinet authorized Chamberlain to negotiate with Hitler – and to sacrifice Czechoslovakia in the process. Like Hitler, Chamberlain despised the French, detested the Russians and dreamed of an Anglo-German *entente*.

Whichever way one looked at Hitler's new bloodless victory the *Luftwaffe* had been a dominant factor in bringing it about. Hitler understood perfectly the *Luftwaffe*'s capacity for intimidating the Western Powers. *Capitaine* Stehlin rightly concluded after Munich that 'the disproportion between the air forces of France and Britain on the one hand and of Germany on the other was one of the main factors in our moral defeat and the loss of our position in Central Europe'.

On 31 September 1938 the Munich conference ended as ignominiously as it had begun. Before leaving the Fuehrer, Chamberlain produced from his pocket a sheet of paper on which he had written, among other things, 'We consider the agreement signed yesterday . . . as [one of] the symbols of the desire of our people never to go to war again with one another.' Hitler read the paper and signed it, without any apparent enthusiasm. A few hours later Chamberlain was on his way back to London. Long before he reached the English coast the radar chain picked up his aircraft and plotted it. When he stepped from the aircraft at Croydon he waved the paper that Hitler had signed. 'I believe . . . that it is peace in our time,' he said amidst wild applause.

At Tangmere we stood down. There was no applause, only heartfelt relief. But we did not feel proud of ourselves. We knew that as Britain's first line of defence we should have been overwhelmed by the *Luftwaffe* onslaught had it come. Of the 750 fighters that Fighter Command possessed only ninety were Hurricanes. The rest were out-of-date biplanes.

Chapter 13

In the controversy following Munich there were two main currents of opinion. The distinguished exponent of one was Mr Winston Churchill. 'We are in the presence of a disaster of the first magnitude,' he declared in Parliament on 5 October. 'And do not suppose that this is the end. It is only the beginning of the reckoning.'

As expressed by the Parliamentary Under Secretary of the Air Ministry, Captain Harold Balfour, another opinion was that Munich afforded to Britain 'a year of salvation'. It was he who in 1917 had admired the gaily painted Albatrosses of Richthofen's Circus looping and rolling, 'like puppies playing with each other'. He was then Flight Commander of B Flight 43 Squadron. I would shortly assume this command.

The 'year of salvation' was not lost on the *Luftwaffe*. It gave the Germans time to establish new air-crew training bases in Austria and to recruit new blood from the Austrian population. A new Messerschmitt factory was set up at Wiener Neustadt and helped considerably to augment Germany's lagging fighter production. Czechoslovakia too was to provide new bases and production facilities for the *Luftwaffe*, but few pilots: hundreds of them would escape to freedom.

Perhaps the most explicit comment on the 'year of salvation' comes from Major Sholto Douglas, another member of 43 Squadron, who was its first commanding officer in 1916 and in 1938 Deputy Chief of the Air Staff. 'In the air in 1938 we had practically nothing; during 1939 we went a long way towards catching up; and by 1940, "when the test came", as Churchill has put it, we were in a position to wage successfully the most vitally important battle that has ever been fought in the air.'

Less than two weeks after Hitler had given Chamberlain an assurance that Germany and Britain would never again go to war, Hitler started to hurl threats and insults at Britain. 'It would be a good thing if people in Britain would gradually drop certain airs which they have inherited from the Versailles period. We cannot tolerate the tutelage of governesses . . .' he said during a speech at *Saarbrücken*.

On 18 October he invited the French Ambassador, André François-Poncet (who was transferred to Rome), for a farewell visit to 'Eagle's Nest' in the Obersalzburg above Berchtesgaden. *Capitaine* Stehlin accompanied the Ambassador. The road cut into the mountain and climbed for ten miles in hairpin bends to a height of six thousand feet. The visitors arrived in front of a high and solid bronze door which slid open as they left their car, revealing a long tunnel at the end of which was a brilliantly lit room. They looked at each other wondering whether they would ever see the light of day again. They were taken by a lift to the chalet, 350 feet above, where they stepped out into an immense circular room. They had the impression of being suspended in space with fantastic views all around. François-Poncet wondered, 'Is it the work of a normal mind or of a man tormented by a wild desire for greatness, by a terror of domination and solitude?' He described the scene as 'bathed in the twilight of an autumn evening . . . grandiose, wild, almost hallucinating'.

Hitler fulminated against England. He expected after his interviews with Chamberlain that England would continue with further peace talks but instead she assumed a superior air and broadcast appeals to rearm.

Hitler did not mention that in a speech only four days earlier Goering had said, 'Hitler has ordered me to organize a gigantic armament programme which would make all previous achievements appear insignificant. I have been ordered to build as rapidly as possible an Air Force five times as large as the present one.'

In contrast to his feelings about England, Hitler held nothing against France and would welcome closer relations with her. From then on German diplomacy would be directed at separating the two allies. England was to take the place of France as Germany's principal enemy.

Immediately after Munich the British Air Minister and his staff went to work to study the mistakes and shortcomings of the past. In the master plan (Plan M) which resulted, top priority was given to re-equipping Fighter Command.

In 43 Squadron the 'catching up' process started on 29 November 1938 with the arrival of Hurricanes L1725 and L1727. By mid-December we had our full initial equipment of sixteen aircraft. The Fury had been a delightful play-thing; the Hurricane was a thoroughly war-like machine, rock solid as a platform for its eight Browning machine-guns, highly manoeuvrable despite its large proportions and with an excellent view from the cockpit. The Hurricane lacked the speed and glamour of the Spitfire and was slower than the Me. 109, whose pilots were to develop contempt for it and a snobbish preference for being shot down by Spitfires. But figures were to prove that during the Battle of Britain, machine for machine, the Hurricane would acquit itself every bit as well as the Spitfire and in the aggregate (there were more than three Hurricanes to two Spitfires) do greater damage among the *Luftwaffe*.

At first the Hurricane earned a bad reputation. The change from the light and agile Fury caught some pilots unaware. The Hurricane was far less tolerant of faulty handling, and a mistake at low altitude could be fatal. One day a sergeant pilot glided back to Tangmere with a faulty engine. We watched him as with plenty of height he turned in – too slowly – to land. The Hurricane fell out of his hands and before our eyes dived headlong into the ground. The unfortunate young pilot died as the ambulance arrived.

There were certain problems with the Merlin engines. At night the normally excellent visibility from the cockpit was badly reduced by a torrent of blue flame pouring from the engine exhausts. We occasionally experienced a phenomenon known as 'surging', accompanied by a sudden loss of power. It was most disconcerting at night – and more spectacular – for with loss of power the blue Bunsen flames faded to an unconvincing yellow.

When this happened to me one night I decided to return to base. Then I smelt castor oil in the cockpit – a smell I had dreaded as a boy and thrilled to when, as burnt blue smoke, it had poured forth from the exhausts of the Bulldog's Jupiter VI engine. But I could think of no connection between castor oil and a Hurricane.

I landed fairly short and, as regulations required, opened up the engine to taxi to the end of the flare path. On the spade-grip of the control column was a curved brake lever. I squeezed it. Nothing happened. Again I squeezed, but the Hurricane did not slow in its course toward the end of the flare path. Then, slamming on the rudder, I managed to slew it into a horrible grinding turn and avoid the far hedge which (along with gravity) we all acknowledged as the chief enemy of aviators.

Had I known my Hurricane better the smell of castor oil would have spelled a leak in the hydraulic brake system, which contained two pints of it – and had failed completely.

Back on the tarmac around 3.00 a.m. I stood talking with my rigger and watching the navigation lights of a Hurricane coming in to land. Suddenly there came a rending crash and the lights disappeared. I yelled for the fire tender and ambulance. But a moment after they had roared off into the dark a column of flame burst from the direction of the crash and lit up the airfield.

In the mess, shortly before dawn, we mourned Charles Rotherham in our own particular way. Fred Rosier fetched his violin and did his best to accompany a record of 'Orpheus in the Underworld'. The idea was to make us laugh, and it succeeded. When the can-can passage came we all danced hilariously round the ante-room. Two days later we trod the familiar road to Tangmere's peaceful graveyard and as the earth was heaped on his coffin, saluted our comrade for the last time.

And so we came to know ourselves and our Hurricanes better. There grew in us a trust and an affection for them and their splendid Merlin engines, thoroughbreds and stayers which changed our fearful doubts of the Munich period into the certainty that we could beat all comers.

The Messerschmitt 109 had begun to enter the *Luftwaffe* fighter units long before our own started to re-equip with Hurricanes and Spitfires. It was a faster fighter, armed with two twenty mm. cannons and two 7·9 mm. machine-guns – compared to the eight machine-guns of the RAF's Hurricanes and Spitfires. It was less manoeuvrable than our fighters but its Daimler-Benz engine was equipped with fuel injection, enabling it to go abruptly into a dive from level flight. With us, the Merlin cut out momentarily under 'negative G', as in going over the top of a switch-back, and lost us a few precious seconds.

The Me. 109s of Hans-Heinrich Brustellin's unit (*JG* 51) were at Vienna during the Munich crisis. But there was no excitement, no sense of emergency. 'The only thing we felt,' said Brustellin, 'was that it was about time the French did something.' But Daladier knew better. As he had said, '*Tout va dépendre des Anglais.*' So Hans-Heinrich had a wonderful time with June Sempill and her sister, whose father (as the President of the Royal Aerial Club) was well-known and respected in international aviation. 'They were lovely girls,' said Brustellin, little dreaming that within a year he and they would be at war.

The Sudetenland crisis found Otto Hintze in *JG* 135 near the Sudetenland frontier at Bad Aibling. The unit had Me. 109s and – unlike 43 Squadron with its ancient Furies – was longing for action. In October they moved to Eger in the Sudetenland where they were welcomed with open arms. 'It was the Flower War,' said Hintze.

Paul Temme in *JG* 2 at Berlin-Döberitz did not find the Munich crisis all that droll. The crack squadron was given the job of patrolling Berlin – not in their Me. 109s but in Heinkel 51s. Paul's cooling system failed one morning and he fetched up against a wall in a Berlin suburb. It would have been far less funny in a Me. 109.

Commanded by Major Theo Osterkamp, with Johannes Janke as Chief Instructor and Hannes Trautloft as *Staffel Kapitän*, the flying school at Berlin-Werneuchen had an assortment of Me. 109s, He. 51s and Arado 68s.

The day the first Me. 109 arrived *Hauptmann* Lutzow told his commanding officer, 'I expect you want to be the first to fly one.' But the wily old Uncle Theo, who had never sat in a Me. 109 in his life and did not intend to make a fool of himself in front of his pupils, replied, 'Go ahead yourself. I've flown one.' He planned to wait until the week-end when there was nobody about. Unfortunately Milch telephoned next day: 'Osterkamp, I want you to send five of your instructors to collect a Me. 109 each from the factory and fly them to Belgrade. You'll probably want to lead the formation yourself.' '*Jawohl, Herr General,*' was all Uncle Theo could say as Milch hung up.

Osterkamp sweated during that flight but he landed perfectly at Belgrade and was greeted by Carl von Schoenebeck, then air attaché there. That evening, writes Osterkamp, 'the five Me. 109s were lined up alongside the old and trusty British Hurricanes which till then had been the pride of the Yugoslav air force. *Sic transit gloria mundi.*'

But Osterkamp must have been seeing things. The first Hurricane was delivered to the Yugoslav air force on 15 December 1938. Incredible though it may seem, approximately the same priority was accorded to them as to 43 Squadron, which, with its outmoded biplanes, only three weeks earlier had faced the prospect of war with Germany. Not only that, but the Hurricane was thus made available for inspection and trial by the Germans.

In July 1938 the Me. 109s at Werneuchen formed into a new *Gruppe* (IV JG 132). *Leutnants* Janke and Trautloft accompanied it to Leipzig-Oschatz where it covered the Sudetenland occupation. Among the young officers was a universal admiration for Hitler, because he always came out on top without firing a shot. It never occurred to either Janke or Trautloft that they were on the brink of war. Janke and his friends were out every night drinking in the *Weinkellerei*. On 6 October IV JG 132 moved on to Karlsbad in Sudetenland, Czechoslovakia, flying over

Pilsen and Marienbad *en route*. A few days later Goering arrived in an
enormous Mercedes. In glorious weather he picnicked with the officers
and men in the open, helping himself to the cook-house stew.

A *Luftflotte* was a self-contained unit, possessing about a thousand aircraft of
all types – bomber, dive-bomber, single and twin-engined fighters and
reconnaissance units all integrated under one command. Each *Luftflotte* was
subdivided into *Flieger Korps*, or *Flieger Divisionen*. In each *Luftgau* were
'lodger-units' which managed supply and administration.

In February General Kesselring was succeeded as Chief of Air Staff by
the young General Hans Jeschonnek. Erhard Milch, then Inspector General,
had been his *Gruppe Kommandeur* in World War I. He found him 'courageous, but too slow on the draw'. Jeschonnek was a loyal disciple of
Hitler's and a personal friend of Goering. Unfortunately, he lacked the
character to stand up to either of them. The weight of his divided loyalties
would eventually drive him to suicide.

On 1 February Ernst Udet became *Generalluftzeugmeister* (Director of
Equipment), responsible for the entire development and testing of the
Luftwaffe's aircraft and weapons. He could have become the most influen-
tial man in the *Luftwaffe*, but he was not equal to his task. In time it would
drive him, like Jeschonnek, to suicide.

There were also rumours of change in the RAF high command. On 23
February the London *Evening Standard* announced that the C-in-C of
Fighter Command, Air Marshal Dowding, would shortly retire to be
succeeded by Air Vice Marshal Christopher Courtney. The next day the
Chief of Air Staff, Newall, telephoned Dowding that, 'no change will be
made during the present year ...'

The last news Dowding had had concerning his retirement was the
official letter which had arrived as the air exercises started in August 1938,
announcing that the Air Ministry would be unable 'to offer him any
further employment' after June 1939. Newall's telephone call was the
first indication that the Air Ministry had changed its mind.

Dowding thought about the situation for a few days, then put his
thoughts on paper. In his own hand he wrote, 'I have received very
cavalier treatment at the hands of the Air Ministry during the past two
years. I have no grievance over these decisions, except as regards the
discourtesy with which they were effected.

'There was no need to inform me that I was next in succession as Chief of Air Staff so that I might expect to be retained up to the age of sixty (he was now fifty-six). But the reversal of these intentions were baldly conveyed to me.

'I can say without fear of contradiction that since I have held my present post I have dealt with and am in the process of dealing with a number of vital matters which generations of Air Staff have neglected for the last fifteen years: putting the Observer Corps on a war footing, manning of Operations Rooms, identification of friendly aircraft, unserviceability of aerodromes and adequate Air Raid Warning System. This work had to be carried out against the inertia of the Air Staff, a statement which I can abundantly prove if necessary.'

It was with a heavy heart that Dowding recorded his decision to abandon his mission. 'In spite ... of my intense interest in the Fighter problems of the immediate future ... there is little in my past or present treatment at the hands of the Air Ministry to encourage me to undertake a further period of service.'

Two weeks later he told the Air Minister, Kingsley Wood, of his intention to leave the RAF in June, and the reasons. Then on 17 March he wrote to Kingsley Wood, '... At our interview last week I told you that I was not anxious to remain ... after the end of June for reasons which I explained to you.

'If it was desired to extend my period of Command, I felt that I should have a letter from you asking me to stay on and telling me that I ... should have the support of the Air Council.'

Three days later Dowding received a letter from the Chief of Air Staff, Newall: 'In view of the importance of ... Fighter Command and the desire to avoid ... changes in the high appointments of the operational commands, it has been decided to ask you to defer your retirement until the end of March, 1940. I hope this will be agreeable to you.'

Although Newall only asked Dowding to 'defer his retirement', the implication was that he would remain as C-in-C of Fighter Command until he retired. But neither Providence nor the Air Ministry had finished with Dowding.

Intrigue and dissension within Czechoslovakia now gave Hitler the chance for 'peaceful intervention'. The Czech President, Hacha, was summoned to Berlin, where he arrived by train – he was too old and too ill to travel by air – at 10.40 p.m. on 14 March.

Not until 1.00 a.m. did Hitler receive Hacha and his foreign minister at the Chancellery. He told him that he no longer had any confidence in the Czech government and that German troops had orders to advance into Czechoslovakia at 6.00 a.m. that very morning; the *Luftwaffe* would occupy Czech airfields.

At 2.15 a.m. the two Czech statesmen found themselves in an adjoining room in the presence of Goering and Ribbentrop. The necessary documents were laid out on the table for signature. 'If you don't sign, half of Prague will be destroyed within two hours.' When Goering remarked sardonically, 'I should be sorry if I had to bomb beautiful Prague,' the overwrought Czech president collapsed in a dead faint. He was brought round by a couple of injections, and staggered back into Hitler's office to sign the *communiqué* prepared by Hitler's staff.

At 6.00 a.m. the German army began to advance into Czechoslovakia and the *Luftwaffe Geschwader* took off.

Part of the *Geschwader* to take part in the massed flight over Prague on 15 March was *KG* 2, Werner Borner's unit. As Werner looked down on Prague from his Ju. 86 he remarked to himself: 'How calm everything looks.'

That night the swastika flag fluttered from the battlements of the Hradschin Palace, where Adolf Hitler had just arrived to spend the night. Since the time, twenty years earlier, when the Czechs had claimed equality with his own people the Fuehrer had never ceased to burn with hatred and contempt for the Czechs. This was his hour of triumph over that upstart race whose presidents, Masaryk and Beneš, had so recently lived and worked in the Hradschin Palace.

Before leaving Berlin Hitler had proclaimed, 'Czechoslovakia has ceased to exist.'

But Major Osterkamp had apparently failed to get the message. He did not feel absolutely happy about the 'justice of our cause' when he arrived in Prague next day with a special commission to take over the Czech air force. Staggered by the majestic beauty of the capital, 'I shuddered to think', he wrote, 'that those magnificent buildings had only just escaped destruction by the *Luftwaffe*'s bombs.'

He called at the headquarters of an airfield thirty miles from Prague. 'I met a young officer who stared at me, petrified . . . I asked him to take me to his CO . . . who was equally astonished to see a *Luftwaffe* officer in uniform . . . He turned pale when I told him what had just happened . . . He had no idea . . . and I felt terribly sorry for him.'

Pulling himself together, the Czech air force officer addressed Osterkamp: 'My good friend . . . although I must await orders from Prague I want to assure you that we air force officers have always wanted to co-operate with our German comrades.'

Judging by the hundreds of Czech air crew and ground staff who left their homeland for France and England, his feelings were not universally shared.

Uncle Theo, a kind of flying Don Quixote, addressed the assembled Czech air force officers. 'I see no humiliation', he told them, 'in this occupation of your country, which is only so that we can help you, as good friends, to prevent your being invaded by a powerful neighbour who wants to attack us. I am convinced that the Fuehrer will welcome you as allies, as I do myself.'

This dangerous deviation from the party line earned Osterkamp a monumental rebuke from his Commander-in-Chief. Goering told him that his attitude was 'incomprehensible and senseless'. And sure enough, a few months later as the German tanks advanced in an endless stream across Czechoslovakia towards the Polish frontier, Osterkamp watched Czech airmen being kicked out into the street. Far from being attacked by her powerful neighbour, by then Germany had agreed on a pact of non-aggression with Russia.

The fighter unit (IV *JG* 132) formed from Uncle Theo's Werneuchen Fighter School moved into the Olmuts airfield at Brno. *Gruppe Kommandeur* Johannes Janke was in a hospital at Vienna, but Hannes Trautloft, *Kapitän* of *Staffel* 10 was there. And like Osterkamp, he had misgivings about the Czech invasion. Everyone was amazed by Hitler's power and audacity. What were France and England doing? Why were they so powerless? Yet Trautloft was sure there would be a war and he felt nervous. It was like waiting to take off, but once in the cockpit all was well. He felt better once they had settled in at Brno.

In the north, at Lüneberg, after completing a two months' air firing course, Karl Missy had just joined the 'Lion' *Kampfgeschwader* 26, specialists in shipping attacks. The target was a drogue, or sleeve, towed by another aircraft, similar to what we used in the RAF. Missy proved to be a steady and proficient gunner with the MG15 machine-gun. As a radio operator he felt he had the perfect job. It was even better than being a pilot. Thoroughly happy and far from the events in Czechoslovakia he never gave a thought to the possibility of war. Yet Missy would be among the *Luftwaffe's* first casualties. Within less than a year he would be lying in an English hospital mutilated by bullets from my Hurricane.

Chapter 14

In 43 Squadron at Tangmere we were quickly becoming skilled with our aircraft. The Hurricanes had completely changed our fearful mood occasioned by the events at Munich.

All our flying was designed to gird us for the war which was bound to come: battle climbs to thirty thousand feet, where the engine laboured and the controls were sluggish and we inhaled the oxygen which came hissing into our face-masks from a black steel cylinder behind the armoured bulkhead; air drill and practice attacks and firing our guns into the sea, where they raised a jagged plume of foam. The recoil of those eight Brownings could slow the aircraft in a climb by forty m.p.h.; cloud flying and night flying, which no one really enjoyed – ever since I first came to a fighter squadron I was told, 'only fools and owls fly by night'.

Quick refuelling and re-arming practices gave ground crews the sleight of hand which speeded their tasks and gained precious seconds. Between them and the pilots existed an understanding on which our lives depended. The slightest grumble from an engine, or any other functional defect – it might occur five miles above the ground or ten miles from the coast – had to be explained to our fitters or riggers, or to the armourers and radio mechanics, in the terms and nuances of their technical language. We would provide the clue but we relied implicitly on their vigilance, skill and devotion to keep our machines free of defects which could cost us our lives.

Hurricanes and Spitfires were flowing steadily if slowly into the fighter squadrons. Gus Holden in 56 Squadron at North Weald found the Hurricane 'was built with the strength of a battleship, had an engine of great power and reliability and was throughout an excellent and accurate fighting machine. Training in 56 hotted up and we were all convinced that the Second World War was well on its way.'

Toward the end of March Bob Tuck collected the first Spitfire of 65

Squadron, Hornchurch. So enchanted was he with the Spitfire that he believed that in time it affected his character, maturing him and giving him an inner balance.

No. 41 Squadron at Catterick (where Norman Ryder was now a Flight Commander) was getting to know – and to love – its Spitfires. 'Superb', Norman calls them. 'If an aircraft looks right it so often is right. Our Spitfires were so well-balanced they would fly themselves. Many pilots owe their lives to this property of the early Spitfires. If a pilot passed out through lack of oxygen the Spitfire would fall away in a dive and correct itself.'

In 54 Squadron, Hornchurch, Al Deere could speak from experience. Not long after the squadron was re-equipped with Spitfires Al was climbing through 25,000 feet of cloud, concentrating so hard on his instruments that he forgot to increase the oxygen flow. At 27,000 feet he passed out, recovering after a four-mile dive just in time to pull out above the sea. A Hurricane might not have forgiven him quite so readily. 'Both fighters', Norman concludes, 'were extremely rugged, the Spitfires faster and more nimble, the Hurricane more manoeuvrable at its own speed and undoubtedly the better gun platform.' The Hurricane had a better fighting view than the Spitfire.

Everywhere there was an unmistakable feeling that war was inevitable, if not imminent. When Air Commodore Trafford Leigh-Mallory, the air officer commanding No. 12 Group, visited 611 Squadron in March he told James McComb that in the event of war he would become the Squadron's CO. But he cautioned James sternly: while he had heard that his conduct was entirely satisfactory on the tarmac he understood that, off it, he was a buffoon. Flight Lieutenant McComb of the Auxiliary Air Force informed his air officer commanding that what he did away from the tarmac was entirely his own affair. Which was indeed the case, for he was a private citizen. In the end he became quite friendly with 'LM'. 'He was not an easy man to know and was rather pompous, but I suspect this covered up for some shyness.'

At the height of the Battle of Britain Leigh Mallory would become involved in a bitter conflict with a brother officer, commander of 12 Group's neighbour, No. 11 Group to the south. He had once done me a good turn when station commander at Tangmere. Now as Senior Air Staff Officer at Fighter Command, he was Dowding's right-hand man. His name was Keith Park.

Five days after Hitler's brief sojourn in conquered Prague, Ribbentrop turned his attention to Germany's next problem. He sent for the Polish Ambassador, Monsieur Josef Lipski. When the Ambassador presented himself at midday on 21 March, he found Ribbentrop cold and aggressive. The Fuehrer, he said, was more and more surprised at Poland's attitude and required an answer on the question of improving road-rail traffic across the Polish Corridor which linked Germany across Polish territory with the free port of Danzig.

Lipski was back from Warsaw on Sunday 26 March with a flat refusal to the German claims on Danzig from Colonel Jozef Beck, the Polish Foreign Minister. And on 28 March Beck warned the German Ambassador, von Moltke, that 'any attempt by Germany to interfere in Danzig will be a *casus belli*'. On 31 March the House of Commons heard Chamberlain announce that 'France and Britain would lend the Polish government all support in their power' if Poland were attacked.

Admiral Canaris, the German Chief of Intelligence, was with Hitler that afternoon when the news of Chamberlain's speech was received. Hitler, his face distorted with rage and his fists beating the marble table, screamed, 'I'll cook them a stew they'll choke on.' From now on England was to stand squarely in the path of the German dictator.

The next day, 1 April, Hitler spoke at the launching of the battle-cruiser *Tirpitz* at Wilhelmshaven: 'Me, you will never tire. I am resolved to pursue the course to which I have committed myself.' And only two days later in a top secret directive, the first under the head *Fall Weiss* (Case White), he ordered the army to prepare for the defence of the frontiers, for war with Poland, and a surprise attack on Danzig. Preparations were to be completed 'at any date after 1 September'.

Goering was glad to be back in Rome on 15 April to see his old friend Benito Mussolini. During his secret talk with Mussolini on 16 April he raised the question of Russia. He had been struck by something Stalin had said in a recent speech: 'The Russians would never agree to serve as cannon-fodder for the capitalist powers.'

Goering concluded, 'I'll ask the Fuehrer if we can't send up a trial balloon with a view to a possible get-together with the Russians.' Mussolini welcomed the idea.

That day in Moscow, the Soviet Commissar for Foreign Affairs, Maxim Litvinov, received the British Ambassador, Sir William Seeds, and proposed a pact of mutual assistance between France, Britain and the

USSR. But hardly had Paris and London been advised of the Soviet proposal, when the Soviet Ambassador in Berlin called at the Wilhelmstrasse. He explained to the Secretary of State, Baron Weisaecker, that 'Russia saw no reason not to maintain normal relations with Germany'. And nothing, he added, should prevent these relations from becoming closer.

Nothing could have suited Hitler's game better. His need to pin down Russia was becoming more and more urgent. Now that Britain and France had no intention of leaving him free to act in the east, Hitler would have to settle with them first. Having done so, he would then turn and attack his ally Russia. Poland was an annoying complication, but if she obstinately refused to co-operate it would be necessary to liquidate her. But the first thing was to square things with Russia.

Goering had told Mussolini that he would see the Fuehrer about sending up a trial balloon to test Russian reactions to a *rapprochement* with Germany. On 17 May the Soviet *chargé d'affaires*, Georgei Astakhov, told Dr Julius Schnurre of the German Foreign Office, 'there is no motive for hostility between the two countries. But, in fact, the USSR feels strongly that it is threatened by Germany.' It would be possible, he added, to dissipate the Russians' mistrust and anxiety. The trial balloon was producing results.

Meanwhile a trial balloon of a very different kind had been cruising off the east coast of England. Registered as L127, it was more familiarly known as 'Graf Zeppelin'. On board was Major General Martini, Chief of *Luftwaffe* Signals, plus a load of high-frequency receivers and an elaborate aerial array. The object of all this paraphernalia was to 'interrogate' the British radar system.

Since February 1939 Martini had been directly responsible to the Secretary of State, Milch. Martini was urgently required to find out details of the British system.

Even before the *Luftwaffe* was 'decamouflaged' in 1935, Martini had established the ground work for a communications and radio-reporting system. Realizing all too well himself the importance of air intelligence he warned that if its own radio-reporting units were not linked by efficient communications the *Luftwaffe* would be in serious trouble. Martini hoped to discover from the Graf Zeppelin's gondola not only how British radar worked, but how it fitted into the air defence system.

The three hundred foot masts with lattice aerials which now extended from the Orkneys to the Isle of Wight were the kind used by the Germans for their own Freya and Wurzburg radars.

As the Graf Zeppelin cruised north of the English coast, its receivers emitting nothing more revealing than a horrible and continuous crackle, the operators at Canewdon and Bawdsey radar stations were placidly watching its outsize 'blip' travelling slowly across their cathode ray tubes. As it was picked up and reported by one station after another, Fighter Command Filter and Operations Rooms leisurely followed its course northwards.

Over the Humber estuary the British Radio Intelligence Service intercepted a message from the great airship reporting its position to base a few miles off the coast.

The men at Fighter Command smiled: they had the Graf Zeppelin accurately plotted – in cloud, well inland, over Hull. The duty signals officer, Flight Lieutenant Walter Pretty said, 'We were sorely tempted to radio a correct message to the airship, but this would have revealed we were seeing her on radar, so we kept silent.'

Had the Graf Zeppelin really mistaken her position or had Martini purposely laid a trap? In any case Walter Pretty did not fall into it and Martini returned, none the wiser about British Radar.

A few days later around lunchtime the watchers at Bawdsey radar station had another surprise. 'The Germans are coming!' they cried as the 'blip', which they estimated as fifty aircraft, steadily approached the coast. Seven miles out it turned and headed back towards Germany. For the radar girls it was a taste of things to come, as it was for the *Luftwaffe*, who this time were only exercising.

Early in May the Chief of Air Staff, General Hans Jeschonnek, had told General Helmuth Felmy, 'The role of your *Luftflotte 2* will be to support the army in Holland and Belgium and to attack England.' Felmy and his staff held numerous conferences and '*Kriegspielen*'. Then came a five-day air exercise.

But the lessons drawn from all this activity were not encouraging. The *Luftwaffe* Operations Staff reported that 'there were not enough aircraft to cope with the large number of targets and the wide area of operations'. Western and south-western England would be out of range of bombers operating from bases in Germany. Small attacks against armament factories in the London area and south-east England might be feasible, but terror-raids against London, far from subduing the British, might even stiffen their resistence.

The OKL Operations report of 22 May concluded that *Luftflotte 2* lacked the necessary strength for a decisive victory against England: General Felmy's conclusions which had so irritated Goering the year before had been proved absolutely correct in practice – not that Goering, for all that, was prepared to forgive Felmy.

The OKL report was not the only thing that day which made Goering disgruntled. The Italians – headed by their Foreign Minister, Galeazzo Ciano – were in Berlin to sign the pact of steel, by which Mussolini hitched his chariot to Hitler's star. It was a great occasion, with the Fuehrer present in person. Around Ribbentrop's neck hung the Collar of the Annunziata, a personal favour from the Italian King. This was too much for Goering who, half crying with rage and disappointment, exclaimed in a loud voice, 'It is I who ought to have the Collar.'

A veteran naval pilot seconded to *Luftflotte* 2 Headquarters, General Hans Geisler, now got down to a detailed analysis of the recent '*Kriegspielen*'. His object was to determine the best strategy for the '*Luftkrieg gegen England*' (the air war against England). It would take him over two months to get to the bottom of this knotty problem. But none could doubt that twenty-one years after the RAF had put an end to German bombing raids on England the German air force was preparing to resume hostilities.

On 23 May, the day after OKL Ops. had decided the *Luftwaffe* were at present incapable of a decisive victory against England, Hitler summoned fourteen of his war-lords to a secret meeting in the Chancellery. Among them were Goering and Milch, the Army Generals von Brauchitsch, Halder and Keitel, and Admiral Raeder. But Hitler did all the talking, while his personal staff officer *Oberstleutnant* Schmundt, took notes.

Hitler harped a lot on England. 'England is hostile and we shall have to go to war against her if we want to survive.' But with the lesson of all those 'war games' how would the *Luftwaffe* ever manage to carry out those 'devastating attacks' that the Fuehrer had in mind? He had the answer: 'The Dutch and Belgian air bases must be captured. Any question of neutrality can be ignored.' But, he added prophetically, 'It is not the attacks of the *Luftwaffe* in the English skies which will force England to capitulate.' The annihilation of the British fleet, he thought, would produce immediate surrender. But with the building programme as it was at present, the German *Kriegsmarine* would not reach parity with the Royal Navy for another six years.

No, the *Luftwaffe* would be the greatest menace to the British Navy.

'The aim must be to hit the enemy a shattering and absolutely decisive blow at the start ... No consideration of right or wrong or of treaties must be allowed to intervene ... If we can occupy Holland and Belgium and conquer France we shall then have established the bases for a victorious war against England.' Hitler concluded, 'The aim will always be to force England to surrender.' Not one of his war-lords demurred.

That day the RMS *Otranto*, homeward bound from Sydney, docked at Colombo. On board was Bill Millington, a twenty-one-year-old Australian boy. Like thousands of other sons of Australia, New Zealand, Canada, South Africa, Rhodesia and a score of other outposts of the British Empire, Bill was sailing 'home' with an uncanny feeling in his heart that England needed him.

The arrival of Bill Millington aboard the *Otranto* at Tilbury Docks on 14 June passed unnoticed. So (at least for the Russians) did the arrival in Moscow of Mr William Strang at the head of the British mission charged to negotiate with Stalin and Molotov. The slow race to Moscow was on. Hitler, for his part, was no keener to be hugged by the Russian bear than the British. He had been blowing hot and cold for a good month. Then the Russians made a move, which led to a dinner date in a Berlin restaurant between the Soviet chargé d'affaires, Astakhov, and Dr Schnurre of the Wilhelmstrasse. Schnurre declared, 'There can be no question of Germany threatening the Soviet Union ... German policy is directed against Great Britain.'

The delighted Astakhov promised to contact Moscow right away, while the Germans waited with growing anxiety. They knew France and Britain had accepted the Russian offer for military talks. But instead of taking a plane to Moscow, the Allies made a five-day boat journey via Leningrad. By the time they arrived in the Russian capital on 11 August Hitler was a good jump ahead.

In the intervening days there had been intense and varied activity on other fronts. One of the more unusual instruments of Hitler's policy against England – the Graf Zeppelin – had again been poking her inquisitive nose into the RAF's radar business.

Although the moon was only two days on the wane there was plenty of cloud cover when, on the night of 2 August, the great airship headed out across the North Sea towards Britain, with *Oberstleutnant* Gosewisch in charge of the radio interrogation apparatus. His object was to note the wave-length, strength and position of all high-frequency transmissions.

But the Germans were again out of luck. Not a squeak came from the British side as the Graf Zeppelin cruised northwards about fifteen miles out. At 3.00 p.m. on 3 August she ran out of cloud off the Kincardineshire coast and was sighted by coast guards and two Auxiliary Air Force fighters. She was then tactless enough to cruise low over the Girdleness Lighthouse.

By 4.00 p.m. on 4 August the disappointed *Oberstleutnant* Gosewisch was back in bed when the telephone rang. The chief of Air Staff, Jeschonnek, was on the line. The London *Daily Telegraph* had reported the Graf Zeppelin over the British coast – was it true? Quite untrue, said Gosewitch.

Later that day the Reich Air Ministry denied the Graf Zeppelin had intentionally left Germany or approached the British coast. The statement continued, 'There have, however, been severe storms during the last day or two and it is possible that the airship could have been blown off her course . . .'

As Fighter Command Signals observed on the first flight in May, navigation aboard the Graf Zeppelin was not always faultless. But there was no need to take unfair advantage of the fact.

Fortunately the Graf Zeppelin was not prying forty-eight hours later when, on 6 August, the RAF's air exercises started. Otherwise she might have picked up the radio chatter between ground controllers and the fighter formation leaders – and this could have given away the whole show. For while radar – the 'eyes' of Fighter Command – was fundamental, a great deal more was involved in the air defence system. Between the radar 'plots' of approaching hostile aircraft and the fighters which climbed to intercept them, and the guns, searchlights, balloons and air-raid sirens (all of which had their vital functions) there existed a highly intricate system of communications manned by hundreds of men and women. It was an air defence system without parallel in the world and was based on what Dowding would call 'science thoughtfully applied to operational requirements'.

The CH (Chain Home) radar stations 'looked' seawards only, within a fixed 120 degrees arc and with a range of 120 miles. They could determine the range, bearing, height and strength of a hostile raid. Their three hundred foot masts precluded any question of mobility. Inland, the Observer Corps plotted the 'hostiles' by sight or sound, depending on the visibility.

The radar 'plots' were passed to Fighter Command near London at Bentley Priory, Stanmore, and received in the 'Filter Room'. Here a filter officer – one for each radar station – shifted the plots and checked them against 'friendlies' and other 'hostiles'. The filtered plots were passed to the adjoining Operations Room. This was the control centre of the Commander-in-Chief, Dowding, where at any second of the day or night he could see on the map table below the exact situation anywhere in the British Isles. In addition to Dowding's duty controller were liaison officers in touch with the Anti-Aircraft Command (guns and searchlights), Observer Corps, Bomber and Coastal Commands, the Admiralty and the Home Office (air-raid warnings).

The Fighter Groups covered a limited area each with its corresponding hinterland: 11 Group from Portsmouth round to the Thames Estuary; 12 Group north from the Thames Estuary to Yorkshire. Other groups were to be formed within the coming year. Each Fighter Group received filtered radar plots from Fighter Command and Observer Corps plots direct from the Observer centres. Balloon barrages too were in direct touch with Group Operations Room.

In the Group Operations Room the Group Commander and his Controller could see simultaneously at any moment the exact situation on the table map of the group area. Around the map sat WAAF girls with headphones and croupiers' rakes, moving coloured discs which represented aircraft according to the plots received. The Group Controller directed the appropriate Sector to deal with a raid.

Sectors in turn each represented a limited geographical area within the Group. A Sector possessed numerous airfields, of which one, the Sector airfield, had its own Operations Block consisting of a D/F (Direction Finding) Room and the 'Ops. Room' proper. The D/F Room followed its own fighters by means of radio 'fixes' which it obtained from the IFF, Identification Friend or Foe (or 'Pip Squeak') – a small automatic transmitter fitted in every aircraft.

The D/F Room passed the fighters' position on to the Ops. Room. There, two deputy-controllers and two navigators rapidly calculated the fighter's interception courses and passed them to the Controller. From his raised dais the Controller had a perfect view of the table map of his Sector and its aircraft discs, swiftly and silently manipulated by the girls with headphones and croupiers' rakes.

The Sector controller directed his fighters to intercept a hostile raid. A simple code was used between them: Scramble, take-off; Angels (ten), height (ten thousand feet); Orbit, circle (a given point); Vector (one-eight-zero), steer (course of 180 degrees); Buster, full throttle; Tally-ho!, enemy sighted; Pancake, land.

Each Sector station and each fighter squadron had a code name – curious two-syllable inventions like: Jaunty, Tennis, Waggon, Lumba and so on. A tactical unit of twelve aircraft, each squadron was divided into four sections of three aircraft: Red and Yellow in A Flight; Blue and Green in B Flight, with the pilots in each numbered 1, 2, and 3. Blue 1 led Blue Section, followed by Blue 2 and Blue 3.

The whole was an intricate and highly organized system of communications – from the hostile target to the Radar Station by radio-magnetic waves then on by telephone line to Fighter Command, to Group and to Sector then by radio-telephone from Sector Ops. to the fighter pilot in the sky. A serious rupture at any stage in this elaborate system would more or less paralyse it.

In sending the Graf Zeppelin to intercept British radar, the Germans were looking only for half the answer. They could have found it more easily and less expensively. For years the radio research station at Bawdsey, Suffolk, had no surrounding barbed wire fence and from the beach lay open to any intruder. With its three hundred foot masts, Dover too could be photographed from the beach – and often was – and any German 'tourist' innocently clad in shorts with a haversack containing the necessary equipment on his back could have picked up the radar signals. For all the good it did, the Graf Zeppelin was really a costly failure.

At Rechlin a month before, on 1 July, Hitler, Goering and Milch had inspected the two types of German radar, Würzburg and Freya. Würzburg was a small, highly mobile set capable of very accurate plotting up to twenty-five miles range. It was just what the *Flak* needed, although judging by his absence at Rechlin that day the *Flak* C-in-C did not seem unduly interested.

An 'early-warning' type, Freya had a range of seventy-five miles with a 360 degree coverage and full mobility. But it could not measure height. Eigh thundred Würzburgs and two hundred Freyas were on order.

The Germans had still given no thought to harnessing their excellent radar to an air defence system – for the good reason that they were bent on offence, not defence. On this score Milch was worried by a serious shortage of bombs. He mentioned the fact to Hitler at Rechlin, but was met by the firm reply, 'I have no intention of getting involved in a general war.'

However, certain realists in the *Luftwaffe* High Command were giving serious thought to an air war against England. One was General Hans Geisler. While the RAF was holding the dress rehearsal of its air defences on 7 August, Geisler produced his plan for attacking England by air. He submitted that the *Luftwaffe*'s objectives should be:

1. Gain air superiority
2. Cripple the British war economy
3. A blockade of shipping
4. Attacks on the British fleet
5. Attacks on British troopships and transports to the Continent and to threaten, or carry out, invasion.

This was one of the earliest references to invasion. The first appears to have emanated from the Intelligence Chief, Beppo Schmid, who in July had warned that Britain could not be defeated by air attack alone, but that for a decisive success invasion would be necessary.

Geisler was pessimistic about the *Luftwaffe*'s chances of subduing Britain in 1940. He estimated that in another year the *Luftwaffe* would become a true threat.

The *Luftwaffe* held its own dress rehearsal almost simultaneously with the R.A.F. *Capitaine Aviateur* Stehlin was not invited, as he always had been in the past. *Luftflotte* 2, whose job it would be to attack Britain in the event of war, was fully engaged. Ports, industrial centres and military installations were the targets for the fully-loaded bombers which, to give a realistic touch, were routed over the sea and issued with full life-saving equipment. The *Luftwaffe* was to find the sea a redoubtable enemy.

Then there were manoeuvres in the Cottbus area, south-east of Berlin. On 10 August scores of generals were assembled in the training area at Neuhammer to watch a dive-bombing demonstration. Already, said Rudolf Braun, who took part with his unit (I *St. G* 3) there was a feeling of war in the air.

Normally the order of attack was the *Kommandeur*'s *Stab Kette* (Staff Flight) first, followed by *Staffels* 1, 2 and 3. For some unknown reason *Staffel* 1, led by *Oberleutnant* Peltz, was this time ordered to attack last. It would save Rudolf Braun's life.

The Met. reported cloud from 6,000 feet down to 2,500 with clear visibility below. At 6.00 a.m. *Hauptmann* Sigel led his *Gruppe* into attack at 12,000 feet. Half-rolling his Ju. 87 he plunged nearly vertically earthwards, with *Oberleutnants* Eppen and Mueller on each side.

On the ground below, the generals (including Wolfram von Richthofen, the *Stuka*'s chief) listened to the whining crescendo of the dive-bombers. as they plummeted towards the ground. Horrified, they knew that nothing could avert disaster. The Met. report was wrong. Cloud base was at three hundred feet.

Hauptmann Sigel, yelling into his microphone, 'Pull out!' managed to do so himself a few feet above the trees. But Eppen went in, Mueller went in, and both burst into flames. The nine Ju. 87s of *Staffel* 2 and two of *Staffel* 3 all went in.

Rudolf Braun and his comrades of *Staffel* 1 had heard Sigel's warning and remained circling above the cloud layer through which columns of black smoke were now rising from the wreckage of thirteen dive-bombers. I *St. G* 3 lost twenty-six young aircrew that day.

Another mission had still to be flown, but orders were given to cancel it and to disband the unit. *Hauptmann* Sigel insisted on carrying on, and none of his few remaining pilots hesitated. Rudolf Braun was among them and was convinced that the second mission saved him from losing his nerve forever.

The Commander-in-Chief of the *Luftwaffe* was unable to study General Geisler's plan for the *Luftwaffe*'s attack against Britain when it came out on 7 August. Instead, he kept an appointment the same day with a group of British industrialists at Soenke Nissen Koog, near Wenningstedt.

They had gathered there to meet him at the instigation of Mr Birger Dahlerus, a Swedish industrialist known to Goering through Carin's family. Dahlerus had extensive business interests in Germany and England and had offered his services to Goering in the sincere belief that he could help to avert a world war. He had emphasized to Goering that the British Government was deadly serious in its guarantee to Poland. The British were there that day to confirm to Goering that British industry was behind the Government.

After looking in on Emmy and their young daughter Edda who were holidaying at Sylt, and, looking hot and bothered in spite of his white summer suit, Goering arrived to shake hands with the British group. He spoke to them and answered their questions in a frank and friendly manner. He felt that because of their hostility to Nazism, the British lacked understanding of the changes which had taken place in Europe since the re-birth of Germany. In spite of the friction between Germany and England, Goering intended to strive with all his might for peace, and asked his listeners to use all their influence for the same end.

Voices were raised among his audience against Hitler's aggressive and unscrupulous methods. Replying, Goering gave his 'solemn assurance as a statesman and an officer' that Germany had no intention of encircling Poland and that after the solution of the Danzig and 'Corridor' problems there would be no further claims on Polish territory.

After his meeting with the British industrialists, *Luftwaffe* chief Goering went on to tour the Ruhr in his capacity of Economic Chief. Back in Berlin on 9 August he declared, 'If an enemy bomber ever succeeds in reaching the Ruhr my name is not Hermann Goering. You can call me Meier.' Only nine months later the whole of Germany would be doing so.

War was preparing. About 10 August a certain Alfred Helmut Naujocks of the SS received orders from the SS Deputy Chief, Reinhard Heydrich, to make preparations for a fake attack on the German radio station at Gleiwitz, near the Polish frontier. 'We need material proof,' Heydrich told Naujocks, 'that this attack is the work of the Poles.'

Meanwhile Heydrich had received a quantity of Polish uniforms and fire-arms from the Intelligence section of OKW.

On 11 August von Ribbentrop and the Italian Foreign Minister, Ciano, met near Salzburg. Their talks, which Ciano described as 'icy', convinced him of Ribbentrop's 'unreasonable obstinate determination to bring about this conflict'.

Next day the unhappy Ciano went on to the Obersalzburg to see Hitler. He found him implacably decided on going ahead with the attack on Poland. Before leaving, Ciano managed to drag out of the Fuehrer a date for his catastrophic enterprise: 'the end of August at the latest.'

On 14 August, in his lofty redoubt, Hitler held a small conclave; Brauchitsch, Raeder and Goering were there. So was Dr Todt (who would later build the Atlantic Wall) and General Halder (Chief of the General Staff), who noted Hitler's words in his diary. 'The great drama is now approaching its climax,' Hitler told them. 'The men I got to know at Munich are not the kind to start a new world war ... England may talk big [but] she is sure not to resort to armed intervention ...' A *Blitzkrieg* of a couple of weeks would crush Poland before anyone could come to the rescue.

Once again, not one of Hitler's listeners uttered a word in protest. Not even Goering, who exactly a week earlier had given the British industrialists his 'solemn assurance as a statesman and an officer' that Germany had no intentions against Poland.

During the week that followed, a fantastic game of political poker had yet to be played out between Berlin and Moscow. Late on Monday night (14 August) Ribbentrop telegraphed the German Ambassador in Moscow, von Shulenburg. The telegram said in effect 'See Molotov and suggest I come to Moscow to discuss Russo-German relations.' A confirmatory telegram followed, and the Fuehrer waited anxiously for a reply. But no word came, and it was not until 19 August that Moscow replied saying the Reich Foreign Minister could arrive on 26 or 27 August.

This was too much for Hitler, who decided to swallow his pride and send on Sunday 20 August a long-winded personal telegram to Stalin begging him to see Ribbentrop on 22 August or at the latest 23 August, and asking for a prompt reply.

For the next twenty-four hours Hitler was nearly prostrate with anxiety. Unable to sleep, he telephoned Goering in the middle of the night. Then at last Stalin's answer reached the Berghof; he agreed to a date. Ribbentrop left for Moscow early next morning, 22 August.

As Ribbentrop winged his way to the Kremlin, Hitler's war-lords again gathered round their Fuehrer at the Berghof. Fourteen in number – representing the *Luftwaffe* were present C-in-C Goering, his personal staff officer Bodenschatz, Milch and Jeschonnek – they sat in a half-circle facing him. Beyond, they could see the Obersalzberg bathed in glorious sunshine.

The hour had struck, Hitler said. 'We have nothing to lose, we can only gain. I am only afraid that some *Schweinehund* will make a proposal for mediation.' The meeting then broke up for lunch, but not before Goering had led a round of applause for the Fuehrer, thanked him warmly and assured him that the armed forces would do their duty.

Lunch over, Hitler worked himself into a frenzy as he exhorted his commanders: 'No shrinking back from anything ... A life-and-death struggle ... I shall give a propagandist reason for starting the war – never mind whether it is plausible or not ... Close your hearts to pity! Act brutally! ... The stronger man is right ...'

When the Moscow meeting was announced in London, the British cabinet immediately published a communique followed by a personal letter from Chamberlain to Hitler. Both made it clear that a Russo-German pact would not change Britain's obligations to Poland.

But when on 23 August Hitler handed his reply to the British Ambassador, Henderson, he told him: 'I am fifty years old; I prefer war now to when I shall be fifty-five.'

That evening at the Kremlin champagne and vodka flowed. Ribbentrop had arrived in Moscow at midday. It took only two meetings before everything was settled: a non-aggression pact, with a secret protocol giving Russia half of Poland and a 'sphere of influence' from the Baltic to the Black Sea.

Stalin's deal with Germany would then enable Germany to go to war against France and England.

For the airmen of the *Luftwaffe* and the RAF who in only twelve months' time would vie with one another for supremacy in the air, the times now were nonetheless enjoyable. 43 Squadron was in top form. We were at one with ourselves and our machines. It was the Hurricane, really, which gave us such immense confidence, with its mighty engine, its powerful battery of guns, and its feel of swift, robust strength and the ability to outdo our enemies. Months would go by before the real test of combat, but we believed in the Hurricane. Performance figures – those of the Me. 109 and Spitfire were in many respects superior – did not in the least dismay us. The Hurricane was our faithful charger and we felt supremely sure of it and ourselves.

Caesar Hull, Sergeant Frank Carey and I had clubbed together in a strictly illegal aerobatic flight. I led – it was the easiest position – with Caesar on the right and Frank on the left – the most difficult position. Flying wing to wing we practised loops, barrel rolls and stalled turns, taking a layer of cloud below as ground level until we could 'roll off the deck' in unbroken harmony. Thus we revelled in the supreme sensation of flying – the imperceptible psycho-visual contact between pilots in an aerobatic formation.

Opposite the guard-room, Tangmere Cottage saw many a hilarious evening. It was there that Lord Willoughby de Broke and his beautiful wife kept open house for fighter pilots. John Willoughby had brought his squadron (605 County of Warwick) to Tangmere, its war-station. His and Rachel's warm, unfailing kindness created a profoundly human bond between us assassins of the regular air force and John's auxiliary squadron of 'mercenaries'.

Our squadron adjutant, John Simpson, was everybody's friend. He always flew with my flight and not even I, his Flight Commander, could see that behind a shield of reticence lay uncommon skill and courage. John was half-Jewish – perhaps that partly accounted for the mixture of sensitiveness, steely resolution and gaiety which made him remarkable. He was also a faithful correspondent. On 23 August he wrote to his friend Hector Bolitho, 'At the moment we are busy preparing for another war scare. Thursday (24 August) is supposed to be zero hour ... I fly all night tomorrow.'

'Tomorrow', 24 August, was B Flight's night. I did a sector reconnaissance that night – it was the last time we should see the friendly lights of Horsham, Brighton and Portsmouth spread out below. Our next night flight would be in the inky darkness of the blackout. After 24 August we would practically cease flying in 43 Squadron, only to wait for the inevitable.

To Werner Borner it was clear that zero hour was approaching. Earlier in the summer *KG* 2 had switched from its old diesel-engined Ju. 86s to Dornier 17s – a 'bird' to which it would become very attached. They realized the situation was growing more serious. Training was intensified – flights in *Gruppe* formation, at high and low level, night flying, air firing. Borner concentrated most of his energies on the machine-gun practices. He was determined, when the moment came, to shoot it out with any enemy fighter which ventured within range.

On 22 August, II *KG* 2 did its last massed formation practice. Then the 'nervous time' began. As dawn on 25 August brought an end to 43 Squadron's night flying Borner and his comrades felt certain they were within hours of war.

By the end of that day one would feel more nervous than the Fuehrer of the Third Reich. Zero hour was fixed for 4.30 a.m. on 26 August. At that moment a million and a half German troops would surge across the Polish frontier and hundreds of *Luftwaffe* planes would take off to bomb Polish targets.

All through the hot, sultry afternoon tension had been mounting in Berlin. Then, just after 6.00 p.m., Hitler received two extremely disagreeable surprises. The first was the news that Britain had just extended her guarantee to Poland into a pact of mutual assistance; the second was a letter from Mussolini which made it clear that he was ready to run out on the Germans. The Pact of Steel was worth no more than the paper it was written on – with only ten more hours to zero hour.

Hitler at once ordered Keitel, Chief of the OKW: 'Stop everything immediately. I need time to negotiate.'

And Halder noted in his diary, 'Fuehrer considerably shaken.' Next day he scribbled, 'Attack starts 1 September.'

The adjutant of 43 Squadron at Tangmere wrote on 27 August, 'Everybody here is remarkably gay and everything is being taken very calmly.' This was anything but the case at government level. In the last six days of

August frenzied efforts were made, notably by Henderson, the British Ambassador, and his friend Hermann Goering, to save the peace. But in the ceaseless comings and goings between Whitehall and the Wilhelmstrasse there was a third man, Mr Birger Dahlerus – he had brought Goering and the British industrialists together on 7 August.

Their efforts culminated in the Germans offering to the Poles a sixteen-point proposal for negotiation. However, Hitler never had the slightest intention of cancelling the invasion of Poland. Later, to his interpreter Dr Carl Schmidt, he said of the proposals, 'I needed an alibi, especially with the German people, to show them that I had done everything to maintain peace.'

Just after midday on 31 August he signed Directive No. 1 for the Conduct of the War. It began, 'Since the situation on Germany's eastern front has become intolerable and all political possibilities of a peaceful settlement have been exhausted, I have decided upon a solution by force.

'Date of the attack, 1 September.'

The tasks allotted to the *Luftwaffe*, should it come to operations against England, included the dislocation of English imports, armaments industry, transport of troops to France and 'concentrated units' of the English Navy.

'Attacks on the English homeland are to be prepared . . .' stated the Directive, but 'the decision regarding attacks on London is reserved for me.' Exactly one year later he would cancel this veto.

When an officer delivered one of the eight copies of Hitler's 'Most Secret' directive the commander of *Luftflotte* 1, General Albert Kesselring, was with the C-in-C of the *Luftwaffe* in his special train, *Asia*, at Wildpark, a suburb of Berlin.

On reading it, Goering lost his temper and asked to be put through immediately to Ribbentrop. 'Now you have got your god-damned war,' he yelled at him. 'You are the only one to be blamed.' And he hung up, white with rage.

However, every detail of the *Luftwaffe*'s operations was fixed, as were other more gruesome details of the imminent German attack. Alfred Helmut Naujocks of the SS had not been idle during his two weeks' stay at Gleiwitz. At 8 o'cjock on a beautiful clear evening, Naujocks launched his sordid but vital little operation, 'Canned Goods', the object of which was to 'recapture' the radio station reported in Polish hands.

Mueller, the head of the Gestapo, had 'prepared' a dozen German convicts, by dressing them up in Polish uniforms, giving them each a lethal injection, then for appearances' sake having them shot. Dead or dying, the convicts were strewn at the approaches to the radio station. Then according to Naujocks, 'we seized the radio station . . . fired some pistol shots and left'.

All through that warm summer's night the German Army was moving up towards the Polish frontier. Before first light on 1 September the *Luftwaffe* was ready to take off. Then with the II *Gruppe Lehrgeschwader* 2, *Hauptmann* Adolf Galland relates how 'it was still dark on the morning of 1 September as we climbed into our cockpits. Blue flames spurted from the exhausts of our engines as they warmed up, and at the first signs of dawn the fireworks started . . .'

Part Four

BAPTISM
OF
FIRE

Chapter 15

On 1 September Goering addressed his men: 'Born of the spirit of the German airmen in the First World War, inspired by faith in our Fuehrer ... thus stands the *Luftwaffe* today, ready to carry out every command of the Fuehrer with lightning speed and undreamed-of might.'

This was not exactly the spirit which imbued Werner Borner's unit (4 *KG* 2) as it waited at dawn to attack the airport of Brest Litovsk. Whether it was the effects of a TAB injection the day before which half knocked them out, or nerves before their first war flight, all experienced a strange, almost sinister feeling. In silence they boarded a Dornier 17 bomber. Then Borner in the radio-operator's seat, like a robot, began checking his radio equipment and his MG17 machine-gun. At 4.46 p.m. the *Staffel* took off from Schippenheim in East Prussia.

Now the *Staffel* were cruising at fifteen thousand feet with the rest of the *Gruppe* – some thirty aircraft in all. Suddenly one of the aircraft, caught in another's slipstream, heeled over and dived. To Borner's surprise one of the crew (Flight Mechanic Holewa) jumped out. Werner watched his body falling over and over, then realized with horror that he must have forgotten to clip on his parachute pack. Holewa disappeared from view and from this life – one of the first German airmen to die in Hitler's war.

In his Ju. 88 bomber of *Lehrgeschwader* 1, Hans Joachim (Jocho) Helbig roared off the ground just after 4.00 a.m., also heading for Brest Litovsk. Suddenly he sighted a Polish fighter below. Helbig's hunting instincts got the better of him. He put his bomber into a dive and tore down on the fighter while his observer and rear gunner poured bullets into it until its wings collapsed. The observer photographed the wreckage.

When Helbig reported the combat to the *Gefechtsmeldung* back at base no one would believe this tall story of a bomber attacking a fighter. But Helbig had the photo as proof and *Lehrgeschwader* 1 recorded its first victory.

Karl Missy was at Gabbert near the Polish border, with the 4th *Staffel* of the II *Gruppe KG* 26. During many missions over Polish territory he never met any serious opposition. The Polish fighters were slow and the *Flak* always far behind. But like Borner, Missy felt uneasy. Everyone in his unit thought Poland only a beginning, and even though the Polish Air Force would obviously be knocked out quickly Missy and his friends were sure the war would not end there.

In Fighter Command our particular concern was the 'knock-out blow' the *Luftwaffe* was expected to deliver as soon as hostilities began. And in the fighter squadrons not one of us doubted that they would. Leave had been stopped. Mobilization of the Auxiliary Air Force and Volunteer Reserve had begun a week before and most of these peacetime pilots were then in uniform.

Now commanding 611 (West Lancashire) Squadron as Leigh-Mallory had promised, James McComb had taken it on 4 August to annual camp at Duxford, its war-time station. Twenty-five years ago to the day his father had been called up to fight the Germans in World War I. On 1 September they waited in their Spitfires at readiness (five minutes' notice for take-off). They would remain in 'camp' for the next six years with no last leave to say good-bye or arrange their affairs.

The Legal Department of the Lancashire County Council, where James worked, wrote, 'You are in a reserved occupation, come back immediately,' and James replied in so many words, 'I ain't coming.'

McComb was engaged to be married. While not actually expecting to be killed, he did not rate his chances of survival higher than fifty-fifty. He checked in King's Regulations the amount of a squadron leader's widow's pension – it would have paid the grocer's bill with a bit left over, that was all. After talking to his fiancée about 'being left with triplets and no money' they both agreed it was best not to marry. But two months later they would decide – as Hitler also feared – that the war might last ten years. So James did the obvious thing – 'We married and lived happily ever after.'

In 56 Squadron at North Weald, where Gus Holden was adjutant, the pilots had been issued with tents and parked themselves twenty paces or so from their aircraft around the airfield. Our grass fighter airfields were comparatively small and a loud-speaker system relayed orders from Station Headquarters and the Operations Room.

The aircraft of 54 Squadron at Hornchurch were dispersed away from the hangars along the far side of the airfield. Fighter Command understood – the Polish Air Force unfortunately did not – that the greatest danger lay in attack *from* the air against aircraft and installations on the ground. Al Deere of 54 Squadron spent much of his time 'filling and humping sand bags' to build dispersal pens for each aircraft. 'We worked stripped to the waist alongside civilians who were being paid a very generous hourly rate to do the same job.'

Norman Ryder, now a flight commander in 41 Squadron at Catterick, was similarly employed. Pilots and aircrew set to and hacked down two openings in the airfield boundary hedge so that aircraft might pass to an adjoining field conveniently surrounded by woods. With 'strange feelings of kicking the orthodox way of life overboard' Norman and his men worked feverishly to build their dispersal point. Tents, wooden huts, openings in the woods for each aircraft, sand bags, equipment, stores, fuel and ammunition were all in place by 1 September.

Tom Gleave would always vividly remember that day. He was then Bomber Liaison Officer in the Fighter Command Operations Room and lived, 'blissfully happy', with his wife Beryl and their little boy John in a cottage near Iver, Buckinghamshire. He was off-duty when at about mid-morning his landlady came running to the cottage and blurted out, 'Those bastards have invaded Poland!' Tom thought it the understatement of the century. 'How I loathed their guts, the lot of them!' he said.

Soon after, a call from Fighter Command broke up the Gleave family. Tom was told to report immediately. Sadly he and his wife began to pack. The same unhappy scene was being enacted throughout Britain as the evacuation of children from the big towns began. Tom managed to get an hour off next day to see Beryl and John off to her parents. Not for years would they again have a home of their own.

On 2 September the British insisted on an ultimatum to Hitler. But the French were in no hurry. General Gamelin knew only too well the failings of the French Army and that it alone would have to withstand an immediate German onslaught – without the British lifting a finger.

At 6.00 p.m. Halifax telephoned to Paris: 'The French attitude is considerably embarrassing to His Majesty's Government.' France and Britain were now out of step and on 2 September while Bonnet prevaricated and Chamberlain waited, an angry debate in the Commons that evening threatened to overthrow Chamberlain's government.

At the Air Ministry in London, the Chief of Air Staff, Sir Cyril Newall, gazed in blank dismay at Air Vice Marshal Jack Slessor. Word had reached them that there was a possibility of the Government backing out. 'It was a horrible moment,' said Slessor. Then suddenly the CAS exclaimed, 'Come on, we must find the Secretary of State.' They hurried off to the House of Commons and sent in a message to Sir Kingsley Wood asking him to come out. Slessor continues, 'Newall told him very briefly that we could not possibly run out now – if we did, we were sunk. Kingsley Wood was reassuring . . .'

The debate over, Halifax called on Bonnet at 10.30 p.m., begging him to agree to present an ultimatum to Hitler at 8.00 a.m. next day, Sunday 3 September. Bonnet would not hear of it. So Halifax told him that if the French could not decide, Britain would go ahead on her own.

Although Ribbentrop had been requested well beforehand to receive the British Ambassador, Henderson, he was 'not available' when His Majesty's plenipotentiary called at the Wilhelmstrasse at 9.00 a.m. on Sunday 3 September. Dr Carl Schmidt – who made it by the skin of his teeth through a side door – was there instead. The Englishman shook hands with the German, but refused Schmidt's invitation to sit down. Standing stiffly upright Henderson read the British ultimatum. Recalling the British warning of 1 September that Germany should cease hostilities, he continued, 'I have the honour to inform you that if today, 3 September, at 11.00 o'clock at the latest, satisfactory assurance have not been given . . . to His Majesty's Government in London, a state of war will from that hour exist between the two countries.'

At that moment on the grass at Tangmere airfield I was lying beside my Hurricane watching flaky white clouds drift across a blue sky, while hovering larks shrilled and voices came to me from pilots and ground crew also lying beside their dispersed aircraft. Never in my life had I experienced so peaceful a scene.

At 11.00 a.m. squadron adjutant John Simpson walked into the hangar and said to Warrant Officer Chitty, 'The balloon goes up at 11.15. That's official.'

We all forgathered in the mess where we had listened to Hitler's shrieking voice just a year ago. Our station commander, Fred Sowrey, looked grave. But the presence of this veteran was reassuring for us who did not know war. Twenty-three years earlier to the very day, Fred Sowrey had been on patrol with Lieutenant Leefe Robinson when Robinson sent a Zeppelin crashing in flames near London. Then Zeppelin L32 had fallen to Sowrey's guns, and in May 1918 he was in at the kill of the last German raider to crash on English soil. This veteran of the first generation of airmen was about to see the horror of a second attempt by the Germans to reduce England to her knees by bombing. He steadied us in our ardour to 'get at the Hun'. He told us, 'Don't think a fighter pilot's life is one of endless flying and glory. You will spend nine-tenths of your time sitting on your backsides waiting.'

Macey and Hoskins, two imperturbables in white jackets, served us each a mug of bitter. The swing door by which they entered the ante-room seemed to creak louder as the silence grew and the fateful hour approached.

Then suddenly the radio came alive and the sombre, leaden tones of Prime Minister Neville Chamberlain fell on the silence of the ante-room. 'It is a sad day for all of us ... Every aim for which I have worked, everything I had hoped for, all the principles in which I believed ... have fallen down in ruin. I hope to live long enough to see the day when Hitlerism will be destroyed and a free Europe will exist again.'

Chamberlain would never live to see that day. Neither would most of us who listened to him. The ebullient Caesar Hull jumped from one foot to another exclaiming, 'Wizard!', and turning to John Simpson, 'Never mind, John, you'll be killed early on.' And he punched him in the back and laughed.

John, however, would come through (like me) by pure luck. But not Caesar, nor Wilkinson nor 'Wombat' Woods-Scawen in A Flight. Nor Tiger Folkes, Eddy Edmonds, Pat Christie or Joe Sullivan in B Flight. Within twelve months or so these valiant young men who cared for nothing more than the joy of flying, would die in the fight to destroy Hitlerism. Not counting the wounded and the burnt, escape was a one-in-five chance.

But no such thoughts troubled us then. As John wrote, 'It's the war we've been expecting, so we can't grumble.'

That was not exactly the view of Major Hoelcke of *Kampfgeschwader* 51. Like us, he and the other officers of the *Eidelweiss Geschwader* were sitting around the radio, but in their comfortable furnished mess at Memmingen near the Austrian border. These bomber men (among them Joachim Poetter) felt at home in their rustic surroundings – the open fireplace, the

Reidinger engravings of the chase, and the stags' heads which adorned the walls. In the morning of 3 September the warm sun shining through the windows glinted on bronze candelabras.

But the atmosphere was grim. For days there had been rumours of war and now the radio announcer was confirming their worst fears. Britain had declared war on Germany. Everyone was silent – except Hoelcke who yelled, '*Gott strafe England!* The Anglo-Saxon countries should stick together. Why the hell must England fight Germany?'

As we in 43 Squadron returned to watch and wait beside our Hurricanes at Tangmere, at his Headquarters in Watford the thoughts of Air Vice Marshal Sholto Douglas (Assistant Chief of the Air Staff) were, 'My God . . . we've got to take on those bastards all over again. We finished them off twenty years ago. Why do we have to start all over again?'

Then the air raid siren went. The last time he had been in an air raid, twenty-one years ago at Bertangles, he had dived under a piano. Now he went down to the air raid shelter. 'We all sat around there looking rather stupid and waiting for the Germans to knock hell out of us.'

In the Filter Room at Fighter Command, Squadron Leader Walter Pretty (who had followed the airship Graf Zeppelin as she meandered round the radar network in May) was, 'like everyone else, very busy doing nothing'. Just as the Prime Minister finished talking plots started coming in from France.

Walter Pretty called the Controller who decided to take no chances. 'Commence to tell,' he ordered and immediately the entire vast complex of Britain's air defence system came into play. The air raid sirens began to wail. That is why Air Vice Marshal Douglas went down to the air raid shelter.

As we waited at Tangmere the atmosphere was so tense that in the end we dismissed it as unreal, and relaxed on the grass in the warm sunshine. Like sleek, powerful thoroughbreds our faithful Hurricanes seemed to be more patient than we as they waited for us to jump up into the cockpit and be off.

At Reichenbach, Wurtemburg, Hans-Heinrich Brustellin (now *Kommandeur* of I JG 51) expected as much as we did that the sky would darken and bombs descend. He whiled away the day playing cards and reading *Mein Kampf*. It was not a good palliative for his nerves. 'It made me feel sick, the language was rough, the style poor.' Then, as neither French nor British bombers appeared the pilots of I JG 51 relaxed.

At the controls of his Ju. 88 Hans Joachim Helbig had no time to relax on the morning of 3 September. Over Warsaw he was hit by Polish anti-aircraft fire. He suffered a flesh wound which was stitched up and did not prevent his flying. Another ten days and he would be back home with an Iron Cross 2nd class.

Hopelessly inferior in numbers and equipment, the Polish airmen fought back with desperate gallantry. In a second assault on Lublin airfield Hajo Hermann's Heinkel 111 was attacked by a Polish fighter. 'He was a marvellous fellow – he rolled over on his back and shot at me,' said Hermann, who had to limp back on one engine.

But the valiant resistance of the Polish airmen soon foundered in chaos. By 8 September the end was in sight. 'The supply situation had become hopeless,' says Major Kalinowski. 'More and more of our aircraft became unusable. There were no spare parts . . .' This was the crux: aircraft could no more fly without an efficient ground organization than without wings – a fact that the C-in-C Fighter Command fortunately understood very well.

Meanwhile, bulldozing ahead of the army, the *Luftwaffe* was giving the Poles – and the world – the first *Blitzkrieg*. Hordes of bombers were blasting a path for the Panzers. Sometimes German tanks were met by horse-drawn gun limbers and cavalry armed with lances. The two sides were a century apart.

Werner Borner saw it all from his Dornier 17 at noon on 3 September when with II *KG* 2 he took part in a synchronized bombing attack in support of a Panzer assault near Mlawa. While Heinkel 111s bombed from high level, *Stukas* spread terror and havoc. Seconds later the Dorniers of II *KG* 2 streaked in at low level, front and rear guns blazing in every direction. The *Stukas*' bombs were bursting just ahead. Before the stunned and shattered defenders had time to recover, the Dorniers came blinding in through the smoke and dust to send their bombs hurtling down into the inferno. Borner could see the Polish soldiers below lying on their backs shooting back with rifles. His MG15 machine-gun answered, as did the sixty-odd machine-guns of the combined *Gruppe*. The carnage was frightful. Then the Panzers moved in and what was left of the defence was quickly mopped up.

II *KG* 2 continued to harass the retreating Polish army against negligible opposition from fighters and AA. By 16 September, when the Polish resistance was practically overcome, II *KG* 2 was withdrawn. But there still remained deadly work for the *Stukas*: Warsaw and the fortress of Modlin were holding out. On 17 September the pilots of I *St. G* 3 (among them Rudolf Braun) were called to the tent of *Hauptmann* Sigel for briefing. Target Modlin. They breakfasted lightly as usual because of the 'G' (gravitational pull) in coming out of a dive. Engines were warmed and immediately after the *Gruppe* was airborne at 10.50. Under strict radio silence they approached the target at twelve thousand feet, cruising at 150 m.p.h. (250 k.p.h.). Sigel led the *Stab Kette* (Staff Flight), followed by *Staffel* I in *ketten* of three aircraft with the two other *Staffeln* to left and right. Then came the *Kommandeur's* order, 'Ready for the attack.' Automatically each pilot acted: switch on bomb sites, dive-brakes out, close radiator flap, move into line astern. In the glass panel in the floor of the Ju. 87 the pilot could see the target below.

Then one after another the *Stukas* rolled over and plunged in a seventy degree dive – 220, 250, 300 m.p.h., the sirens on each undercarriage leg screaming in an unearthly crescendo of sound. Down went the HE bombs onto Modlin fortress and its valiant defenders.

For another ten days the city held out against a combined onslaught of the *Luftwaffe's* bombs and the guns of the army artillery. Above the beleaguered city great columns of smoke rose 10,000 feet. From 16–24 September the *Luftwaffe* dropped millions of leaflets calling on the population to surrender, but the proud obstinate Slavs still refused to bow to the Hun invader. Then on 25 September Kesselring ordered the *Luftwaffe* to deliver a devastating *coup de grâce*. Three days later the city capitulated.

In the 'eighteen days campaign' the *Luftwaffe's* part had been decisive, mainly in disrupting communications and paralysing the Polish army and air force – a feat it would come near to repeating against Fighter Command. Udet's cherished *Stukas* had proved themselves instruments of the *Blitzkrieg*. They would continue their bloody, devastating career – but not indefinitely. Within less than a year, decimated by the RAF's Hurricanes and Spitfires, they would be withdrawn from the battle.

The day that Rudolf Braun was dive-bombing Modlin fortress in his Ju. 87, I was engaged in the gentle pursuit of balloon-bursting. The equinoctial gales had played havoc with the barrage balloons and in a few days 43 Squadron had downed several. Wallowing lazily in the air currents at thirty thousand feet, where the Hurricane was very sluggish, a balloon was a surprisingly difficult target. I last saw the one I was chasing sag half-deflated into a field near Selsey Bill and drift onwards with the wind, pursued by the local inhabitants like a wounded animal with a limp.

The Under Secretary of State for Air, Captain Harold Balfour, visited

43 Squadron. So did the C-in-C of Fighter Command, 'Stuffy' Dowding. It was just as the airfield was being camouflaged by spraying the grass with soot. Aloof and silent, Dowding regarded us sadly; we looked more like chimney sweeps than fighter pilots. This was the first and last time I ever set eyes on our Commander-in-Chief during the war. Harold Balfour, on the other hand, was warmth itself. He had been B Flight Commander in 1916 and found that 'nothing had really changed in 43 except the machines'.

Karl Missy's unit, the II *Gruppe* of the '*Lion Geschwader*' (*KG* 26), withdrawn from Poland in mid-September, was settling in at Westerland on the island of Sylt. Two weeks later they were joined by I *KG* 30 under *Hauptmann* Pohle. A *Kette* of I *KG* 30 led by *Gefreiter* Carl Francke had, with the generous aid of Dr Goebbels's propaganda, 'sunk' the aircraft carrier *Ark Royal* – which was then steaming serenely toward the South Atlantic.

On 9 October Pohle landed at Westerland in his Ju. 88, furiously angry. I *KG* 30 had joined forces with *KG* 26 and *LG* 1 (Jocho Helbig's unit) in an Armada of some one hundred and fifty bombers to attack the Home Fleet.

Missy enjoyed these anti-shipping missions. At the *Flugbesprechnung* (briefing) he did not feel a qualm. His *Gruppe* took off – forty-eight aircraft, followed by the other *Gruppen*. Before sighting the ships they had to fly some two hundred miles in poor weather. Then came the leader's warning, '*Bomben zum Abwurf klarmachen!*' (ready for bombing) and one *Kette* at a time, the *Gruppe* ran in over the target.

Whether it was heavy AA or bad weather, the operation was a failure. Hence Pohle's rage. And Goering's too when he presided over a meeting the next morning at the Air Ministry in Berlin. 'Pohle, we've got to score a success,' said the C-in-C. '.... Everyone who helps in getting rid of these ships will have a house of his own and all the medals that are going.' Less than a week later Pohle would make another attempt.

Goering was at that time anxious for the *Luftwaffe* to step up the bombing war against the British fleet, which lurked in the naval bases of Rosyth on the Firth of Forth and Scapa Flow in the Orkneys ready to strike out at any German challenge. 'There's no fear of our bombers running into British fighters up there,' Major Beppo Schmid, Chief of *Abteilung* 5 (Intelligence), assured Goering, who believed him implicitly. But Beppo Schmid – not for the last time – was wrong.

At 11.00 a.m. on 16 October *Hauptmann* Pohle took off from Westerland at the head of his I *KG* 30 *Verband*. At about 12.30, after circling Rosyth he put his Ju. 88 into a steep dive. Squarely in his sight ten thousand feet below was the cruiser *Southampton*. Pohle pressed the bomb release button and down went a one thousand kilogramme bomb. Immediately the automatic mechanism took over to bring the 'wonder bomber' out of its headlong dive.

Leading two other Spitfires of Red Section 603 Squadron, Flight Lieutenant Gifford was at that moment closing in on Pohle. First the Ju. 88's port engine, then the starboard one, were hit. With the rest of his crew dead, Pohle managed to 'ditch' in the Firth of Forth where a trawler picked him up unconscious. Though he had failed again – the *Southampton* was only slightly damaged – Goering's rocket would not reach him. He was a prisoner of war in Port Edwards Hospital.

Attacking after Pohle, *Leutnant* Horst von Riesen caused casualties aboard the destroyer *Nohawk*. Then Spitfires of 602 and 603 Squadrons pounced on him as he streaked low down for the open sea. 'I saw what looked like raindrops hitting the water,' said von Riesen. They were the Spitfires' bullets and they found their mark. White smoke suddenly belched from one of the Jumo engines and it stopped. At that moment the Spitfires, now several miles from the coast, miraculously disappeared.

The bomber staggered along just above the water, von Riesen barely able to hold it straight against the violent torque of the other engine. The observer lashed his belt to the rudder-bar and heaved. It helped to take the weight off von Riesen's leg. But could they last out like that for another four hundred miles back to Westerland? 'What about turning back to the coast?' someone asked on the intercom, but von Riesen shook his head. 'We preferred to risk drowning than having to face those Spitfires again,' he said. Four hours later the exhausted crew sighted the lights of Westerland.

The next day *Hauptmann* Doench (I *KG* 30's new *Kommandeur*) led four Ju. 88s in the teeth of heavy AA fire to attack Scapa Flow. But this time Beppo Schmid was right about the British fighters. There was not one within a hundred miles.

The Navy decided that Rosyth and Scapa Flow were obviously too hot and withdrew to the west coast. Four months passed before fighter squadrons were installed near Scapa. One of them would be 43.

While on 17 October I *KG* 30's bombs were raining down on Scapa

Flow the Air Staff and its Chief, Newall, were racking their brains to find a way of stiffening Britain's still utterly inadequate fighter force. The situation looked desperate. Before the outbreak of war Fighter Command's needs had been estimated at forty-six squadrons for general defence, plus six for the protection of coastal convoys and Scapa Flow – a total of fifty-two. Northern Ireland was also to get a squadron. With this force Dowding felt sure of crushing any onslaught the *Luftwaffe* might make from its bases in Germany.

But on 3 September he was faced with the bleak reality that his squadrons numbered thirty-five, not fifty-two. Of this meagre force four squadrons had left for France and in answer to the urgent demands of the British and French armies six more had been put on a mobile footing. Dowding protested strongly that this decision had 'opened a tap through which will run the total Hurricane output' – prophetic words. Its immediate result was to reduce his potential Home Defence fighter force to twenty-five squadrons – less than half of what was required.

Dowding demanded twelve more squadrons but was informed that only three could be provided, equipped with twin-engined Blenheims – a good bomber, but a mockery as a day fighter. Dowding countered by reducing his bid to eight squadrons, but he was not averse to wrangling the arithmetic somewhat. The three squadrons could be six half-squadrons; two more whole squadrons would make eight potential squadrons which could be brought up to strength later.

Newall readily agreed. But he did much more. He was only too aware of Dowding's needs for fighters, but with Hurricanes and Spitfires only trickling off the production line he had nothing to build on – save faith. So, spurred by 'the stream of forceful, cogent and entirely outspoken protests' of the C-in-C Fighter Command and trusting in his own judgement, the Chief of Air Staff calmly informed those who met on 17 October that not only must the eight new squadrons be ready within the next two weeks, but in the following two weeks ten more squadrons must be formed! It was an amazingly bold and imaginative stroke which would ensure victory to Fighter Command, if only by the 'narrowest of margins', in the great air battle of the next summer.

Meanwhile, the protection of shipping within five miles of the coast was added to Fighter Command's task of defending the British Isles.

Chapter 16

This was the reason for 43 Squadron's move on 18 November to Acklington, near Newcastle. A bleak and windswept sward, its black iron hangars and drab buildings provided a dismal contrast to Tangmere. In a way it helped, toughening us to the notion that we were there to fight and possibly to die. We became more rugged, coming to readiness in the icy dawn before flying out to sea, more often than not in the filthiest weather, to patrol above the coast-bound convoys.

From our snug cockpits we looked down on the brave merchant ships trying valiantly to get from trough to trough while the gale tore along. Frayed lines of smoke rose from their thin funnels. Cramped in our tiny cockpits above the convoys our relation to rain, wind, ice and snow differed from that of the sailors, but we both faced the weather and the immense wastes of sea. Our own lives depended on the single Merlin engine thrumming steadily in front. If it failed we should suffer a sailor's fate, or possibly worse, for we had no dinghies. In those icy, tempestuous seas our Mae Wests would merely prolong the agony.

One man who was beginning to take an unusual interest in the coastal waters and beaches of England was the chief of the German *Kriegsmarine*, Admiral Erich Raeder – a God-fearing sailor, short in stature and quietly efficient. Every day at 11.00 a.m. the Admiral met with *der kleine Kreis* (a small 'inner circle' of senior naval officers) in the *Kriegsmarine* Headquarters at Tirpizufer on the banks of the winding river Spree in Berlin. At the meeting of *der kleine Kreis* on 15 November Raeder directed that Naval Headquarters should examine 'the possibility of troop landings in England, should the future progress of the war make the problem come up'. Raeder's admitted personal views on the project were that it was *verrückt* (mad). The risks were prohibitive.

Within five days *Kapitän* Hans Jurgen Reinicke of the Operations Staff had produced a short paper on the subject. Reinicke was convinced that invasion was impossible, one of his main reasons being that hostile air reconnaissance would forbid any element of surprise. One of the essential prerequisites to invasion was to knock out the opposing air force. Another obvious one was to eliminate all hostile naval forces in the operational zone. But at that moment, he argued, the enemy would in any case be reduced to impotence, so why bother to invade? However, if invasion there must be, 'a large scale landing over the North Sea . . . would appear as a possible means of forcing readiness for peace', *Friedensbereitschaft*. For the English the Germans now envisaged a kinder fate than for their continental enemies, for whom *zerschlagen* (break in pieces) was the word. But in time the Germans would harden their hearts to England.

Luftwaffe Intelligence Chief, Major Beppo Schmid, aired his own views on England in a document issued on 22 November entitled 'Proposal for the Conduct for Air Warfare against Britain'. Schmid believed that 'from Germany's point of view Britain is the most dangerous of all possible enemies'. Germany would never win 'as long as Britain has not been mastered'. Germany's aim should be to strike at Britain with the *Luftwaffe* and the *Kriegsmarine* – the sooner the better and certainly that year. Schmid's idea was to strangle Britain by cutting her supply lines, sinking her warships and merchantmen, and smashing her ports and food depots. 'The intermingling of residential areas with dockyards . . . is no reason for failing to attack such ports.'

But the strangulation of Britain was not going to be as easy as it apparently looked to Beppo Schmid. He made no allowance either for British radar, or for the *Luftwaffe*'s lack of marine aircraft or for the need for air superiority.

All the same, Schmid was barking up the right tree. His aggressive intentions towards England were strongly endorsed by his Supreme Commander when, the very next day in the Chancellery, Hitler delivered a speech to his war-lords. It was about time, too, for there had been a deliberate go-slow by Brauchitsch and the generals on Hitler's Western offensive, set for 12 November. The generals heaved a sigh of relief when on 7 November bad weather caused its cancellation.

Hitler ran through his past achievements, concluding that 'the moment is favourable now'. Never one to be bashful about his own feats, he said, 'As a last factor I must in all modesty name my own person irreplaceable . . . I am convinced of my powers of intellect and decision.

'My decision is unchangeable. I shall attack England at the most favourable and quickest moment. Breach of the neutrality of Belgium and France is meaningless . . . Victory or defeat! The question is . . . who is going to dominate Europe in the future . . . I have led the German people to a great height, even if the world does hate us now. I am setting this work on a gamble . . . I shall shrink from nothing and shall destroy everyone who is opposed to me . . .'

Six days later on 29 November Hitler issued another Directive. It contained distinct echoes of Beppo Schmid. 'In our fight against the Western Powers England has shown herself to be the animator of the fighting spirit of the enemy and the leading power. The defeat of England is essential to victory.' And the way to defeat England was 'to deal an annihilating blow to the English economy'.

Once the Franco-British armies were defeated and a sector of the Channel coast in France was under German domination '. . . the task of the *Kriegsmarine* and *Luftwaffe* to carry the war to English industry becomes paramount.' Bases in northern France were vital to the *Luftwaffe* and the *Kriegsmarine*. French ports were not to be attacked just because they were French, but 'only . . . in so far as they are involved in the siege of England'.

Whether it was Hitler's exhortation or professional pride that was injured by the Navy's invasion study, on 13 December Brauchitsch woke up with invasion fever. A paper to the other services said, 'The Commander-in-Chief has ordered examination of the possibilities of a landing in England . . . in a study designated *Nordwest*. Collaboration is requested . . .' The Army was more optimistic than the Navy about invasion. Once in England – getting there was the Navy and *Luftwaffe*'s problem, not theirs – the Army would carry out a mixed airborne and infantry assault between the Wash and the Thames.

For the time being Goering had the last word. On 30 December he commented on *Studie Nordwest*, 'the planned operation can only be considered under conditions of absolute air superiority . . .

'A combined operation with a landing in England as its object must be rejected. It could only be the last act of a war against England which had already taken a victorious course . . .' To the C-in-C of the *Luftwaffe* there was only one way of pursuing that victorious course. The essential condition for invasion was the destruction of the Royal Air Force. His *Luftwaffe* would look after that. Without air defences England would be impotent. Invasion would then be unnecessary. To the C-in-C of the *Luftwaffe* it was as simple as that. The C-in-C of Fighter Command agreed.

Caesar and I, who had kept up our formation aerobatics, saw the old year out with a flourish. Our neighbours, 152 Squadron, were changing their Gladiator biplanes for Spitfires. They felt they were one up on us. So Caesar and I innocently asked if we could try out one of their machines and Freddy Shute, their CO, agreed.

It was the first time we had flown a Spit., but after putting it through its paces we exchanged delighted opinions. 'Wizard!' Caesar called out on the blower. 'Let's show them.' In close formation we dived on Acklington. John Simpson was on the tarmac watching. 'In full view of the whole aerodrome they did a loop and roll in formation ... You can imagine what our ground crews were like ... It might have been a race-horse stable with rival trainers. They were jumping with joy when they saw Caesar and Peter put those Spitfires in their place ... Freddy Shute was angry but charming.'

Only one month later we were to mourn this good and gentle man when he disappeared in foul weather at sea – not in a Spitfire, but in one of the old Gladiators.

By mid-January winter tightened its grip. Thick snow clogged the wheels of our Hurricanes, making take-off impossible. No such thing as a snow plough existed at Acklington and shovels were scarce. Like every other airfield in the north we were paralysed. But not for long. We wrenched a door off the dispersal hut, wrapped up three men in the thickest woollies and Balaclava helmets, and sat them on the door. The whole lot was tied behind a tractor. Up and down it went, gradually flattening and pressing the snow into a hard surface. When the men became frozen three others took their place and soon we had a perfectly good runway. The convoys were not left unprotected.

Heinkel 111s had been snooping around them recently and Caesar had actually shot at one which returned his fire. The result was a single bullet through his Hurricane and a claim by the German radio that it had been shot down. Every other time, the Heinkels eluded us by pulling up sharply into low-lying cloud. So instead of patrolling just below cloud where they could see us we kept down low, only a few feet above the water. Our green and brown camouflage made us less visible and with the Merlin pushed to full throttle we would have the power to zoom up and catch the raider before he slipped into cloud. This tactic would prove the undoing of Karl Missy.

When, on the morning of 30 January, I led Blue Section low down past the end of Blyth Pier, a mountainous sea was breaking against it. Tiger Folkes complained that the spray had splashed his windscreen. Tiger was a timid boy, his hair a sandy-orange colour. His melancholy purple-blue eyes looked questioningly from a pink, oval face and when offered a drink he had a stock reply, 'It might be dangerous not to.' But though outwardly timid, he was a tiger at heart whom I could count on to follow me through all weathers – until he disappeared forever, another victim of the sea.

That afternoon we were rushed out over a convoy which was being attacked, but in the foul weather we saw nothing. Landing back at base I passed Caesar, who was having trouble taxying out in a strong cross-wind, and hurled a few jibes at him over the R/T. Throwing his head back and baring his big white teeth, he laughed. Then he was gone.

Twenty minutes later he returned and jumping down from the cockpit of the machine which the German radio had claimed was destroyed the day before, told us how he had just shot down a Heinkel – 43 Squadron's first. All Caesar's wild excitement could not conceal that he was shaken too. He had never killed in his life before. Now he had killed four men at a single blow.

Reports of a British convoy southward bound from Sweden sent II *KG* 26, the *Lion Geschwader*, flying from their permanent base in Westerland to Schleswig on 2 February. Take-off was timed for first light on 3 February. The crew of Heinkel No. 3232, like most of the others, spent that evening quietly in the mess playing cards and having a few drinks.

Unteroffizier Missy felt it was good to belong to such a close and efficient team: the pilot Hermann Wilms, the observer Peter Leushake and the flight mechanic Johann Meyer – all of them *Unteroffiziers* like himself. They welcomed the change from Westerland, a bleak, isolated strip off the Danish coast where they were not even allowed off the base. There were compensations, of course: the food was good, and despite cramped living quarters they enjoyed each other's company.

Next morning they were up at 2.00 a.m. A snowplough and a hundred soldiers were already at work clearing three feet of snow from the runway. Despite the five hour flight ahead Missy and his companions set to and gave a hand. At last the runway was clear and they reported for the *Flugbesprechnung* (briefing). As usual Missy felt no qualms. The only fear that lurked in his mind was the sea. But he knew everyone else in the *Gruppe* felt the same.

The convoy was now reported to be steering south off the north-east coast of England. Orders were to take off in pairs at three minute intervals and steer west. After two and a half hours' flying one or two aircraft should intercept the convoy. They were to attack and shadow to report first position. The others would then close in.

The crew of Heinkel 3232 left the briefing room for the aircraft. Then an odd thing happened: they met a chimney sweep, no ordinary one either for he wore a top hat, a rare sight in those days. They waved happily and Karl Missy thought, 'That's bound to bring us extra good luck.' At least it would to him.

While Karl Missy and his friends were sleeping in the barracks at Schleswig we in B Flight 43 Squadron were dozing fitfully in the cold and discomfort of our dispersal point at Acklington. On the morning of 3 February I plodded out in a cutting wind with the other pilots in my flight to fetch our aircraft dispersed on the far side of the airfield. As usual some starter-batteries went flat and some engines had to be cranked by hand. This could at best scrape the skin off your knuckles, or break your wrist through a kick-back, or at worst decapitate you if you slipped forward into the propeller. One by one the Merlins burst into raucous life and we taxied back to the dispersal hut as the blood red sun began to mushroom in the east. Then all colour faded from the sky and left us staring at a Siberian landscape. The corporal wound the telephone and reported to sector headquarters, 'Blue and Green Sections B Flight 43 Squadron at readiness.'

Far away, at Danby Beacon Radar Station the duty operator picked up the telephone. It was 9.03 a.m. In the cathode ray tube the observer had seen one 'blip', then another. Unidentified aircraft some sixty miles out to sea were approaching the coast at one thousand feet. Now the Danby Beacon Teller was reading off the 'plots' to Fighter Command. From Fighter Command they were relayed simultaneously to 13 Group and to Acklington sector.

Within minutes the telephone jangled in 43 Squadron dispersal hut. 'Sector ops. here. Blue section 43 scramble base. Angels one.' Moments later I was climbing away from Acklington airfield, Folkes and Sergeant Hallowes in my wake. 'Vector 190, *Bandit* attacking ship off Whitby. *Buster.*' Our throttles wide-open we raced south at wave-top height, spread out in search formation, Hallowes on my left, Tiger on my right. I searched the low cloud-base anxiously. Then suddenly there it was, a Heinkel above and to my right. 'Tally-ho! two o'clock.' There was not a second to lose, for the Heinkel was just below cloud. I banked right in a climbing turn. Now the Heinkel was in my sights. My thumb was on the firing button.

At that instant Observer Peter Leushake yelled out, '*Achtung, Jäger!*'

Then I was firing at Missy, Wilms, Leushake, and Meyer, who at Schleswig only a few hours earlier had been shovelling snow and enjoying coffee and sandwiches. It never occurred to me at the time that I was killing men. I saw only a big Heinkel with black crosses on it. But in that Heinkel Peter Leushake was already dead, and Johann Meyer (his stomach punctured by bullets) mortally wounded.

Closing in fast on the Heinkel I passed it as it entered cloud – a vague black shadow uncomfortably close above. Then Folkes, the Heinkel, and I tumbled out of the cloud almost on top of one another. And the German turned shorewards with a trail of smoke behind him.

Karl Missy knew he had been badly hit in the legs and back, but he kept firing while with great skill Wilms handled the disabled aircraft. It grazed the high cliffs at Whitby and passed over house tops. A girl heard the screaming of seagulls and then the Heinkel seemed to be passing in front of her window.

Seventeen-year-old J. D. H. Armstrong, who worked for a Whitby tea company, seeing that the Heinkel was going to crash, jumped into an Austin van and headed out to the spot. Mr Arthur Barratt, a Special Constable, was drinking a cup of tea at his house in Love Lane when the bomber passed two hundred feet overhead 'with three of our fighters round him like flies round a honey pot'. He dashed for his car and sped up towards Sneaton Castle in the direction of the doomed bomber.

A woman who had just got off the Castle Park bus at the Parade watched astonishedly as the bomber passed low overhead. She could see the pilot through the cabin window and on the tail a black swastika.

During the entire action Missy had not left his swivel seat in the rear upper gun position. The Heinkel was done for and everything now depended on Wilms getting it down safely. When he left Schleswig Missy had never dreamed that three hours later it would all end like this. If he survived, and that was by no means certain, he would be taken prisoner. Suddenly this worried him. How would they treat him? He could not be sure. He knew what the English thought of the Nazis.

Looking down at the ground covered with snow as it had been at Schleswig when they took off, Missy felt impotent. Then gardens and houses and trees were coming closer. He could see people looking up. Suddenly a line of telegraph poles was in front. The Heinkel smashed through the wires and headed straight for a barn. He felt Wilms's desperate effort to lift it over the roof. Then they were slithering across the snow.

I too watched them from where I was circling a few hundred feet above. I could see snow and mud flying up behind the Heinkel as it careered across the ground towards a line of trees. Its right wing hit one, snapping it in half. Then it slewed round and came to rest a few yards from Bannial Flat Farm.

Hardly had the flying snow settled when, with some farm workers, Special Constable Arthur Barratt dashed up to the Heinkel. Barratt climbed on to the wing, 'the first Englishman to enter a German plane ... in England since the war started'. He saw Wilms kneeling inside burning the aircraft's papers, 'with two of his mates leaning against him, groaning'. Hanging head down inside the cockpit, Constable Barratt grabbed Wilms by the collar. But the German pilot struggled free and finished the job. Then Wilms came and Barratt 'told someone to look after him while we lifted his pals out, but ... he got to the front of the plane and set fire to the blinking thing while we were struggling with the wounded'.

Young Armstrong, who had arrived in the Austin van seconds after the Heinkel crashed, saw Wilms raise his hands and shout, 'Boom, Boom!', at which the little crowd backed away. It took five fire extinguishers and shovels full of snow to put the fire out. But, despite Wilms's efforts, Intelligence officers were able to recover valuable papers from the German bomber.

Mrs Smales and Miss Sanderson were among the first on the scene. Mr Smales called several times to Karl Missy to get out of the aircraft and it was only when he tried to leave his swivel seat that Karl realized how badly he was hit. His legs were shattered and useless. So with his powerful arms he lowered himself down to where Johann Meyer lay huddled in the 'bath' below.

With several bullet wounds in his stomach, Meyer was screaming with pain. With a frantic effort Missy tried to release his friend, but collapsed half on top of him. Blood was pouring from his own wound but he never lost consciousness. He called to Wilms, 'Hermann, come and help Johann.' Then he dragged himself up and heaved himself out of the top gun position on to the wing. He slid down to the ground and from there watched while Wilms dragged out the body of Leushake. He then realized that Leushake (who had been hit in the head) had died instantly as he lay in the observer's position in the aircraft's nose. Then Wilms came back to get Meyer. He dragged him forward to the front of the aircraft and got him out. Amazed at his own efforts to get clear, Missy realized as he watched Wilms that in such moments men are possessed with some supernatural strength.

Armstrong went to assist Johann Meyer, who was trying to crawl in the snow. Blood was pouring from his wounds and all Johann could say was, '*Kamerad, Kamerad*', very weakly. The boy Armstrong then turned to help Karl Missy, who 'cried out in agony as he was dragged clear'.

Later in a nearby field Armstrong found 'a trail of red spots in the snow'. It was blood which had dripped from the Heinkel as it came in to land.

Mr Smales helped Wilms carry Missy and Meyer into the house. They were frozen stiff and Mrs Smales and Miss Sanderson brought them hot water bottles wrapped in blankets and made them tea. Missy gestured that he wanted to smoke and he and the other were given cigarettes.

A doctor arrived and immediately knelt beside Meyer, giving him morphine. Then he cut off Missy's boots and put splints on his legs. The left one was broken, the right terribly mutilated. The kindness these people were showing to Missy and his comrades made him feel certain for the first time that he would be well treated. Meanwhile, the body of Peter Leushake had been laid in an out-house.

Missy would always remember the drive in the ambulance to the hospital, the agony of Johann Meyer, and the pitiful cries of his dying friend. On arrival he was carried straight to the operating theatre. Karl Missy never saw him again. That night it was his turn to be wheeled to the operating table. His right leg was amputated high up – he was losing so much blood it had to be. In the broken left leg there were wounds which did not appear to be too serious, so it was put in plaster.

When on the morning of 4 February Missy regained consciousness he saw a guard at the end of his bed. Sure enough he was a prisoner. He felt weak and in terrible pain and it occurred to him that he might die. He thought of his fiancée and his family. The home at 43 Dohlerstrasse, Rheydt, seemed to belong to another world and another century. He remembered the day he had left his father after a quarrel and how the harsh old man had turned up at the station next day, tears in his eyes, to see him off.

Then he thought of his comrades, of the brave Wilms who had handled his aircraft and himself so well; of Peter Leushake who had left this world with the dreaded words '*Achtung, Jäger!*' on his lips; of poor Johann Meyer's long agony; of the whole ghastly catastrophe which had broken up their little team after the day had started so well with the snow clearing, the coffee and sandwiches and that sudden meeting with the sweep. Some luck this had brought them!

Missy would never be able to shovel snow again. Never again would he feel the wonderful comradeship which had grown up among the crew of Heinkel No. 3232. Only one thing gave him any desire to live. He had already noticed the care – it was really tenderness, devotion – which the sister-in-charge was showing him. In his pain and misery it touched him. She could speak no German, he no English, but she somehow managed to convey a spark of hope to him. Besides, they allowed Wilms to stay for a while to help with the language problem.

Missy thought how odd it was that yesterday the English had tried to kill him – even now he was not sure he would live – but here was this Englishwoman who cared for him as if he were one of her own people. Her name was Sister Oldfield. At that moment she came in and said to Karl Missy, 'There is a visitor to see you. He will only stay a couple of minutes.' Wilms translated.

A moment later Sister Oldfield met me in the corridor. 'He is very ill indeed and we can't tell yet whether he is going to pull through. So only two minutes,' she said to me. Then she opened the door of Karl Missy's ward. I entered and walking straight up to his bed held out my hand. Turning to me he clasped it with both of his until it hurt. But it was the way he looked at me that I can never forget. We had no common tongue so could only communicate as the animals do, by touch, by expression, and by invisible means. As he took my hand Missy had in his eyes the look of a dying animal. If he had died I would have been his killer. He said nothing and only looked at me with a pitiful, frightened, and infinitely sad expression in which I thought I could recognize a glimmer of human gratitude. Indeed Missy felt no bitterness. He sank back on the pillows and I held out the bag of oranges and the tin of fifty Players I had brought for him. They seemed poor compensation.

Then I left Karl Missy and went back to Acklington and the war. Perhaps I should end up like him, with no legs, or burnt and disfigured, or pieced together to be buried in some strange cemetery, with other pilots saluting – for such was the custom – as my broken remains were lowered into the earth.

Peter Leushake and Johann Meyer were buried with full military honours at Catterick. A wreath was placed on their coffins. It read, 'From 43 Squadron, with sympathy.'

Three days after Karl Missy lost his leg, a telegram came for Douglas Bader, in the south of England. It said, 'Posted to 19 Squadron, Duxford.'

Bader had no legs at all; the last time he had seen Duxford was seven years before when he had driven away from the airfield and out of the RAF, with a hundred per cent disability pension.

After the Munich crisis Bader felt sure that there would be a war. He wrote to the Air Ministry offering to serve as a pilot, but was told, 'It is not possible for you to be taken on in a flying class of the reserve. But . . . if war came we would be only too glad . . . if the doctors agreed.' War had come, and Bader had been summoned before for a medical board at the Air Ministry. He found himself standing before the president, Air Vice Marshal Halahan, his commander years before at the RAF College. Halahan had once reprimanded Bader, 'We want men, not schoolboys, in the RAF . . .'

The tests over, Bader faced the senior medical officer, a man 'slightly bald, but with a pleasant face', who handed him a note he had been reading. It was from Halahan, and said, 'I have known this officer since he was . . . at Cranwell (RAF College). If he is fit . . . give him A1B category. [Fit for all ground and air duties.]' Bader would later write, 'I think I stopped breathing.' During the interminable silence which followed he stared straight at the doctor, 'willing him to think my way'. At last the doctor said slowly, 'I agree with Air Vice Marshal Halahan.'

The legless pilot, who still enjoyed a hundred per cent disability pension, returned to Duxford on the evening of 7 February and reported to 19 Squadron for flying duties. Within six months both the RAF and the *Luftwaffe* would be feeling the effect of this heroic and turbulent character.

Chapter 17

On 22 February, one of *KG* 26's Heinkels ran the gauntlet of 43 Squadron once more – a black speck etching a white vapour trail across the blue sky. Pat Christie, my No. 2, saw it first.

Four miles above our heads the enemy bomber flew eastwards toward home. In it were four young airmen oblivious that death was creeping up on them and that they had only a few more minutes to live. Fate had picked me as their executioner. The horrible reality never struck me during those last seconds as the Heinkel grew larger in my sights. The Heinkel was my target, not the man inside it.

The effect of my guns was devastating. The bomber staggered, emitting a cloud of oily vapour which obscured my windscreen. Then, as if the pilot had collapsed over the controls, it tipped into a steep dive at a terrifying speed. Suddenly both wings were wrenched off with fearful violence and the dismembered fuselage plummeted straight into the sea, followed by a trail of fluttering debris. Only at that moment did I realize what I had done to the men inside. I felt utterly nauseated.

The next morning 43 Squadron left Acklington. An hour later we landed at Wick, near the north-east tip of Scotland, John o'Groats. Across the sea from there, in the Orkneys, lay the naval base at Scapa Flow. Our job was to defend it.

Never had we known the elements to be more savage. At hurricane force the wind wrenched our aircraft from their iron pickets. Sheets of ice formed on the wings and when it thawed, mud wheel deep clogged the radiators. Day and night we careered above the seething whirlpools of the Pentland Firth and the angry spume of the open sea beyond. There the loyal and timid Tiger Folkes disappeared one morning in blinding rain. A convoy forged through the tempestuous seas below. Suddenly the escorting destroyer altered course, heeling over and churning the seas white as its engines went full ahead. I knew at once that something was wrong and turned. There was Plenderleith, but no sign of Tiger. I flew ahead of the destroyer and then I knew that Tiger was lost. A jagged patch of oil, a map, and some debris were all that marked Tiger's watery grave.

Guarding the Yorkshire coast, the pilots of 41 Squadron decided to remove the kapok from their Mae West life-saving jackets and let out all the air, as it interfered when dealing cards. On 3 April Flight Lieutenant Norman Ryder was hurriedly called from the card table to patrol over some fishing vessels off Redcar. Weather conditions were tricky: 'grey sea, grey visibility and grey, low cloud, all blending into a featureless backcloth.

Suddenly a Heinkel 111 appeared against the grey. Norman fired at the port engine and 'could hardly believe my eyes when it burst into flames'. Moments later the Heinkel ditched.* During the attack he had heard two bangs 'like hammer blows on a slate roof', and then his Spitfire's engine began to run rough. The oil temperature was off the clock, the pressure zero. Soon after, Norman was gliding towards the sea, which 'looked more and more angry every second'. He slammed on the rudder at the last moment and landed parallel to the swell. There was a resounding bang and he heard himself say, quite reverently, 'Christ!' Then all was eerily quiet, and in a cathedral-like green light he looked down the long nose of the Spitfire, watching bubbles from the propeller boss running up the engine cowling. Some broke left, some right. In a relaxed calm he watched them, wondering which way they would break. The water was getting darker, 'but still I played the fascinating bubble game'.

At last he decided it was time to get out, yet he wondered 'why hurry, there is plenty of time?' By then it was totally dark, and he realized his predicament. Yet he never thought of releasing his parachute harness and floating free. Instead he wriggled out, parachute and all. It seemed an age before he broke surface only to find himself helpless in the trough of the waves. Once with a supreme effort he made a crest, only to slide down the other side and disappear below the surface. After a long struggle he was free of his parachute harness and as if in celebration he rode another wave crest, but slid down the other side until he thought he would never see daylight again. Then something hit him on the head – it was his parachute pack, which he grabbed and clung to for dear life.

Twenty minutes later, Norman was dragged aboard a trawler by the old skipper and a boy in his 'teens. When the escorting destroyer signalled

*Slang for alighting on the sea.

the trawler to transfer Norman, the skipper snarled, 'We'd be knocked to pieces by that bleeding tin can alongside in a sea like this.' So, hours later, the trawler landed Norman at West Hartlepool.

Back in the pilots' room next day, he noticed everyone now had their life jackets stuffed with kapok.

To airmen (friend and foe) the sea was a common grave. On the night of 8 April it claimed more victims. That evening we were at stand-by strapped in our cockpits. Enemy jamming was heavy on our wavelength and that meant a raid. The nerve-racking tension made us sick. Then suddenly, 'Off you go', called the controller. And I was heading out to sea, Hallowes following. 'Twenty plus', the controller called, and then the darkening sky above Scapa was an inferno of anti-aircraft fire.

In the north-west the 'afterglow' of the sun (long since set) provided a luminous background, but I searched that sector of the sky in vain. Then the vague silhouette of a Heinkel appeared high above me heading south-east into darkness. His mission was accomplished, but not mine. All through the long, stealthy climb my eye was riveted immovably on the retreating bomber. The minute of truth was upon us. In the next few moments someone would die. The chances were – and it was certainly my intention – that it should be they, but one never knew. You never even thought of it as killing men. All you could see was the aircraft.

My fire blasted into it. Down came the undercarriage – a frequent phenomenon with Heinkels – and the usual clouds of Glycol vapour poured from the engines. I pulled aside, followed by a stream of tracer. The rear gunner could see me against the afterglow and now it was going to be a desperate gun-battle. The Heinkel came alive. Someone in it was out to kill me. The fight became personal. Him or me.

I forgot the dark abyss below and in its depths the sea, waiting for the vanquished. I thought no more of the coast I had left fifty miles behind. Nor was I any longer normally conscious of myself. I had become incensed with resolve to kill the man who was now very understandably trying to kill me.

On my second attack I flew straight down the cone of fire marked by his darting red tracer bullets – for every one there were four others, invisible, of ball, and armour-piercing. Our fire crossed until it met at point blank range. At that moment I actually heard the MG15 firing just above my head as I dodged below the Heinkel to avoid collision.

The Heinkel was now doomed. Its navigation lights came on and I could just discern it in the dark as it settled on the water. Then the lights disappeared.

Twenty minutes later the flashing beacon at Duncansby Head told me I was nearing base. When I arrived above it I saw, not the flarepath, but a confusion of lights. 'Don't land yet,' called the controller. But my tanks were nearly empty so I touched down clear of the lights and taxied over to them.

In the middle of the airfield lay a Heinkel 111, wheels up, propellers bent. Apparently Hallowes had hit it and the pilot had turned back to the coast. Mistaking our flarepath for lights on the sea he decided to 'ditch'. Before the astonished eye of the airfield control officer the Heinkel ground to a standstill. A door was opened, a dinghy thrown out and two of the crew – bootless, for easier swimming – dived out onto dry land. Rumour even had it that they climbed into their dinghy and began rowing.

Later they insisted that a Spitfire had attacked them. It was the first sign of the *Luftwaffe's* 'Spitfire snobbery'. There were no Spitfires within miles.

The next day I looked ruefully at my own Hurricane. It was riddled with bullet holes and the tail plane was badly damaged. It wouldn't have taken much more to have knocked me down into the sea.

While I was shooting it out over the North Sea that night with the Heinkel, and later when its crew of four men were drowning or suffering the agonies of exposure, Goering was dining with his commanders in Berlin, preparing the final orders for his *Luftwaffe's* next conquest – Denmark and Norway.

At 5.00 a.m. on 9 April German naval and land forces, with the *Luftwaffe* in support, had begun to invade those two neutral countries.

The next day four more of Goering's airmen would perish in the sea after a skirmish with 43 Squadron. The weather that afternoon was too lovely for dying. For the sea placidly reflected the sky's rich blue. Led by our squadron commander George Lott, we were a formation of seven, as we flew out to sea toward the island of Ronaldshay. 'Tally ho!' I think we all bellowed at once: a lone Heinkel was dodging among the clouds just ahead. With seven of us lining up for a crack at that pitiful target the attack was a shambles. As I came in I could see the tail unit was already wobbling and the engines streaming vapour. I turned aside and as the Heinkel glided down I flew in very close alongside it. Caesar Hull stationed himself on the other side. The rear cockpit bore the signs of a charnel

A Heinkel 111 bomber explodes in mid-air, its petrol tanks pierced by incendiary bullets.
More usually aircraft went down streaming oil and coolant liquid from their engines.
Occasionally they disintegrated under the stress of a headlong dive.

Marshal of the Royal Air Force
Lord Trenchard inspecting a
RAF unit. Trenchard (nick-
named 'Boom'), the veritable
'Father of the RAF' – a title he
disliked – fought for its survival
in the early twenties.

Air Chief Marshal Sir Hugh
Dowding, known affectionately
as 'Stuffy'. Dowding's 'Security
of the base' strategy was opposed
to Trenchard's 'Attack is the best
defence'. Dowding, appointed
first C-in-C Fighter Command
in 1936, was the architect of
victory in the Battle of Britain,
but his foresight and obstinacy
led him into conflict with the
Air Ministry.

Adolf Hitler and his senior air commanders. From left to right: Erhard Milch (Secretary of State for Air, in 1940 Inspector-General *Luftwaffe*); Hugo Sperrle (general commanding *Luftflotte* 3 during the Battle); the Fuehrer and Supreme Commander Armed Forces (*Wehrmacht*); Hermann Goering (Air Minister and C-in-C *Luftwaffe*); Albert Kesselring (general commanding *Luftflotte* 2 during the battle).

Luftwaffe C-in-C Goering with his *Luftzeugmeister* (Director of Equipment) Ernst Udet. Udet, a brilliant stunt flyer and commercial pilot, was popular with the RAF between the wars. He later committed suicide.

The Heinkel 111 bomber of K926, piloted by *Unterofficezer* Wilms, which was shot down on 3 February 1940 by Peter Townsend and his Blue section, 43 Squadron, near Whitby, Yorkshire. It was the first enemy aircraft to fall on English soil since 1918.

Karl Missy, the radio-operator (*opposite*), though badly wounded, remained at the upper dorsal machine-gun which is seen pointing skyward. Bullet holes from British fighters are visible in the fuselage and tail.

Peter Townsend with his rigger Duxbury (*left*) and fitter Hacking (*right*) with 43 Squadron at Wick, Scotland, in Spring 1940. 43's role was the protection of Scapa Flow naval base.

General Hans von Seeckt talking to (*left*) General von Blomberg. Von Seeckt, member of the German peace delegation at Versailles in 1919, became chief of the 100,000-man army, the *Reichswehr*. It was to him that German military aviation owed its survival during the post–World War I years, when it was officially prohibited by the Versailles Treaty.

Young trainee pilots of the *Deutsche Verkehrsflieger Schule* (German Commercial Pilots' School) in 1928. Many pilots of the DVS, while ostensibly being trained as airline pilots, were transferred to the 'Black' (secret) *Luftwaffe*, so-called before its existence was officially announced in March 1935.

The town of Lipezk, on the banks of the River Voronezh, south of Moscow, favoured by Peter the Great as a watering-place. The Germans had a secret military air-base there from 1924 to 1933.

General Werner Junck (*right*) with his flight engineer (*second from left*) at Lipezk, where he was chief instructor. Both wear civilian clothes. Junck became *Jafu* 3 (Fighter Leader, *Luftflotte* 3) in the Battle of Britain.

"Get me Messerschmitt 109."

An aspect of the Battle, as seen by Pont (*Punch*), 21 August 1940. That day, a week after Eagle Day, Goering was visiting *Luftwaffe* fighter units in the Pas de Calais.

A Heinkel 111 bomber over the famous U-bend in the Thames, the heart of London's dockland, and a landmark known to every *Luftwaffe* bomber crew.

house with the gunner slumped inside it mutilated beyond recognition. His fair hair streaming in the slipstream which rushed through his shattered windscreen, the young pilot bent over the controls trying to urge his stricken machine to fly. Through the window panels the two other members of the crew regarded me in silent despair. I pushed back my hood and signalled them to turn toward the coast. Those men were no longer enemies but airmen in distress. If only we could have borne up their doomed aircraft with our own wings. But there was nothing we could do to help. I knew I was watching the last moments of three brave men as they went down to perish in the sea. I watched the Heinkel until, unable to fly any more, it alighted awkwardly on the sea. The fuselage broke in half. One wing tipped crazily in the air then slithered under the surface. As I circled low overhead I could see the three men in yellow life-saving jackets struggling free and beginning to swim. Like some of the others I called base to fix our position and ask for help. We were some twenty miles from the coast. The three Germans would be dead long before help could reach them.

The sea had claimed more victims. Before long I should nearly become one myself.

Soon after dawn on 10 May the German Ambassador at The Hague, Count Julius von Zech-Burkersroda, called at the Foreign Ministry with a note announcing that German troops were entering the country to protect its neutrality against a threat from the Franco-British armies – despite what Hitler himself had admitted, that the allies would never violate Dutch or Belgian neutrality. Twenty-six years earlier Burkersroda's illustrious father-in-law, Chancellor Bethmann Hollweg, had called the German guarantee of Belgian neutrality 'a mere scrap of paper'.

At Brussels, the Belgian Foreign Minister, Paul Henri Spaak, faced the German Ambassador squarely as the latter entered his office bearing a similar note. Spaak cut the German short. 'Forgive me, but I wish to speak first. The German army has just attacked our country. It is the second time in twenty-five years that Germany has committed a criminal aggression against a neutral Belgium . . . What has just happened is even more odious . . . than in 1914. No ultimatum, no note, no protest has ever been laid before the Belgian Government. It is through the attack itself that Belgium has learnt that Germany has violated her promises . . .'

But in Hitler's own words a 'breach of the neutrality of Belgium and

H

France is meaningless . . . No one will question that when we have won.'

Winning – that is, carrying out their declared threat to crush all resistance – would take the Germans only a few days. Their opponents would soon surrender. As the German Ambassadors were delivering their notes in The Hague and Brussels the *Luftwaffe*'s bombs could be heard crashing down on nearby airfields. Since dawn the German army had been pushing forward on a 175-mile front and *Luftwaffe* bombers had swept down on seventy allied airfields.

Their tasks were threefold: to destroy the enemy air forces, to support the army, and to attack ports and shipping. The *Luftflotten* used (No. 2 under Kesselring and No. 3 under Sperrle) included 1,400 bombers and dive-bombers, and 1,260 short- and long-range fighters.

On 10 May the Franco-British air forces in France were pitifully inadequate against this mighty host: twenty-five RAF squadrons totalling four hundred aircraft. Six were Hurricane fighter squadrons and eight 'Battle' light bombers – which with tragic swiftness would prove their reputation as 'flying coffins'. The rest were Blenheim medium bombers and Lysander Army co-operation aircraft.

On the critical part of the front the French *Armeé de l'Air* in General Augereau's northern air zone were more numerous on paper but even less battleworthy than the RAF: their 275 day fighters, Morane 406s and Curtiss fighters were no match for the Me. 109s. Nor was their paltry force of fifteen day bombers and fifty-five night bombers likely to make much impression on the enemy. Not even the supreme and selfless gallantry displayed by the allied airmen could make up for such mediocre equipment and meagre numbers.

Recently transferred to 501 Squadron at Tangmere Gus Holden got to bed at his club at 3.00 a.m. on 10 May after dancing all night at the Dorchester in London. At 8.00 o'clock the valet brought him tea. 'Bad news, sir,' he said, 'the Germans have walked into France.' After a break-neck drive back to Tangmere at 11.30, Gus was greeted by his squadron commander: 'We take off at one o'clock sharp for France.' The six Hurricane squadrons in France had been laying into *Luftwaffe* bombers since first light. One of them was 85, the squadron which in 1918 Billy Bishop had led to join forces with 43 at Bertangles. It was the squadron for which 'Bish' and Mick Mannock and the 'War Birds' (Callahan, Mac Grider, and Elliot White Springs) had won such a great name with their desperate combats against the German *Jastas*. Two decades had passed and now the young generation of 85 Squadron was as furiously at grips with the German flyers as its forebears had ever been.

85 Squadron's most brilliant pilot was Dicky Lee, in 1918 a two-year-old already with a claim to fame: he was godson of the great Boom Trenchard. Dicky began to make a name of his own. 85 flew forward to meet the German bombers over Belgium and Holland. All day Dicky was in the thick of the fighting. Wounded, he got back safely. The next day he would be back in the fight.

That day the job of *Hauptmann* Werner Streib (of I ZG 1) was, with his *Schwarme* of four Me. 110s, to escort eight Ju. 52s packed with airborne troops to Waalhaven airfield near Rotterdam. One of the Ju. 52s would carry General Kurt Student, chief of the German airborne troops. Before take-off, Streib asked Student, 'Tell me, Herr General, which is your aircraft? I want to make sure you get the best protection.' 'Never mind,' replied Student, 'your job is to look after them all.' They left their base (Gütersloh) at 7.30 a.m. and were due over Waalhaven at 10.00 a.m.

At Manston, Kent, B Flight 600 Squadron had been briefed soon after dawn. German parachutists and airborne troops had taken Waalhaven. B Flight 600 were to patrol Waalhaven, engage enemy aircraft, and shoot up the airfield. Led by the CO, Squadron Leader Jimmy Wells, the six Blenheims were soon off on their hazardous mission. Twin-engined two-seater Blenheims, with a top speed of 260 m.p.h. and a modest armament of five machine-guns firing forward and one aft, would be easy prey for German Fighters.

Flying Officer Norman Hayes flew No. 2, on the CO's right. As they approached Rotterdam he saw 'great columns of smoke from fires burning in the city.' Then the CO moved the flight into line astern and dived to attack. 'I shot up a Ju. 52 standing on the airfield and as I climbed away to the right . . . I saw . . . Me. 110s about 800 feet above and just peeling off onto our tails,' said Norman.

The leader of those Me. 110s was *Hauptmann* Werner Streib. He got onto the tail of a Blenheim which tried in vain to outmanoeuvre the Me. 110. Then it dived for the ground. Once again in vain. Against the Me. 110's murderous fire its rear gunner with his single machine-gun had no chance. Streib sent the Blenheim crashing into the ground.

Meanwhile, Norman Hayes was having a strenuous time. No sooner had he shaken off an Me. 110 from his tail than he turned to attack a Ju. 52. Another Blenheim (Hugh Rowe's) got in ahead, but was pounced on by a Me. 110 and shot down. Norman closed with the Ju. 52, setting its port engine on fire. At that moment a Me. 110 attacked from behind, holing the Blenheim's starboard tank. Petrol gushed into the cockpit and with his gunner (Corporal Holmes) shouting directions, he avoided the Me. 110 and dived for the ground. It was high time to go home. A few minutes later he realized to his consternation that he was flying straight towards Germany. Turning back over Rotterdam again he spotted three Heinkels below and immediately dived to attack. Discretion then got the better of Norman's valour and he sped off westwards. His was the only Blenheim of B Flight 600 to return to Manston.

The Commander of the British air forces in France, Air Marshal Arthur ('Ugly') Barratt, had waited all morning for orders from *Généralissime* Gamelin to unleash his bombers against the advancing German columns. And with what pathetic hope! Disaster awaited them when at midday, with still no word from Gamelin (who with Vuillemin wanted to avoid a 'bombing war'), Barratt sent his Battle squadrons in to attack. One of them was No. 12, the 'Dirty Dozen'.

One of its pilots, Flying Officer Bill Simpson, approached a German column at tree-top level. Then the *Flak* ripped a hole in his engine. He staggered on, dropped his bombs, noting despite his own predicament that they fell 'on helpless mules as well as men' – and with flames and molten metal streaking past the cockpit he crash-landed a few moments later in the Ardennes. The aircraft immediately exploded and before he could undo his straps sheets of flame rushed up at him. 'In the first rush of flame my hands and legs were burnt to stiff sticks . . . enveloped in white heat; paralysed by flame and fear . . . I waited for death.'

Still burning, Bill was dragged clear by his observer (Flight Sergeant Odell) and his gunner (Corporal Tomlinson). He looked at his hands, 'the hands of a spectre – bloodless, impossibly white . . . the fingers curled into a desperate gesture . . . tapered like the claws of a bird.' His was one of many vain sacrifices made by the RAF bombers. Of the thirty-two Battles that attacked, thirteen were lost and the rest damaged. And the field-grey columns kept surging forward.

All that day Joachim Poetter's unit (the *Eidelweiss geschwader*, KG 51) now equipped with Heinkel 111s, kept up a non-stop attack on allied airfields. Joachim bombed Lyon-Bron airfield but some of the bombs got hung up. At that moment a Morane 406 attacked, hitting Joachim in the arm and stopping one of the Heinkel's engines. In great pain he flew it back on the other.

Joachim's adventure was hardly noticed beside the catastrophe which befell *Oberleutnant* S – his name is never mentioned in connection with it. At 2.23 p.m. S took off from Landsberg, near Munich, leading a *Kette* of three Heinkels in the 8th *Staffel*. Target Dijon-Longvic. S's *Kette* became separated from the other two in cloud so he had to go on with it alone. He saw an airfield he took to be Dole-Tavaux. The *Kette* bombed.

At that moment (3.40 p.m.) the *Flugwache* (Air Guard) at the German town of Freiburg, near Baden, saw 'three aircraft . . . clearly recognized as Heinkel 111 P, cross (German national markings) clearly seen through binoculars.' At 3.59 p.m. it was reported, 'Airport Freiburg bombed . . . two aircraft sighted with German national markings . . .' These and other details were contained in a report dated 10 May from the Officer Commanding *Luftgau* VII. *Oberleutnant* S and his *Kette* had brought tragedy to the peaceful town of Freiburg. Fifty-seven civilians including several children, were killed by their bombs – sixty-nine in all, of which twenty-four were duds. So there was no problem in identifying their German origin.

When Goering read the *Luftgau* VII report that evening he was beside himself. His *Luftwaffe* bombing an open German town – and on the first day of the Western offensive! 'That's a fine way to start the campaign,' he raged. 'The *Luftwaffe* and myself look quite ridiculous – how can we account for it to the German public?'

That was left to Goebbels. First he accused the French, then shifted the blame to the British. 'In reprisal . . . the German air force will reply in the same manner . . . every further attack will be paid back five-fold on English or French towns.'

So the British were made the culprits, and the blame would stick to them for years afterward. When the *Kommodore* of KG 51 (*Oberst* Josef Kammhuber) read the accusation against the British in the newspapers next morning he suspected a propaganda trick. But his pilots all believed it was the British. Even when the secret enquiry confirmed that *Oberleutnant* S. was responsible there was no court martial – it would not do for the truth to get out, for the Freiburg incident would soon serve Hitler as an alibi for bombing allied towns.

Oberleutnant S. would have to go on living with the dreadful facts – but not for long . . .

Gus Holden still had a bit of a hangover when, with the rest of 501 Squadron, he landed in the early afternoon at 'an obscure field', Bethnivielle, near Reims. Almost immediately disaster struck 501. The Bombay transport aircraft bringing reserve pilots, ground crews, and baggage crashed, killing nearly everyone.

At 4.00 p.m. Gus was sent off to reconnoitre near Sedan where the German forces were concentrating. For some minutes he gazed down on the smoke of battle below, keeping an eye out for 'any unfriendly person' behind. Suddenly a whole *Staffel* of Me. 109s was on his tail. That cured Gus's hangover. He whipped over on his back and dived vertically at full throttle, not daring to look at the A.S.I.* Skimming the tree-tops, 'the whole pack were still after me with the leader pushing out shells in my direction'. But Gus made it back to Bethnivielle. The day which had begun with morning tea in his London club had ended with him a much wiser young man.

All day in London a Government crisis raged. 'Perhaps the darkest day in English history,' wrote Chips Channon. Harold Balfour had telephoned first thing to tell him about the German invasion. 'Another of Hitler's brilliantly conceived coups,' wrote Channon, '. . . England is politically divided, and the ruling caste riddled with dissension and anger.'

The future of the Premiership lay between Chamberlain, Halifax, and Churchill. But the Labour Party refused to serve in a coalition under Chamberlain. Halifax, 'the Pope', firmly refused to be Premier. When Mr R.A.Butler called on him for a last attempt to persuade him he was out at the dentist's. Did England's destiny hang on this visit to the dentist? It is not impossible, but soon afterwards the die was cast. The King would receive the Prime Minister at 6.00 p.m.

Chips Channon 'sat numb with misery and mused on that fantastic day . . .' on his drive along the Strand with Harold Balfour, where they had seen placards, 'Paris raided' – 'Brussels bombed' – 'Lille bombed' – 'many killed in Lyon'. (Had Joachim Poetter's bombs gone astray while the Morane attacked?')

Channon had tea with Mr Van Kleffens, 'a tall thin youngish man with a nose rivalling Cyrano's.' Van Kleffens's seaplane had finally landed off Brighton, where he was taken for a German and promptly arrested.

Just after 6.30 p.m. news came through that Winston Churchill had kissed hands with the King. At the moment Churchill took the destiny of the British people in his hands, Hitler's armies were advancing to invade Europe – and perhaps Britain.

* Air Speed Indicator.

Chapter 18

All through 11 May the *Luftwaffe* kept up a ferocious assault on allied air-fields. The 4th *Staffel KG* 2 were briefed to attack Vaux, near Sissonne la Malmaison, No. 114 Bomber Squadron's base not far from Reims.

Werner Borner was there in *Gustav Marie*, one of the nine Dornier 17s which *Oberleutnant* Reimers was now leading straight at the Maginot Line, hedge-hopping to avoid detection. They skipped over the defences and were gone before the French gunners could fire.

Not long after dawn the Blenheims of 114 Squadron taxied out for their first operation of the day, a mission they would never accomplish. As they waited, lined up for take off, Reimers and his 4th *Staffel* swept low across the airfield raining down fifty-kilo bombs on the concentration of Blenheims. Werner Borner watched the havoc spreading as the percussion of the Dorniers' bombs touched off the bombs in the Blenheims. The attack over, Borner coldly took his 8 mm. cine camera and while *Gustav Marie* circled he filmed the columns of black smoke and flame which rose from the wreckage of what a few minutes ago had been an entire proud bomber squadron.

But Reimers's devastating success nearly cost the lives of his crew and himself when they ran into AA fire. With a terrible wound in the leg Reimers was pulled from the pilot's seat by his observer, *Ober Feldwebel* Kruger, who took the controls. Kruger had never flown before but shepherded by *Gustav Marie* he got his Dornier back to Frankfurt and landed like a professional.

The *Flak* got Dicky Lee too. Like every other Hurricane Squadron, 85 fought back all day against the *Luftwaffe* bombers. Dicky Lee brought down two in the morning, was then hit by ground-fire and crash-landed in a field near some tanks. A peasant said they were Belgian, but Dicky soon found out he was mistaken. He was promptly made prisoner by the

Germans, but they were mistaken too about Dicky, who was wearing an overcoat. Taking him for a refugee they locked him into a barn. He then climbed up to a window and looked out. Under his nose was a ladder. The next day Dicky Lee was on patrol with 85 Squadron.

On 12 May the invader's grip on Holland tightened. Elsewhere the German invasion thrusts were concentrated at Maastricht and, through the Ardennes, near Dinant and at Sedan. 12 May: the date coincides with the squadron in a selfless and poignant act of youthful heroism. No. 12 Squadron was asked for volunteers to destroy the two vital bridges near Maastricht, keys to the Albert Canal defence line. The six crews next for duty at once agreed to go – to almost certain destruction. Finally, five Battles took off.

They were to fly in two sections. The leaders, Flying Officers Garland and Thomas, had a 'heated discussion' at the last moment about the approach – high dive? or low level? 'It will be interesting to see the result, and may we both be lucky enough to return,' was Thomas's parting shot. He did return – after five years in prison. But Garland, a boy of twenty-one, was killed with his crew, Sergeant Grey and Leading Aircraftsman Reynolds.

For their valour Garland and Grey were each awarded a posthumous Victoria Cross. But no award went to Reynolds, who had as willingly as they accepted the risk of almost certain death. What a gross mockery of their noble deed to discriminate between the sacrifices of these three young heroes. Was it a question of rank or the scarcity of VCs? Not that either mattered in the world where they had gone – any more than they do in this one, where most saints and heroes go unsung.

None of those five Battles returned to base, although one crew got back on foot. Of the original British bomber force of 135 aircraft that evening only seventy-two remained.

Losses among the six squadron fighter force (ninety-six Hurricanes) had been heavy too. But loyal to a promise given to the French, Fighter Command dispatched four more of its squadrons (64 aircraft) to France by 12 May, making the fighter force ten squadrons. Thirty-two more Hurricanes reached France on 13 May. Twelve squadrons had now been drawn off from the Home Defence fighter force through the 'tap' through which C-in-C Dowding had always feared 'will run the entire Hurricane output'. And even now, that tap was not yet fully open.

On 13 May General von Kleist's armies forced a crossing of the Meuse at Houx, near Dinant, and at Sedan. Before them went wave after wave of *Stukas* in a terrible, pulverizing assault of the French defences. Twice that day Rudolf Braun took off with I *St. G* 3 from their advance base at Dockendorff. 'There seemed to be swarms of Me. 109s everywhere and this was comforting,' he said. Not a single enemy fighter, French or British, was to be seen.

I *St. G* 3's tasks were to attack French troop concentrations and destroy the Meuse bridges, thus blocking a possible French counter-attack. Rudolf Braun's Ju. 87 was one of two hundred which hurtled down nearly vertically, sirens screaming, to launch its bombs into the carnage and wreckage below. They paralysed, petrified, the French defences. After all he had seen Rudolf was convinced the French army would fold up in face of the speed, fury, and clockwork organization of the German advance – infantry, tanks, and *Stukas*, irresistibly smashing down every-thing in their path. The *Stukas* (Rudolf Braun with them) would pound and pursue the allied armies in a turning movement from the Meuse to the English Channel.

With disaster now staring them in the face the French High Command called on their own and the British bomber forces to make a supreme effort on 14 May against the German bridgehead at Sedan – the name was a portent of disaster to every Frenchman. Soon after noon the few re-maining French bombers went in. Their losses were so terrible that further attacks were cancelled.

Between 3.00 p.m. and 4.00 p.m. all that was left – seventy-one aircraft – of the RAF bomber force followed undaunted into the holocaust. They were virtually annihilated. Forty were shot down and many of the remainder damaged. Never again during the war would the RAF suffer a more terrible rate of loss. Their sacrifice was in vain, however. Two hours after the RAF's suicidal effort at Sedan, the Germans were off again on their race to the Channel coast.

Meanwhile a demand had come for more British fighters – from the French Premier himself, Paul Reynaud. 'If we are to win this battle, which might be decisive for the whole war, it is necessary to send at once ... ten more squadrons.' Ten more! The 'Hurricane drain' had already whittled down Dowding's Home Defence fighter force to thirty-six squadrons. Ten more sent to France would leave him with twenty-six – exactly half the fighter force of fifty-two squadrons fixed by the Air Ministry as a minimum for Home Defence.

That day a grim catastrophe would make a strong Home Defence fighter force an absolute necessity. As the first wave of RAF bombers bore down on the Sedan bridgehead, fifty-seven Heinkel III's were ravaging the centre of Rotterdam. Both Hitler and Goering had given very precise orders for a mass attack on Rotterdam – 'Fortress Holland' was proving a tougher nut to crack than expected. 'This resistance must be broken quickly,' Hitler ordered in Directive No. 11. And *Luftwaffe* reinforcements were brought in 'to hasten the rapid conquest of Fortress Holland'.

General Albert Kesselring ordered the attack. But now, at that very moment when a force of forty-three Heinkels and another of fifty-seven (both of KG 54) were approaching the city, surrender negotiations were in progress. Leading the two bomber *Gruppen*, *Obersten* Hohne and Lackner and their *Staffel Kapitän* had marked the target with a triangle on their maps – a small defended area in the heart of the old city. They had been warned: Red Very lights from the ground means 'attack cancelled'.

'The tension was appalling. Would Rotterdam surrender in time?' wrote the German Colonel von Scholtitz, who four years later was to surrender Paris to its rightful owners. Hohne saw the signal at the last second and warned his *Gruppe* not to bomb. But in the smoke and haze Lackner failed to see the red flares. His Heinkels released their bombs, ninety-seven tons of high explosive. In those few seconds the heart of the old city of Rotterdam and in it over eight hundred people (mostly civilians) were wiped out. At 5.00 p.m. the Dutch commandant, Colonel Scharroo, surrendered.

Through a cruel error Rotterdam had suffered the fate of Warsaw. The German air and army authorities concerned had made desperate efforts to avert the catastrophe. Not because they felt any more tenderness for the citizens of Rotterdam than for the Dutch soldiers who were daring to resist, but because surrender negotiations were in progress.

The Germans reasoned that the target was a defended area. Defended by civilians? Most of the casualties were civilians as they were at Guernica and at Warsaw. Twenty-five years earlier when they started bombing London the Germans had invented total air war. Since then they had vastly improved their technique, but the principle had not changed: civilian lives and property must suffer the consequences. Over a decade ago Trenchard had warned, 'There can be no question ... that this form of warfare will be used ... I would therefore urge ... that we accept this fact and face it.'

And what about Freiburg, an open town where the *Luftwaffe* had accidentally killed civilians four days earlier? Dr Goebbels had told the world that the RAF were responsible for the 'Freiburg massacre'. This was a handy alibi which Hitler was keeping up his sleeve.

For Winston Churchill 15 May began dramatically. At 7.30 a.m. (half an hour before he was usually called) the telephone at his bedside roused him from a deep sleep. His voice trembling with emotion Paul Reynaud, the French Prime Minister, was speaking in English. 'We have been defeated,' he began. Churchill did not respond. 'We are beaten,' insisted Reynaud, 'we have lost the battle. The front is broken near Sedan . . . they are pouring through in great numbers with tanks and armoured cars.'

In vain Churchill tried to reassure the unhappy Reynaud, who only kept repeating, 'we are defeated, we have lost the battle'. Finally Churchill said, 'All right, I will come over to Paris and talk to you.'

The War Cabinet met several times a day. Apart from Churchill, the Prime Minister and Minister of Defence, there were four other Ministers: Neville Chamberlain, who was already a sick man; Clement Attlee, the Deputy Prime Minister, timorous in appearance but a 'colleague of war experience long versed in the House of Commons'; the Foreign Minister, Lord Halifax; and the white-haired and bespectacled Arthur Greenwood, Minister without Portfolio, 'a wise counseller of high courage and a good and helpful friend'. These five, Churchill observed wryly, 'were the only ones who had the right to have their heads cut off on Tower Hill if we did not win'. Subject to the support of the War Cabinet and Commons, Churchill directed the war personally.

At the War Cabinet's first meeting on 15 May Churchill reported his conversation with Reynaud. The burning question was how many more fighter squadrons could be thrown into the battle of France without leaving England defenceless and incapable of continuing the war? Already the British air forces in France had lost 206 of their original 474 planes of all types. But both military arguments and 'historical reasons' tempted Churchill to cede to Reynaud's incessant appeals for help. However there was a limit which 'if transgressed would cost us our life'.

Churchill apparently misunderstood what the limit was – the Air Ministry figure was fifty-two fighter squadrons for the defence of Britain. Incredibly, Churchill had got it into his head the figure was twenty-five.

The *Luftwaffe*'s attack on Rotterdam the previous day was also discussed. Both Hitler and the allies had up to then been careful not to provoke a general bombing war on one another. But with no fear of retaliation (as at Warsaw and now at Rotterdam) the Germans had not hesitated to bomb targets in residential areas, killing civilians by hundreds. The War Cabinet now resolved to retaliate against the Germans. They authorized Bomber Command to attack the Ruhr that night – a decision of defiance and sacrifice: London and every other British city would henceforth be at the mercy of the *Luftwaffe*. The utmost strength and vigilance on the part of Dowding's Fighter Command was now vital.

The instructions Dowding had received – to be ready to send ten more fighter squadrons into France – incensed him so much that he dispatched a note to the Air Minister, Sinclair, asking to put his case before the War Cabinet. 'It was a very unusual request and I was very much surprised when permission was granted,' he said later.

The War Cabinet met for the fourth time that evening. Dowding was present as were some thirty others, ministers and chiefs of staff. Churchill presided; his face wore a permanent scowl but Dowding did not feel in the least deterred. Beaverbrook was there – the Minister of Aircraft Production, 'the little nut-brown man', and a good friend of Dowding's. And for the RAF – the new Air Minister, Archibald Sinclair, with his high wing collar and bow tie, and the Chief of Air Staff, Cyril Newall, moustached and pink-faced, his mild eyes showing the strain which one day would blind him. Less prominent, but keenly alive to the dramatic importance of the occasion, was Group Captain 'Bill' Elliot of the Cabinet Secretariat. He felt that the atmosphere was tense and one of the most highly charged he had ever known.

Dowding was seated on the same side of the table as the Prime Minister, about six places to his right. He was invited to state his case, and for five or ten minutes he did so 'as elegantly as possible'. From the outset it seemed that the majority of his listeners were hostile to his view. Churchill 'sat there with a face like a boot. He just didn't register at all.' Or perhaps he resented the fact that a RAF officer (even if senior) was contradicting him. The Air Minister, Sinclair, merely acquiescing with all that Churchill said gave Dowding no support. As for Cyril Newall, whom Churchill had just ticked off for no reason at all, he only sulked and took no notice.

Suddenly Dowding got up and drew from his pocket a piece of paper on which he had hastily sketched a graph in red ink showing the curve of Hurricane losses during the last few days. Beaverbrook, seeing him rise, thought (he recalled the fact later): 'He's going to resign!' But Dowding, going straight up to Churchill, put the graph in front of him. 'I think some of the people thought I was going to shoot him. I felt like it,' Dowding later commented. To the Prime Minister he said: 'This red line shows the wastage of Hurricanes in the last ten days. If the line goes on at the same rate for the next ten days there won't be a single Hurricane left either in France or in England.' 'That did the trick,' Dowding explained, 'because he never uttered another word.' Group Captain Elliot remembered later, 'He had put his case so ably and spoken with such sincerity that there was no room left for further discussion.'

But Dowding had no promise from Churchill. 'Even if I had I would have regarded it with doubt, considering the influences to which the Prime Minister was subjected.' But he thought that his 'absolutely crashing argument' must have 'sunk in very deeply'.

Dowding returned that night to Montrose, his home in Stanmore where his sister Hilda was waiting for him. Miss Dowding was two years his senior and ran her widowed brother's house. He felt worn out after that tense and vital meeting. Despite the fact that he had made his point with the War Cabinet, and above all the Prime Minister, he could not rid himself of the terrible fear that they might go back on their decision. He decided to put his case in black and white. 'I knew that if this wastage, this great flood of Hurricane exports to France, was not checked it would mean the loss of the war.' And so, 'in a mood of desperation', he wrote to the Under Secretary of State for Air:

Sir,

I have the honour to refer to the very serious calls which have recently been made upon the Home Defence Fighter Units in an attempt to stem the German invasion on the Continent.

2. I hope and believe that our Armies may yet be victorious in France and Belgium, but we have to face the possibility that they may be defeated.

3. In this case I presume that there is no one who will deny that England should fight on, even though the remainder of the Continent of Europe is dominated by the Germans.

4. For this purpose it is necessary to retain some minimum fighter strength in this country and I must request that the Air Council will inform me what they consider this minimum strength to be . . .

5. I would remind the Air Council that the last estimate which they made as to the force necessary to defend this country was fifty-two squadrons, and my strength has now been reduced to the equivalent of thirty-six squadrons.

6. Once a decision has been reached as to the limit on which the Air Council and the Cabinet are prepared to stake the existence of the country, it should be made clear to the Allied commanders on the Continent that not a single aeroplane from Fighter Command beyond

the limit will be sent across the Channel, no matter how desperate the situation may become.

7. It will, of course, be remembered that the estimate of fifty-two squadrons was based on the assumption that the attack would come from the eastwards... We have now to face the possibility that attacks may come from Spain or even from the north coast of France. The result is that our line is very much extended at the same time as our reserves are reduced.

8. I must point out that within the last few days the equivalent of ten squadrons have been sent to France, that the Hurricane squadrons remaining in this country are seriously depleted...

9. I must therefore request that as a matter of paramount urgency the Air Ministry will consider and decide what level of strength is to be left to the Fighter Command for the defences of this country, and will assure me that when this level had been reached, not one fighter will be sent across the Channel...

10. I believe that if an adequate fighter force is kept in this country, if the Fleet remains in being, and if Home Forces are suitably organized to resist invasion, we should be able to carry on the war single-handed for some time, if not indefinitely. But, if the Home Defence Force is drained away in desperate attempts to remedy the situation in France, defeat in France will involve the final, complete and irremediable defeat of this country.

> I have the honour to be
> Sir,
> Your Obedient Servant,
> (signed) H.C.T.Dowding,
> Air Chief Marshal.

Dowding remembered the decision not to make him Chief of Air Staff and thought how fortunate, after all, this decision really was. He had to ask for a personal hearing at the War Cabinet to prevent the dissipation of the Home Defence Squadrons in a vain attempt to bolster up the defeated armies in France ... A few days earlier and he would have been unable to convince the Prime Minister of the seriousness of the position; a few days later and the damage would have been irrevocable. As Chief of Air Staff he would have been prematurely committed to battle on this issue. He would have been saying what *would happen* and not what *was happening*. He would have failed in his efforts and it is more than doubtful that he could ever have kept his fighter force intact for the battle which was sure to come.

But as Dowding wrote on the morning of 16 May, the War Cabinet were meeting. Their decision was to send four more Hurricane squadrons to France immediately. Dowding's worst fears were justified. There now remained only twenty-two modern single-seater fighter squadrons (a total of some 250 aircraft) plus nine squadrons with obsolete planes with which to defend Britain – instead of the prescribed fifty-two squadrons. Churchill, with his great love for France, was putting his own country in terrible jeopardy.

At 3.00 p.m. that afternoon, as he left Northolt airfield near London in a De Havilland Flamingo, the British Prime Minister was still under the impression that the number of fighter squadrons needed to defend Britain was twenty-five and not fifty-two. Later he wrote: 'Air Chief Marshal Dowding ... had declared to me that with twenty-five squadrons of fighters he could defend the island against the whole might of the German Air Force. My colleagues and I were resolved to run all risks for the battle [in France] up to that limit – and those risks were very great – but not to go beyond it, no matter what the consequences might be.'

In spirit Churchill was every inch in support of Dowding, but for some inexplicable reason he had got the figures the wrong way round – twenty-five instead of fifty-two. It was all the more inexplicable in view of his statement, 'My colleagues and I were resolved to run all risks ... up to that limit ...' The Air Minister and the Chief of Air Staff were both colleagues. It was the CAS, Newall, whose bold move in October 1939 had laid the foundations of this force of fifty-two squadrons. He would never have let Churchill believe that twenty-five squadrons was the maximum.

Dowding was shocked at Churchill's allegation that it was he who had given the wrong figure: 'How could Churchill have made such an incredible mistake? ... I had just been waging a desperate battle in the Cabinet to be allowed to retain ... thirty-six squadrons against the fifty-two squadrons which was the Air Staff estimate of my requirement. Is it reasonable to suppose that I then told Mr Churchill that twenty-five would suffice? ...'

Churchill arrived at the Quai d'Orsay at 5.30 p.m. There he met Paul Reynaud, Minister of National Defence, Daladier and General Gamelin, *Généralissime* of the French Army. Gamelin spent five minutes explaining how the German armour and infantry had overcome the French Army and were driving west with lightning speed. Churchill then asked, breaking into French ('Which I do indifferently, in every sense of the word'), '*Où est la masse de manoeuvre?*' ('Where is your strategic reserve?') '*Il n'y en a plus*' ('I've no longer got one') replied Gamelin with a shrug. Churchill was dumbfounded. Gamelin had just given him one of the greatest surprises of his life.

Gamelin lamented the French inferiority in the air and pleaded for more RAF squadrons, above all fighter squadrons. Among other things, these were needed, he said, to stop enemy tanks. (The *Généralissime* must have been out of his senses. How could fighters with rifle-calibre machine-guns stop tanks?) Churchill reminded him that the fighters' business was to 'cleanse the skies' above the battle.

The existence of Britain, Churchill knew, turned on an adequate fighter defence. Still obsessed with the figure of twenty-five squadrons being the minimum required he decided to 'cut to the bone'. Ignoring Dowding's warning, the War Cabinet had sent four to France that very morning. Churchill was now to ask his colleagues in London for six more, to make up the ten originally requested by Reynaud. In his view this was the final limit. In reality it would have made certain the defeat of Fighter Command before the Battle of Britain ever began.

In the gardens of the Quai d'Orsay bonfires were blazing and Churchill noticed that 'venerable officials were pushing wheelbarrows of archives onto them'. Gamelin had warned that the fall of Paris was imminent.

Churchill and his Chief of Staff, General Ismay, returned to the British Embassy. At 9.00 p.m. Ismay telegraphed – in Hindustani – to the War Cabinet from the Prime Minister: 'I personally feel that we should send squadrons of fighters demanded (i.e. six more) tomorrow and . . . give the last chance to the French army to rally its bravery and strength.'

At 11.30 p.m. came the War Cabinet's reply – again in Hindustani – which General Ismay translated. Churchill took this reply for an unequivocal 'Yes'. But in fact this was not so.

Meeting late that night the Cabinet were all but won over by Churchill's request. But Newall, whom Dowding took for an 'enemy', barred their way. He had been in touch with Air Marshal 'Ugly' Barratt, commanding the RAF in France, to learn that available French airfields could accommodate only three more RAF squadrons. He had also received Dowding's letter and been so moved by it that he was now determined more than ever to fight for him against the War Cabinet's reckless squandering of RAF fighters. Newall had the intelligent idea of sending three Hurricane squadrons to France in the morning and another three to relieve them in the afternoon. This would bring six squadrons into action, yet avoid their being swallowed up in the imminent debacle in France.

At Wick, Scotland, I had received orders to take command of 85 Squadron in France. That 16 May I led B Flight 43 Squadron for the last time on a defensive patrol. We headed out low over the rocky cliffs near John o'Groats and then soared up above the menacing, tumultuous sea which had claimed indifferently both our own and the enemy's airmen.

Things in France were now going from bad to worse. Rumours had even reached us that 85's two preceding commanding officers had been shot down on consecutive days. I was to be next in succession for the post.

Capitaine Aviateur Paul Stehlin reported on 16 May at Chissey in the Jura as second in command of the III/C Fighter Group. He had called at the Air Ministry in Paris on 13 May and spoken to the new Minister, Laurent-Eyrac. All that he had so closely observed (thanks to his intimate friendship with Goering) of the *Luftwaffe* during those four years in Berlin, all the warnings he had flashed back to the Ministry, warnings which had been largely ignored, were now before them in stark catastrophic reality.

The Air Minister listened, but nothing that Stehlin now said seemed to have any meaning. Stehlin then went off to Chissey; Laurent-Eyrac on a tour of French air units. Back in Paris on 16 May he broadcast 'I return with a feeling of absolute confidence.' It was not the impression gained by Stehlin when he arrived that day among old friends. Nor of General Augereau, who remarked, 'I have nothing left.'

Sunday 19 May passed quietly at my mother's home in Sussex. I walked over the Downs, over the springy, sweet-smelling turf and looked south towards Tangmere and beyond it to the sea. In my first days as a fighter pilot I had come to know that fair countryside from the cockpit of my Fury. Chances were I should never see it again. The next day I would have to call at the Air Ministry, and then be on my way to join the battle in France.

Or so I thought. But on Sunday 19 May, before the relentless German advance towards the Channel coast, the Air Ministry decided to withdraw the majority of the Hurricane squadrons – including 85.

I caught the little train which puffed into Treyford Halt the next morning at 8.00 a.m. Rattling along through the spring-time countryside I mused on this banal 'door-step' aspect of total warfare. There was nothing about me betraying the deadly nature of my journey which might well end that evening or the next day in a pile of smoking rubble. For I looked, and almost felt, as if I were on my way to a London office, not to a battlefield where men were dying in thousands.

At the Air Ministry there was bad news. A stout, middle-aged Flight Lieutenant with scant respect for my 'scraper' ring told me paternally, 'I'm sorry my lad, there's chaos in France and we have lost 85 Squadron.' Squadron Leader John Peel, of Postings, told me 'Go and enjoy the fine weather while I try to find you a squadron.' It would not take him long.

Good news that day for Goering. The Italian Ambassador, Alfieri, had come hurrying to the front to find the *Luftwaffe* C-in-C at his mobile headquarters, *Asia*, installed in his personal train which went by the same name. Preceded by a pilot train, Goering's 'special' was impressive. At each end was an open truck bristling with anti-aircraft guns. Goering's own coach had two bedrooms and a small study.

In the second coach was a salon and a film projection room. A third coach contained the operations room and a fourth the dining-room, where Goering regaled himself and his guests with the finest foods and wines. Guest coaches were hooked on behind.

Well camouflaged, the train was parked as usual near a tunnel into which the C-in-C of the *Luftwaffe* could bolt at the first sign of enemy aircraft. Alfieri came here bearing the collar of Annunziata, the coveted personal decoration of the Italian King which had provoked Goering to such envy and rage when Ribbentrop had stolen it from under his nose a year before. Goering now thanked the ambassador in a voice which quivered with emotion. Then he disappeared, squeezing himself sideways through the narrow door, to return a few moments later wearing the collar. At that moment the photographers were called in.

While Goering in his Annunziata collar was posing for the photographers, his Fuehrer, 'wild with joy' at hearing that the Panzers had reached the Channel coast, began busying himself with peace terms for the French. 'The British,' Jodl noted, 'can have a separate peace after return of colonies . . .'

Hitler's sudden renewal of interest in overseas territory was surprising, considering his aversion for the sea. More surprising was the fact that the mood still possessed him next day when he received Admiral Raeder. The Admiral, as the Naval Staff diary duly noted, 'discusses in private with the Fuehrer the possibility of a later landing in England'. As far as we know it was the first time Hitler seriously contemplated invasion.

Meanwhile, Squadron Leader John Peel had found me a squadron. On 23 May I arrived at Debden, Essex, to take command of the remnants of 85 squadron. Led by the adjutant, Tim Moloney, the ground crews had reached England by boat. A handful of pilots with nothing but their high spirits and the clothes they stood up in had rallied to Debden in any Hurricane that would fly. Those that would not had to be left behind. Dowding's fighter squadrons abandoned 120 unserviceable Hurricanes to the *Luftwaffe*, plus seventy-five shot down in combat. Those 195 fighter aircraft represented twenty-five per cent of Britain's Home Defence force. Sorely weakened, Fighter Command now had to face its sternest trial to date.

That evening Goering's train, *Asia*, was stopped in a siding at Polch and a heavy oak table had been set up beneath a clump of trees as Goering's 'outdoor office'. As he sat chatting with the Chief of Staff, Jeschonnek, and the Intelligence Chief, Beppo Schmid, news came through that the Franco-British armies were almost trapped in Flanders. Goering reacted in a flash. 'This is just the job for the *Luftwaffe*!' he exclaimed. 'Get me through to the Fuehrer at once.'

Over the telephone Goering used every argument to sell his plan to the Fuehrer. The *Luftwaffe* was ideally suited for the job, it was a golden opportunity. Moreover, for the Fuehrer's personal prestige it was not at all desirable that credit should go to the generals for the coming annihilation of the British army. 'Leave it to me and the *Luftwaffe*,' said Goering. 'I guarantee unconditionally that not a British soldier will escape.' All he asked was a free hand; the Panzers must pull back out of the way of the bombers.

'There he goes, talking big again,' commented Jodl, Chief of OKW Ops. at the Fuehrer's headquarters. But Hitler was convinced. 'Go right ahead,' he told Goering, and Jodl and Jeschonnek quickly settled details over the telephone. When Milch heard, he was critical. 'A very extraordinary idea, Hitler thinks he can capture the British Army by bombing them.'

Hitler had other things, too, in store for the British. Bomber Command had been raiding the Ruhr since 15 May. Not that they did much material damage, but Hitler was by now thoroughly irritated, not to speak of Goering whom everyone was now calling 'Meier'.

On 24 May the land battle was at its height. Guderian's Panzers were thrusting from Abbeville, captured Boulogne, surrounded Calais, and reached Gravelines, twelve miles from Dunkirk.

During the previous week Hitler had been very temperamental. On

17 May Halder found him 'terribly nervous'. In the middle of that afternoon the Supreme Commander had visited the headquarters of General von Runstedt's Army Group A. According to General Blumentritt, Runstedt's Chief of Operations, he was by then again 'in a good temper'.

Hitler's opinion was that the war would be over in six weeks. He would be out by only a couple of days – for France. But he was badly mistaken in his reckoning about England. England – General von Sodenstern quoted the Fuehrer – 'once destructively beaten in north France, will be ready to come to terms . . .' This astonished the listening soldiers, 'because we had judged the British otherwise.' How right they were to be.

Then Hitler surprised the high staff officers when, in Blumentritt's words, he told them of his 'admiration for the British Empire, . . . and of the civilization which England had given to the world'. All he wanted was that England should acknowledge German supremacy in Europe, then he would come to a gentleman's agreement with her. He counted at all events on doing a deal. How wrong could he be about the English?

By 18 May, Hitler's mood had slumped again. Halder noted he was 'raging and screaming'. But on 20 May Jodl found him 'wild with joy' about the German Panzers which had reached the Channel. (On 21 May, von Elzdorf of the German Foreign Office told Halder, 'we are seeking [presumably with the Fuehrer's approval] to arrive at an understanding with Britain on the basis of a division of the world.') On 24 May the Fuehrer was once again in a peevish mood, for Army C-in-C von Brauchitsch had been daring to act without his approval.

And now those bomber raids were getting under the Fuehrer's skin and while ready to shower compliments on the British he decided to teach them a lesson. In Directive No. 13 of 24 May he ordered: 'The *Luftwaffe* is authorized to attack the English homeland in the fullest manner . . . This attack will be opened with an annihilating reprisal for English attacks on the Ruhr.'

Apart from this unpleasantness, Hitler's latest directive revealed a remarkable change of intention. In Directives 6 and 9 of the previous autumn the *Luftwaffe*'s role was with the *Kriegsmarine*'s U-boats to blockade England, strangle her, starve her out. Piqued by the RAF's pin-prick raids on the Ruhr he decided to land England a smashing, spiteful blow.

Hitler's Press Chief Dietrich put the Fuehrer's fits of pique down to his obstinate refusal to face reality. In any case it was an emotional reaction without regard to the air strategy needed to defeat Britain. And it was not the last time the irascible Fuehrer would intervene to the detriment of the *Luftwaffe* in the *Luftkrieg gegen England*.

Hitler made another fatal decision about England that day. At 11.30 a.m. he arrived at General von Runstedt's Army Group A's headquarters in Charleville. Von Runstedt's Panzers needed overhauling and his men had to rest. Hitler emphasized, notes Group A war diary, that it was necessary to 'husband the armoured forces for the coming operations (the final conquest of France'.) Furthermore, squeezing the Franco-British army into a tighter pocket 'would only result in ... restriction of the activity of the *Luftwaffe*'. So at 12.45 p.m. orders went out to the Panzers, 'Halt'. 'We were speechless,' commented the Panzers' general Guderian, with victory already within his grasp.

What were the *Luftwaffe*'s hopes of rounding up and annihilating the Franco-British armies? Kesselring was extremely doubtful that his *Luftflotte* 2 could succeed. General Wolfram von Richthofen, the ruthless commander of *Fliegerkorps* VIII (whose *Stukas* having smashed and terrorized the allied armies across France were now straining to take off and swoop on Dunkirk) while rearing to go, did not believe the *Luftwaffe* could go it alone.

On 25 May from his headquarters in a children's convalescent home at Proisy, he was on the telephone to Jeschonnek. 'Unless the Panzers can get moving again the English will give us the slip. No one can seriously believe we can stop them from the air.' 'You're wrong, my friend,' replied Jeschonnek, 'the Iron One [Goering] believes it.'

The hard-bitten Richthofen was ready to have a go. Listening in to the conversation, his Chief of Staff, Colonel Oberst Seidemann later commented, 'Richthofen wanted ... to bring home to the Fuehrer this singular opportunity to strike the British destructively.' Jeschonnek then said something which made Richthofen wonder if he were going mad. 'The Fuehrer wants to spare the British a too humiliating defeat.'

On 21 May Rudolf Braun had landed with I *St. G* 3 at Guise. They had virtually dive-bombed their way across France supporting the left flank of the German advance about which, as Halder had previously noted, 'The Fuehrer keeps worrying ... We are on the way to ruining our campaign...!' The left flank was weak in infantry: the *Stukas* filled in and with more terrible effect.

The Fuehrer's worries did not enter into Rudolf's reckoning. He was doing his dangerous and often unpleasant job which on the get-away took him hedge-hopping and even streaking down through the rides of forests where he could see the havoc he had caused. Far more important to him were the few creature comforts during this tough, non-stop bombing blitz, sleeping – and not for long – in tents and flying from bumpy grass airfields.

At Arras a pleasant surprise awaited the *Stuka* crews – an abandoned British supply depot where they found cigarettes and whisky, enough to last them till Christmas. For Rudolf Braun this was the highlight of the Western offensive – to hell with iron crosses and such heroics. Rudolf became a confirmed whisky drinker from that moment. Only he was sorry for the Panzer boys – they were in such a hurry to push on to the Channel coast that they had no time to plunder whisky and cigarettes.

At each new airfield the *Flughafer Betriebskompanie* was there with fuel, bombs, and ammunition – all transported in Ju. 52s. The organization was faultless. On 26 May I *St. G* 3 reached Cambrai. That night at 6.57 p.m. Operation 'Dynamo', the Dunkirk evacuation, went into action. The *Stukas* would be at the rendezvous next morning.

While the Royal Navy was making hasty plans to carry the British Army across the Channel to England the *Kriegsmarine* had been studying the prospects of transporting an invading German Army to the English shores.

By 27 May, as the first thousands of British began the hazardous crossing, Admiral Fricke (chief of the *Kriegsmarine*'s operations) had produced his '*Studie England*'. The *Kriegsmarine*'s thinking now favoured landing on England's south and south-east instead of east coast. Certain indispensable conditions had to be fulfilled before a landing: destruction of the Royal Air Force, the laying of protective minefields and, finally, good weather.

'Long preparations' were necessary. They involved the survey and collection of shipping, the provision of crews, and the preparation of embarkation ports. Thanks to the German Army more and more ports were being captured. The plan outlined by Hitler in Directive 6 of the previous October was working out admirably. The purpose was 'to win as much territory as possible in Holland, Belgium and Northern France to serve as a base for the successful prosecution of the air and sea war against England . . .' The net was rapidly extending around England.

That day, too, the Naval Staff had an approving word for Hitler's latest directive No. 13. It indicated clearly 'the object of this war, the annihilation of the main enemy England. The way to her defeat lies through the destruction of France . . . to the starvation of the British island empire . . .' Tender thoughts on the northern brothers.

Preliminary work on invasion would begin four days later with instructions for Admiral Schuster to begin a survey of possible invasion shipping. A week or so later the Naval Intelligence Division produced a twenty-one page study on landing beaches, ports, defences, and airfields from the Wash to the Isle of Wight. The *Kriegsmarine* were taking invasion seriously.

At Dunkirk that day British sailors and soldiers, in a reverse invasion of England, were bravely enduring hell from the *Luftwaffe*. At 7.40 a.m. the *Stukas* were over Dunkirk. Rudolf Braun described their attacks as taking place in a general confusion of smoke, AA, and British fighter attacks. I *St. G .3* suffered casualties. 'This,' said Rudolf, 'was our first taste of real war. From the British fighters we met heavy and spirited resistance.' Far from affecting the *Stukas'* morale, it seemed to incite them like a drug.

On approach the *Stukas* were often scattered by the British fighters. Then it was each man for himself – no question of a classic attack. Once in the dive with dive-brakes out they were fairly safe from fighters, which overshot them. And never if possible did they fly out to sea. The Naval AA was too hot.

At briefing they had each been given a specific target. Fuel tanks were the trickiest. They went up in a colossal explosion which would take the *Stuka* with it if it had pulled out too low. Rudolf Braun concentrated only on his target – the rest was total confusion and he could not bring his thoughts to bear on it. In that screaming hell-dive it was the target and only the target upon which his eye was riveted.

For the Messerschmitt 109 pilots it was otherwise. As for us the enemy was until then a *thing*, not a person. They shot at an aircraft with no thought for the men inside it. But now they had the job of ground-strafing as well. Sensitive, highly strung Paul Temme said, 'I hated Dunkirk. It was just unadulterated killing. The beaches were jammed full of soldiers. I went up and down at three hundred feet "hose-piping".' Cold blooded, point blank murder. Defenceless men, fathers, sons, and brothers, being cruelly massacred by a twenty-four-year-old boy.

Seven years older than Paul, Hans-Heinrich Brustellin was, if not more hardened, more philosophical. He did his job of ground-strafing well but it left him revolted. He took off from Guise at 11.00 a.m. on 29 May. The weather was just right – low cloud, affording a concealed approach. All the roads were blocked by trucks streaming towards Dunkirk. First he searched the sky to make sure there were no enemy fighters about. Then he dived. He saw lorries so crowded that there were soldiers hanging onto the sides. When they saw the Me. 109s they jumped for cover. 'It was an awful sight if you looked too closely, a demoralizing business for a fighter force,' said Brustellin.

But Brustellin saw it also with a professional eye. Spread out on the Dunkirk beaches the British Army offered a difficult target. The Me. 109 pilots therefore concentrated on lines of British soldiers embarking. More could be killed that way.

Heading 611 Auxiliary Squadron James McComb saw the tragi-comic side – he typified the attitude of most British fighter pilots. When he sighted his first enemy fighter inland from Dunkirk he was so surprised at its black crosses that he forgot to press the firing button. Then in the general *mêlée* he saw a defensive circle of five Me. 110s with a Spitfire turning round in the opposite direction inside it. He rushed to the rescue, only to find Flight Sergeant Pilot Sadler with hood pushed back, roaring with laughter. Each burst of fire which passed just below the Spitfire's tail was greeted 'by a vulgar two-fingered gesture' from Sadler.

611 were set upon by a 'vast number' of Me. 109s. McComb looked desperately 'for anything with a roundel painted on it, and at last joined up with one of his flight commanders, Jack Leather. His microphone hanging down from one side of his helmet, Jack was grinning all over his fat, pink face. Then he pressed the microphone to his mouth and James heard him say, 'Chee-rist, this is bloody dangerous.'

Meanwhile the other flight commander (Stoddard) joined two Hurricanes – which turned out to be Me. 109s. 'He didn't half get a pasting,' said James. But Stoddard got back to base. On touching down his aircraft 'folded up like a pigeon landing in Trafalgar Square'.

Piloting his Ju. 88, Hajo Hermann approached Dunkirk from the south. Five or six Hurricanes got on his tail, shooting him up badly. With oil tanks holed, instruments shot away, one engine out and his windscreen shattered he glided down towards a ship – and bombed it. The Hurricanes then realized 'that the devil was not finished after all'. Down they swooped again and hit Hajo's second engine. He ditched the Ju. 88. 'Silence, then bubbles. I was dazed – two of the others were free, but one could not swim.'

Hajo got him ashore. They were in no-man's-land with the firing going on from each side. So they went back into the sea, to hide. 'We must have looked ridiculous as we crawled in the water towards our lines.' Ahead were the sand dunes where he could see German soldiers waving. At that moment he ran into a British pilot, also crawling in the water. It was the Hurricane pilot who had shot him down. They now crawled on together until they reached the German lines. There Hajo commandeered a large black limousine from some Belgian officers. Soaked to the skin and shoeless, Hajo drove back to Bruges with his crew and the Hurricane pilot who had shot him down and had become his prisoner.

For days 54 Squadron had been flying out from Hornchurch across the Channel to the Dunkirk area to join in the desperate attempts to repulse the *Luftwaffe's* murderous assault on the Franco-British armies. The survivors in 54, as Al Deere said, 'were literally on their last legs'. On 28 May word came that the next day they were to change with 41 Squadron, Norman Ryder's lot at Catterick.

At 3.30 a.m. on 29 May Al was roused by his batman Roach. 'Lovely day sir and the sun will soon be shining.' Al looked out – it was pitch dark and rain streamed down the window pane. Two hours later Al was at the head of his flight as 54 Squadron headed out to sea for its last Dunkirk patrol.

Over Gravelines Al pounced on a Dornier 17, blasting a hole in its port engine. But the Dornier's rear gunner had a stout heart and a steady aim. Al felt bullets thudding into his Spitfire's engine which enveloped him in a white spray of Glycol coolant. A few minutes later, with a nasty crack on the head, he staggered out of the cockpit onto the beach fifteen miles from Dunkirk. With a last forlorn look at his Kiwi One (by then engulfed in flame) he made off to a Belgian field hospital. At that moment the Germans were entering Ostend twenty miles to the east.

By hopping a lift and stealing a bicycle, Al Deere followed the drift of refugee traffic towards the neighbourhood of Bray-Dune. When the road became choked with refugees he continued on foot into Dunkirk.

'The sight ... on arrival at the beach, I shall never forget ... Discipline and control despite the obvious exhaustion and desperation of the thousands of troops ... in snakelike columns stretched from the sand-dunes down to the water's edge.'

Guided by a naval beach-commander Al made his way to a destroyer alongside the Mole. It had been raining but the weather cleared. Within minutes three Ju. 88s streaked across overhead. 'There was a mad scramble for cover ... mostly the troops just dived into the water, re-emerging at neck level to fire their rifles in desperation and defiance ... A crescendo of bombs ... machine-gun fire descended on the beach. In a few seconds it was all over. A number of British soldiers would not be requiring transport back to England.'

Al never saw what happened to those Ju. 88s, but one of them may have been piloted by *Oberleutnant* Jocho Helbig. His unit (*LG* 1) had been called up from Düsseldorf. 'After dropping our bombs, three Hurricanes discovered us about three hundred feet over the beaches.' They attacked. Wounded, Jocho was bandaged up by his observer and got the aircraft back 'on one arm'.

We called it the 'Hell of Dunkirk', he said. 'We met terrific resistance from the British fighters and battleship AA. It was the turning point. Now we knew what the enemy's mettle was like.'

Meanwhile Al had reached the causeway and was running towards a destroyer. An angry army major blocked his way. 'I am an RAF officer,' explained Al, not feeling much like one – with a tattered ground-sheet over his uniform, a bloody bandage round his head and his face dirty and unshaven. 'I am trying to get back to my squadron which is operating over here.'

'I don't give a damn who you are,' the major shouted furiously. 'For all the good you chaps seem to be doing, you might as well stay on the ground.'

Al told him to go to hell. A few moments later he was aboard the destroyer. Below in the ward room he was greeted in stony silence by a crowd of army officers. 'Why so friendly?' he asked 'What have the RAF done?' 'That's just it,' someone answered. 'What have they done?'

Poor Al. 'For two weeks non-stop I had flown my guts out and this was all the thanks I got,' he wrote later. Then he sank wearily into a chair, 'past caring what the Army thought'.

Back at Dover without money or means of identification he jumped into the first train for London and fell asleep. 'Tickets please.' The ticket collector was standing over him. Al explained where he had come from and why he had no ticket. 'Sorry,' said the man, 'you will have to get off the train at the next station.' A senior army officer in the carriage intervened and Al was saved. 'He has obviously not heard about the RAF at Dunkirk,' Al thought.

Next morning 41, like 54, was patrolling Dunkirk. What Norman saw below 'defied description'. 'Lines of ants were heading for temporary jetties, made out of lorries, to struggle aboard anything that would enable them to reach one of the larger vessels off-shore. Some swam. Black smoke from the burning Dunkirk oil tanks blew inland ...' 'If only,' thought Norman, 'it would blow out to sea and cover our troops.' The smoke did in fact blow down Channel and across to England. 'We smelled it in Sussex,' said John Simpson, who patrolled with 43 Squadron. 'You could fly from Brighton to Dunkirk on the smoke trail.'

Both John and Norman saw the same appalling sight, 'a destroyer crack in two,' Norman wrote, 'it was there one moment, gone the next, and in its place a growing patch of oil, sand from the seabed and debris'. And John saw 'parachutes coming down from wrecked aircraft, landing in the water, on the beach and on the land'. One British pilot who fell in the sea was swimming round when he found a woman clutching a baby He tried to help her, but the baby started screaming. 'Go away you beastly man, you have made my baby cry,' gulped the indignant mother.

Above in his Spitfire Norman suddenly heard a fragment of the National Anthem bursting into the R/T chatter. He felt a sudden lump in his throat and thought, 'even a stone would feel emotion'.

By dawn on 30 May nearly seventy-three thousand men had been taken off. The weather, that unfailing ally of the British, was true to form. When the Armada lay off Gravelines in 1588 'He blew and they were scattered.' Now over Dunkirk a few miles east of Gravelines, He blinded the enemy with fog and rain. The *Luftwaffe* was grounded on 28 May and half of 29 May. On 30 May the weather again clamped down on the German Air Force. About fifty-nine thousand troops were evacuated that day, some fifteen thousand of them French.

Meanwhile forty thousand Frenchmen were fighting doggedly alongside the British, holding the Germans at bay on Dunkirk's perimeter. Loyal allies, the British and French fought on valiantly while their comrades were carried to safety in the Navy's ships and the 'great tide of small vessels' which had flowed forth from England's ports – nearly seven hundred all told, plus one hundred and fifty allied vessels.

Under the murderous deluge of *Luftwaffe* bombs and machine-gun fire who could blame the soldiers and sailors for their bitter reproach, 'Where is the RAF?' But Dowding's fighters were doing their loyal best. Operating a hundred miles and more from their bases it was not possible with available numbers to maintain constant patrols over the beaches. But 'the whole Metropolitan air force, our last sacred reserve, was used . . . Hour after hour they bit into the German fighters and bomber squadrons, taking a heavy toll,' wrote Winston Churchill. But those violent combats, generally miles above or away from the beaches, were seldom seen by the soldiers and sailors who were being bombed to hell below.

Fog grounded the *Stukas* on 31 May, but 1 June was clear and sunny. It was a day that Soldier 2nd Class Michel Nastorg would never forget. To Michel war and soldiers were pure anathema. When called up he was acting in *Peer Gynt* at the Odeon Theatre, Paris. If he had to go to war he would go in style. Besides his rifle he took his camera, a portable radio, shirts made to measure, blue and beige striped pyjamas, and a bottle of *gnole* (a fiery liquor) to help him forget.

He and the rest of the French Seventh Army had pushed forward into Belgium on 10 May. Then came the terrible confusion of retreat, harassed by *Stukas* and artillery. At Hoggstad twelve of his comrades were killed by a single salvo of shells. All but four of the others fled in panic. Michel stayed to help bury the dead. Then he drove on with the wounded towards the coast. They were stopped by the British. 'The wounded must stay put, we are embarking first,' they said. 'Bastards,' thought Michel as he watched them destroying their lorries, guns, and even tea-urns. Then he reached the coast at Bray-Dune, where Al Deere had arrived on a bicycle the same day. Michel saw the corpses of British soldiers floating at the water's edge and felt sorry. 'It could have been us,' he thought. For three more days he crouched in a hole in the sand while German shells whined overhead. 'It was like an aerial metro.'

On 1 June he was cowering with others on the outskirts of Dunkirk while the *Stukas* screamed down. Someone yelled 'take cover' and ran for a nearby coal dump. Michel never made it. He just saw his friends and the coal dump blown to bits in one frightful eruption of black, choking coal dust.

At 12.00 noon he stood on the quay with a crowd of French soldiers. For embarkation the order was: one officer and twenty men at a time. But there were no officers. 'We thought the French Army the best in the world. *C'était un affreux malentendu* (it was a dreadful misunderstanding),' commented Michel.

He and his friends boarded the *Scotia* and were shown down to the saloon – where tea was served. 'We felt we were off on a weekend trip to London,' he said. The feeling did not last long.

At 12.10 Rudolf Braun had taken off at Cambrai with I *St. G* 3. As the *Scotia* pulled out of Dunkirk he was overhead in his Ju. 87, peeling off into a dive. Whether it was his bombs or another's neither Rudolf nor Michel could ever say. The *Scotia* staggered under a terrific explosion and everyone in the saloon ran for the doors. Michel dived through a porthole and fell in a heap on the promenade deck on top of someone whom he immediately recognized – Pierre Dux, of the *Comédie Française*, who had been playing in *Le Misanthrope*. '*Monsieur Nastorg de l'Odeon*,' Michel introduced himself. 'We meet in curious circumstances,' replied Pierre Dux gravely as the *Scotia* heeled over in flames and began to settle.

Michel swam around – he had no life jacket. A drowning man grabbed at him, so he helped him to a floating plank, but ten others got there too. Michel swam on with the dying man's insults and imprecations in his ears. Then a German aircraft dived, machine-gunning. Men folded up and sank all around Michel. Others still clung terrified to the burning hulk of the *Scotia*, calling on their mothers and the Holy Mother to save them. By their accents they must have been from the Corrèze or the Creuse, men who had probably never seen the sea before. Rather than jump into it they clung to the ship and were burned alive.

Michel was hauled aboard a British destroyer and landed at Dover. His first contact with England was unforgettable. 'The English seemed completely oblivious of the war. Half of them were walking round with tennis rackets and golf clubs.' Two weeks later Soldier 2nd Class Nastorg was back at Cherbourg. The war was over for him. He thought ruefully of the line from Giraudoux, '*La Guerre que les Hommes ont inventée pour rester entre eux.*' His mother's comment when he telephoned from Cherbourg was less philosophical: 'Thank goodness I didn't know, or I would have worried about you.'

In the haze and smoke which hung over Dunkirk it was hard to recognize friend from foe. At 4.00 a.m. on 1 June Otto Hintze (I *JG* 186) woke up in his room at the Modern Hotel, Antwerp. After a good breakfast (*thé complèt*) he was driven to Deurne airfield. At 6.00 a.m. he was airborne leading his *Schwarme* (four aircraft) following his *Staffel Kapitän*, *Oberleutnant* Kientzle. Over Dunkirk Otto sighted Spitfires diving out of the haze to attack. He was surprised to see them so far from England. Suddenly his Me. 109 was hit in the cooling system. He managed to pancake on the beach and on his return to Deurne found Kientzle waiting anxiously.

Who had hit Otto Hintze? They reconstructed the combat. It was certainly not the Spitfires – they were out of range. He was convinced it was one of his own pilots. Everyone was jumpy at this first big clash with enemy fighters. The mystery was never solved, but Otto Hintze thinks it was his own wing-man, an 'old' man and happily married. 'He must have been thinking of his wife and family when he pressed the button,' thought Otto.

This domestic aspect of the war was always present. One left one's hotel in the morning to go out and die. If death was not at the rendezvous, one went back to the hotel for a drink with the boys. Or the mess. James McComb (who shared a cottage with Donald Little and Ralph Crompton and their wives near the airfield at Digby, Lincs, had organized a sherry party for the wives in the mess at 12.00 noon on 2 June. Not even a Dunkirk patrol would make him cancel it. His engine was already revving up when Donald Little climbed up on the wing and asked him to feed his dog.

As James led the squadron out over the Channel he wondered, 'Why the hell does he want me to feed his dog?' Then they were over Dunkirk, getting 'well beaten up'. With two Me. 109s on his tail, the pilot officer, Brown, only managed to shake them off by diving under a gantry in Dunkirk docks. 'Apart from the indignity of it,' ran his combat report, 'I do not reckon I raised the morale of the BEF very much.'

Back in the mess at Digby the party had already begun as the last few pilots were still coming in to land. They entered the ante-room by ones and twos until there were two nineteen-year-old wives without husbands. Those girls knew that they need not wait any longer. James was watching them closely. 'They just slid out of the ante-room. There was no fuss, no tears. They just left.' One of them was the wife of Donald Little.

They could have wrecked the morale of the squadron, but they never did. 'They were made of the same stuff as their husbands.' Squadron Leader James McComb felt as proud of those two brave young wives as he did of any of his pilots.

One of the squadrons which (like 611) had refuelled at Martlesham before heading for Dunkirk was Bob Tuck's 92. Bob was not only leading his own squadron but two others which had joined up with his to form a 'wing' of some thirty-six aircraft. Over the French coast they did battle with eight Heinkel 111s – small fry for a wing – and their escort of twenty-five Me. 109s. It was the first time British fighters had fought as a wing. But not the last: the wing idea was to cause a lot of trouble soon.

In his post as Bomber Liaison Officer at Fighter Command, Squadron Leader Tom Gleave was an expert in aircraft 'plots'. Meanwhile he had been deeply involved in a plot of quite a different kind – to get to a fighter squadron. That day, 2 May, he arrived at Kirton-in-Lindsey, not far from Digby, to command 253 Fighter Squadron.

Goering's guarantee to prevent the Allied Armies' escape was proving a hollow one. The *Luftwaffe*'s all-out effort on 1 June did not prevent over sixty-four thousand men being taken off. But it did decide Admiral Ramsay to continue operations only by night, when the *Luftwaffe* stayed grounded. Goering had evidently overlooked the fact that darkness, not to speak of bad weather, was not the problem to the British Navy that it was to his *Luftwaffe*. During the night of 2 and 3 June the rest of the BEF and sixty thousand French soldiers were pulled out of Dunkirk. Deprived of its prey, the *Luftwaffe* turned to the French *Armée de l'Air*, or what was left of it.

Operation Paula was a concerted blow at the airfields and aircraft factories in the Paris region. It was also meant to impress the French public. II *KG* 2 (Werner Borner was with them in *Gustav Marie*) bombed Orly. 'The very few French fighters we met,' he said, 'fought bravely.' *Oberst* Kammhuber, *Kommodore* of the ill-fated *KG* 51 whose *Oberleutnant* S had bombed Freiburg, led his *Geschwader*, now equipped with Ju. 88s, in an attack on Etampes. But trouble with his air-brakes caused him, like the Duke of Plazatoro, to lead his *Geschwader* from behind 'instead of at the fore-oh'. Worse, he was shot down and made prisoner.

It happened that Air Vice Marshal Sholto Douglas and Admiral Sir Geoffrey Blake landed that morning at Villacoublay on a visit to Admiral Darlan and General Vuillemin, Chief of Air Staff. 'We rather expected ... there would at least be someone there to welcome us ...' said Sholto Douglas. As they got out of the aircraft ' ... a little man wearing a tin hat with a gas mask bouncing on his backside ... shouted at us to take cover.'

Sholto, who had not forgotten the night he had dived under the piano at Bertangles, needed no encouragement. He and Admiral Blake bolted for the nearest shelter, 'a not very reassuring mound of sandbags and corrugated iron ...' A second later *Luftwaffe* bombs were plastering Villacoublay's airfield and hangars.

Sholto Douglas had seen three French fighters take off. Of the fifty others parked round the airfield many were blown to smithereens. Sholto wondered why the French fighters did not hurl themselves at the enemy. The British Air Staff had warned the French the day before of Operation Paula.

He entered the mess with Admiral Blake. There they found the French pilots 'sitting down quietly and having their lunch ... They were not at all interested in what had just happened.' His thoughts went back to the French aces of his day, Fonck and Guynemer and their generation. It was not until later, 'when I had Free French pilots under my command that I found ... Frenchmen who could be as keen and gallant ...'

That day Vuillemin told the Deputy Chief of Air Staff that the *Armée de l'Air* was ready, if need be, to bomb Italy. Two airfields in the South of France would be at the disposal of the RAF for the purpose. 'Encouraged by this offer of co-operation from the French,' the RAF made an all-out effort to dispatch the ground crews, equipment and bombers to be ready at the airfields in question.

At dawn on 4 June, leading A Flight 222 Squadron Douglas Bader looked down on Dunkirk harbour. Smoke still rose from the shattered town and harbour. The beach was littered with debris and equipment but not a soul moved. Only the white sail of a yacht proceeding out to sea caught his eye: the last ship to leave Dunkirk. Goering's guarantee had proved worthless. He had allowed 338,226 allied soldiers to escape.

Another man over Dunkirk beach that morning was *Luftwaffe* Inspector General Erhard Milch at the controls of his Fieseler Storch. With him was the Italian air attaché, while in another Storch flew Milch's aide. They landed in a field near a burning village outside Dunkirk. Milch saw scores of dead soldiers. The only live one was a Black. 'I was looking everywhere for English prisoners. I didn't find them. Over three hundred thousand English soldiers had escaped leaving their arms and equipment. But it was the men who were important. Hitler thought he could make the English prisoners with bombs. It was a very remarkable idea.'

Then Milch drove down to the sea. Off-shore were a dozen sunken ships, the beach and dunes were strewn with vast quantities of broken equipment. Thousands of soldiers had escaped but were now defenceless. This, thought Milch, was the moment to strike at England, to invade. Milch's plan – he went to see Goering about it the next day – was to do it with airborne troops: capture the British coastal airfields and give the *Luftwaffe* a foothold in England, fighters and *Stukas* first, then Ju. 52s for transporting ground crews and equipment. Meanwhile army troops would be ferried across the Channel in every available boat.

Fighter Command had 331 Hurricanes and Spitfires left – the equivalent of about twenty-one squadrons. Never as great as needed, its strength had been sorely taxed by the Battle of France and Dunkirk and now it was – if in numbers only – a pathetically reduced force. Even if its fighting remained indomitable it was ill-disposed to counter a serious air assault on England.

As Milch was ruminating on a lightning air invasion of England Winston Churchill told the Commons about Dunkirk. 'Wars are not won by evacuations. But there was a victory inside this deliverance ... It was gained by the Royal Air Force. Many of our soldiers ... underrate its achievements ... This was a great trial of strength between the British and German air forces. Can you conceive a greater objective for the Germans in the air than to make evacuation impossible? ... They tried hard ... they were frustrated in their task. We got the Army away ...

'I will pay my tribute to these young airmen ... May it not also be that the cause of civilization itself will be defended by the skill and devotion of a few thousand airmen?'

He told the British what he expected of them. 'Even though large tracts of Europe ... may fall into the grip of the Gestapo and all the odious apparatus of Nazi rule, we shall not flag or fail ... We shall defend our island ... we shall fight on the beaches, we shall fight on the landing grounds, we shall fight in the fields and in the streets, we shall fight in the hills; we shall never surrender ...'

The British on their island now knew exactly where they stood.

Apparently unashamed at having failed to annihilate the British Army, Goering could not resist a look at the mess his *Luftwaffe* had made of Dunkirk. That evening *Oberst* Werner Junck, newly appointed *Jagdflieger-fuehrer* (*Jafu*) (Fighter Leader) of *Luftflotte* 3, dropped in for dinner with his C-in-C and Jeschonnek in his train, *Asia*, which had been put in a tunnel for the night. 'It is funny,' Junck chided his superiors, 'when I was a boy I was always afraid to go into tunnels. You two seem afraid to go out of them.'

I

Chapter 19

Dunkirk over, the Germans thrust forward the very next morning with a crushing attack against the Somme defence line. The French Army's hour was at hand. The flower of its fighting strength had been cut down in Flanders, and all but one division of the British Army had gone. The *Armée de l'Air* was almost done for and only a few RAF squadrons remained to fight alongside them.

At Debden we never even smelt the smoke of Dunkirk. 85 Squadron was non-operational. With a dozen boys not long out of school and about the same number of new Hurricanes, my job was to reform it into a fighting unit.

In Dicky Lee and Jeffries I had two fine flight commanders. Both had been branded in France and both had been lucky to escape – Jeffries was drinking coffee in an Abbeville café when he saw the Germans coming down the street. No one had ever '*filé a l'anglaise*' quicker than he did. He soon went on to a Czech squadron and a Canadian named Hamilton took his place.

The new boys were a varied group – an air marshal's son, a couple of undergraduates, an ex-insurance clerk, and among them two New Zealanders. They were boys of twenty and sometimes less with only ten hours' Hurricane experience. This was the major problem. In a single-seater you have to do it all yourself. No one can help you. It had taken me years to gain what experience I had and even then my chances of survival were not high. Theirs were infinitely less.

The flight commanders and a few other pilots – Paddy Hemingway, Nigger Marshal, Patrick Woods-Scawen, Sergeants Sammy Allard and Geoff Goodman were the most tested – helped me to provide a lively fund of experience on which the young ones could draw. They could barely fly a Hurricane – a highly dangerous machine in inexperienced hands, as was proved by the swift tragedy which overtook two of them.

All we could do was communicate our experience by touch, talk, and intuition and thus encourage the young ones to have faith in us and follow our examples. They had to learn through the mysterious, intuitive language of single-seater fighter pilots.

We taught them to search the sky, and watch their tails. They jousted with us in the sky to learn the tricks of air combat – above all never climb or dive in front of a Me. 109, but turn and turn again since it was there that the Hurricane outclassed the Me. 109. We led them up to Sutton Bridge to fire their guns. And as they progressed, I sent them out over the East Coast convoys to learn discipline, loyalty and vigilance.

Our superiors were encouraging. First our station commander Wing Commander Larry Fullergood, short of stature, energetic, and warm in his feelings towards us. We called him the Bulgarian General because we were endeared by his swarthy appearance and his real affection. He stood for us, and we loved him. Later he would write to me: '85 to my mind will always be the First Fighter Squadron of the RAF.'

On 3 June Boom Trenchard came into our midst and without asking anything of us, left us feeling determined to be worthy of him. He told us a simple story. 'People in London,' he said, 'tell me how dreadful it will be when the German bombs start falling. So I tell them, "have you thought how many pigeons there are in London?" I've not been hit by one yet.'

Trenchard's godson, Dicky Lee, had his flight at Debden's 'satellite' airfield, a meadow where the sweet-smelling grass mingled with the rank and thrilling odour of aircraft. I was there often, for I preferred life in shirt sleeves under the sun and stars to the formal uniform confines of my office and the mess at Debden. Or else I would fly to join A Flight near the coast at Martlesham and with them patrol over the convoys. Life under canvas was pleasant on the scented heath. The feeling of early days at Tangmere returned. Once again I felt I belonged to the best flying club in the world.

Day by day 85 grew strong again, watching and waiting with growing impatience.

Other squadrons which had been through the fighting in France and at Dunkirk were doing the same. Tom Gleave's 253 Squadron, then at Kirton, had been decimated. Then, it was a squadron of 'inexperienced youth with a leavening of veterans, themselves mostly boys'.

Like 85. But we had patrols over the convoys, an excellent training ground. Tom and 253 grew impatient with no sign of the enemy. Conversation always centred round one question, 'When is the Hun going to show?'

'We were thirsty for action,' Tom said. 'The squadron was fanatically keen for real, live ops.' So, their flying done, they kept up their spirits with crazy games at dispersal and regular sorties to the local pubs. Never was there any drinking on duty, but at the end of the day they would foregather at the Sarazen's Head or the White Hart, always to talk on the same theme, 'When will the Hun show up?'

This was a question which exercised the C-in-C of Fighter Command. Just after Dunkirk Dowding had forecast three major threats: invasion, for which the Germans would first have to win control of the air; night bombing; and the submarine menace. He believed the most serious was invasion preceded by the destruction of Fighter Command.

With that, he applied all his abundant energy to its re-organization. He was left with 331 Hurricanes and Spitfires. The Air Ministry's estimated strength of the Home Defence fighter force was over eight hundred fighters. Beside the three hundred odd Hurricanes and Spitfires, another one hundred and fifty obsolete fighters were shown on the order of battle, but Dowding had no illusions about them. They were slower than even the enemy bombers. 'I want speed as the paramount quality in a fighter,' he said. This meant the Hurricane and, above all, the Spitfire, 'which is why I hung on to the Spitfire so desperately'. The slower Hurricane was 'a jolly good machine . . . a rugged type, stronger than the Spitfire'.

But on 14 May a magician with a fiery dynamism had appeared on the scene in the person of Lord Beaverbrook. Fighters were the key to Britain's immediate survival and fighters, Minister of Aircraft Production, Beaverbrook, decided was what Britain would get. In February 1940 one hundred and forty-one fighters were produced. When Beaverbrook took over in May the figure became three hundred and twenty-five. June would end with four hundred and forty-six new fighters produced and there would be more in the following month.

Human relationships play a big part in the running of a war – as was soon to be proved. Despite their totally different characters, Dowding and Beaverbrook were luckily the best of friends.

Behind the great aircraft constructors and their 'shadow' factories (Swinton's clever idea) were fifteen thousand sub-contractors making components ranging from wings to the nuts and bolts which held them together. The sub-contractors themselves varied from full-blown engineering works down to old ladies and schoolboys, who in 'filing parties' at home or in the classroom, did their vital bit to help answer the urgent cry for more fighters.

The activities of Beaverbrook's Ministry of Aircraft Production went beyond the mere production of aircraft. Damaged aircraft had to be made new and a formidable organization existed to this end: the Civilian Repair Organization. In February 1940 it repaired a total of twenty machines; in July it would repair one hundred and sixty. Of all the fighters supplied during the Battle of Britain thirty-five per cent would be repair jobs – as good as new.

No. 50 Maintenance Unit was given the job of conveying crashed aircraft to the Repair Units. Aircraft beyond repair, the heaps of twisted metal – as my own beautiful Hurricane (No. 3166) would one day become – were collected by the Salvage Organization and along with enemy aircraft all were melted down in the same pot.

Because the Germans surrounded Britain from the North Cape in Norway to the Cherbourg Peninsula, the watch on Britain's coasts and countryside had to be extended and improved. It was a gradual operation, posting extra sentinels – in the radar and Observer Corps – who were so vital to the British fighters. But it was begun immediately: Radar stations and Observer Corps posts sprung up in the West of England, in Wales and finally in Scotland.

In barrage balloons Dowding was not too badly off. Nor in searchlights either. But there was a woeful lack of AA guns – only twenty-five per cent of the eight thousand needed. The AA guns were sent to protect not British cities (which at first were left relatively defenceless) but aircraft factories and other vital targets. The British people faced up to the grim reality of total air warfare: the defence of military targets came first.

Of Dowding's problems, most serious by far was his shortage of fighter pilots. The Battle of France and Dunkirk had claimed 435 killed, missing and imprisoned. By mid-June Dowding was 360 pilots short of his full complement of 1,450. The Canadian Prime Minister Mackenzie King's refusal in 1937 to co-operate in the Empire Training Scheme now hit the RAF at its most critical hour. Output from the training schools was lagging – so seriously that Churchill stepped in and instructed the naval and air staffs to comb their pilots' ranks for any who could be spared for Fighter Command.

From Bomber, Coastal and Army Co-operation Commands volunteers came forward to swell the fighter pilots' ranks. The Navy's response was immediate. Fifty-eight naval pilots converted to eight-gun fighters and joined their land-lubber comrades in Fighter Command. What a bold, magnificent contrast to the miserable bickering fifteen years ago between the Navy and the RAF. Trenchard had insisted then that pilots of both services should be 'trained on a single system, imbued with a single doctrine'. Now that policy was paying off.

In this critical hour the need for solidarity was desperate and it seemed that the Admiralty was showing the way. Jock Colville (the Prime Minister's secretary) told Chips Channon, that 'the Admiralty is fantastic now; people who were at each other's throats a few weeks ago are now intimate and on the best of terms. Winston darts in and out, a mountain of energy and good nature . . .'

France's courage was already failing. On 11 June Churchill flew for the fourth time to see Reynaud, who had left Paris and was now at the Château at Briare, near Orléans. Descending from his Flamingo aircraft he 'displayed the smiling countenance and confident air which are thought suitable when things are very bad . . .' But the French were in no mood for smiles.

At 7.00 p.m. Churchill sat down with Premier Reynaud, Marshal Pétain, General Weygand (now commanding the French armies), the Chief of Air Staff, General Vuillemin, and another young General – de Gaulle. All through the 'miserable discussion' that followed Churchill was 'haunted . . . by the grief . . . that Britain . . . had not been able to make a greater contribution'. And that almost all the 'slaughter . . . and the suffering had fallen upon France and upon France alone'.

Churchill urged the French Government to defend Paris. He reminded Marshal Pétain how Clemenceau had said, 'I will fight in front of Paris, in Paris and behind Paris.'

Then Weygand spoke. He demanded more British fighter squadrons. 'Here is the decisive point. Now is the decisive moment.' But Churchill had not forgotten Dowding's dramatic plea before the War Cabinet on 15 May. All the same, Dowding's warning had gone home. Churchill's answer to Weygand was, 'In accordance with the Cabinet decision, taken in the presence of Air Marshal Dowding . . . twenty-five fighter squadrons must be maintained at all costs for the defence of Britain.' It was evidently then that he had got the numbers wrong – the bottom limit which he took for twenty-five squadrons instead of fifty-two.

To Weygand, Churchill retorted, 'This is not the decisive point and this is not the decisive moment. That moment will come when Hitler hurls his *Luftwaffe* against Great Britain. If we can keep command of the air, and if we can keep the seas open . . . we will win it all back for you.'

In the middle of dinner ('soup, an omelette or something, coffee and light wine') Churchill's personal staff officer, General Ismay, was called to the telephone. It was Air Vice Marshal Barratt. There was trouble at Salon, one of the airfields in the south of France that Vuillemin and Sholto Douglas had agreed should be used by the RAF for bombing Italy. 'The Wellington bombers are there, but the local authorities are objecting to their taking off tonight. They're afraid of reprisals,' Barratt told Ismay.

In fact No. 99 Bomber Squadron had hardly touched down at 3.30 p.m. that afternoon when the nearest French Bomber Group telephoned Group Captain Field (commanding the RAF ground force 'Haddock' at Salon) to say that in no event were the RAF bombers to take off. The local authorities reinforced the veto.

What had Vuillemin been up to? At 9.45 p.m., just before sitting down to dinner with Churchill, he had telephoned Barratt telling him to cancel the raid on Italy. Hence Barratt's call to Ismay who told him, 'the PM thinks the bombers should go ahead.'

But from Field's point of view, this was easier said than done. Despite orders from the French to countermand the raid, he ordered the first Wellington off just after midnight. But the French were determined to stop the RAF bombers. To the Wellington pilots' astonishment a number of French lorries rushed out and blocked the runway. The raid on Italy was off.

After his meeting with the French, Churchill informed President Roosevelt, 'The aged Marshal Pétain, who was none too good in April and July 1918, is, I fear, ready to lend his name and prestige to a treaty of peace for France. Reynaud . . . is for fighting on and he has a young General, de Gaulle, who believes much can be done. Admiral Darlan declares he will send the French Fleet to Canada . . .'

On 13 June Churchill returned to France, this time to Tours. He made for the prefecture, where he conferred with Premier Reynaud and Georges Mandel, Minister of the Interior and 'faithful former secretary to Clemenceau'. Unknown to Churchill the French Cabinet was at Cange and was vexed that he had not gone there. But as he had never been invited, and as no one met him at the airfield, he felt the reproach unjustified.

Reynaud was depressed. Weygand had just declared that the French should ask for an armistice. Churchill answered that the British were determined to win the war and urged Reynaud to put the question 'squarely' to President Roosevelt before seeking armistice. Reynaud agreed and promised to hold on until he had an answer. He also promised to hand over the four hundred *Luftwaffe* prisoners in French hands, who included *Oberst* Kammhuber of *KG* 51 and the top ace *Hauptmann* Werner Molders. Events would prevent the transfer. 'Those German pilots all became available for the Battle of Britain,' wrote Churchill, 'and we had to shoot them down a second time.' Kammhuber escaped being shot down and Molders, who was hit, managed to get back all the same.

As he left, Churchill saw General de Gaulle 'lofty and expressionless' standing in the doorway, and as he passed him he muttered, '*l'homme du destin*'.

Before going to bed in London in the early hours of 14 June Winston Churchill drafted a message (it was dated 13 June) to Reynaud: 'We renew . . . our pledge and resolve to continue the struggle . . . in France, in this island, upon the oceans and in the air . . . We shall never turn from the conflict until France stands safe and erect in all her grandeur!'

Dawn had just broken on Friday 14 June when General Fedor von Bock (commanding German Army Group B in the north of France) alighted in his Fieseler *Storch* at Le Bourget, almost as the van of his 9th Division was marching down the road past the airfield towards the gates of Paris. Having greeted them, the General drove ahead to the Place de la Concorde. There he took the salute of the 9th. Bock then drove up the Champs-Elysées to the Arc de Triomphe, its white granite inscribed with countless French victories, where he reviewed the 8th and 28th Divisions. The swastika flag floated from the Eiffel Tower. Impressed by the *Luftwaffe*'s Operation Paula, Paris remained an open city. It had fallen without a shot.

On 13 June, Churchill and Reynaud learned Roosevelt's position. The United States would do 'everything in its power' to supply the French and British with the 'material they so urgently require' to carry on the fight.

Two days later Reynaud resigned, and Pétain took over. The new Premier asked for an armistice the following day. That day, the RAF flew General de Gaulle to London, where he made his famous appeal to the Free French over the radio.

And on 18 June, Churchill announced to the House of Commons that the Battle of Britain was about to begin: 'The whole fury and might of the enemy must be turned upon us. Hitler knows that he will have to break us in this island, or lose the war.'

J*

Part Five
OVERTURE

Chapter 20

Hitler himself was confident that faced with air attack and possibly invasion, the British would prefer to settle with Germany and watch with the rest of the world while he proceeded to achieve his greatest ambition, the liquidation of Soviet Russia.

But Britain and Russia took the edge off Hitler's joy. While Germany's back was turned, Russian troops had marched into Lithuania on 15 June. Halifax remarked when informed, 'that leaves me cold'. Not so his German opposite number Ribbentrop, who became hotter and hotter as the Russian Army proceeded to occupy Latvia and Estonia during the following two days.

Then England: Admiral Raeder came to badger the Fuehrer about England on 20 June. Raeder was fundamentally against invading England; his policy was blockade, or 'siege'. But you never knew with the Fuehrer – it was better to be prepared. Raeder had therefore been working on invasion for several months, not that he now felt any more enthusiasm for it. But the Army and the *Luftwaffe* had had their triumphs. What about the *Kriegsmarine*? England, the *Kriegsmarine*'s particular 'last enemy', was still there. With France out, this was the moment to have a crack at her. Blockade or invasion, the *Luftwaffe* help was needed. Hadn't the Fuehrer a couple of weeks before ordered priority for U-boats and aircraft? And if it was to be invasion, what was the army doing about it?

The main trouble about working with the *Luftwaffe* was its dreadful C-in-C. When Raeder had asked him for air protection for his base in Norway at Trondheim, Goering had merely replied with a rude telegram which Raeder now read aloud to his Fuehrer.

It was already obvious that with his *Luftwaffe* Goering was out to win the war single handed. But Raeder also had a job to do – siege, invasion, or both – which depended on Goering's co-operation. The two Commanders-in-Chief would never hit it off, a bad augury for the coming Battle of Britain.

The air was a leading topic at the conference that day. Everyone agreed: successful invasion depended on the *Luftwaffe* gaining command of the air over the Channel and the English coast. Raeder demanded vigorously that the *Luftwaffe* should immediately begin attacking British ports and naval bases. (He missed the point entirely. The *Luftwaffe* was not going to gain 'air superiority' by attacking the Royal Navy. It could only gain it by destroying the RAF and first and foremost its fighters, which guarded the ports, the bomber bases and the aircraft factories.)

But Raeder saw the essential: 'Command of the air is a necessary precondition for invasion . . .'

Meanwhile, Raeder asked if the Fuehrer would agree to the *Kriegsmarine* going ahead with the development of special landing craft? Hitler did so, but his reaction to the project was lukewarm. Losses would be too terrible, and feeling generous in his hour of triumph, he did not now feel like crushing the British. He hoped instead to talk them round.

The Army, which would have to do the fighting on the other side of the Channel, entirely agreed. The next day, on 21 June, the Army Ops. Section noted: 'OKH (Army General Staff) entirely opposed to operation.' Surely they had already done a good enough job in France? At present they could only stare idly across the Channel and ask, '*Was nun?*' ('What now?').

The *Luftwaffe* had every reason to feel that the fight with the RAF would be hard. However, some (including the C-in-C) were so enthusiastic about their overwhelming successes in the Polish and French campaigns that they thought the *Luftkrieg gegen England* would be a walk-over. Even young *Leutnant* Vogel, who was with Paul Temme in I *JG* 2 at Beaumont-le-Roger, wrote on 27 June, 'We hope the Tommies will come in crowds so that our guns will not rust . . . We bathe in the sea in order to get used to the salt water.' A wise precaution. Many of them would soon be swimming far out of their depth.

'After the Battle of France,' said Rudolf Braun, 'everyone was convinced of victory.' The 'arch enemy', France, had been defeated so quickly – thanks largely to *Stuka* pilots like Braun – that they felt nothing could go wrong. They thought the war was over – it would be possible to come to an arrangement with England.

They even felt a sympathy for the English, an 'admiration' for their sporting spirit and sense of fair play. Goebbels's propaganda had said some hard things about the English. For example, that *Luftwaffe* airmen would be murdered if they landed in England. But Rudolf Braun and his friends did not believe it. They hoped for a reconciliation with the English; Braun himself had a deep conviction that Germany and England should come to terms.

On 24 June Braun's unit (I *St. G* 3) went to Caen on the Normandy coast. He had married after the Polish War and now spent some time in Graz with his wife. On returning to Caen he again found the war. His heart sank. His and his friends' views about war with England were mixed. There was no overwhelming enthusiasm. The glorious feeling of adventure as they crusaded through France, sweeping all before them, was gone. Now the war would begin in earnest. A feeling of doubt and apprehension crept into their minds: Things will be harder; our chances of survival less; maybe we shall not return.

Their forebodings were justified. The massacre of the *Stukas* was not far off.

Goering had no qualms about thrashing the RAF, although the Fuehrer did cool him off one day when he became over-pugnacious. *Oberst* Walter Warlimont (Chief of Plans OKW) was present when, on the village square of Brûly-de-Pesche, Goering was 'talking big' (again) about retaliating for a few British bombs which had fallen on residential areas in the Ruhr. 'He wanted to "give them back ten bombs for every one of theirs." ' To hit back *'mit ver-ex-fachter Kraft'* (to the *nth* degree). 'Without hesitating for a second Hitler expressly forbade anything of the sort ... he thought we should wait for a time before taking counter-measures.'

Meanwhile, Monsieur Laroche, Mayor of the little village of Le Coudray (south of Beauvais), had been visited by a party of *Luftwaffe* officers. Monsieur Henri Masselin, Mayor of Neuville d'Amont (a mile and a half to the north) had been warned too. They were not the only ones. Within the bounds of the villages of La Boissière, Parfondeval, le Coudray-en-Thelle, and Le Déluge it was obvious that something was cooking. In the forest near Le Coudray was a tunnel. The Germans came and blocked up one end of it. Farms were requisitioned, and so were the presbytery of Neuville-d'Amont and the *café-tabac* of Le Coudray. Then the Germans started laying down barbed wire and *Feldgendarmes* arrived with their police dogs. The *Luftwaffe* was setting up its headquarters at Le Coudray.

Then one day *Asia* puffed through Le Coudray and stopped in front of its bolt-hole in the forest. Goering had arrived.

The time had come for the *Luftwaffe* to attack the RAF. Goering's friend General Bruno Loerzer's II *Fliegerkorps* was based on the Pas de Calais. It included *KG* 2 (Werner Borner's lot) under *Oberst* Johannes Fink, and two *Stuka Gruppen*. *Oberst* Theo Osterkamp's *JG* 51's Me. 109s were there to escort them. Down Channel behind Le Havre was General Wolfram von Richthofen's *Fliegerkorps* VIII. It included I *St. G* 3 (Rudolf Braun's unit) and *JG* 2 (the Richthofen *Geschwader* in which adventure awaited Paul Temme). The job of these two *Fliegerkorps* was to clear the Channel of British shipping.

Jeschonnek had been working hard on the plans and on 30 June a directive was issued, signed 'Goering, Commander-in-Chief.' It was more preliminary than definite instruction. 'As long as the enemy air force is not defeated, the prime requirement is to attack [it] ... by day and by night, in the air and on the ground, without consideration of other tasks.' Proved in Poland and France, this was the classic method of defeating an enemy air force.

Attack the RAF: in the air, on the ground, by day and by night. Continental air campaigns were one thing, cross-Channel ones another. To say 'without consideration of other tasks' was all very well, but already the chief of *Kriegsmarine*, Raeder, had been screaming for attacks on ports and harbours. The Army and OKW would soon come up with other such 'strategic' targets: food stores, imports, exports, power stations, and the rest.

The principle of 'attacking the enemy air force, its ground organization and its own industry' was fine, and the only way the *Luftwaffe* could gain command of the air – at least, within range of its escort fighters, and that meant from Portsmouth round to the Thames estuary and up to London. (As an escort the Me. 110 was to prove a flop. The Me. 109 could just reach London from the Calais area and get back.) Within that vital sector the *Luftwaffe* could stick to tactical warfare, in which it had proved so terrifyingly adept, and thereby stand a good chance of knocking out the RAF fighter force.

But ordering (as did the directive) to wage an 'overall war against enemy imports, provisions, ... harbours ... transports and warships,' plus any other target which might later be thought up, was to steer it clean away from the avowed task – destruction of the RAF.

Moreover, that kind of strategic warfare called for heavy bomb loads. Well might Kesselring lament the absence of four-engined bombers, but, abetted by Milch, it was he who in 1937 signed the fatal order cancelling them. Jeschonnek, his successor as Chief of Air Staff, was extremely keen on the Ju. 88 – the 'wonder bomber' which could carry but two tons of bombs for short ranges and half that load to the north of England. And then of course there were Udet's *Stukas* . . .

The *Luftwaffe* High Command was already showing signs of muddled, if not downright ignorant thinking. More was to come.

OKW, and notably its chief of operations General Alfred Jodl, had also been thinking what they would do to England. But within OKW was a band of 'young Turks' – headed by *Oberst* Warlimont and *Oberst* Lossberg. For them, blockade or siege of England was too slow, too old-fashioned. Lossberg later wrote, 'As our troops stood around Calais after the victory . . . they saw before them the chalk cliffs of Dover on the other side of the Channel . . . Those German soldiers were brimming with confidence, they believed they could carry the day against any defence. More out of the mood at the front than from sober evaluation . . . the thought was born in them to land in England.'

But Jodl was not to be rushed. Like Keitel, he had 'words' for the Fuehrer – 'the greatest military genius' – and hung on to Hitler's every word. And Hitler was still cool about invasion. So the six-page memorandum that Jodl put out on 30 June was a mixture of his own and his Fuehrer's thinking. It was called 'The Continuation of the War against England', and it said in substance, 'If political measures do not succeed, England's will to resist must be broken by force.'

Force could be applied either 'by direct attacks on the English homeland', or 'by extending the war to the periphery, (e.g. attacks on Suez, Gibralter etc.). For the English homeland Jodl recommended three possibilities: naval-air siege; terror attacks on heavily populated areas; and invasion. But whatever the method, Jodl was comfortably sure of the outcome: 'Germany's final victory over England is only a matter of time.' First and foremost the RAF had to be knocked out. This would allow the *Luftwaffe* to set itself against the British aircraft industry and pluck from the Englishmen's hands arrows they might otherwise let fly against Germany. The RAF was the main objective. Jodl saw it going down under the blows of the *Luftwaffe* and with it Britain's precious aircraft industry.

The treatment reserved for the RAF would be extended to Britain's food supplies, with nasty jabs as required – 'occasional terror attacks' on the civilian population. Jodl believed this mixture would 'paralyse and finally break the will of the people to resist and thereby force their government to capitulate'.

A landing in England could be undertaken 'only if the command of the air has been gained by the *Luftwaffe*'. Jodl did not believe that the object of a landing should be to defeat England by arms. That was the job of the *Kriegsmarine*, and above all the *Luftwaffe*. The German Army would land 'only to deal a *coup de grâce*, if still necessary, to an England economically paralysed and impotent in the air'. He forecast England would be thus brought low by August or early September. But invasion plans must meanwhile go ahead.

Jodl ended on a hopeful note: there was every expectation that England would 'be inclined to peace when she learns that she can now get it at relatively low cost'.

At Tannenburg (his new headquarters in the Black Forest region) Hitler, according to the Italian Ambassador, Dino Alfieri, was in 'one of those periods of isolation that precede great decisions.' This put it a bit strongly perhaps, for next day on 1 July Hitler received Alfieri, who then found him restless. He was 'considering many alternatives ... raising doubts'. If Hitler's mind were not on a great decision it was certainly much occupied by England. Jodl's memorandum was before the Fuehrer, who then told Alfieri that Germany was preparing an attack against Britain. It would be 'bloody', and a 'horror'.

In Berlin, General Fritz Halder was spending a busman's holiday. He had celebrated his birthday the day before with his family and, combining pleasure with business, had dropped in on a few friends. Baron von Weizsaecker, State Secretary of the Foreign Office, said that there was 'no concrete basis for any peace negotiations', adding that 'Britain will probably need one more demonstration of our military strength before she gives in and leaves us a free hand in eastern Europe.'

Halder was worried by what would become of the thirty-five divisions which he had orders to demobilize. How would they ever find employment? The General need not have worried. Millions of young Germans would yet be needed for the charnel house of the Russian front, where Hitler was so longing for England to allow him a free hand.

Halder then called on his friend Admiral Schniewind, Naval Chief of Operations, to get the latest on the invasion. The two talked alone and at some length. As usual, command of the air was agreed to be the first need. Hopefully, a calm sea too. Halder estimated that one hundred thousand men would go across in the first wave – the *Luftwaffe* would provide artillery cover. The General and the Admiral talked of submarines, mines, underwater net barrages, concrete landing barges, and the beaches where they would run ashore. Schniewind was anxious about the

British Navy's overwhelming strength. It cooled the *Kriegsmarine*'s interest in invasion.

Halder, however, was now filled with enthusiasm. 'After 1 July a landing operation in England was, on the part of the Army General Staff, considered feasible.' From that date the Army did not count on peace talks, but 'the elimination of the British island as a basis for counter-attack later against the German-occupied Channel coast'. Their reasoning was well founded.

Halder next called on the Chief of Army Ordnance, General Emil Leeb, to find out his position on amphibious tanks. Leeb protested that 'he was told all along that invasion of England was not to be considered'. But Halder warned him: 'Possibilities must be examined, for if the political leadership requires a landing, they will want everything done at top speed.' Leeb thought again.

On 2 July, back at Army General Headquarters (now at Fontainebleau), Halder immediately got down to discussion with his C-in-C (Brauchitsch) about 'the basis for a campaign against England'. After that Brauchitsch went off to Berlin.

That day OKW came back with an answer to Hitler's parting request, as he left Brûly-de-Pesche, for basic invasion plans. For the first time Supreme HQ breathed the word 'invasion'. 'The Fuehrer and Supreme Commander have decided that a landing in England is possible,' stated the directive, 'provided air superiority can be attained and certain other conditions fulfilled ... Preparations are to be begun immediately.' The *Kriegsmarine*, Army and *Luftwaffe* were to submit plans – the *Luftwaffe* to say whether and when air superiority could be achieved. Everything hung on air superiority.

However, plans were subject to the proviso that 'invasion is still only a plan, and has not yet been decided upon'. Hitler firmly believed that the end of the war was at hand, that Britain had no chance of victory and that he could talk her into peace. He did not even trouble to put his signature to that directive. Keitel signed it instead.

Meanwhile, the Supreme Commander took time off for picnicking in the lovely country around Tannenburg. One of those who shared with his Fuehrer these al fresco meals, the Secretary of State, Otto Meissner, averred, 'Hitler spoke repeatedly of this ... that he saw the time had arrived ... for making a peace proposal on a grand and generous scale to Great Britain. He would therefore, in a *Reichstag* speech, make an offer ... of a covenanted peace; ... he hoped that the English people ... would concur and exert pressure on the warmonger-led cabinet.'

But on 4 July his optimism was rudely challenged. Word came that the British fleet had attacked the French ships at Oran to prevent them from falling into German hands. There was consternation at Hitler's Tannenberg headquarters. In Berlin, three days later, he told Ciano that he was prepared to 'unleash a storm of fire and steel on the British'.

Chapter 21

The Commander-in-Chief of Fighter Command viewed the imminent air assault with quiet confidence. His Order of Battle of 7 July reflected the immense efforts made in the last months. Fifty-two squadrons were shown, of which twenty-five had Hurricanes and nineteen had Spitfires. Six had Blenheims (suitable only for night fighting) and two had Defiants. The two-seater Defiants had a brief, spectacular success over Dunkirk before the Me. 109 pilots got wise to their four-gun rear turret. Subsequently their gallant crews were cut to pieces, and the Defiants became night-fighters.

On the ground a fighter squadron normally possessed sixteen aircraft. The forty-four squadrons therefore represented a force of 704 Hurricanes and Spitfires – single-seater, eight-gun fighters. However, in the air, a squadron was a unit of twelve machines only. Assuming sufficient serviceability 528 single-seater fighters stood guard over Britain to meet the *Luftwaffe*'s assault in the air by day.

Dowding's Fighter Command was divided into Groups: On 7 July No. 11 Group (Air Vice Marshal Keith Park) covered the whole of the south of England with twenty-three single-seater squadrons, a fighting force of 276 aircraft. But ten days later a new Group, No. 10 (Air Vice Marshal Quintin Brand), took over half of 11 Group's territory (from Portsmouth westwards) and seven of its single-seater squadrons – a fighting force of eighty-four aircraft. This left Keith Park's 11 Group covering the approaches to London from Portsmouth to the Thames estuary, with sixteen single-seater squadrons – a fighting force of 192 aircraft. The thick of the fighting would obviously be in 11 Group.

The East Coast and Midlands were guarded by No. 12 Group (Air Vice Marshal Trafford Leigh-Mallory) with eleven single-seater squadrons, a fighting force of 132 aircraft. No. 12 Group (Air Vice Marshal R.E. 'Birdie' Saul) defended the north and north-east with ten single-seater squadrons – a fighting force of 120 aircraft.

The 'eyes' of Fighter Command, No. 60 Group, comprised a network of some fifty stations. They detected enemy aircraft and passed the 'plots' to Fighter Command Filter Room where they were sorted out and passed on to Fighter Command Ops. Room, from where they were passed on again to Group and to Sector Ops. Rooms. The Sector controller guided or 'vectored' the fighters to intercept. Overland the Observer Corps took over from radar and passed on direct to Group Ops. Rooms up to the minute information of everything within view or earshot.

The Germans knew about British radar but never dreamed that what the radar 'saw' was being passed on to the fighter pilot in the air through such a highly elaborate communications system. As they approached the 'island' it was a brutal surprise to the *Luftwaffe* to find RAF fighters waiting for them.

Behind the fighters were the AA batteries, searchlights and balloons. AA Command and Balloon Command came under Fighter Command's operational control.

In the opposite camp, *Luftflotte* 2 (General 'Smiling Albert' Kesselring) and *Luftflotte* 3 (General Hugo Sperrle) were arrayed against the South of England. *Luftflotte* 5 (General Hans Juergen Stumpff) in Norway were to enter the day battle for but one disastrous day.

At this time *Luftflotten* 2 and 3 could muster between them a total force of approximately 1,800 serviceable aircraft (2,500 were available).

This force of 1,800 serviceable aircraft consisted of a round 1,000 bombers (including dive-bombers), 650 Me. 109 single-seater fighters, and 160 Me. 110 two-seater long-range fighters. This was its nominal day fighting force. There was no lack of pilots.

In July, just over 500 English single-seater day fighters were ready to join battle in the air against an array of 1,800 *Luftwaffe* aircraft. (Milch's figures are slightly higher: 2,105.) This gives a rudimentary idea of the strength of the opposing forces. They never met in a pitched battle in those numbers, but were deployed in lesser cohorts. But those were the basic fighting strengths in the two camps as the RAF fighters waited for the *Luftwaffe*'s onslaught during the warm summer days of July 1940.

With his doughty little band of fighters Air Chief Marshal Dowding waited for the *Luftwaffe* to open the battle. Only one question continued to disturb him. Would that little band of pilots be able to hold out long enough? Or would they be cut down before they could turn the battle against the enemy? Dowding had no serious shortage of machines. They were replaceable, but not the skilled pilots who flew them.

But another anxiety now came to trouble Dowding's mind on the very eve of battle: his future as Commander-in-Chief of the fighters. On 5 July the Chief of Air Staff had written, 'I am writing to ask if you will again defer your retirement beyond 14 July. I should loathe [*sic*] for you to leave the Fighter Command on that day and I would be very glad if you would continue until the end of October.' Dowding was understandably irritated. His retirement date seemed of little consequence at this moment when the whole responsiblity for Britain's survival was in his hands, and his alone.

He replied on 7 July inviting the CAS to 'cast his eye' down a list of the numerous occasions when his retirement had been raised. He protested vigorously at 'the lack of consideration involved in delaying [this] proposal . . . until ten days before the date of my retirement. I have had four retiring dates given me and now you are proposing a fifth.

'Before the war I should have been glad enough to retire; now I am anxious to stay, because I feel there is no one who will fight as I do when proposals are made which would reduce the Defence Forces of the Country below the extreme danger point.' This fighting spirit was as fierce as ever it was on 15 May last. But maybe he was a little unjust to Newall who had since then become 'one of his supporters'.

Then came the bombshell: 'I suggest that I should not . . . retire . . . before the first retiring date given me, 24 April 1942, or the end of the war, whichever is the earlier.' At that date he would reach the age of sixty.

Dowding was so angry that he dispatched a copy of his letter to the Air Minister, Archibald Sinclair, who replied on 10 July: '. . . it was my wish that you should remain in command of our Fighter Squadrons upon whose success in defeating the German attack . . . during the next three months will almost certainly depend the issue of this war.

'I could give you no higher proof of my confidence in you and . . . the assurance of my full support.'

That day 85 Squadron was ordered forward to Martlesham, near the East Coast. With enemy action warming up I had been there myself for some days with A Flight, patrolling convoys. Ten years had passed since the day when as an air-crazy schoolboy I had seen the Beardmore-Focke Wulf 'inflexible' at Martlesham, and at Felixstowe nearby had sat in the slender streamlined Schneider Cup Supermarine seaplanes. Little did I dream that a 'return to Felixstowe' was to be included in the next day's programme.

When not over the convoys we basked drowsily in the sun, enjoying the pastoral life of Martlesham's scented heath. Across the Channel, pilots of the *Luftwaffe* (also in their early twenties) bathed in the sea and thought life very pleasant. But the time for killing was at hand.

On 10 July, at noon, two German reconnaisance aircraft were shadowing a west-bound convoy as it entered the Channel off Ramsgate. They were driven off by British fighters, but too late. The telephone rang at the omnibus HQ at Cap Blanc Nez of *Oberst* Johannes Fink (*Kanakafu*).* An hour later the Dornier 17s of Major Fuch's III *KG* 2 were climbing away from the Arras St Leger airfield. *Hauptmann* Hannes Trautloft too, leading twenty Me. 109s of his III *JG* 51 was airborne from St Omer to rendezvous the bombers. The escort was completed by thirty Me. 110s from the one-legged Major Huth's *ZG* 26. The attacking force numbered seventy.

Six Hurricanes of 32 Squadron, Biggin Hill, patrolled the convoy as it passed the cliffs of Dover just before 2.00 p.m. Diving out of a rain cloud they ran slap into the German formation and engaged immediately. Meanwhile, elements of 56, 64, 74 and 111 Squadrons were coming to the rescue. 'Suddenly the sky was full of British fighters,' Hannes Trautloft remarked. 'Today we were going to be in for a tough time.'

That evening in the House of Commons the Minister of Information, Sir Edward Grigg, described the engagement as 'one of the greatest air battles of the war'. The Battle of Britain had begun.

Thirty British single-seater fighters against twenty Me. 109s. But it was nonsense to think the Me. 109s were outnumbered. In addition to them were twenty Dorniers and thirty Me. 110s, all part of a fighting force the British fighters had to oppose.

The Germans (and Uncle Theo Osterkamp was one of them) vainly believed that the Battle of Britain was going to be a romantic jousting contest in the clouds between the fighters of the RAF and of the *Luftwaffe*. But we RAF fighters were not in the least interested in the German fighters – except in so far as they were interested in us. Our job was defence. German fighters could do no harm to Britain. German bombers with their deadly loads were the menace. Our orders were to seek them out and to destroy them. Only when their Me. 109 escort interfered did

*Full title: *Kanal kampfuehrer* (Channel-war-leader).

it become a fleeting battle between fighter and fighter. But we tried to avoid them, not to challenge them.

The Me. 110s were another matter. Long-range fighters with a tremendous forward fire power (twice that of the Me. 109E), they were, however, highly vulnerable to Hurricanes and Spitfires which could easily out-manoeuvre them and then have to face only a single machine-gun firing rearwards. Menaced by our single-seater the Me. 110s immediately went into a 'defensive circle', covering each other's tails, as they did that day.

Finally there was the Me. 109 pilots' contempt for our Hurricanes. We thought they were great and we would prove it by shooting down around one thousand *Luftwaffe* aircraft in the Battle. The *Luftwaffe* airmen often mistook Hurricanes for Spitfires. There was the crew of their famous Heinkel which landed 'in the sea' on Wick airfield, who swore a Spitfire had downed them. During the Battle of France, Theo Osterkamp seemed to see Spitfires everywhere. There were no Spitfires in France, only Hurricanes. Even General Kesselring said, 'Only the Spitfires bothered us.' The *Luftwaffe* seemed to be suffering from Spitfire snobbery.

Three Hurricanes and four Me. 109s were lost in the Channel engagement that day. At Martlesham there was no shooting but a feeling of increasing danger made us stick closer than ever to our protégés, the convoys. In four patrols I flew for nearly six hours. It was a long day, and half-clothed I went to bed early in the tent on the edge of the airfield. I was due to come to readiness with Yellow section at 5.00 a.m. the next day.

Over at Arras St Leger four men also slept early that night. One of them was Werner Borner. He and his comrades, *Oberleutnant* Genzow (his pilot); *Leutnant* Bernschein, navigator; and *Feldwebel* Lohrer, flight mechanic, were due off at dawn next morning, 11 July.

Dornier 17 *Gustav Marie* was airborne just about as I telephoned to Sector Ops., 'Yellow section 85 Squadron at readiness.' Mist hung low over Martlesham Heath as the fitters warmed up our Hurricanes. I watched mine, VY-K, the tug of its roaring Merlin engine straining against the chocks. K had been my 'kite' since I came to 85. A pilot has a feeling of belonging to his aircraft, and when I had been strapped into the cockpit of my Hurricane I felt we became an integral whole. K felt good in my hands, and smelt good – the reek of an aircraft was always thrilling, nostalgic.

Back in the tent we dozed on our beds, waiting. What would the day bring forth? Useless even to wonder; better to live for the moment. Suddenly the telephone rang. 'One aircraft only, scramble and call controller when airborne.' Within minutes I was off the ground, cleaving through a soft blanket of low-lying mist. Guided by the controller, I climbed up through drifting rain cloud and headed out to sea.

Always the sea. For the last eight months I had been flying convoy patrols in all weathers and in all seas. 'In' was perhaps not the exact word. – our Mae Wests would keep us afloat. But we had no dinghies. If we fell in the sea too far from land to swim, a lot would depend on luck.

I was at eight thousand feet and still climbing in and out of grey soggy rain clouds. Below yawned a dark, blue-grey void and somewhere at its bottom the sea. Suddenly an aircraft appeared out of the cloud above, going the other way. A Dornier 17! Through the miracle of radar we had met in a cloud.

I wheeled my Hurricane round, craning my head backwards, my eyes riveted on the Dornier. It must not escape. My only hope of not being spotted was to keep directly underneath, stalking and climbing until I could draw level astern and in range. It was my only hope of getting in a decisive burst of fire before being seen.

The going was bad that morning. I felt enormously visible, and could only dimly see the Dornier through my rain-washed windscreen. I opened up the hood and slanted my head out into the battering slipstream. It helped a bit. Another hundred yards and I would have to risk a pot shot.

After leaving Arras St Leger, Dornier *Gustav Marie* headed out over the North Sea, toward England. 'The nearer we came to the English coast,' said Werner Borner, 'the lower the clouds. Heavy rain pattered on the cabin windows. There was no "trade" to be seen.' All the same, Werner Borner was keeping a sharp look-out. He had the best view astern, and the lives of his crew depended on him.

Then through a break in the cloud he saw the English coast. 'Looks a bit like Schleswig-Holstein,' said someone. Another voice on the intercom complained, 'What a bind having to fly in weather like this.' They were forbidden to bomb the mainland by day. Vaguely they had heard that it was to avoid upsetting the Fuehrer's peace plans. But they flew inland for some 'aerial sightseeing'.

Over Lowestoft Gonzow decided to bomb the shipping lying in the harbour. *Feldwebel* Lohrer opened the bomb doors and down went ten hundred-pound bombs. Then Gonzow turned *Gustav Marie* south for home and the whole crew began singing, 'Good-bye Johnny ...' They were still singing a few minutes later when there came a yell in the intercom of '*Achtung, Jäger!*' Werner Borner had seen me.

He grabbed his MG15 and opened fire. His bright-red tracer came darting towards me and I remember thinking, 'It's too early to fire.' I had to get closer. Then I pressed the tit and things warmed up inside the Dornier. 'Pieces of metal and other fragments were flying everywhere,' said Werner. One of the ammunition drums was hit and bounced onto Werner's knees. Then *Leutnant* Bernschein, on the starboard rear gun, was hit in the head and fell onto the floor of the cabin. A second later *Feldwebel* Lohrer collapsed on top of him wounded in the head and throat. Blood was everywhere.

Only Werner was left to shoot it out with me. As he reached for a new drum of ammunition there was a violent explosion just above his head, and he saw three fragments whip past pilot Gonzow's head, missing it by a fraction and smashing the windscreen. Unscathed, Gonzow flew on but Werner now felt blood trickling down his cheeks. 'I took no notice – things were too hot. With a last effort I shot at the Hurricane which was so close, I could see the pilot. I shall never forget that sight of yellow-orange flashes from its guns criss-crossing with the incendiary and tracer from my own guns – all of it silhouetted against a ghostly-looking bank of dark thunderclouds. Then my gun was knocked out of my hands.'

But not before Borner had used it to good effect. I was still firing when suddenly there was a bright orange explosion in the cockpit in front of me. I suppose I must have kept firing a second longer – those last bullets knocked Borner's gun from his hands. When I broke away Borner saw my Hurricane diving down, trailing a plume of black smoke. A moment later *Gustav Marie* was swallowed up in the clouds.

The cabin of the Dornier was a shambles. 'Bits and pieces everywhere, blood-covered faces, the smell of cordite, all windows shot up. There were hits everywhere: in the wings, in the fuselage, and in the engine. But what a surprise: no one was really seriously wounded and our good old *Gustav Marie* was still flying!'

Which was more than could be said for my Hurricane VY-K. The engine was hit. Powerless, I could only glide down through the rain clouds. I called Kiwi One, the ground station: 'Wagon leader calling. Am hit and bailing out in sea. One, two, three, four, five. Take a fix if you can.' Then I was clear of cloud and the sea opened up below – twenty miles to England, two hundred to the other side. Not a ship in sight. Now only two things mattered, life and death. The next few moments would decide. Meanwhile, I was far more concerned about trying to spot a ship, and peering below I banked my aeroplane steeply to left and to right. Then below my right wing a little ship appeared. It looked like a toy, as if someone had put it there at the last moment.

The sea was waiting for me. It was the minute of truth: life or death. It occurred to me that to survive was only to run the chance of dying all over again a week, or a month later. Faced with the simple alternatives of death or survival, instinct takes over from reason and the mind works with clarity and precision. I was surprised to feel so calm about the whole thing, perhaps because neither death nor life was yet certain. The sea would decide.

As I stood in the cockpit to dive out into space there came to my mind a story I had read as a boy: a German airman of the First World War, grabbing vainly at the ripcord ring, had crashed to death. I crossed my arms in front of me, my right hand firmly on the vital ring. Then I dived out head first, and down to the sea. I was falling on my back, in total silence, my feet pointing at the sky, when I pulled the ripcord. The parachute canopy clacked open and the harness wrenched my body violently from its headlong fall. Far below I could see Hurricane VY-K diving vertically towards the sea to disappear in an eruption of spume and spray.

Swinging there high above the sea I felt safe for the moment. Having first attached the ripcord ring to the microphone wire, I took off my helmet and dropped it. That rid me of one encumbrance. Clad as I was only in a light sweater and trousers, there remained but one more thing, my flying boots. Oddly enough I preferred to stick to them. If necessary I would kick them off in the sea.

When the big splash came I hit the harness release knob and sank, it seemed fathoms deep, into green obscurity. The harness was gone and long seconds followed while I thrashed out vigorously with arms and legs. When at last I broke the surface I saw the little ship lying less than a mile away. Luckily they had seen me and were lowering a boat. I kicked off my boots and feeling tiny and impotent in that immense sea swam around rather relaxed, supported by my Mae West. The bulbous yellow life-jacket filled with kapok could be inflated only by mouth. I blew through the pink tube, but swallowed mouthfuls of sea water. So I took to swimming again and steered towards my helmet, a small dark blob floating a hundred yards away, with the ripcord ring still firmly attached. This precious souvenir more than compensated for my boots.

When the little boat, rowed by four stalwart sailors, approached, a fifth stood up in the stern brandishing a boat-hook and shouted, 'Blimey, if he ain't a fucking Hun.' Only one answer was possible: 'I'm not, I'm a fucking Englishman,' I shouted back, and the boat hook was quietly lowered. A moment later brawny arms were around me and a warm Yorkshire voice was speaking, 'Come on lad, we've got you. It's all right.' And they hauled me into the boat. Unknown, willing hands had saved me from certain death.

Ten minutes later I was aboard the trawler *Cap Finisterre*, out of Hull. Her burly pink-faced master, Mr Samson, put me in his cabin where I changed into a blue sailor's jersey and a pair of bell-bottom trousers. Mr Samson handed me a double ration of rum, but I protested. It was only 6.30 a.m. and I had not eaten. 'Swallow it down,' he said, 'then you can go below and have breakfast.' There I met the crew. One of the seamen was just down from Oxford. The ship's engineer was a Burmese.

More rum was served to toast the survivor. Then I went up on deck, tottering slightly, and sat with the mate on the fo'c'sle as we sailed back to Harwich. It was he who had brandished the boat-hook and I learned from him then that when she picked me up the *Cap Finisterre* was well off course and in the middle of a minefield. I had been luckier than I thought. I gave the mate my flying helmet as a souvenir, and he said it would be handy in bad weather.

In *Gustav Marie* the wounded were roughly bandaged. Gonzow brought the Dornier down to six hundred feet where he could see the water. The crew tried to jettison the remaining bombs, but they hung up. The wiring circuit was shot through and the manual release smashed. By deflecting my bullets, the ten remaining bombs had probably saved *Gustav Marie's* crew from a worse fate.

But when at last they were over Arras St Leger, the undercarriage would not come down. They would have to belly-land – sitting on top of the bombs. They could see fire crews and an ambulance waiting near the runway.

Then *Gustav Marie* was ploughing a deep furrow in the grass. Dirt and sand shot up into the cabin and the aircraft jerked to a stop. Said Werner Borner, 'Our brave Do. 17m Y 5 GM – *Gustav Marie* for short, had got us home, despite 220 hits in the engines, fuel tanks and other vital parts.'

Meanwhile, I was steaming back to Harwich, where the *Cap Finisterre* arrived just before noon. Sloops and mine-sweepers were berthed beam to beam three or four deep. We came alongside the outside one of a group and gratefully I took leave of Mr Samson and his crew. Then I climbed over the gunwale of the *Cap Finisterre* on to the deck of the adjacent mine-sweeper. The word had gone round, 'a survivor'. I was led below immediately and asked, 'What will you take for it?' 'Rum, please,' I said, already well steeped and, with my blue jersey and bell-bottoms, beginning to feel every inch a sailor. I had to down two more rums before these big-hearted men of the sea would let me go. It was with considerably less agility that I climbed over the gunwale of the next ship, dismayed to see that there was still one more to go before I reached the jetty. Despite my protests I was led below once more. 'A survivor,' people keep repeating and they gathered around me and raised their glasses.

The warm little ceremony was repeated in the last ship and then at last I stepped – it was hardly the word – ashore. Waiting for me was Flight Lieutenant Hamilton ('Hammy') Commander of A Flight. I felt slightly heroic at that moment. After all, I had been shot down. And what fighter pilot can honestly deny that it is more romantic to be shot down than to shoot others down? Also, I had been shot down in the sea, and this was really something since I had been rescued and now stood (with some difficulty it is true) ready once more to command my men. But the subordinate officer who now faced me just roared with laughter. Hammy said I looked a scream in my bell-bottoms. And how come I had got myself shot down by a Dornier, of all things? So the word was already going round. Shot down by a Dornier.

Hammy led me to a benign-looking naval officer. On the chit he gave me I signed off as a shipwrecked mariner and became once more an airman. Then I was bundled into a boat and ferried across to Felixstowe. There, on a summer's day years ago, flying had been for me but a youthful dream. Now it had become a stern reality. That evening – when the rum had worn off – I went up on patrol again in a new Hurricane.

As I was leaving Harwich, Flight Lieutenant Al Deere was leading six Spitfires of B Flight 54 Squadron from their forward base at Manston. Crossing the coast near Deal, Al looked down at the shimmering sea. Suddenly a glint of silver caught his eye. It took a fraction of a second before his mind – conditioned to the silhouettes of German combat planes in green and brown war paint – registered this strange apparition – a silver seaplane with red crosses (not black) standing out boldly on its wings and fuselage. A Heinkel 59 rescue plane. A dozen Me. 109s were weaving behind it.

What was a German rescue plane doing there, so close to the English coast? Looking for a *Luftwaffe* pilot in the sea? Or pretending to, hoping to find a British convoy? Those Me. 109s were not out on a joy-ride. The possibility of attacking a Red Cross rescue plane had never occurred to Al Deere. When he had an enemy plane in his sights he shot to destroy the plane, not the men inside it. If they were killed he thought, 'Poor devils, but it might have been me.' If they baled out, and especially if they were fished out of the sea and saved from drowning, he thought, 'Good luck to them', and hoped he should have the same good fortune.

We were not, thank God, involved in the intimate, personal killing of men which is the lot of the infantry – though we fired with the same bloody end in view. The men inside the aircraft must be killed or maimed or taken prisoner, otherwise they would return to battle. Very few of us thought of it that way, and this gave to our battle in the air the character of a terribly dangerous sport and not of a dismal, sordid slaughter.

Yet there were nuances to this genial situation, and Al Deere was at this instant faced with one. If the German Red Cross Heinkel rescued a German pilot he would probably, like me, be on patrol again that day. This was one reason to attack the rescue plane. Another was that if the Red Cross plane spotted a British convoy it would certainly not refrain from reporting its position. A third, the simplest of all, was that the escort of twelve Me. 109s was an admission that the Red Cross plane was expecting to be attacked.

Al Deere warned his Spitfires over the 'blower' and then dived to attack. A minute later, Spitfires and Me. 109s were milling in violent combat. A Spitfire plunged into the sea. Then a Me. 109 went down a 'flamer'. Someone peeled off and went for the Heinkel 59. It wobbled and slowed up and finally plumes of spray flared out behind its floats and it came to rest on the sea.

As Al hauled his Spitfire out of a steep turn a Me. 109 was coming at him head-on. Too late to avoid it. It was on top of him. He ducked and felt his Spitfire stagger as the Me. 109 crashed past overhead. The Spitfire shuddered horribly as the propeller slowed and Al saw the blades bent back nearly horizontally.

Bruised and shaken, he crash-landed in a field near Manston. 'Unlikely that I shall ever have a closer shave than that,' he said to himself. But he was wrong.

In 1940 the *Luftwaffe* looked after its ditched crews better than did the

RAF. The German airmen had a better chance of surviving, because they had inflatable dinghies. Their chances of being spotted were better because they carried a chemical that stained the sea around them a yellowish-green. And they had a better chance of being picked up because the *Luftwaffe* had an organized air-sea rescue service of some thirty aircraft and high-speed launches.

After the He. 59 incident German rescue aircraft would be camouflaged and armed. Major-Doktor Greiling, medical officer of *JG* 52, was also a rescue pilot. When 'rescue alert' was given he immediately stood by his aircraft, which carried two spare dinghies. He spent many hours searching for ditched aircrews – dropping them a dinghy if needed. Often RAF crews were picked up by German rescue aircraft. Some would perish in them, shot down by their own comrades.

The Air Ministry pondered the question of shooting down German rescue aircraft. We then received an official order to shoot them down. I never saw the order. If I had I might well have thought, as did James McComb, 'Better look the other way.' But the Air Ministry had a case. They maintained that British convoys and minefields were reported by the rescue aircraft. Major Greiling agreed.

Our own hopes of survival in the sea depended first on luck. With luck you would be spotted and picked up by the gallant crews of the lifebout service, or by a passing ship. It was luck for the *Cap Finisterre* to be there that morning. Two weeks later she was sent to the bottom by enemy bombs.

Hitler had retired to the Berghof and on the morning of 11 July he received Admiral Raeder. The Admiral spoke frankly of his lack of enthusiasm for invasion. It was riddled with problems such as sweeping mines near the enemy coast and laying them on the flanks of the crossing. Assembly and preparation of the invasion fleet would take time, and Germany's economy was bound to suffer. No one had yet solved the question of unloading vehicles on the enemy shore, although landing craft were being tried out. He really could not advise invasion. England's defeat lay through siege and for that the combined efforts of the *Kriegsmarine* and the *Luftwaffe* were needed. Invasion should only be a last resort.

Hitler, who was in pensive mood, agreed: invasion would be a last resort although, let it be noted, he had given orders the day before for all available heavy artillery to be mounted on the Channel coast opposite Dover. In his mind, the covering fire thus obtained would be vital to a Channel crossing.

But he was still hoping that his forthcoming *Reichstag* speech would tempt England into making peace. What did Raeder think of the idea? Raeder was frankly not so sure. While against invasion, he believed that any talking to England should be backed by force. The U-boats should tighten their grip on her, the *Luftwaffe* should hit her ports and principal centres of population – Liverpool for instance, or London. Be brutal, and that way cool England off and put her in a mood for talking.

Over at *Luftwaffe* headquarters Jeschonnek had just come out with an OKL order in line with Raeder's thinking: 'Directive for the Intensive Air Warfare against England.' It was not in Raeder's fire-eating spirit – unusual for him – but it did stress the now familiar theme: destruction of the enemy air force and armament industry was 'a prerequisite condition to a successful air war against England'.

A copy went to General Otto Stapf, Army Liaison Officer at OKL. He informed his chief, Halder: 'The *Luftwaffe* estimate that it will take two to four weeks to beat down (*niederschlagen*) the enemy air force.'

On 12 July it became Jodl's turn to pronounce on invasion, which he did in a paper entitled, 'First Thoughts on a Landing in England.' The landing would be difficult, for Britain had command of the sea. But here the *Luftwaffe* would be the key: 'We can substitute command of the air for the naval supremacy we do not possess . . . The role of artillery will fall to the *Luftwaffe* . . .' The OKW Chief of Operations was thinking big: the landing must take place in the form of 'a mighty river crossing on a broad front', but he admitted that strategic surprise would be impossible, with the RAF snooping all the time.

The first condition for a successful invasion, said Jodl, was the moral and actual defeat of the RAF until they could not attack the crossing. This would leave the *Luftwaffe* free for its second task: 'The crossing and disembarkation will take place under the protection of the entire *Luftwaffe* . . . mines . . . long-range coastal artillery.' The *Luftwaffe* would be fully extended. They must: 'prevent interference by the enemy air force – attack naval forces far away from the crossing – reduce coastal defences at the landing beaches – pin down enemy ground forces – annihilate reinforcements and destroy their roads of access.' It was a big assignment.

And then the invasion operation was baptized 'Lion'. In a few days its proud sponsor would change its name to a more appropriate one.

The soldiers' growing enthusiasm for invasion left the *Kriegsmarine*'s chief cold. Admiral Raeder knew that his navy, already partially crippled by the loss of a dozen destroyers in Norway, could not fight on equal terms with the Royal Navy. Again, the *Luftwaffe* was the key, as Jodl and

K

everyone else (including Raeder himself) insisted. But Raeder wondered if the *Luftwaffe* could really tip the scales against the British Navy? As a sailor he had taken good note of Dunkirk. The *Luftwaffe* had sunk 240 out of the total of 860 allied ships – all types – engaged: 28 per cent. Of naval vessels alone – including a cruiser, destroyers, sloops, gunboats, and minesweepers, 85 in all – they had sunk and damaged 40: nearly fifty per cent, an impressive figure. Could the *Luftwaffe*, at the mercy of RAF fighters and the weather, repeat this figure if it came to an 'opposed crossing'? This brought him back to the same old problem – air superiority: the *Luftwaffe* was the key. It had to weigh in to the British Navy and soften them up.

Kanakafu Fink had already started. But with his one bomber *Geschwader* (*KG 2*, a crack unit) and two *Stuka gruppen*, was he ever going to achieve his grandiose task of destroying British shipping in the Channel and the Thames estuary? Richthofen's *Stukas* were further down Channel, but before reaching a convoy they had to cross more than fifty miles of sea. For RAF fighters the *Stukas* were 'a piece of cake'. Fink and Richthofen versus Britannia (who firmly ruled the Channel and North Sea waves) while the RAF's eagle hovered overhead, ready to strike. Could these two dent Britannia's shield? The month of July would show.

Meanwhile, they had had a poor start. In the first three days three convoys were attacked. One small ship was sunk at a cost to the *Luftwaffe* of twenty-three aircraft, to Fighter Command of thirteen fighters.

85 Squadron flew daily from dawn till dusk over the convoys – they had peculiar code-names like Agent, Booty and Bread – in our sector. Action was rare – Fink was busier further south – but we never relaxed our guard. Nor did the convoys. They were distinctly trigger-happy and sometimes fired on us. We forgave them. Recognition was difficult and sailors were never masters of it. One day my brother Michael, Captain of the destroyer *Viscount*, wrote me, 'My guns are so old I do not think they could even deal with a Hun plane. But a Dornier flew over us the other day and I let her have it – not for long because she was an Anson (of RAF Coastal Command). We could not do without them . . . our morning paper is now delivered . . .'

On the dawn patrol we would fly low past the escorting destroyers, waving good morning to the men on the bridge – but one morning they answered with an angry shake of the fist. We had given them a fright.

We admired the sailors and were out to do our best for them. We faced similar dangers. On the 12 July 85 Squadron lost Sergeant Jowitt, claimed by the sea while helping to fend off an attack on the convoy Booty.

Theo Osterkamp, *Kommodore* of *JG* 51, hence official Grand Protector of 'Papa' Fink's bombers, was not interested in naval warfare. He was after fighters. 'Our enemy is the British fighter,' he told his pilots. 'Be as cunning as a fox . . . wait patiently . . . then strike like lightning and get out as fast. We have now got a hard battle against a particularly obstinate enemy . . . good luck in your fight against the "lords",' as he called us. Once the skies were cleared of British fighters the *Luftwaffe* would have it all their own way. That would even make Admiral Raeder feel better.

But how to destroy the British fighters, especially as the *Luftwaffe* was supposed to be destroying British shipping? Osterkamp sent for 'Papa' Fink, 'luckily a reasonable man'. Fink's view was that 'the British fighters are sure to attack the *Stukas*, then you can deal with them'. Osterkamp thought differently. A fighter escort was too tied to its bombers, it was not free enough to get in a good crack at the enemy fighters. Fink saw the point and they came to a gentleman's agreement.

The *Stukas* would be escorted by Me. 110 *Zerstörer* (destroyers). This would leave the Me. 109 escort free. Secondly, Me. 110s would occasionally act as 'bait' for the British fighters while the Me. 109s waited above to pounce. 'The twin-engined Me. 110s were so powerful that they required no escort.' Here Osterkamp was mistaken; he let himself be carried away by false illusions. As an 'old eagle' of the first war he remembered that Zeppelins and Gothas bombed London. But that was nothing compared with today, when he could 'cruise unmolested over British territory for half an hour' at the head of his Me. 109s. Daily he did so and concluded that it must have left a 'profound effect' on the British.

But Dowding and Park were not in the least impressed. Their attitude was: if the Me. 109s like joy-riding over England at twenty-five thousand feet, let them go ahead.' Freedom from British fighters did not mean the Germans had air superiority, but only that we were not playing ball with Osterkamp. Galling for him, but good tactics. Dowding's fighters were there to stop bombers, not fighters. They concentrated on the *Stukas* attacking convoys and ignored Osterkamp's Me. 109s.

On 13 July a new crowd of Me. 110s made their first appearance: the

'Jaguars' of *Erprobungsgruppe* 210. They carried bombs – and RAF fighters were on them in a flash.

Formed at Cologne-Ostheim on 1 July, *Erp Gr.* 210 had three *Staffeln* – Nos. 1 and 2 of Me. 110s and No. 3 of bomb-carrying Me. 109s. Otto Hintze was *Staffel Kapitän* of 3rd *Staffel*. They were a brave, determined lot with a magnificent leader, *Hauptmann* Walter Rubensdorffer, 'tall, lean, always in a good temper, even in the worst situations,' was how Otto described him. 85 Squadron was to have several brushes with them.

At 7.00 a.m. on 13 July *Erp Gr.* 210 moved forward from its base at Denain to St Omer for a convoy attack. An early lunch – meat, potatoes, red cabbage, no alcohol – and at 12.15 p.m. the *Gruppe* was climbing away from St Omer. The target: a convoy off Harwich which took violent evasive action. *Erp Gr.* 210's results were not brilliant, but from then on they were in the battle. It was going to be a hard one for them.

Generals Brauchitsch and Halder arrived at the Berghof at 11.00 o'clock that morning to report to the Supreme Commander. They unfolded the Army's plan for invasion produced by the new OKH Section E (for England). Hitler studied it briefly and approved. 'Recommendations are accepted ... practical preparations ... are to start immediately ... noted Halder. Only two days earlier Raeder thought he had won Hitler over with the argument of siege, with invasion as a last resort. Hitler had actually agreed, but he then told the Army to go ahead with invasion preparations.

On 16 July Hitler signed Directive No. 16, which began: 'Since England in spite of her hopeless military situation shows no signs of ... coming to an understanding, I have decided to prepare a landing operation and, if necessary, carry it out.

'The aim of this operation will be to eliminate the English homeland as a base for the prosecution of the war against Germany and, if necessary, occupy it completely ...'

It was a logical, necessary aim. If it could be achieved Germany would win the war, then turn unhindered to 'exterminate' Russia. If not, it could in the long run prove fatal to Hitler's ambition.

Preparations for the operation, which was now called 'Sea Lion', were to be completed by 15 August. They were to create conditions which would make a landing possible. First on the list: 'The English Air Force must be so reduced morally and physically that it is unable to deliver any significant attack against the German crossing.'

At Fighter Command, Dowding was minutely informed of the battle, but he left the tactical deployment of his squadrons to his group commanders. So far his 'fighter boys' were handling their side of the business well. They seldom saw their C-in-C but they felt his presence and trusted him. So did the Minister for Air. A letter came from Sinclair in which Dowding read about 'the decision for which I am personally responsible to Parliament . . . to request you to remain in command of our Fighter Squadrons until the end of October.

'I did not look beyond this period, in which I believe the issue of the war will probably be determined . . . my only preoccupation was to ensure that the best available commander was now occupying this key position.' Just the evening before, Dowding had dined with the Prime Minister at Chequers, his official residence. 'He was good enough to tell me that I had secured his confidence,' wrote Dowding.

Dowding was the only man for the job.

Section E of the German Army General Staff was working overtime on 'Sea Lion'. Their naval adviser, Captain Loycke, might well have admonished, '*Kinder, kinder*, you don't know what you've got hold of,' but the Army was bent on invasion. OKH issued orders for thirteen picked divisions to be moved to embarkation points: six of General Busch's 16th Army to the Pas de Calais for landing between Ramsgate and Bexhill; four of General Strauss's 9th Army to the Le Havre area for landing at Brighton and Hove; and three of Field Marshal Reichenau's 6th Army to the Cherbourg Peninsula, destination Lyme Bay – the entire force was under Field Marshal von Runstedt. The initial assault comprised 90,000 men; by the third day 260,000 should be ashore in England on a 230-mile front.

Raeder discussed invasion with the Army C-in-C, Brauchitsch. When on 15 July news of Directive 16 had been telephoned to him Raeder had been staggered. Accompanying groans came from his naval staff, but he instructed them: 'The task of preparing Invasion of England takes precedence . . . the C-in-C . . . therefore requires all departments . . . to take up the new task with energy and vigour.'

That did not prevent him warning Brauchitsch of the risk: the entire invading force might be lost. But Brauchitsch was not to be deterred. Having started the invasion idea, the Navy was now getting cold feet. He told Raeder, 'It should be quite easy and should all be over in a month.

Over the Channel, the RAF Defiants of No. 141 Squadron were being decimated. Taking off from Hawkinge, near the coast on 19 July they were ordered to patrol Folkestone at 5,000 feet.

Punctually at 1.00 p.m. *Hauptmann* Hannes Trautloft leading III *JG* 51 made rendezvous with *Hauptmann* Rubensdorffer's *Erp Gr.* 210 over St Inglevert. In perfect visibility fighter-bombers and escort climbed north toward the English coast in search of the target, an armed trawler northeast to Dover. They could see it miles off, already zig-zagging, and as the *Zerstorers* dived Trautloft could see it 'firing furiously from all "buttonholes".' Then the ship disappeared in a mountain of spray. Hannes's *Gruppe* escorted the Me. 110s back to the French coast then decided to return for a *Frei-jagd* ('free-hunt', or 'sweep'). A voice – *Leutnant* Wehnelt's – yelled over the radio, 'On the right, below, several aircraft.' They were the nine Defiants of 141 Squadron flying in 'close *Staffel* formation' led by Squadron Leader Richardson. But it was not until half a mile away that Trautloft 'noticed a turret behind the Defiant's pilot. The sun was behind me . . . I made sure there were no Hurricanes or Spitfires about.' Trautloft checked his watch: It was 1.43 p.m. Then he dived with his *stab Schwarm*. 'I aimed at the right Defiant . . . the rear gunner's tracers streamed towards me. Suddenly . . . a violent blow somewhere on my Me. 109. But the enemy had to go down . . . my guns fired . . . pieces of the Defiant . . . broke off and came hurtling towards me . . . I saw a thin trail of smoke . . . then suddenly just a fiery ball.'

Trautloft turned back quickly for France with a juddering engine and strong smell of burnt oil in his nostrils. A few minutes later he crawled in low over Cap Blanc Nez to crash land at St Inglevert.

Only three of the nine Defiants returned to Hawkinge; one was piloted by twenty-year-old Pilot Officer Ian MacDougall. As the Messerschmitts pressed home their attacks he had seen their tracer streaking through the British formation 'like small bright glow-worms'. He had watched as first one, then another Defiant dropped away, pouring smoke and flames. One had plunged into the sea, leaving a widening ring of foam; close to him, another was going down while two parachutes floated above it.

Suddenly, bullets slammed into his own Defiant. The engine stopped and the cockpit filled with smoke. MacDougall dived, undoing his harness and calling to his air gunner to bale out. There was no reply, so he kept shouting, 'Sergeant, are you all right, are you all right?' Then the sea was coming up at him and as he levelled out the engine spluttered into life.

A few minutes later Ian MacDougall crash-landed at Hawkinge.

Turning to look into the gunner's turret, he was astonished to see it was empty. His gunner was never found.

As that hot summer's day closed on the *Kanalkampf*, A Flight 43 (my old squadron) was ordered off from Tangmere. John Simpson felt the warm air buffeting him as he passed through the slipstream to climb into the cockpit of his Hurricane. Flying east at ten thousand feet he spotted a dozen Me. 109s just above, flying the other way in a thin layer of wispy cloud. The six Hurricanes of 43 Squadron continued climbing into the sun, then turned and dived. 'In a moment the battle began. Our six Hurricanes against the enemy's twelve.'

It would have done Osterkamp good to have seen them, because he believed that 'the feeling of having machines inferior to the Me. 109s had an effect on the British fighter pilots' morale. This inferiority was very marked with the Hurricane . . .' Well, there were six Hurricanes actually daring to attack twelve Me. 109s. The truth was, we knew we were better than the Me. 109s if they would stay and 'mix it'. We could turn faster. The 109s could beat us in the dive and in the climb, and they were nearly always above us. That is where the danger lay.

The eighteen fighters chased each others' tails in and out of cloud. Then a Me. 109 gave John his chance. 'He seemed to be dreaming . . . I gave him a short burst which damaged him . . . I flew in closer for a second dose . . . he dived out of control and I followed him down to six thousand feet. There I . . . watched him dive vertically into the calm sea . . . I opened my hood for a breath of fresh air.'

Then John was alone. He climbed back to the thin cloud layer. Three Messerschmitts crossed in front of him, so close he could see the black crosses on their wings and fuselage. He opened fire on the last one. 'We went round and round in decreasing circles, as I fired . . . Pieces of his wings flew off and black smoke came from behind the cockpit. He dived and I fired . . . from astern. We were doing a phenomenal speed. Then my ammunition gave out just as the other two Messerschmitts attacked me.'

John was in a fix. He was at sixteen thousand feet, eight miles from the coast. He dived, twisting and turning. But the Me. 109s had him. 'I could hear the deafening thud of their bullets hitting the armour plate behind my back, and . . . see great hunks being torn off my wings . . . my engine was chugging badly.' There came a cold, stinging pain in his left foot, and the controls went solid as black smoke filled the cockpit. 'Jump!' John said to himself, undid his harness straps, and opened the hood.

The rushing slipstream did the rest. 'It felt like a hand lifting me from the cockpit, by my hair . . . I found myself in mid-air, beautifully cool and dropping . . . it seemed hours before I reminded myself to pull my ripcord . . . there was a terrific jerk,' and John was swinging like a pendulum on the end of his parachute. Then he vomited. He was drifting towards the long lines of villas on the coast at Worthing.

One of the Me. 109s began circling him. 'I was alarmed. He was near enough for me to see his face. I felt . . . he would shoot me . . . But he behaved very well. The noise of his aircraft was terrific. He flew round me . . . then he suddenly . . . waved to me.' And the chivalrous German fighter pilot then dived for home.

John was lucky. He was fair game for that *Luftwaffe* pilot. Even Dowding thought so. On 'the ethics of shooting at aircraft crews who have baled out', it was his opinion that 'Germans descending over England were prospective prisoners and should be immune, while British pilots descending over England were still potential combatants. German pilots were perfectly entitled to fire on our defending airmen.'

John hung in mid-air, drifting shorewards. 'I took out my cigarettes and lit one with my lighter . . . ages seemed to pass and I was quite happy.' He heard the 'All Clear' siren go as he swung over the beach, and saw soldiers looking up. He was relieved that they were not aiming their rifles. 'I must have looked English, even at one thousand feet,' said John. Then he thought, 'I'm going to end up being killed against the wall of a sea-side villa.'

Then everything was rushing up at him. 'I hit the roof . . . of a house . . . I was going through a garden fence backwards, and then, bang, into a cucumber frame.' He was badly knocked about, but heard himself whimpering 'because I was grateful to be alive'. A woman brought him tea and a policeman leaned over the garden wall and handed him a glass of whisky. He had survived another day.

As John stepped out of his cucumber frame Adolf Hitler was climbing on to the raised dais in the Kroll Opera House, Berlin. It was the evening of 19 July. Hitler had truly weighed every word of his speech, which was to be his last before the *Reichstag* and his most brilliant.

Before the Fuehrer were arrayed row upon row of Nazi Delegates; up in the balcony the cream of Germany's military might and in the boxes, decked with the red-white-and-black Nazi colours, the high Party pundits. In the centre of the stage, behind his beloved Fuehrer and backed by a giant swastika dropcloth, sat Hermann Goering, the *Reichstag*'s President and C-in-C of the *Luftwaffe*.

Hitler began with a review of the miraculous feats of German arms. He showered promotions on his Army generals – nine were promoted Field Marshal, with three more from the *Luftwaffe*: Milch, Kesselring and Sperrle, the two last having the enviable task of wiping England off the map. But to the Chief of the *Luftwaffe* he made an exceptional gesture, promoting him to the unique dignity of *Reichsmarschall*. Goering wore a special white uniform for the occasion. While the honours were being doled out, William Shirer noticed Goering chewing on his pencil as he put finishing touches to his speech, and clapped his hands with Gargantuan gestures.

Then Hitler turned to more serious business. After insulting Churchill and warning the British of the terrible sufferings that awaited them, he offered them a last chance: 'In this hour I feel it to be my duty before my own conscience to appeal once more to reason and common sense in Great Britain, as much as elsewhere. I consider myself in a position to make this appeal, since I am not a vanquished foe begging favours, but the victor speaking in the name of reason ... the continuation of this battle will result in the total destruction of one of the opponents. Mr Churchill may believe that it will be Germany. But I know it will be England.'

The next day, 20 July, the *Reichsmarschall* got down to some hard talking with his three *Luftflotte* commanders (Kesselring, Sperrle and Stumpff) on the air war *gegen England*. For that reason he had to miss the Fuehrer's conference with his top commanders at the Chancellery, but Goering dispatched Jeschonnek with a message to the Fuehrer asking leave 'to launch attacks against Britain's fighter pilots, air force, aircraft industry, ports, industries, oil centres and the Channel area'.

The *Grosseinsatz der Luftwaffe* (the big air offensive) was to begin. *Luftflotten* 2 (Kesselring) and 3 (Sperrle) would concentrate on Southern England. *Luftflotte* 5 (Stumpff) would pin down the British fighters in the Midlands and North. The first objective was to wipe out the RAF fighters. Nothing less than total elimination. After which the *Luftwaffe* bombers, unescorted, could range free and annihilate the aircraft factories. The Royal Navy was a new target to be included on the list. But Goering warned them that the attacks must not destroy the docks since they would be needed for invasion, not that he had the slightest faith in 'Sea Lion'.

Grosseinsatz was a clumsy word. Something more romantic, more Wagnerian, was needed: *Adlerangriff*, for instance, Eagles' Attack.

Luftflotte commanders could submit plans as soon as possible. 'Meanwhile,' warned Goering, 'those fighters of ours had better wake up. We are losing too many bombers and dive-bombers. The Me. 109s should clear enemy fighters out of the way before our bombers arrive.'

Luftflotte 3's fighter leader (*Jafu* 3) *Oberst* Werner Junck did not take kindly to Goering's remarks. He realized that far from romping home, the *Luftwaffe* was in a weak position. 'You might as well ask a housemaid to make war against England,' was his comment.

At the Chancellery in Berlin Hitler was meanwhile in conference with his Commanders-in-Chief – Brauchitsch, Raeder, and Jeschonnek, who deputized for Goering. Hitler had obviously been contaminated to some extent by the *Kriegsmarine*'s pessimism. He was now thoroughly alive to their problems. Russia too was playing on his mind. He was convinced that Britain was counting on the Russians, but in his view 'Russia would make no effort to enter the war against Germany of her own accord.' There was no hope therefore for Britain. 'We have won the war; [Halder noted the Fuehrer's words] it is impossible now that events can turn against us.'

As for 'Sea Lion', Hitler realized that there was no question of its being just 'a river crossing', as Jodl had fondly imagined, but 'the crossing of a sea which is dominated by the enemy . . . an utterly determined enemy . . .' The main operation was to be completed by 15 September.

But trouble had arisen between the Army and the *Kriegsmarine*. The Army insisted on forty divisions spread over a 230-mile front. The *Kriegsmarine* said this was impossible; it should be thirteen divisions on a narrower front.

Hitler emphasized: it all depends on the *Kriegsmarine*. At this Jeschonnek chimed in with Goering's message: can the *Luftwaffe* have permission to go ahead with the *Grosseinsatz*? The Fuehrer would let them know in due course.

After the meeting had broken up Hitler raised the question of Russia. The English, it seemed to him, had been down for the count. But now they seemed to be up on their feet again. Russia must be behind this sudden recovery. Halder noted, 'Take Russian problem in hand.' He had his orders from the Supreme Commander: study campaign against Russia, possibly this autumn. It was the first indication Hitler had given for the realization of his life's ambition. It was, too, his first step to a war on two fronts, and to Germany's ruin.

The *Kanalkampf* continued. On its shadier side was the *Luftwaffe*'s nightly mine-laying in British harbours. *Luftwaffe* mines were to destroy more British ships than Papa Fink's bombers. On the night of 22 July *Hauptmann* Hajo Hermann (then *Staffel Kapitän* in III *KG* 30) was briefed to drop mines in Plymouth Sound. Aerial mining was a tricky business. The mines had to be dropped in the shallow waters of regular shipping channels at slow speed to prevent the parachute tearing.

Hermann took off that evening in his Ju. 88 from Zwischenahn in western Germany, with a thousand pound mine under each wing. He had planned things carefully. He would approach the Sound from the landward side over Plymouth itself, letting down to three hundred feet over the water and then make his get-away out to sea.

In the half moon he could clearly see Plymouth and its breakwater. From north-east of the city he began his descent, silently, throttle back, dive-brakes out. Halfway down a weird bulbous object suddenly lay right in his path. It was a barrage balloon. Hajo kicked on rudder, but too late – the Ju. 88 flumped straight into the balloon, sticking to it so that bomber and balloon continued earthwards as one. The next thing Hajo saw was 'searchlights shining from above. We had fallen off the balloon ... upside down, and were going down out of control. I felt as if I were playing a piano as it fell from a fifty storey building.'

Hermann slammed the air brakes shut and banged open the throttles. Still no feel on the controls, as the bomber plummeted down. So, 'Bale out,' he yelled to the crew and felt a blast of cold air as the escape panel broke away. At that instant he righted the Ju. 88. He was a few hundred feet over the Sound, exactly where he meant to drop his mines – only heading straight for Plymouth and its AA defences. Down went the mines. Despite blazing searchlights and a storm of AA fire, Hajo somehow managed to get out of the 'cage'.

Chapter 22

With prospects of the *Kanalkampf* intensifying, Western Approaches to the English Channel had been closed and shipping re-routed through St George's Channel to Northern ports like Liverpool. This put one more burden on the back of the Fighter Command, which had then to guard the coastal waters all around England.

Dowding had to keep enough squadrons in hand around London to protect the capital and as a strategic reserve against possible invasion. But he resisted the temptation to strengthen the south-eastern sectors of 11 Group, whose main battle area in the precincts of Dover had by then earned the name of 'Hellfire Corner'. Dowding held firm in face of strong criticism; but he knew better than anyone that if he weakened the sectors covering the West and above all the North and Midlands, he would lay Britain open to an outflanking attack by the *Luftwaffe*. That flank attack would surely come, only to find Fighter Command ready and waiting.

Dowding now demanded more squadrons to meet his increased commitment; and also that the Navy work very closely with Fighter Command to perfect the protection of convoys.

Despite the closing of the Western Approaches British ships often continued to sail (not always unscathed) under the nose of *Kanakafu* Fink and his battle group. The morning of 24 July saw a convoy entering the Thames estuary, and another off Dover. At 8.15 a.m. Al Deere led 54 Squadron off from Rochford, on the estuary's northern shore. At twenty thousand feet east of Dover the controller warned, 'Red Leader, two big raids approaching, one heading for Thames estuary. This one for you.'

At that moment Colin Gray, leading B Flight 54, spotted the other formation. 'Tally-ho! Red Leader,' he called Al, 'big formation south of Dover.' But Al had now sighted his own lot. 'Leave your lot alone,' he called to Colin, 'and follow me.' The enemy formation, a phalanx of 18

Dorniers protected by large numbers of fighters criss-crossing above and behind, was boring on towards the estuary. It was the biggest enemy formation Al had yet seen: 'I reported the unpleasant facts to Control and requested immediate assistance.'

Al found 'an attack against such numbers was a frightening prospect'. The Me. 109s 'presented a formidable looking defence'. He shot a glance down at the convoy 'sailing unsuspectingly towards the estuary, presenting an ideal target'. The enemy bombers must be running up to attack. 'We must break them up,' Al thought to himself, 'or it will be too late.'

'Blue Leader,' Al called to Colin, 'cover with your flight while we get at the bombers.' Back came an indignant Colin, 'What the hell d'you mean Red Leader, we're already stuck in the fighters!' 'You clot,' Al bellowed, 'you're after the wrong formation.' But it was no time for recriminations.

Al called to his Red and Yellow Sections, 'Try to get a shot at the bombers before the 109s get us.' With his six Spitfires in echelon, he swooped on the Dorniers. 'The right hand one received the full impact of my eight Brownings.' Then the Me. 109s were on the Spitfires. In a 'frenzy of twisting and turning' Al got in a pot shot at three without observing results. Suddenly the sky was clear and he was alone. 'One moment the air was a seething cauldron of Hun fighters, and the next it was empty.'

Apparently unharmed, the convoy sailed blithely on drawing away from the group of brown circles which marked the fall of enemy bombs.

Adolf Galland was in one of those Me. 109s leading his III *JG* 26. It was his first action over England. 'We got into a heavy scrap with Spitfires screening a convoy,' he said. In that 'frenzy of twisting and turning' he picked out a Spitfire. 'I glued myself to [its] tail and . . . managed to get in a long burst. The Spitfire went down almost vertically. I followed it . . . until the pilot baled out, then followed him down until he crashed into the water. His parachute had failed to open.'

Back at Caffiers, Galland and his pilots looked at one another gravely. 'We were no longer in doubt that the RAF would prove a formidable opponent,' he wrote.

Spitfires of 65 Squadron were also involved. 'This little shindy,' wrote the squadron diarist, 'has eased the browned-off feeling and put our tails up, and at least there will be a few Huns u/s [unserviceable] for some time.' There were at least two such Huns from Adolf Galland's *Gruppe*.

During two weeks of operations *Kanakafu* Fink's battle group had not closed the Channel to British shipping, but not every convoy got off as lightly as the one in the Thames estuary. In the small hours of 25 July, convoy 'Peewit' sailed from the estuary toward the Straits of Dover. By then German Freya radar stationed near Cap Gris Nez at Wissant was watching the Straits. At first light nine German E-boats streaked out across the grey waters to launch their torpedoes at Peewit. Two merchantmen went to the bottom.

From his motor-bus HQ at Cap Blanc Nez Fink watched through his binoculars as the convoy, escorted by the destroyers *Boreas* and *Brilliant*, steamed on. Then his bombers – Dorniers and Junkers 87s – were overhead. Peewit lost three more small ships. As if maddened by this cruel onslaught, *Boreas* and *Brilliant* made a brave dash straight to the French coast and loosed off several salvos at Fink's headquarters. Their daring cost them dearly. Back came Fink's bombers and took them severely to task.

The air-sea battle that day merely underlined the *Kriegsmarine*'s views on 'Sea Lion': everything depended on the *Luftwaffe*. Their successful action augured well. As the gallant *Boreas* and *Brilliant* limped back to Dover, Raeder was giving Hitler a more hopeful picture: provided there were no special problems, provided – as always – that the *Luftwaffe* would clear the RAF out of the sky, then the *Kriegsmarine* should be able to manage the invasion. Save one battery, even the long-range artillery would be in place opposite Dover by 15 August. Then and there the Fuehrer fixed a further conference for 31 July.

But Raeder could not leave without spreading his usual cloud of gloom: 'Sea Lion' would be ruinous to the German economy and cause havoc with the transport system. Foodstuffs, including the harvest crops, might pile up and rot for want of transport. With trawlers requisitioned, Germans would have to go short of fish. Even the output of U-boats, vital for starving Britain out, would suffer. Hitler was thus forewarned. Yet he insisted on priority for 'Sea Lion,' as confirmed by Keitel in a memorandum the next day.

Our responsibilities as squadron commanders often weighed on us heavily. None was worth his keep unless he could do any job he expected of his pilots, and tackle the most dangerous ones himself. The squadron in the air was a compact little band of twelve men who – if worth *their* keep – might follow you to destruction.

Some squadron commanders, like James McComb, 'lived in terror of leading my friends, the Squadron, into a trap and getting them all annihilated'. What haunted me most was the inability to be 'there' at a young pilot's side to help him out of a tight corner, or admonish him for his faults. The half dozen veterans (and we were always learning) among us could do much to teach the young ones by means of a language of hyperbole and onomatopoeia into which we insinuated the message of our experience and authority. But a single-seater fighter pilot in his cockpit, be he sergeant or squadron leader, was eventually master of his own fate. No one sat beside him to help.

We had already lost two young pilots in flying accidents. No one could be sure of the error they committed – one moment they were flying with the sense that training had instilled in them, the next moment they had fallen helpless to earth. I knew for sure that one of the reasons was overkeenness. Those young ones were loyal and fearless, their morale superb, but with battle so close they were over-eager, infected by our own burning zeal to get at the enemy and beat him down. Shocking news now came to me at Martlesham: Rickerdyke (a fine, burly New Zealander) had crashed near Debden, our base airfield fifty miles inland. The Commanding Air Officer, Leigh-Mallory, wished to see me. The next day I stood before him in his office at HQ 12 Group. There must be no more accidents in my squadron, 'L-M' told me. He was firm, but fair, and he wished me good luck.

It was not the moment to remind him that he had done so once before, eleven years ago at Old Sarum when I was a boy of fourteen who had just made his first flight. The schoolboy had grown up into one of his squadron commanders.

Since Raeder's Fuehrer-conference on 25 July the *Kriegsmarine* had been working hard to implement their chief's assurance to Hitler that technical problems on 'Sea Lion' would be overcome. But their solution, which they trotted out in a memorandum on 28 July, brought dismay to the Army: The *Grosse Admiral*, who was in 'full agreement', then went back on everything he had told Hitler: the sailors reckoned it would take them ten days to get the whole invasion across; they could not accept responsibility for it this year, and they doubted whether it would ever succeed. The only hope lay in narrowing the front to a single, direct crossing of the Dover Straits.

Halder raged: the plan 'upsets all previous calculations ... if true, previous estimates of Navy have been nonsense; in that case landing not possible.' And General Grieffenburg was dispatched posthaste to *Kriegsmarine* HQ in Berlin.

He returned on 30 July to Army HQ at Fontainebleau – with depressing news, which led Brauchitsch and Halder to the conclusion that the *Kriegsmarine* would probably not 'provide us this autumn with the means for successful invasion of England'. But then came the dilemma: to postpone invasion to later in the autumn would make worse the weather problem. To put it off until spring 1941 would allow the enemy to strengthen his defences. Better, after all, to have a go now?

Installed in the train *Atlas*, *Oberst* Warlimont's Plans Section L of OKW was drawn up on 29 July in Bad Reichenhall Station, Berchtesgaden. That day Jodl, Chief of Ops. OKW, sent a message saying he would like to speak to Warlimont and his senior assistants. 'Four of us were present,' related Warlimont, 'sitting at individual tables in the restaurant car ... Jodl went round ensuring all doors and windows were closed then, without any preamble, disclosed to us that Hitler had decided to rid the world "once for all" of the danger of Bolshevism by a surprise attack on Soviet Russia ... at the earliest possible moment, i.e. May 1941.' The effect of Jodl's words was 'electric' ... His listeners were all the more filled with consternation when Jodl told them that 'since war with Russia was supposed to be the best method of forcing England to make peace' the West war and the East war could be carried out independently. They themselves would soon be pushing on with redoubled energy in their planned invasion of England, in the fervent hope that this mad idea of the Fuehrer's might drop into second place. War with Russia? Why, the Friendship pact was not yet a year old. And war on two fronts? This was folly.

Jodl brushed their chorus of objections aside. The Fuehrer had made an *unabanderlicher Entschluss* (an unalterable decision). No argument was possible. War with Russia was bound to come anyhow, said Jodl, and victory would take a matter of weeks. Then Germany would turn back west again and smash England. Planning for the *Aufbau Ost* (Eastern build-up) must start. May 1941 was the target date.

On 30 July Halder began to see through the Fuehrer's cryptic thinking: 'If we can not reach a decision against England, the danger remains, England will ally herself with Russia,' he wrote in his diary. 'The question is whether we should carry on war on two fronts, one of which would be Russia?' That indeed was the question, and Halder, old and tried campaigner as he was, entirely disagreed with his Fuehrer. 'Better remain friends with Russia,' he noted.

It still remained to eliminate England while yet there was time before the bad weather set in. Apart from the *Kanalkampf*, which was really not raising much dust on the far side of the Channel, or even much spray in it, the German war machine had ground almost to a standstill in its operations against England since Dunkirk. A week had passed since Goering had begged his Fuehrer's leave to unleash the *Luftwaffe's Grosseinsatz*, the big offensive on Britain, and ordered *Luftwaffe* commanders to draw up the plans.

Waiting on 30 July for his commanders to join him on the cool heights of the Obersalzburg, *der Grosste Feldherr* was wondering what on earth Goering was up to. So he fired off a stiffly worded teleprinted message to the lethargic *Reichsmarschall* that morning. Goering received it at 12.20 p.m. 'The Fuehrer has ordered that the preparations for the *Luftwaffe's* great air battle against England should be completed immediately and with great dispatch.'

Half the trouble was that Kesselring (*Luftflotte* 2) and Sperrle (*Luftflotte* 3) could not see eye to eye – a petty quarrel between two men of different make-up and experience, but it held matters up. Finally the Chief of Staff, Jeschonnek, accepted as a basis the ideas of *Oberst* Paul Deichmann, Chief of Staff of Loerzer's *Flieger Korps* II. Deichmann's plan was to destroy the RAF fighters *in the air*. This had to be done within range of the short-winded Me. 109s which from the Pas de Calais could reach London, fight for twenty minutes, and just get back. But the RAF fighters had so far shown an irritating tendency to refuse combat with the German fighters. How then, to flush the RAF fighters and get them to rise so that the Me. 109s could shoot them out of the sky? There was only one sure method in Deichmann's mind – bomb London.

Oberst Paul Deichmann was only half right. He did not understand that RAF fighters would rise in the defence of every target menaced by bombers, and by far the most important ones to them were their own installations: radar stations, and sector airfields with their ops. rooms and telephonic communications. Both these vital targets were above ground, fully exposed to *Luftwaffe* bombs. These destroyed, Fighter Command would be blind, its brain and nervous system paralysed. The *Luftwaffe* had knocked out the Polish and French air forces in a few days, principally on the ground where damage to communications threw everything into confusion. And here was Fighter Command's vital, vulnerable radar/ground control system, wide open to the heavens. Yet the *Luftwaffe* planners forgot the lesson of Poland and France and decided to go first for the RAF fighters in the air. What was the Intelligence Chief, Beppo Schmid, up to? He evidently hadn't a clue about the real workings of Fighter Command.

So a London attack was to goad the RAF fighters into the air. This suited Goering perfectly. From Wever down to the present young Chief of Air Staff, the *Luftwaffe* chief and his men were Douhet men. 'The disintegration of nations ... will be achieved by aerial forces.'

But there was one hitch. Hitler would not have it. Since the war began he had repeated in each directive, 'I reserve the decision on terror attacks to myself.' And although he had talked of 'annihilating reprisals' for the RAF's Rühr attacks, he had not yet withdrawn his veto. London was *verboten*.

Only Theo Osterkamp saw the facts clearly. He and his JG 51 had tried everything to lure up the RAF fighters, yet the RAF had refused to shoot except in self-defence. But hit them where it really hurt – on the ground – and that would bring them up to where they were vulnerable. Swing low, swing high. But no one listened to the wise old eagle.

On 31 July with Keitel and Jodl for the OKW, Brauchitsch and Halder for the Army, and Raeder for the *Kriegsmarine*, Hitler went into session at about midday at the Berghof. At Carinhall Goering was meeting his own commanders. None of his men was at this important briefing of Hitler's.

How was the *Kriegsmarine* coming along with 'Sea Lion', asked Hitler, and Raeder replied that preparations were in full swing. Barges should be ready by 15 September, and the manning of them completed. The requisitioning of trawlers was in hand and they should be ready by 1 September; it was a pity, thought the *Grosse Admiral*, that the Baltic herring catch should have to suffer. It promised to be exceptional. Minesweeping depended on the *Luftwaffe*; given proper air cover there should be no problem. But no one should have any illusions; the *Kriegsmarine* would not be ready before 15 September.

There were details too, which were capital as far as the sailors were concerned: the landing must be made two hours after high tide, as then the ebbing tide would leave the landing craft firmly stuck in the sand. Next, if the Army insisted on a dawn landing (the *Kreigsmarine* was against this) a certain amount of moonlight would be needed to navigate such an ungainly fleet to the enemy coast. This would mean crossing between 19–26 September.

The *Grosse Admiral* added his usual warning: 'Sea Lion' would put a crippling load on Germany's economy; *Kriegsmarine* could only cope with a narrow-front crossing and finally, it would be better to put back the invasion until May 1941.

But Hitler stuck to his decision, and Halder noted: 'The air war will start now. It will show our relative strength.' If the results were not satisfactory, invasion preparations would be stopped. But if the British looked like giving in under air bombardment, 'then we shall attack'. Landing preparations were therefore to be continued.

Meanwhile, Russia continued to irk Hitler; he was convinced that Britain was still counting on Russian support. Halder noted, 'If we smash Russia, Britain's last hope will vanish. Decision: Russia must be liquidated.'

But if Russia were the stuff of Adolf Hitler's dreams, England was the problem that gnawed at his dark soul. During the coming weeks he would concentrate all his thoughts on the defeat of England.

The next day, 1 August, Fuehrer Directive No. 17 established the main principles: 'I intend to intensify air and sea warfare against the English homeland. I therefore order:

1. The *Luftwaffe* is to overpower the Royal Air Force . . . in the shortest possible time.
2. After achieving . . . air superiority the air war is to be conducted against ports . . . food stores.'

Finally, the *Luftwaffe* was to be ready to take part 'in full force' in 'Sea Lion'.

Hitler ordered D-day to be any time from 5 August, depending on *Luftwaffe* readiness and the weather. For himself, he reserved the prerogative to order terror attacks.

Keitel followed up in an ultra-secret directive: preparations for 'Sea Lion' were to be completed by 15 September. A week or two after the start of the air offensive, the Fuehrer would decide if the invasion would or would not take place that year. 'His decision will depend largely on the result of the air offensive.'

So the *Kanalkampf* was folding up. For the *Luftwaffe* it was now to be *Wir fliegen gegen England* in deadly earnest. 'During the last days of July,' wrote *Oberst* Werner Kreipe, 'Hitler sent for the commander of *Luftflotte* 3, vehemently demanding the violent and maximum commitment of the Luftwaffe against Britain.'

The *Luftwaffe's* chief summoned his commanders to the HQ (at The

Hague) of General Christiansen to tell them how. Theo Osterkamp wrote: 'Everybody with a name or a rank worth mentioning was there. The weather was perfect so the party took place in the garden. The "Iron One" appeared in a new white ceremonial uniform.'

Goering announced the Fuehrer's orders to his commanders: 'The Fuehrer has ordered me to crush Britain with my *Luftwaffe*. By delivering a series of very heavy blows I plan to have this enemy, whose morale is already at its lowest, down on his knees in the nearest future so that our troops can land on the Island without any risk.'

He then turned to the plan's execution. Osterkamp reported that, 'according to the information of the Intelligence Service, Britain disposed in its southern sector of at the most four to five hundred fighters. [Actually the air fighting force consisted of some three hundred single-seater fighters.] Their destruction in the air and on the ground was to be carried out in three phases: during the first five days, within a radius of 150 to 100 kilometres south and south-east of London; in the next three days within 50 to 100 kilometres, and during the last five days within the 50-kilometre circle around London. The whole operation, then, should be over in thirteen days. That would irrevocably win absolute air superiority over England and fulfil the Fuehrer's mission.

'I must have made a terribly stupid face, but in my case that should scarcely attract any attention. Goering looked up, saw me and said, "Well Osterkamp, have you got a question?"'

Uncle Theo explained that during July when his *JG* 51 was alone in combat over England he had reckoned that 'about 500 to 700 British Fighters were concentrated in the area around London'. If we call that 11 Group Uncle Theo was way out in his reckoning. He believed too, that 'their numbers had increased considerably ...' Here again he was wrong. Dowding had resisted the temptation to reinforce 11 Group at the expense of 12 and 13 Groups in the Midlands and North. Finally, he told his C-in-C that 11 new units had been equipped with Spitfires, which he considered as good as the German fighters. It was true that the Spitfire was as good as the Me. 109, but of the new fighter squadrons forming some had Spitfires, some Hurricanes.

Goering cut him off angrily: 'This is nonsense, our information is excellent, and I am perfectly aware of the situation. The Messerschmitt is much better than the Spitfire because the British are too cowardly to engage your fighters.'

Uncle Theo stuck to his guns: 'I reported only that the British fighters were ordered to avoid combat with our fighters.' 'That is the same thing,'

Goering shouted, 'if they were as strong ... as you maintain, I would have to send my *Luftzeugmeister* [Udet] before the firing squad.'

Osterkamp asked, 'How many fighters will be used in the combat against Britain?' Goering answered, 'Naturally all our fighter *Geschwader* will be used in the battle.' Uncle Theo had counted on having some '1,200 to 1,500 fighters'. In this he was to be 'bitterly disappointed'. In fact the German Quarter Master General's figure was 929 fighters, of which 700 were Me. 109 single-seaters, the rest twin-engined Me. 110s.

The bomber figures gave Osterkamp a bigger shock. 'I was completely staggered when the two *Luftflotten* reported that they had not even seven hundred bombers ready for combat duty.' Goering looked round. Shocked and as if in search of help, he murmured, 'Is this my *Luftwaffe*?' It was his *Luftwaffe* all right, but a *Luftwaffe* of which the RAF had been taking a steadily increasing toll since Karl Missy's Heinkel had crashed in February.

But the German Quarter Master General's fighters were not quite as depressing: 875 long-range bombers and 316 dive-bombers (total 1,191) of *Luftflotten* 2 and 3. *Luftflotte* 5 possessed 123 long-range bombers, 34 Me. 110 twin-engined fighters.

The thirteen-day campaign discussed at that meeting paled before the *Reichsmarschall*'s dream-plan, outlined in an OKL directive next day: the object of the exercise, then called *Adlerangriff* (Eagle-attack) was to destroy the RAF as the Polish and French air forces had been destroyed.

Luftflotten 2 and 3 would crack off on *Adlertag* with three mighty successive attacks. On Eagle plus one *Luftflotte* 5 from Norway would join in. After only four days the RAF should be out of business. The criterion for Fighter Command's defeat: trim it down to below three hundred aircraft.

What were the fighting forces ranged against one another *in the air*? Fighter Command's Order of Battle a week later would show a total of 48 single-seater fighter squadrons – 768 aircraft (including reserves) with an air fighting force (squadrons of 12 aircraft) of 576. But in the South, 'the only sector which interested us', as Uncle Theo put it, there were but 7 squadrons in 10 Group, 19 squadrons in 11 Group – a total air fighting force of 312 aircraft disposed on a score of airfields.

In the opposite camp, *Luftflotten* 2 and 3 between them mustered 43 bomber *Gruppen* and 33 fighter *Gruppen*, an air fighting force of upwards of 2,000 aircraft disposed on 48 airfields. The figures are based on 12 aircraft per RAF fighter squadron, 12 aircraft per *Luftwaffe* fighter *Staffel*, 9 aircraft per bomber *Staffel*. *Stab* (staff) flights are not included. The battleground was, after all, in the air. Over the South of England 312 RAF fighters faced 2,000 *Luftwaffe* bombers and fighters.

Nos. 12 and 13 Groups, each with 11 single-seater squadrons, covered the Midlands and North with an air fighting force of 264 aircraft.

Oberst Kreipe was listening to Goering that day: 'For the first time in modern history,' he said later, 'the people of England were now to feel the full and direct impact of war on their own soil: their morale was expected to deteriorate in consequence.'

Meanwhile the Germans were busy on the diplomatic front in a last effort to get Britain to come to terms. Once again the good offices of the King of Sweden were sought, and on 3 August he addressed the British Government. But Churchill did not flinch; before Britain would even listen to any peace proposals, 'it would be necessary that effective guarantees, by deeds not words, should be forthcoming from Germany which would insure . . . free and independent life of Czechoslovakia, Poland, Norway, Denmark, Holland, Belgium and above all France . . .'

In our own little world we were hardly aware of the great issues at stake. Our thoughts did not go far beyond the narrow confines of our cockpits and the job in hand, which was to boot the Hun out of our sky. Nothing could be allowed to get in the way of that.

But for Tom Gleave something did. At thirty-two, he was already above the age for a squadron commander, which Dowding had fixed at twenty-six. Tom was one of the few exceptions. But on 20 July he had been promoted to wing commander. That did it – he was now too senior to lead a fighter squadron. His appointed place was in the Group Ops. Room. But Tom thirsted for battle. 'I hared down to Group HQ to see my Commanding Air Officer, "Birdie" Saul. I found him in the mess, apologized for intruding and asked, "Could I stay with 253 Squadron?" ' When Saul said he could, Tom felt like a man reprieved.

But on 5 August a new CO, Squadron Leader Starr (once a pupil of Tom's at Sealand) arrived to command 253. But that did not prevent Tom from suggesting, 'Let me stay on as an "ordinary bloke",' and Starr agreed. 'We will share the squadron' – a gentleman's agreement for which fate was to show a cruel contempt.

On the German side from the Supreme Commander downwards doubt and discord were rife. Was invasion necessary, or would the *Grosseinsatz* do the trick? If invasion took place, should it be on a wide or narrow front?

Even within the *Luftwaffe* there were divisions of opinion between the *Reichsmarschall* and his *Luftflotten*, and between the two *Luftflotten* commanders themselves. On 5 August, the day set for Eagle to swoop on his prey, he was still busy preening his feathers.

Yet the *Luftwaffe* had already struck some heavy blows. It had sunk and battered many of the Royal Navy's destroyers in the narrow waters of the Channel and in the North Sea. If it could win supremacy in the air from the RAF's fighters the British fleet would be at its mercy. Although the Navy's thirteen battleships and its heavy cruisers were keeping out of harm's way in the west and north, a 'ceaseless, vigilant patrol' was being maintained by the lighter fighting vessels – nearly eight hundred of them. This was the answer to Goering's boast that Britain was no longer an island. Island she still was, as Goering's airmen were soon to discover. Only, the RAF had taken over the first line of defence from the 'senior service'. To the RAF fell the tasks of protection, of spying out the enemy's movements, and of counter-attack.

Churchill defined Britain's lines of defence: first, the enemy's ports. These must be watched from the air and by the Navy's submarines. They could be hit by the RAF's Bomber Command and by the Navy. The second line of defence, patrolling, was for the Navy and the RAF's Coastal Command. The interception and destruction of invasion convoys would fall to the Navy and the RAF. The last line of defence consisted of the beaches of Britain. If the enemy got that far, everything would be thrown at him, from land, from the sea, and from the air.

Working together 'in harmonious and detailed agreement', Churchill and his advisers were confident that 'anything that got ashore' would be hurled back into the sea. They half hoped that invasion would come – it would be a chance of 'striking a blow at the mighty enemy which would resound throughout the world'. The same hopes were echoed by the men who waited vigilantly for the invader. And there was always that personal grudge against Hitler. 'Do you think Hitler is coming, sir?' a Home Guard asked his General. 'It will be an awful pity if he doesn't.'

Another who prayed for invasion was *Unteroffizier* Karl Missy. In Whitby Hospital Sister Oldfield's devotion had helped him on the way to recovery. Then he was transferred to the Royal Military Hospital at Woolwich, East London, where he would soon be in the front row of the stalls. Missy and his comrades expected invasion and their optimism grew with every new batch of wounded prisoners. 'Invasion's round the corner,' was the invariable story. Karl Missy was cheered by the thought of an early return home to Dohlerstrasse, Rheydt.

The Navy's harbours, the RAF's airfields, radar and aircraft factories, the Army's depots and concentrations, public amenities (food, light, fuel, communications) were all listed in Beppo Schmid's *Studie Blau* – his blue-print for the *Luftkrieg gegen England*. Their protection was the responsibility of Fighter Command. For years Dowding had maintained that attack as a means of defence is all very well, but security of base is the essential prerequisite. Now the moment had come for him to prove it.

He had no false illusions about winning the war. His sole aim was to prevent the Germans from winning. 'If the Germans could win command of the air for just one week they would win the war,' he said.

The *Luftwaffe* was now ready to snatch air supremacy from Dowding's fighters. If they succeeded Britain and her Navy would be at the mercy of the Nazi bombers, and 'Sea Lion' could if necessary – put to sea.

At Carinhall Goering threw a final party for Eagle on 6 August, a day after it was supposed to start. The *Reichsmarschall* seemed in no particular hurry. Four or five days of good weather was all that he needed. 'He was entranced by the ideas of General Douhet,' remarked *Oberst* Kreipe. That meant bombing Britain to blazes, driving the people to terror and despair, the government to submission.

But the *Luftflotten* staffs were not so sanguine. Kesselring, it is true, was all for the saturation attack – it was he who had laid it on at Warsaw and Rotterdam, and it had worked like a charm. But Kesselring was an admitted Goering man. He respected him in spite of his brutality and found him on the whole 'generous and kind'. He liked to work with him.

But he differed with his C-in-C over the aims of the *Grosseinsatz*: 'I recommended the invasion very strongly to the *Reichsmarschall* .... believed in it too.' His own preparations for invasion were 'very simple, because I and my *Luftflotte* 2 were opposite the target and it was only mental preparation ... and bringing up additional operational groups and finding airfields, then conferences ... with the Army and Navy ...'

It all looked too simple, but things were not to turn out that way. From Goering's verbal instructions on 6 August Kesselring was led to presume 'that the air offensive ... was intended to be the prelude to "Sea Lion" ...' But from the outset the offensive 'was conducted on lines quite at variance with those instructions ...'

Sperrle did not get on with Goering. The massive, anvil-jawed Commander of *Luftflotte* 3 had been fighter-ace Goering's superior in the First World War, and Goering had never forgotten the rocket he received from Sperrle for indiscipline. He showed a calculated contempt for Sperrle.

Sperrle had not forgotten his 'act of force' at Guernica, but at his *Luftflotte* 3 HQ (his Chief of Ops. Kreipe observed) no one seriously believed the *Luftwaffe* could conquer Britain alone. 'We did believe that a strong air force could strike the decisive blow against the United Kingdom, provided the Army and Navy were fully committed to invasion. At that period the *Luftwaffe* was probably strong enough ... to carry out the part assigned to it in "Sea Lion".'

The next few weeks would show. Anyway, as Kreipe admits, Goering 'never had much faith in "Sea Lion".' He had the lowest opinion of the *Kriegsmarine* and its conscientious chief, Raeder, upon whom he vented both hatred and contempt. It was dangerous, said Rieckhoff, 'even to mention anything in favour of the *Kriegsmarine* in Goering's presence'.

Goering's relations with the Army C-in-C, Brauchitsch, were hardly better. As did almost every other top-ranking officer, Brauchitsch mistrusted him not least for his underhanded way of bringing the top brass into discredit in front of Hitler, and so gaining his Fuehrer's favour.

The Fuehrer's favour was everything to Goering, who was frankly frightened of him. 'I often make up my mind to say something to Hitler,' he once admitted, 'but then when I come face to face with him my heart sinks into my boots.' But Hermann knew that his Fuehrer knew little about aerial combat. Press Chief Dietrich described Hitler's attitude as 'tragic'. He had no 'inner feeling for aircraft; he did not like to fly and almost ignored aviation'. The feeling was so strong that 'he felt uneasy before the development of any instrument so strange to his nature'. No wonder that Goering had so easily persuaded Hitler to leave it all to the *Luftwaffe* at Dunkirk and then had managed to sell the Fuehrer the same bill of goods once again. In Raeder's opinion Hitler was at one with Goering in believing that *Luftkrieg gegen England* would force Britain to her knees before invasion ever became necessary. Yet Raeder himself was convinced there was no bluff about 'Sea Lion'. No one was better placed to judge than he.

The Eagle party at Carinhall ended on a cheerful note – four or five days of good weather. But the weather turned sour and Goering began to grow fidgety.

The dispute between the Army and *Kriegsmarine* over a wide or narrow front, came to a head on 7 August. After the Fuehrer-conference on 31

July Raeder had instructed his naval staff to plan the crossing for the Dover Straits. He told them to forget the Army's wide-front plan, with landings as far west as Brighton and Lyme Bay. Then the Admiral went off with Generals Brauchitsch and Halder to inspect landing craft at Sylt, without breathing a word to them about his instructions.

Halder's copy was waiting on his desk at Fontainebleau, where he returned on 4 August. Fuming, he telephoned OKW. Jodl calmed him; the Admiral must have misunderstood. *Kreigsmarine* Chief of Staff Schniewind came speeding from Berlin to have it out with his irate Army opposite numbers. A staff train with both chiefs of staff on board puffed out of Fontainebleau late on the evening of 7 August, bound for the embarkation points on the Channel coast.

Their discussion, which began quite calmly, ended in a bitter quarrel. Schniewind explained that a 230-mile front from the Nore to Lyme Bay was beyond the capabilities of the *Kriegsmarine*. Even if it were possible to gather the armada of transports necessary for such enterprise, the British Navy would play havoc with them. The only hope of not losing the entire invasion fleet would be to concentrate on a narrow-front crossing of the Dover Straits, covered by the *Luftwaffe* and long-range coastal artillery.

Normally calm, Halder exploded. 'I absolutely reject the navy plan. It would be pure suicide. I might as well put my assault troops through a sausage-machine.' Stung by this gruesome picture, Schniewind retorted that a wide-front crossing would be equally suicidal, as it meant sailing under the noses of the British fleet based in Portsmouth and Portland. Only the Supreme Commander could solve this cruel dilemma.

Exasperated by the *Kriegsmarine*'s quailing, Halder noted that evening in his diary that it was 'afraid of the British fleet, the more so now that the *Luftwaffe* is incapable of guarding against this danger'. Halder had a poor opinion of his brothers-in-arms. Only the evening before, he had written, '. . . the *Kriegsmarine* is full of misgivings . . . the *Luftwaffe* is very reluctant . . . and OKW . . . just plays dead. The only driving force . . . comes from us.'

And now the *Kriegsmarine* was beginning to grumble that the *Luftwaffe* was missing opportunities despite good weather. But sailors' weather is not always good for airmen. Fixed for 8 August, *Adlertag* again had to be postponed although on the 8th the *Luftwaffe* made a ferocious attack on a westbound Channel convoy.

The twenty merchantmen of 'CW8' had sailed from the Thames estuary the previous evening. The idea was to nip through Papa Fink's backyard in the dark and give the slip to his *Stukas*. At least that part of the plan worked. But how could anyone have thought that CW8 could escape a terrible mauling on its way down the Channel? The Freya radar station at Wissant had been operational since the end of July. If *Stukas* could not see CW8 in the dark, Freya could. E-boats were alerted. Before dawn they were streaking across the grey waters of the Dover Straits to launch their torpedoes among the convoy. Three good ships and the men aboard them were sent to the bottom.

Down Channel, *Fliegerkorps* VIII was waiting. Richthofen ordered his *Stukas* to wipe out the convoy. They did their damnedest. Three times the massed *Stuka Geschwaders* with fighter escort swept down on the merchantmen.

Rudolf Braun dived with them. He knew the Me. 109s could not stay long for lack of fuel, but as long as they were there the *Stuka* crews thought, 'Nothing can happen to us.' Then there was a Spitfire on Rudolf's tail. As it closed in the *Stuka*'s gunner shouted, 'Now,' and Rudolf jerked his Ju. 87 round in a steep turn – it could turn on a postage stamp. He fired a quick burst for luck, then cleared off quickly – the air was unhealthy for *Stukas*.

Battered and torn asunder, CW8 forged on below, leaving a trail of foundering ships and debris in its wake, while Hurricanes and Spitfires fought it out desperately with the *Stukas* and their Me. 109 escort. It was a field-day for Tangmere sector. Twelve Hurricanes of 43 Squadron advanced to meet the third raid. 82 *Stukas* with swarms of Me. 109s were stepped up in tiers 'looking like an escalator on the Piccadilly underground', as Squadron Leader Tubby Badger (43's CO) put it. Frank Carey, with whom Caesar and I used to have fun doing formation aerobatics, was there. Life was not fun then. What Frank saw was 'a raid so terrible and inexorable it was like trying to stop a steam roller'. Brave as a lion and blind as a bat (we called him Wombat) Tony Woods-Scawen flew clean through the *Stukas*, firing as he went.

Leading 145 Squadron John Peel climbed from Tangmere seawards to 16,000 feet. *Stukas* below! As 145 dived to the attack the Me. 109s, from higher still, leapt on the Hurricanes. 'The enemy fighters (painted silver) were half-rolling and diving and zooming . . . I fired two five-second bursts at one and saw it dive into the sea. Then I followed another in a zoom and got him as he stalled.'

Quite a change from John Peel's dingy Air Ministry office where he had told me a couple of months ago, 'Go away and enjoy the fine weather.' Since then 85 Squadron had been rebuilt. Apart from sporadic convoy attacks our sector had remained quiet. But ceaseless patrols had put a heavy strain on men and material. In July alone I did a good three months' peacetime flying.

With CW8's gallant but reckless voyage the curtain rang down on the *Kanalkampf*. Luckily such disasters were rare: since 10 July only some forty thousand tons of shipping had been sunk out of four million which had run the gauntlet between the Nore and Land's End. *Kanakafu* Fink and Richthofen had not succeeded in cleansing the Channel of British shipping.

And General Theo Osterkamp's early feeling of triumph as he rode unchallenged with his Me. 109s through the British skies had positively subsided. In five weeks of action against Fighter Command, *Luftwaffe* losses rose to 286, of which 105 were Me. 109 and Me. 110 fighters. Fighter Command lost 148 fighters.

One evening Mr Garfield Weston wrote a cheque for £100,000 to replace the fighters lost in the day's battle – a patriotic gift like Lady Houston's £100,000 which ten years before had spurred the development of those fighters and their Merlin engines.

General 'Hap' Arnold of the US Air Force would later write: 'On 8 August 1940 the RAF Fighter Command took off to save everything, and between then and the end of September they saved it.'

But at *Luftwaffe* HQ at Le Coudray, Goering's weather men were getting frantic. So was Goering. A belt of high pressure from the Azores which should have given him four to five days of good weather, obstinately refused to materialize. *Adlertag* was put back again to 10 August, but when that day dawned Goering would still not release the Eagle. The *Kriegsmarine*'s diarist commented tartly on the bird's reluctance.

The *Luftwaffe* offensive was now increasing, and Dowding made a move which strengthened the 'fighter belt' round London: Debden (85's sector) was transferred from Leigh-Mallory's 12 Group to 11 Group. This gave Air Vice Marshal Keith Park command of the approaches to London from Bournemouth on the Channel all the way round to Great Yarmouth on the east coast.

Next day Park landed his Hurricane at Martlesham. As my station commander at Tangmere he had done me a good turn two years earlier which was the reason I was now commanding one of his squadrons. I was lucky to still be there for earlier that morning I had had a strange encounter with the enemy.

It began with a Dornier 17. I spotted it lurking near convoy 'Booty' and chased it in and out of big tufts of cotton-wool cloud, their shadows mottling the glassy sea. During this game of hide and seek there came into my earphones a blurred singing which grew louder until I recognized the tune – 'September in the Rain'. Then came a series of lazily spoken orders – in German. At that moment (thirty miles from the coast) the cloud gave out. Not a sign of the Dornier, but instead twenty Me. 110s just below circling in twos and threes while their leader – I suppose it was he – continued to enchant them, and me, with his catchy refrain.

I'm almost certain I thought to myself, 'Pretend you're Richthofen – the Red Knight.' He always waited above to pounce on a straggler. Round came the one I was looking for, and down I went at him head-on, holding my aim as long as I dared. In fast and out as fast; Uncle Theo's advice was sound. I soared up from the circus of Me. 110s to be met by one, more crafty than the rest, which must have pulled up well above me. It then dived head-on, pumping what looked like streams of red-hot ping-pong balls – the tracer – uncomfortably close. We passed within spitting distance and I climbed on into the nearest tuft of cloud.

Viewed from the wrong end, the Me. 110s two 20 mm. cannons and four machine-guns were disconcerting. When I had recovered I swooped down from my cloud on another straggler. Head-on, it was impossible to see the result, especially as this time when I pulled out of the circle I was pursued from behind with a hail of lead. A Spitfire had come from nowhere to rescue me from the angry Me. 110. I couldn't help chuckling as I looked down and saw the Spit. standing on its tail as I had just done, to reach a friendly cloud.

An E-boat of the excellent German rescue service was patrolling below the Me. 110s. I saw it suddenly veering towards something which had splashed into the sea. I could not say what it was.

I had, of course, been clammering loudly to Hornpipe (ground station) for help. 'Get the rest of the squadron over Booty.' Six of our Hurricanes were there when *Erprobungs Gruppe* 210 attacked. They sent two Me. 110s into the sea.

This was a mere skirmish in the wings. Heavy fighting was going on down south – a dress rehearsal for *Adlertag*, which still hung fire because of the weather. Hans-Heinrich Brustellin's I *KG* 51 had a record day at balloon-busting with the Dover barrage – an operation which puzzled and almost offended Al Deere for its apparent pointlessness – unless it were to clear the way for the *Stukas*. But that day the *Stukas* did not dive on Dover. Nor were the formations of Dorniers which swept in over Dover looking for action. They were out to act as 'bait' (*Lock-vogel*) for the British fighters. Among the bomber crews this was a highly unpopular sport. II *KG* 2 was playing at it that day and Werner Borner (whose courage no one could doubt) admitted, 'I must honestly say we did not feel very happy with these flights.'

To the west, over Portland naval base, German fighters were assigned to pin down the British fighters, in order for the bomber *Geschwader* to concentrate on Portland. It was the chance the *Jagdgeschwader* had been longing for: they believed that free combat, fighter to fighter, was the best way of knocking out the Hurricanes and Spitfires. That was the fighters' real job: 'Cleanse the air' – much better than this dreadful escort business, where one was tied to the bombers like a hound on a leash.

JG 2 (Richthofen) had a tough fight that day.

'We had strict orders,' said Paul Temme, flying with the *Stab-schwarme*, 'to tie down the British fighters, come what may, for 35 minutes. No quitting before time.'

Towards 11 a.m. approaching German formations were picked up by Ventnor (Isle of Wight) radar station – the last job it would do for some time. *JG* 2 first clashed with RAF fighters over the sea south of Portland. The 'coffee grinder' started. Round and round they went. From 20,000 feet down to sea level it was a nightmare of snap-shooting and near-collisions.

A Spitfire dived at Temme head-on. He fired, then banged the stick forward. Negative G sent dust flying up from the floor of the cockpit into his eyes. Then two Hurricanes set on him – and there were still ten minutes to go. Paul had to stay with them – and it needed all his will power to do so. He swung this way and that in a series of violent 'tele-curves'. Luckily there was scattered cloud, otherwise the more nimble Hurricanes might have got him.

When Temme landed back at Beaumont-le-Roger he was all in. Mechanics heaved him out of the cockpit and he flopped onto the grass next to *Leutnant* Helmuth Wick, *JG* 2's rising star. Wick was too exhausted to speak. He had had a herculean combat and claimed three of the 22 British fighters that *JG* 2 had believed they had shot down that day. But in a furious combat like that the counting went all awry. Two or three pilots might claim the same enemy aircraft. It happened on both sides. Along the entire air front, from Harwich via Dover to Portland, 32 British fighters were lost. The German news bulletin claimed 90 and admitted the loss of 26. But the *Luftwaffe* Quartermaster General – he at least had to be realistic – wrote off 38 machines.

'A bag of 90 British planes on the day before the famous beginning of the grouse season is a matter on which sportsmen can congratulate themselves ...' Such was the cynical attitude of the propaganda pundits towards the sacrifice, reeking of blood and burning flesh, in which so many British and German youths were to be immolated.

In the end, it was the lessons gained from the air fighting not the 'scores' which counted. *Luftflotte* 3 commander Hugo Sperrle was pleased. 'Fighter protection near Portland was excellent,' he signalled the *Jagdgeschwader*. Dowding on the other hand could ill afford to lose 32 fighters particularly as of the 38 *Luftwaffe* losses, the bomber *Geschwader* (which had knocked hell out of Portland) had only lost 15. The remaining 23 were fighters – Me. 109s and Me. 110s. RAF fighters would have to concentrate more on enemy bombers and avoid getting tangled with enemy fighters, which needed no encouragement anyway.

Goering called at the Berghof, where Hitler waited impatiently for Eagle to spread its wings. '*Mein Führer*,' Hermann promised, 'the moment I get three clear days of fine weather I shall give the "go" signal.' The very next day *Luftwaffe* Met. signalled all clear for the 13th. Jeschonnek double-checked with the *Luftwaffe* Liaison Officer at OKW (Major Freiherr Sigismund von Falkenstein) and reported to Jodl, 'The weather forecast is favourable ... order for a major attack ... expected ...'

But first, *Erprobungs Gruppe* 210 had a special job to do. On 3 August Chief of Staff Jeschonnek had signalled *Luftflotten* 2 and 3: 'Known British radar stations to be attacked with the first wave ... in order to eliminate them as early as possible.' Then the order was confirmed – it was the signal for the *Grosseinsatz* to begin.

Hauptmann Walter Rubensdorffer briefed his leaders: he himself would take Dunkirk (near Faversham, Kent) with the *stab-schwarme*; *Oberleutnant* Martin Lutz was to attack Pevensey (near Eastbourne) with 1 *Staffel* (Me. 110s); and *Oberleutnant* Rossiger, leading 2 *Staffel* (Me. 110s), would bomb Rye (near Hastings). *Oberleutnant* Otto Hintze, with his 3 *Staffel* (Me. 109s) was to go for Dover. Each of Hintze's 8 Me. 109s carried a 250 kg bomb. Otto Hintze led his *staffel* off Calais-Marck at 10.30 a.m. and headed north.

On Monday 12 August the night watch at Rye radar station went off duty at 8 a.m. Leading Aircraftswoman Daphne Griffiths, one of the relief watch in the Receiver hut, noticed that they all looked tense and exhausted. Something was brewing. 'Change quickly and quietly, girls,' the duty corporal told them. Daphne slipped on the Converter's head-set. From that moment she was 'reading' plots at record speed: 'Track one, now range 25, Read,' called Helen, watching the cathode tube. 'Robert 8426. Height 20,000.' Daphne read the co-ordinates direct to the Filter Room at HQ Fighter Command, Stanmore. 'Hostile 4 now at 18 miles, Stanmore. Read.' 'Robert 7129.' 'Twenty plus on both tracks,' it was Helen. 'Track one is now hostile 6,' the Stanmore plotter told them.

After 9.00 a.m. the pressure eased but a lovely August day was beginning to warm up the inside of the hut. Betty the Dalmatian came in and took up her favourite position under the Converter. Suddenly Daphne picked up a new response from the French coast, where *Oberleutnant* Rossiger and 2 *Staffel* were still climbing. 'Robert 9433,' Daphne read. 'Can I have a height?' asked the Stanmore plotter. 'Height 18,000. Range decreasing fast.' Stanmore said, 'We've put an X (unidentified) on your plot.' At Rye they watched the plot coming straight for them. 'Warn the guns.'

Meanwhile Otto Hintze and 3 *Staffel* were attacking Dover. Holding their Me. 109 *Jabos* (fighter-bombers) in a steady dive of 45 degrees into the wind, they aimed at the foot of one of the giant aerial masts. Concentrate solely on the mast, and some of the vital buildings will certainly be hit. It never entered Otto's head that in those buildings girls like Daphne Griffiths were sitting at their sets refusing to budge as the *Jabos* roared down on them.

'Warn the guns!' At Rye no one doubted the intentions of the approaching X-raid. Corporal Hempson seized the telephone. Before he could speak to the AA battery the troop commander yelled back 'Three dive-bombers – duck!'

Suddenly the noise was unbelievable – diving aircraft, exploding bombs, guns, voices; Daphne's reaction was one of 'incredulous amazement'. Then she felt so frightened she could neither speak nor move. A distant voice (Stanmore) was asking, 'Rye, what's happening? What's all the noise?'

'Your X-raid's bombing us. Here they come again!'

The whine of diving aircraft became louder and shriller. A terrific explosion rocked the hut, which filled with acrid fumes. Then the telephone rang. Helen, the girl on the tube (which had now gone black), picked it up. 'Air raid warning Red,' said the voice. 'Hell's teeth, you're telling us,' screamed Helen as she slammed down the receiver.

In the Filter Room at Fighter Command the usual hum of activity increased as running commentaries came in from radar stations Dunkirk, Rye, Pevensey, and Dover – all had reported. Then the plotting table called up to the Duty Filter Officer, Flying Officer Robert Wright: 'Ventnor's being attacked!' He threw one of the battery of switches beside him and was on the line to Ventnor, where the corporal in charge was giving a blow by blow account. 'Are you all right?' Wright asked.

'We're being properly beaten up,' came the reply.

'What about the girls?'

'They're all right so far,' shouted the corporal above the din of bombs and aircraft engines, 'Blondie's yelling at us from outside. She's trying to count the buggers!'

Poor Blondie. She never got to the end of counting those fifteen Ju. 88s which were screaming down on Ventnor. When they searched later among the burning shambles she was missing.

The radar station went off the air. In one swift blow the *Luftwaffe* had forced a vital breach in Fighter Command's defences. Fortunately they never realized it: by sending out impulses on another transmitter Fighter Command foxed the Germans into thinking that Ventnor was still functioning.

At Rye casualties were slight: an A A trooper killed, six others wounded. Daphne Griffiths surveyed the damage: clods of earth and mud had been thrown up into the three hundred foot transmitter towers which had not been budged. The road was pitted with craters, the water main was cut, and where the cookhouse had once stood there was an enormous lake with splintered planks and kitchen utensils floating on it. Daphne returned to the Receiver hut. 'Already the stand-by Diesel was providing us with power and we were back on the air – and plotting.' It was the same at Dunkirk, Dover and Pevensey. Despite more or less serious damage, all were back on the air within hours.

Just after noon, convoys 'Agent' and 'Arena' were passing one another in the Thames Estuary. A mile above, with six Hurricanes, I looked down

L

on some eighty vessels – Britain's life line. Controller's orders were vague and hard to hear at that range. AA bursts blotched the haze below – were they shooting at us? I never saw the twenty-two Ju. 87s, led by *Hauptmann* von Brauchitsch (son of the Army chief), which were ineffectively attacking Agent and Arena.

Then six white incisions appeared above in the immense blue. Me. 109 vapour trails? 'Pull the tit and stick with me,' I called to the others. I pulled my own emergency boost knob and pushed the throttle wide open but the white trails stopped abruptly and six black dots came down at us, growing wings as they approached. The leader must have said 'Hurricanes'. I thought 'Spitfires', but was not sure, even less so when Nigger Marshall (my No. 2) rolled over and disappeared. I myself dodged and then again saw the six of them below. I had height and the sun in my back – the fighter pilot's dream. I closed. Heinkel 113s? We had heard that a few had been seen and looked like Spitfires. Could be: they had attacked my flight; my No. 2 had disappeared. Still I closed, thumb on the firing button, sights glued on the leader. But careful! They could be Spitfires. Then one small feature confirmed it: the radiator under the starboard wing. Mistakes in identity were not infrequent. That very day a Ju. 88 over the Cherbourg peninsula was less fortunate than those Spitfires.

With one radar station knocked out the *Luftwaffe* had made a good start (even if they did not know it) in the battle to smash Fighter Command. They landed damaging blows too on fighter airfields – Manston, Hawkinge and Lympne – on the south coast. Those airfields were not indispensable, but the strategy was right.

Papa Fink nearly bought it over Manston, which his *KG* 2 practically demolished in the space of five minutes. The Dorniers streaked in low in close formation. 'We met no fighters or AA,' said Werner Borner, 'and everything went fine.' *Oberst* Fink wanted to do better, but on their second run in *KG* 2 was pounced on by 56 Squadron.

Led by Flight Lieutenant 'Jumbo' Gracie, an inveterate 'Hun-hater', 56 had scrambled from Rochford airfield near Southend. Innes Westmacott was with them. 'York Blue Leader Lumba calling. Seventy plus bandits approaching Charlie Three,' called the North Weald controller, Wing Commander John Cherry. 56 caught them over the sea – Do. 17s with Me. 109 escort. Innes first saw them some way off. 'They look like pretty toys,' he thought. In those pretty toys were living men like Fink and Borner and Hannes Trautloft, ignorant of their fate which the next few minutes would decide. Another was Geoffrey Page who, sweating hot in his Hurricane, had pushed back the hood. Home from a party in the early hours of the morning, he had written to a friend, 'It's only an hour before dawn. To me it will mean just another day of butchery . . . it makes me feel sick . . . how will it all end?'

Then Jumbo was calling, 'Echelon starboard, Go!' And he dived on Papa Fink's leading Dornier. The rear guns of thirty Dorniers opened up. It was Innes Westmacott's baptism of fire. 'We were received with a hot fire from their rear guns.' He aimed at a Dornier and saw his bullets striking home. Then down came the Me. 109s and he had to break away. All he could say was 'I've fired my guns in anger and with reasonable accuracy for the first time.'

Jumbo had aimed well. In the leading Dornier, Papa Fink had his map shot clean out of his hands; but he had hit Manston hard.

Or were they Geoffrey Page's bullets? He had closed in to fifty yards on the leading Dornier and he could see his bullets striking the port engine. He had one thought: kill them before they kill me. Then something exploded in his ears – a gaping hole appeared in his right wing. The fuselage tank, just ahead of the cockpit, blew up in his face. Sheets of flame. 'Dear God, save me!' he prayed and grabbed at the pin of his Sutton harness, watching his hands shrivel in the flames.

Then somehow he was clear and falling. The Margate lifeboat found him bleeding and burned to the bone, still trying to swim with his charred and blistered fingers and blinded by the scorched and swollen flesh about his eyes. Well might the 'sportsmen' of Nazi propaganda congratulate themselves on a 'good bag'. Geoffrey Page was but one of the bag. On both sides hundreds of others were yet to fall.

This was the first day of the Manston saga, a story of selfless courage and stark, degrading fear.

Diving his Ju. 88 nearly vertically over Portsmouth Harbour, Joachim Poetter held his sights on the battleship HMS *Queen Elizabeth*. *KG* 51's attack was an ill-conceived operation. First, Joachim's 7 *Staffel KG* 51 had no real experience of dive-bombing in Ju. 88s. Next, though the sinking of the *Queen Elizabeth* might please Admiral Raeder it could hardly further the *Luftwaffe*'s avowed aim of destroying Fighter Command. *KG* 51's efforts were wasted and it cost them six of their best crews.

Joachim's bombs fell short of the *Queen Elizabeth*. On pulling out, his air brakes jammed. He was a sitting duck, but it saved him. Lagging behind the rest of the *Gruppe*, he saw British fighters closing in on it. He watched as his comrades fell flaming into the sea – one of them was his best friend Noelken. Another was *Oberleutnant* S. Thus was his fatal error at Freiburg expiated honourably on the field of battle.

At 5.00 p.m. OKM flashed a signal to *Luftflotten*: *Adlertag* begins 7.30 a.m. 13 August. It meant nothing to Paul Temme and his friends in their château near Fécamp: the next would be a day like any other. You had to believe it, otherwise there was no going on. Yet Temme felt unaccountably depressed. Was it the memory of that Blenheim he had driven (a raging furnace) into the ground a few days earlier? He was proud of his victory – he kept a fragment of the aircraft. Then he saw the photos and letters in the young pilot's wallet and he realized what he had done.

Helmut Wick was dejected at the thought of having shot down a Ju. 88 in error. Paul and Helmut talked despondently until 10.00 a.m when Wick stood up and smashed his glass into the fireplace. Then he stalked off to his room.

Temme tried to sleep on a sofa in the library. No good. So he sat up and wrote to his mother. Then he tore the letter up. His eye had fallen on a book, the poems of Rainer Maria Rilke. He opened it at random and read, '*Wer nun weint in der Nacht, weint für mich*' (who now weeps in the night, weeps for me). Paul felt a terrible loneliness, as if the sorrows of the world were weighing on his heart. Then he fell asleep.

Earlier that day Dowding had received a letter from the Chief of Air Staff, Newall: 'I am now glad to be able to say that it has been decided to cancel the time limit in the period of your appointment as C-in-C Fighter Command.' Dowding at last felt free to fight the Battle of Britain.

Part Six

THE
ATTACK

Chapter 23

For the last few days Goering had been growing more and more nervous, pacing up and down beside his half of the train *Asia* inside a tunnel in the woods near Le Coudray.

During the Battle of Britain the C-in-C of the *Luftwaffe* was to travel thousands of miles in his train but despite the gypsy life he was well cosseted by a trio of faithful servants: ex-sailor Robert Kropp, his valet; Fedor Radmann of the German Wagon Lits, his chef; and Christa Gormanns, his private nurse, or 'needlewoman', as Milch called her. Christa was a remarkable girl whose activities went far beyond Goering's somewhat exacting clinical needs. She answered his telephone, took down his orders, dictated them to the Signals section, and occasionally barked them out on the telephone straight to the *Luftflotten* commanders.

Goering did himself well. He was not a heavy eater, but he liked the best – choice dishes, fine wines, strawberries flown in from Spain.

His Chief of Staff Hans Jeschonnek was never far away in his own train, singularly named *Robinson*. On the morning of 13 August, Jeschonnek and his staff officers – *Oberst* von Waldau (Ops.) and Major Beppo Schmid (Intelligence) – read the Met. reports. The forecast of the previous evening had been good; then reconnaissance aircraft reported a deterioration. Fink's *KG 2* were already signalled airborne. Their target: Eastchurch Airfield, east of London. Goering immediately ordered: operation cancelled.

Werner Borner (II *KG 2*) noted in his log, 'Airborne Arras St Leger 0550.' 74 Dorniers all told, the *Geschwader* formed up with Papa Fink leading I *Gruppe*, Major Weitkus following at the head of Werner's II *Gruppe*, and Major Fuch's III *Gruppe* in the rear. *KG 2* headed for St Omer to rendezvous with its escort – Me. 110s of *Zerstörer Gruppe* 76 led by the one-legged veteran, *Oberstleutnant* Joachim Huth. But *KG 2* had never before seen an escort like this. The Me. 110s dived and zoomed over the Dornier's heads as if attacking and one (Huth himself) flew head on at the bomber formation, missing it by feet. 'What the hell are they up to?' wondered Borner – a question that *KG* 2's angry leader also was trying to answer.

Had Fink's wireless not been useless that morning, he would have understood. From the 'Holy Mountain', *Luftflotte* 2's advanced HQ at Cap Blanc Nez, frantic messages were relaying Goering's order: '*Angriff beschranken*' (attack cancelled). Weitkus's machine actually picked up the message, but his operator got it wrong: '*Angriff ausfuehren*' (go ahead). 'There was a slanging match against Weitkus because he had left his radio on "transmit",' said Werner Borner. That jammed all the others. Unheeding and unescorted Papa Fink led *KG* 2 on to England.

The weather worsened. Fink ordered his *Gruppen*: '*Ausschwarmen*' (break up). Far away to the north Borner could see the London barrage balloons. Then Weitkus led the II *Gruppe* down to fifteen hundred feet for the run in over Eastchurch. They bombed with devastating effect and made for the clouds again.

The other *Gruppen* were not so lucky. III *Gruppe* had been badly shot up on the way in by 'Sailor' Malan's 74 Squadron. And on the way back, Fink's own I *Gruppe* was caught by 111 Squadron (Squadron Leader 'Tommy' Thompson) which sent five Dorniers into the ground.

As *KG* 2 climbed away from Arras, Haerle, a mechanic at Beaumont le Roger in Normandy, was warming up the engine of Paul Temme's Me. 109. Then he switched off and jumped down from the cockpit to report to his pilot. Immediately he saw that something was wrong. 'What's the matter?' he asked. Temme did not answer, but simply handed him a fragment of the Blenheim he had shot down.

'Keep it if you like,' he told Haerle. Then he turned to join Helmut Wick and Rudi Pflanz for a last cigarette. Rudi lit Wick's cigarette, then his own. Temme leaned forward for a light.

'Stop! It's a bad omen,' cried Rudi, but Paul just answered, 'What the hell!'

Dawn had hardly broken when they took off with orders: *Frei-jagd* (free hunt) Brighton. The British coast seemed clear of the enemy but Temme kept saying, 'Something's going to happen.' It did. He spotted a Hurricane attacking a Ju. 88 and dived on it, with two Spitfires on his tail. He hit the Hurricane, which exploded. Then the Spits. got him. Oil pressure dropped, coolant temperature rose off the clock; he would never make it home. A few moments later his Me. 109 was slithering through a potato field near Shoreham. Shorn of its wings, the dismembered fuselage came to rest upside down against a railway embankment. Paul wriggled out, covered from head to foot in mud. Not since the days when he helped clear the glider strip at Lippstadt had he seen such mud. The boy with a craze for flying was now a prisoner of war.

As Temme breakfasted with the station commander at Shoreham, Hurricanes of 43 Squadron from Tangmere battled overhead with Ju. 88s of *KG* 54, heading for the airfields of Odiham and Farnborough. Harried by the Hurricanes and frustrated by cloud, the bombers never found their targets. After its crew had baled out a Ju. 88 which fell to 43's guns almost crashed on top of Arundel Castle. One crewman wearing gaudy pyjamas under his uniform was found near Poling radar station. For his pilot, *Hauptmann* Wilhelm Strauch, a resting place was found in Tangmere churchyard, where more of his comrades were soon to be.

KG 54 was briefed for a second raid, this time on Portland. But the *Luftwaffe's* C-in-C, raging and screaming at all Met. men who ever drew breath, once more sent out a personal order at 11.00 a.m.: Delay attack until 2.00 p.m.

It merely added to the confusion. *KG* 54 received the message, its escort, V (*Zerstörer*) *LG* 1, did not. Despite the 'Ventnor Gap' other stations in the radar chain had already seen them, 'twenty plus', over the Cherbourg Peninsula. *Hauptmann* Leinsberger and his twenty-three Me. 110s were watched all the way over to Portland, where RAF fighters rushed down on them. Six of Goering's 'Ironsides' – his pride and joy – went down, while the rest beat it back to France.

In the afternoon bad bombing weather prevailed over England. Fifty-two Ju. 87s from Richthofen's *Fliegerkorps* VIII cruised around looking for Middle Wallop Fighter Airfield, near Salisbury. 'The attack was a flop,' wrote Richthofen in his diary, ' . . . our formations returned without releasing their bombs . . .'

Not all returned: thirteen Spitfires of 609 Squadron slipped under the Me. 110 escort while it was mixing with 238 Squadron's Hurricanes and dispatched nine of the *Stukas*. One of the Spitfire pilots remarked, 'I missed the Glorious Twelfth, but the glorious thirteenth was the best day's shooting I ever had.' Just like the Nazi 'sportsmen' the day before.

It was sport all right, a terribly dangerous one, as long as you thought of it as shooting aeroplanes. Only when you could not keep your mind off the charred and mangled remains of the men inside them, did the sporting side wear thin and become, as Geoffrey Page had written, 'Another day's butchery.' So thought Major Hozzel as he watched with horror the *Stukas* of his *Gruppe* exploding in mid-air, or plunging earthwards like fiery rockets. Another *Stuka* leader (Major Eneccerus) said, 'They ripped our backs open to the collar.'

The German fighters did a good job that afternoon. While Me. 109s (JG 27) and Me. 110s fought it out with Hurricanes (213 and 238) and Spitfires (152), six Ju. 88s attacked Middle Wallop — without effect; another twelve bombers damaged the old bomber airfield at Andover. Meanwhile Major Kern's I *LG* 1 inflicted heavy damage on Southampton docks. Southampton – a peaceful sea-faring town where in better times luxury liners berthed, where I had stood with my mother at the foot of the *Neuralia*'s gangway bound for Singapore. Southampton ravaged by Nazi bombs. It was a bit much.

As black smoke settled over Southampton, ten Hurricanes of 43 Squadron tried to catch the Ju. 88s as they dodged home through the clouds. Sergeant Hallowes attacked one head on, 'a frightening experience', he called it, because of the high closing speed. He fired at another which had already been winged: 'Pieces fell from the aircraft, which dived into clouds.' Position, thirty-five miles south of Selsey Bill. At Selsey during those carefree peace-time summers we had galloped along the broad sands, swum in the chilly sea, and watched the big liners. Now Hallowes was knocking pieces off a German bomber a few miles south. Well, a bloody good thing too. But for them we would have still been having fun.

Nine Hurricane pilots landed at Tangmere; the tenth, 'Wombat' Woods-Scawen, rolled up in a car. His parachute had worked for the fourth time.

Eastwards over Kent, two *Stuka Gruppen* of Loerzer's *Fliegerkorps* and another borrowed from Richthofen's made for Detling airfield near Maidstone and Rochford, North Weald's satellite near Southend. Above wheeled the Me. 109s of *JG* 26, led by Major Hendrick, Olympic gold medallist in 1936, but by then a bit old for single-seaters. Leading III *Gruppe* was his dauphin, Adolf Galland. 'Destroyed' at Manston the day before, 65 Squadron now charged energetically into the Me. 109s. Once again German fighters had lured the defence. Unhindered below, *Stukas* were demolishing Detling. Cloud saved Rochford from a similar fate. With their bombs the *Stukas* turned for home, but leapt upon by 56

Squadron, they jettisoned over Canterbury. 'We were taught a sharp lesson,' said Innes Westmacott, 'by the enemy rear gunners' excellent shooting.' 56 lost a Hurricane, with six others badly damaged. It was the last time they tried attacking from astern. In future it would be from the beam or quarter.

Luftwaffe air crews had fought courageously and inflicted serious damage on 'the English homeland': Eastchurch, Detling and Southampton docks were very hard hit. But as an opening to the *Luftwaffe*'s great air offensive against their particular enemy, Fighter Command, Eagle Day was a complete failure.

Ranting in the woods near Le Coudray, Goering had no reason to feel proud. After all, he had given the orders, as a result of which two attacks had been completely botched up with the loss of five of *KG* 2's Dorniers and six of V (Z) *LG* 1's Me. 110s. In all, the *Luftwaffe* lost forty-five aircraft to thirteen of the RAF's fighters. It was a heavy price to pay for the achievements of Goering's bombers, which contributed absolutely nothing to the *Luftwaffe*'s hoped-for victory against Fighter Command. Neither Eastchurch nor Detling nor Andover were Figher Command's airfields. Nor were Odiham or Farnborough, which the bombers in any case had failed to hit. The fighter airfields of Middle Wallop and Rochford were unharmed. The successful attack on Southampton made no breach in Fighter Command's defences. And not a single radar station was touched.

The *Grosseinsatz* was off to a bad start, far worse than the *Luftwaffe* high command imagined. But Kesselring and Sperrle expressed satisfaction. They deluded themselves into believing they had hit Fighter Command in the vitals. They were lured by the rosy accounts from the units. Airfields like Manston were blue-pencilled off the map as if they no longer existed; the thirteen RAF fighters lost swelled into 134. It is true that Johannes Janke's I *JG* 77 destroyed eleven RAF Wellington bombers that day over Denmark. That meant a serious loss to Bomber Command, but it had no essential effect on the outcome of the Battle of Britain, a battle which depended before anything else on Fighter Command.

Rightly, the British measured results against overall losses of the *Luftwaffe* only by their own fighter losses and installations damaged. The *Luftwaffe* had to destroy Fighter Command. It was the first step in defeating Britain.

Hearing that Eagle had begun to flap its wings, Hitler returned to Berlin at noon on the 14th. At 5.30 p.m. he was closeted in the Chancellery with Admiral Raeder and his Chief of Staff Schniewind; Keitel and Jodl were in attendance. Raeder went off on his favourite tack: the army had a case for a wide front crossing, but *Kriegsmarine* just couldn't make it. Tides, winds, lack of boats – and the British Navy . . .

'The admiral's right,' Hitler agreed, 'and we cannot risk failure. If we failed the British would gain immense prestige.' But if he wouldn't say yes, he wouldn't say no to invasion. 'We must wait and see the effect of the *Grosseinsatz*.' He would also like to check out with Brauchitsch. . .

Jodl had been to work on his Fuehrer. He had summarized his own views in an appreciation. To the essential prerequisite 'destroy the RAF', he had now added another, 'destroy the Royal Navy' at least in Channel waters. 'Within a week we should know,' that is, by 20 August.

Then 'Sea Lion' would roll. But only if the *Kriegsmarine* could manage a wide front, at least as far west as Brighton. If not, invasion would be 'an act of desperation which would have to be chanced in a desperate situation'.

But Britain, said Jodl, remained Enemy Number 1. The 'decisive battle against England' was beginning. Her resistance had to be broken by the next Spring (1941). If *Grosseinsatz*, *Unter-zeebooten* and *Seeloewe* would not bring her to her knees, there were other ways: through Gibraltar, and Egypt (with Mussolini's help). Meanwhile all other operations not essential to the conquest of England should be postponed until England was defeated. None of this would upset Hitler's dream-conquest of Russia, scheduled for Spring 1941 – when Britain would be in the bag. It was a neat plan.

On 14 August the Fuehrer kept a date with his eight new marshals. It was baton-giving day. Just to remind everybody that he had done one better *Reichsmarschall* Goering turned up, already fondling his. He had left the five-day air war intending to liquidate the RAF for the more sophisticated surroundings of his beloved Carinhall. A conference with the *Luftwaffe* commanders was set for the next day. Meanwhile, to everyone's surprise, he was hob-nobbing with his *bête noire* Erich Raeder. He had even apologized to the Admiral for his rudeness over the Trondheim defences. Now he 'warmly seconded the view of the *Kriegsmarine* chief'. Raeder thought Goering had buried the hatchet, but the wily *Reichsmarschall* was only supporting his views on 'Sea Lion' so that the *Luftwaffe* could gain all the honours.

The glittering investiture over, Hitler spoke of 'Sea Lion'. 'I do not intend to carry out an operation (Raeder noted the Fuehrer's words) whose risk is too great. I take the view that . . . Britain's defeat does not depend on invasion alone. It can be achieved by other means (*Grosseinsatz*, for example). But I want to continue the threat of invasion. Preparations must therefore go ahead.'

Hitler was not bluffing. When the *Kriegsmarine* put up a suggestion for a 'deception operation to maintain the threat', Hitler replied that preparations must be genuine and be ready by September. That was enough for Raeder. Opposed as he was, he was now convinced that 'Sea Lion' was no bluff.

After its shaky start, *Grosseinsatz* dwindled on 14 August to a few desultory attacks. A gallant little incident brightened the grey dawn. The lifeboat *Charles Cooper Henderson*, returning to Dover about 7.00 a.m. with two survivors from a British bomber, came upon a canoe. Paddling it was Miss Peggy Prince, with another survivor.

While JG 26's Me. 109s lured British fighters into combat above the clouds, *Oberleutnant* Roessiger with II *Staffel Erp Gr.* 210 nipped in below and bombed Manston. The Blenheim night fighters of 600 Squadron were grounded by day. But the officers and men did not shirk their duty to defend the airfield. They helped refuel the day fighters and while others crouched in the deep chalk shelters, 600's air gunners let fly from improvised gun mountings as the fighter-bombers came diving down. A Bofors 40 mm blew the tail off *Unteroffizier* Steding's Me. 110. Somehow gunner *Gefreiter* Ewald Schank baled out, landing on the tarmac a few seconds after the Me. 110, engines screaming, hit the airfield. Completely dazed, Schrank could only keep muttering, 'the big lick, very soon the big lick'.

At that moment *Luftwaffe* bombers were sinking the Varne Lightship and its fighters shooting down eight Dover balloons. This kind of fun did not help to defeat Fighter Command.

Red Tobin, a lanky American from Los Angeles whose new home was with 609 Squadron, was walking over to hangar 5 after lunch at Middle Wallop fighter airfield when three Ju. 88s suddenly dived out of the clouds. 'I hit mother earth and stayed there . . . sprayed with debris . . . it was awful. One man's foot was blown off, another one's arm up to the shoulder blades. At least three ... crushed under the hangar door. Red saw Sergeant Alan Feary in his Spitfire dive on the Ju. 88 and shoot it out of the sky. 'I am convinced,' wrote Red in his diary, 'that war is now ... playing the most brutal game.'

Red and his friends Andy Mamedoff and Shorty Keough had been looking for a fight with the Germans. After many adventures they reached England, where an MP friend put in a good word for them and the RAF gladly took them on. Later I was to know Red, a fine and gentle man who might have stepped straight out of a Western. His language was coloured with phrases like 'Saddle up boy, I'm ridin'' that sent his fitter running to start up his Spitfire.

At Fighter Command HQ Dowding discussed the fighting with his friend General 'Tim' Pile, C-in-C of Anti-Aircraft Command. Dowding could not know that the day before was the first day of the *Grosseinsatz*, any more than when the great air offensive would end. He knew only that there would be fighting more or less every day for weeks, perhaps months, until one side gave up. So far he was satisfied with the battle's progress. Miraculously, all the radar stations had survived except Ventnor for which a mobile set at Bembridge was filling in. The sector airfields with their vulnerable Ops. Rooms had not been touched; three advanced airfields, though badly hit, were again serviceable for landing. That was all they were needed for. The *Luftwaffe* had wasted most of its bombs on non-fighter airfields.

At Fontainebleau Halder studied the report of his *Luftwaffe* Liaison Officer, General Staff. 'Results of fighting on 8–12 August, first aim, reduction of enemy fighter strength in Southern England. Results, very good. Overall ratio of losses: 1 *Luftwaffe* to 3 RAF. For fighters only 1 *Luftwaffe* to 5 RAF. Ground organization: eight major airfields virtually destroyed.'

All this of course was nonsense. Dowding was never to take the claimed 'score' as an index of the battle's progress. If the *Luftwaffe* believed their fantastic claims, all the better. Let them fall into the trap of false optimism. On the other hand, if the RAF's claims were exaggerated, this could only help to boost public morale. Dowding was only interested in hard facts: his own losses in machines, and the damage done to fighter installations and above all, pilots. These were the gauge of Fighter Command's success. One thing irked Dowding: the criticism, levelled at him from on high, of his deployment of squadrons (a fighting force of 228) in 11 Group, and 7 squadrons in 10 Group. In the opinion of the critics it was a pathetically small force to oppose massed cohorts of enemy which concentrated on the south and south-east of England.

But Dowding had carefully calculated his deployment. For one thing neither airfields nor ground control in 10 and 11 Groups could accommodate more squadrons. For another, Dowding believed it would be fatal to weaken his northern flank – guarded by 12 and 13 Groups, each with 11 single-seater squadrons. The 'big lick' would prove who was right.

Thirty miles from Berlin, Goering was back at Carinhall. There he amended the *Luftwaffe*'s operational plan for 15 August. Stumpff's *Luftflotte* 5 were to participate. For *Luftflotte* 5 it was a momentous decision. Weather permitting, all was set for the 'big lick'.

A ridge of high pressure over Britain promised warm, sunny weather. Five hundred miles away at Carinhall, Goering (in his *Reichsjaegermeister* hunting outfit – white shirt with puffed sleeves, high boots, and a hunting knife stuck into his belt) tried to relax in his private loggia overlooking the lake. In summertime he always worked there. That morning he felt in no mood for mincing words with his *Luftflotten* commanders, Kesselring and Sperrle, who had to be with Stumpff and the *Fleigerkorps* commanders at noon. Then, of all days, there was no top brass on the air front.

His friend Bruno Loerzer (II *Fleigerkorps* chief) had left *Oberst* Paul Deichmann, his chief of staff, in charge. From his headquarters in a rat-ridden farmhouse at Bonningues, Deichmann gave the 'go' to his bomber and fighter units. Then he drove over to the Holy Mountain, *Luftflotte* 2 HQ at Cap Blanc Nez. *Oberstleutnant* Rieckhoff, Chief of Ops., was minding the shop for his absentee chief, Kesselring. Rieckhoff was astonished on hearing that the *geschwader* of *Fliegerkorps* II were already airborne. 'Berlin's just cancelled,' he told Deichmann. It was too late. The fuse was already ignited: the whole air front from Norway to Cherbourg was about to explode into activity.

Deichmann's *Stukas* were already pounding Hawkinge and Lympne when a force of *Luftflotte* 5 bombers with long-range fighters were leaving the Norwegian coast, steering for the Tyneside area in north-east England. Allowing for the usual safety margin it was a long hop, some eleven hundred miles there and back. No question of the Me. 109s of Johannes Janke's I *JG* 77 escorting. So twenty-one Me. 110s of I *ZG* 76 took on the job, each carrying an auxiliary 'Dachshund' fuel tank.

Every effort was made to deceive the British defences. Leading the *Stab-schwarme, Hauptmann* Werner Restemeyer's Me. 110 'Dora' was fitted with a special radio array to intercept the enemy's ground control directions and thus avoid their fighters. *Hauptmann* Hartwich (X *Fliegerkorps* chief signals officer) came along in the back cockpit of 'Dora' to work the set. It was a tragically unsuccessful attempt to outwit the British radar control system.

In a further attempt to fox the defences, twenty seaplanes were sent ahead, steering for the Firth of Forth, well north of the real target. Alas for the 63 Heinkel 111s of 'Lion' *Geschwader KG* 26 (Missy's old unit), their own navigation was sadly out. They made a landfall almost at the same spot as the seaplanes, seventy-five miles off course.

At 12.08 p.m. radar picked up a plot of 'twenty plus' some ninety miles off the coast. It swelled to 'thirty plus'. 13 Group had plenty of time to dispose their squadrons. When Squadron Leader Ted Graham (leading Spitfires of 72 Squadron) sighted the German formation twenty-five miles from the coast he gasped in astonishment. 'Thirty plus' had now blown up into eighty-four Heinkels and Me. 110s all told.

Down went the Spitfires, one section going for the Me. 110s, the rest for the Heinkels. 'Dora' was one of the first to be hit. Its 'Dachshund' tank exploded and the brave Restemeyer and Hartwich plunged in flames into the sea, and with them the apparatus they hoped would save them from the enemy fighters.

After 72, came more Spitfires of 79 and 41 Squadrons and Hurricanes of 605 and 607. Five more Me. 110s went down. Some of the Heinkels pressed on tenaciously, but were forced back, with a loss of ten, before reaching their targets – the bomber airfields of Dishforth and Linton.

Seventy-five miles south, fifty Ju. 88s of 'Eagle' *Geschwader KG* 30 were dead on course for the bomber airfield at Driffield. They aimed well, hitting four hangars and wrecking twelve Whitley bombers. *KG* 30 lost six Ju. 88s which, with the ten Heinkels and six Me. 110s of the northern force, was a heavy price to pay. No RAF fighters were lost. The Germans however claimed eleven, two Spitfires having been seen to 'hit the sea'.

Impressions in combat were always deceptive; only facts counted with Dowding. *Luftflotte* 5 would never again attack in daylight.

Further south, the luncheon hour at Manston was rudely disturbed by twelve ground-strafing Me. 110s. Then, just after 3.30 p.m., fifty Dorniers of II and III *Gruppen* of *KG* 3 were massing over Cap Gris Nez waiting for their fighter escort, an exceptionally strong one comprising about 150 Me. 109s from four *Jagdgeschwader* – Handrick's *JG* 26 (Adolf Galland leading I *Gruppe*), Trubenbach's *JG* 52, and Mettig's *JG* 54. This host of some two hundred aircraft bore down on Eastchurch and Rochester airfields while *Hauptmann* Rubensdorffer slipped unnoticed around by the East Coast with his *Erp Gr.* 210. Six Hurricanes and one Spitfire squadron (84 fighters) closed in on the main force, but were held off by the powerful escort. While III *KG* 3 bombed Eastchurch, II *KG* 3 scored a bull's-eye on Rochester.

In the Comte de Beauvais's château near St Inglevert (where he was quartered) Brustellin had breakfasted off cold partridge brought by a black servant. At 3.30 p.m. he led his I *JG* 51 off St Inglevert airfield following the *Geschwader Kommodore* (Moelders) and climbed up over the Channel. *JG* 51 was to act as fighter screen – to 'cleanse the air' in front of the bombers.

And the air over England seemed full of aircraft. So poor was Brustellin's eyesight that he relied on the eyes of his wing-man. 'Hurricanes in the sun!' the wing-man called, and Brustellin opened up and drew away from his *Schwarme*. A fighter approached on his left – 'one of ours,' he thought, but as it closed – Spitfire! Both aircraft were converging, throttled back, trying to get on the other's tail. It became a slow-flying contest which the Spitfire won. Brustellin's Me. 109 stalled and dived away. In a flash the Spit. was on his tail, pouring lead into the Me. 109 and its pilot. Wounded in the legs, with petrol gushing from a fuel pipe, Brustellin dived for France and safety. A belly-landing at St Inglevert did not improve his Me. 109. And two weeks in hospital put a temporary stop to the pleasures of *la vie du château*.

The violent and scattered combats between British fighters and the escorting Me. 109s caused confusion on the plotting tables. Four more squadrons were dispatched. One was 85; another, 17 Squadron, our sister-squadron in the Debden sector which had remained at Martlesham. I led 85 down to the Thames Estuary at full bore, searching frantically in the thick haze for the enemy. But the controller seemed to have lost the thread of the battle. 17 meanwhile was 'vectored' here and there over the North Sea, and then ordered to land at Martlesham. From afar they could see it had been properly plastered. Rubensdorffer had been and gone, leaving Martlesham 'a heap of smoking rubble', a description which before the day closed would more aptly fit his own Me. 110. The gallant Rubensdorffer had but three more hours to live.

The enemy withdrew (*KG* 3 to its bases in Belgium, *Erp Gr.* 210 and the *Jagdgeschwaderen* to theirs in the Pas de Calais) while Fighter Command's squadrons went winging back to their airfields, there to refuel and re-arm. It was a chance for the *Luftwaffe* to catch them on the wrong foot, but they did not take it. Co-operation between the *Luftflotten* was poor.

Small wonder, considering the *Luftflotten* and *Fliegerkorps* commanders where closeted with their Commander-in-Chief 500 miles from the battle front. Goering was in a raging temper. Nothing was going right: *Stuka* losses were appalling. That was the fault of the *Jagdgeschwaderen*. In the future fighter escort must be strengthened, three *Gruppen* to every *Stuka Gruppe*. And the Me. 110s: that business on the 13th with V (Z) *LG* 1 was a disgrace. 'The Me. 110s are being squandered needlessly, and there are all too few of them.' The truth was that despite the extraordinary courage of their crews, Goering's 'Ironsides' and Udet's *Stukas* were proving a dismal failure before a resolute fighter defence. The Me. 110 long-range escort itself now needed escorting. The *Stuka* was impossible to escort effectively; it was so slow.

Losses in officer aircrew were too high – in the future only one officer per crew would be allowed. And effort was being wasted on useless targets. What was this nonsense about sinking the Varne Lightship? Bombing Southampton docks? 'Operations are to be directed exclusively against the enemy air force, including their aircraft industry.' *Kampfgruppe* 100, the night bombing experts, must get busy on this. Night raids, even on a small scale, would allow 'the enemy defences and population no respite'.

All this was reasonable enough. But Goering lacked the wisdom, judgement and scientific knowledge needed to win against a highly organized defence backed by twenty years of professional experience and managed by a technician like Dowding. Besides Southampton docks, the Coastal and Bomber Command airfields, though courageously and successfully attacked, were a complete waste of the *Luftwaffe*'s finest aircrews and equipment. Goering's incompetence as an air commander had proved disastrous to the German cause at Dunkirk. It was to have a fatal effect on the decisive battle against England.

Now came the first imperial blunder: 'It is doubtful whether there is any point in continuing the attacks on radar sites,' opined the C-in-C, 'in view of the fact that not one of those attacked so far have been put out of action.' Little did he know. Ventnor had been wrecked in one attack. Half a dozen attacks on the four others already damaged would have wrecked them too. Only good Intelligence, in which Beppo Schmid was sorely lacking, and a little application (e.g. better tactics, like carpet bombing) and those stations would go for a Burton. The Air Ministry had already done half the job by leaving the technical buildings, not to speak of the girls inside them, above ground to be blown to bits by a few well-aimed bombs. Incredible – were it not for the fact that the equally vital Sector Ops. Rooms (and the girls inside them) were similarly exposed.

Yet Beppo Schmid and his Chief never saw it. 'Don't waste time on radar stations, they are no more important than the Varne Lightship or Brighton Pier.' Even *Oberst* Paul Deichmann agreed, but for a more subtle reason. 'Leave the British their radar,' he said, 'it will enable them to find our fighter formations who will thereupon destroy them.'

While his commanding general and his C-in-C were sunning themselves on the terrace at Carinhall five hundred miles away, Paul Deichmann was running the biggest air battle yet known in world history. But his theory was not working. RAF fighters were finding the *Luftwaffe* formations all right, but instead of being cut down themselves, they were inflicting serious losses on the invaders.

Nearly two hours after the withdrawal of *Luftflotte* 2 in the east *Luftflotte* 3 advanced on Portland in the west. From Lannion in Brittany came Ju. 87s of Hozzel's I *St.G* 1 and Eneccerus's II *St.G* 2; from Orleans, *LG* 1, 'Jocho' Helbig leading IV *Staffel*. Above and behind flew Me. 110 'destroyers' of Vollbracht's *ZG* 2, while higher still swarmed Me. 109s of Ibel's *JG* 27 and Taubadel's *JG* 53 – some 60 bombers escorted by 170 fighters. Destination: Worthy Down naval airfield. The Me. 109s would be stretched to the limit of their range – worse still, they had already burnt up precious fuel waiting to rendezvous with the bombers. With nearly a hundred miles of sea to cross, it was a 'dicey' operation, to say the least.

A mixed force of 180 British fighters rose to meet the advancing columns. The enemy's escort became locked in combat thousands of feet above the bombers, leaving them exposed. As the youngest *Staffel Kapitän*, Jochem Helbig brought up the rear of Major Kramer's II *Gruppe* with his 4 *Staffel*. When enemy fighters swooped out of the sun, 4 *Staffel* caught the full impact. 'For twenty minutes we were caught in a furious shoot-up with three British fighters.' The Ju. 88s closed in to concentrate their fire, but the fighters were not letting go. One Ju. 88 after another fell out of formation. At last Jochem was able to break away, but a fourth fighter then fixed on him. Only the coolness of his gunner (*Oberfedlwebel* Franz Schlund) saved the day: following his directions over the intercom, Helbig threw the Ju. 88 around like a fighter.

But it couldn't last. With the navigator wounded, starboard engine hit, and rear gunner out of ammunition, they all thought 'This is it.' They were in for a surprise. 'For five minutes the fighter played cat-and-mouse with us, coming right in close to peer at us – then he tipped his cap and cleared off.' Jochem Helbig was the only one of his *Staffel* to return. Eight crews were lost. Jocho did not know that of those thirty-two men, twenty-four were prisoners. 'The worst part,' he said, 'was writing to the next of kin.'

The rest of II *Gruppe* pressed on valiantly, attacked in turn by no less than eight RAF fighter squadrons. Three Ju. 88s got through to Worthy Down, but their bombs caused no serious damage. Leading I *Gruppe*, *Hauptmann* Kern reached Middle Wallop. The Germans believed their attack 'all but wiped out two British squadrons on the ground'. But one of them (609, Red Tobin's outfit) chased the Ju. 88s all the way to the coast. Said Red, 'They hit hangar 4, burnt three Blenheims and generally raised all kinds of hell, but nobody was hurt. So it wasn't so bad after all. It didn't pay the square heads because all eight of them were knocked down before they got home.'

Luftflotte 2 now followed up with a quick punch which caught some of Park's 11 Group squadron refuelling. But he had enough in hand to meet two bomber *Gruppen* of Dorniers headed for Biggin Hill Sector airfield, south of London. *Hauptmann* Rubensdorffer led the other. The target for Erp *Gr.* 210's fiftteen Me. 110s and eight Me 109 fighter-bombers was Kenley sector airfield, a stone's throw from 'Biggin'. Searching in the haze with the setting sun in their eyes they spotted West Malling (near Maidstone) a forward airfield in the Biggin Hill sector but without the Sector Ops. Room that made 'Biggin' so valuable a target. Luckily for Fighter Command the Dorniers unloaded their bombs on West Malling – they put the airfield out for a week.

It was perhaps to avoid attacking with the sun in his eyes that Rubensdorffer suddenly turned north. He would then dive southwards on Kenley with the sun on his right. At that moment escorting Me. 109s of JG 52 lost touch with Erp *Gr.* 210 and turned back. Rubensdorffer was already over the London suburbs. Overflying London was *verboten* – Fuehrer's orders. *Erprobungs Gruppe* 210 wheeled south and dived. Leading 3 *Staffel* (eight Me. 109s) Otto Hintze heard base calling, 'Attack cancelled,' and Rubensdorffer's laconic answer, 'Too late, we're attacking.' But where was Kenley? Impossible to pick out anything in that haze. Then there it was, an airfield in front. Had Rubensdorffer been one of those senior *Luftwaffe* pilots formerly on the *Lufthansa* London service, the cooling towers to the north would have told him that the airfield was Croydon.

Diving last with his 3 *Staffel* Otto Hintze saw the Me. 110s disappear into the haze, pursued by Hurricanes. He bombed and pulled up, then saw Me. 110s above 'all over the place'. In trouble, they were trying to form a defensive circle while a score of Hurricanes tore into them. Rid of their bombs they were fighters once more, but the Me. 109s had to form their own 'circle of death'. Hintze tried to edge it towards the Me. 110s.

Tommy Thompson's 111 Squadron had been patrolling at eight thousand feet over Croydon, their own base. On the airfield below his fitter had grabbed Pat, Tommy's Alsatian bitch, rushed her off to the nearest shelter and chained her to the bottom of the steel stairway. At that moment her master was plunging with his nine Hurricanes down on Croydon on the tails of the Me. 110s. He caught one as it pulled up vertically. 'Masses of bits flew off' (the German pilot landed what was left in a nearby field). Joined by more Hurricanes of Squadron Leader John Worrall's 32 Squadron, 111 was making it hot for the Me. 110s when Otto Hintze's Me. 109s closed in.

This was Rubensdorffer's chance. With the *Stabschwarme* in his wake he dived towards the coast and vanished in the haze. None of them got back. Valiant to the last, Rubensdorffer heaved his blazing Me. 110 aside from a Kentish cottage to crash on the far side. He and his gunner perished; of his Me. 110 there was left but 'a heap of smoking rubble'. It was a black day for *Erprobungs Gruppe* 210.

After landing, Tommy Thompson searched everywhere for Pat. But the Alsatian was nowhere to be found. People had seen Flight Lieutenant Peter Powell's bull terrier, Gangster, hobbling with a hind leg blown off – but no sign of Pat. It was not until Tommy went to his room in the Aerodrome Hotel that night that he saw a dog's tail sticking out from under his bed. Pat had snapped her chain and made for a 'better 'ole'.

That evening the pilots of 54 Squadron lay about on the grass near their Spitfires at Manston. 'I've had enough today,' said Colin Gray, 'I reckon the Huns have too. I'm just dying for a beer, a good meal and bed.' His flight commander Al Deere just had time to feel his appetite whetted when the warning bell went. Start up! Pilots were running, Merlin engines bursting into life. Then nine Spitfires roared off Manston's green-grass, pock-marked surface. 'Hello Hornet Leader, seventy plus, Angels 20,' said the unruffled voice of the Hornchurch controller, Ronald Adam, 'heading Dungeness-Dover. You are to engage escort fighters.' 'That's a new one,' thought Al. It was a new tactic of Park's to send Spitfires for the high-flying escort, Hurricanes for the bombers.

Squadron Leader 'Prof' Leathart cocked on another five thousand feet to the ordered height and climbed to twenty-five thousand feet. Radar heights were not always accurate and it was as well to take a bit of extra height to avoid being 'jumped' by enemy fighters. As it was, 54 just had the advantage and themselves jumped the Me. 109s from behind. Pandemonium. Al fixed on a Me. 109, following it in a long dive south-wards through a thin layer of cloud. There below was France. Calais – Marck airfield, the circuit infested with Me. 109s. 'You bloody fool,' said Al to himself, swerving away and diving for the sea with two Me. 109s in hot pursuit. Each time they closed Al turned to meet them, but each time they got closer. Suddenly his instrument panel was shattered. Then he felt his engine hit – vibration and oil streaming across the windscreen. Agonizing moments, then, dimly visible was the sight he'd been praying for, the cliffs of Dover. The Me. 109s saw them too, and turned back to France.

Al crossed the English coast with just enough speed to pull up to fifteen hundred feet. He jettisoned the canopy and as the cockpit filled with flames rolled the Spitfire over to drop out. Something snagged his para-chute pack. The Spitfire's nose dropped and it began diving upside down. Al struggled free just in time to pull the ripcord and land, seconds later, not a hundred yards from where his Kiwi II had exploded.

Hardly had he picked himself up when two airmen approached. 'I'm an ambulance driver,' said one, 'and my pal's a nursing orderly. We're on our way to Kenley and we thought we might help.' Excellent service, thought Al. Three hours later he was being treated at East Grinstead by Mr Archibald McIndoe, the wizard of plastic surgery whose magic hands were to transform hundreds of burnt and battered young bodies into presentable human beings. McIndoe kept Al for the night, and seeing he was all in would have held him longer. But the incorrigible Kiwi slipped out during an air raid warning and caught the next train back to Hornchurch.

With the burning wrecks of Rubensdorffer's Me. 110 and Al Deere's Spitfire scattered over the Kentish fields, a nine-hour air battle had ended. First estimates put *Luftwaffe* sorties at nearly 1,790; but later it was confirmed that over 2,000 German aircraft including over 800 bombers had flown against England that day. RAF fighters made just under one thousand sorties. Both sides made wildly exaggerated claims of aircraft destroyed – the invariable consequence of great numbers and confused fighting. The RAF claim of 182 enemy machines was more than twice the *Luftwaffe* Quarter-Master General's loss figure of seventy-five. At OKW Major von Falkenstein reported, '108 enemy planes were downed' *Luftwaffe* losses being 55 (possibly *Luftflotte* 5 figures were not yet in). Of those 108, 82 were believed to be Hurricanes and Spitfires. Fighter Command's real loss was 34 fighters.

But while the Germans persuaded themselves that their figures were true, Dowding was not taken in by theirs or the British claims. When the Air Minister cautioned him, 'There are serious doubts about your pilots' claims,' he cut him short. 'If the German claims were correct, they'd be in England by now.'

Wishful thinking about the 'score' did not alter the significance of the day's air battle, the greatest of all time. Fighter Command had engaged the *Luftwaffe* from Newcastle round to Portland on a front of over five hundred miles. But the *Luftwaffe* once again failed to concentrate a massive, unrelenting assault on achieving the aim in view: the overthrow of Fighter Command. Often heavy, the damage at the secondary airfields – Hawkinge, Lympne, Manston, West Malling and Croydon – was not too serious. The cratered surfaces were quickly repaired, and that was all that mattered. Of the Sector airfields – Middle Wallop had got off lightly. Biggin Hill and Kenley were missed altogether, and the courageous, determined efforts of the German airmen had been largely wasted. Through bad generalship and staff work Goering's five-day air campaign was failing to crush Fighter Command.

Dowding on the other hand had confounded his critics. The attacks he had anticipated in the north had been routed. His relatively small forces in the south-east and south had repulsed the enemy during hours of furious fighting. Winston Churchill had been watching tensely at Fighter Command Ops. Room. He had seen proof of Dowding's genius: 'The foresight of Air Marshal Dowding . . . deserves high praise, but even more remarkable have been the restraint and the exact measurement of formidable stresses which had reserved a fighter force in the north through all these long weeks of mortal conflict in the south. We must regard the generalship here shown as an example of genius in the art of war.'

Driving back to Chequers with General Ismay, Churchill was lost in thought. 'Don't speak to me,' he told him, 'I've never been so moved.' And Ismay heard Churchill murmuring to himself, 'Never in the field of human conflict was so much owed . . .'

Chapter 24

On the 16 August the weather was again warm and sunny. It was four days since the radar stations were attacked – incredible that the *Luftwaffe* had not again hit where it hurt Fighter Command most, or at the Sector airfields with their vital but vulnerable Operations Rooms. Goering had decided to ignore the radar stations, but how much longer would sector airfields remain unscathed? Middle Wallop had been hit twice, and the passes at Biggin Hill and Kenley looked sinister.

During 16 August the *Luftwaffe* came back with another 1,700 sorties against southern England. Manston received its usual visitation. Then, just after 11.00 a.m. Dorniers of *KG* 76 made for West Malling. 111 Squadron (which Tommy Thompson had taken forward to Hawkinge at dawn) was 'scrambled' to intercept. It was Tommy's birthday, but what happened blotted out all thoughts of celebration.

The trouble with Hawkinge was that being right up in the front line you had to climb beneath the enemy at the mercy of his fighters. Tommy led 111 north-west before the advancing bombers. Everything was going well as he brought his squadron round in a wide left-hand turn for a head-on attack. Then the unexpected happened. 'Mike Ferris was slightly ahead of me on the inside of the turn. He just pressed on and collided head-on with a Dornier. There was a tremendous explosion and very little left, except a few pieces floating down.'

The Dorniers broke up and 111 set about them. This was the advantage of the head-on attack. It cut out the leaders and in the confusion you could pick on the enemy singly. But there were disadvantages: the high closing-speed left you little time to aim and fire. Then too, a slight jink by the enemy would upset the attack.

As Dowding himself said, 'The German aircrews showed great bravery.' *KG* 76 flew on as 111 Squadron cut down one Dornier after another. The bombers devastated West Malling, where the rubble from the evening before was still being cleared. For all that, they would have done better to go on another twenty miles and spend their fury on the Sector airfield, Biggin Hill. Was it just Teutonic respect for the form of things that made the *Luftwaffe* work from the outer ring of advanced airfields inwards, instead of stabbing straight to the heart – the inner ring of 11 Group's vital Sector stations? In any case, *KG* 76 was warming up for greater things.

The only Sector airfield on the outer ring was Tangmere. Just before 1.00 p.m., John Simpson (back from sick leave) heard the sirens as he drove up to Tangmere's main entrance. *Stuka Gruppe* 2 and *KG* 51 were overhead and their first bombs fell before John reached the guardroom. 'The noise was terrific... The bombs dropped all around. I was terrified... the smell of cordite and dust was horrible.'

Tangmere was left in ruins. With its curving roof and wooden beams built by German prisoners of the first war, 43 Squadron's hangar was one of the buildings gutted. Where the new sick quarters once stood, John saw 'nothing but a heap of rubble ... the smell made me feel quite sick'. The enemy was closing in on Fighter Command.

Flight Lieutenant J.B.Nicolson of 249 Squadron was patrolling in his Hurricane west of Tangmere at seventeen thousand feet. He dived on some Ju. 88s when suddenly his Hurricane staggered. From somewhere behind bullets and cannon shells ripped through the hood, hit him in the foot, and pierced his centre-tank. A searing mass of flame filled the cock-pit. As he whipped into a steep turn he saw the offender, a Me. 110, slide below, diving hard. A wild resolve, stronger than reason, seized Nicolson. The cockpit a furnace, his dashboard 'dripping like treacle', and his hands fused by the heat onto throttle and stick, he yelled, 'I'll get you, you Hun.' And he went on firing until the Me. 110 fell, until the frightful agony of his burns had passed the threshold of feeling. Then he struggled out of the cockpit and still wreathed in flames fell until the rush of cold air extinguished them. Only then did his mutilated hand fumble for the ripcord and somehow find strength to pull it. As if his sufferings were not already enough, some imbecile of a Home Guard fired at Nicolson and hit him fifty feet above the village of Millbrook in Hampshire.

The gallant Nicolson was awarded the Victoria Cross. Of three thousand fighter pilots who fought in the battle 'to defend the cause of civilization' Nicolson alone among the defenders received the supreme award for valour. It was enough. The twenty-three-year-old pilot was typical of his young comrades. Alone in their tiny cockpits miles above the earth, their courage was of a peculiar kind which no medal, no material standard, could ever properly measure.

Although the *Luftwaffe* had been listening for weeks to the radio chatter between ground control and fighter aircraft, Intelligence Chief Beppo Schmid had not yet tumbled to the fact that Sector Ops. Rooms were located at the airfields, above ground. The Tangmere Ops. Room had miraculously survived. For all the devastation, the sector station could remain operational.

The *Luftwaffe* was again making a mighty effort, battering the naval airfields of Gosport and Lee-on-Solent near Southampton, and the Experimental Establishment at Farnborough. Five Ju. 87s peeled off from this force and bombed Ventnor. They need not have troubled, had Beppo Schmid only known that the radar station was already out. In a daring attack on Brize Norton in the quiet Oxfordshire countryside two Ju. 88s sent fifty trainer aircraft up in smoke. Violating the Fuehrer's veto for the second time in twenty-four hours, other bomber *Gruppen* bombed the London suburbs.

None of these determined but ill-directed attacks made a breach in Fighter Command's defences. But the *Luftwaffe* was closing in, and we braced ourselves to meet the assault.

On the invasion front, the Army-*Kriegsmarine* row had been settled by Fuehrer decisions, contained in an OKW directive: invasion preparations were to be completed by 15 September; Lyme Bay was dropped as a landing point, but Brighton was kept for landing light forces. The new front was now Dover-Brighton, but given a week's notice it could still be narrowed to the *Kreigsmarine*'s Dover crossing.

A lull in air fighting on 17 August gave Goebbels the chance to drop some propaganda bombs. Britain, it was announced from Berlin on 17 August, was under a total blockade by sea and air – a claim which embarrassed Raeder and his sailors who were only too painfully aware of the impotence of their own puny surface forces against the British Navy. Goebbels's statement 'must be regarded as a purely political propaganda measure', sniffed the *Kreigsmarine*'s diarist.

Meanwhile ignoring the unpleasant facts, the Army enjoyed the tang of sea air. Everyone was there, from the C-in-C, von Brauchitsch, downwards, as the cheerful soldiers set sail from Boulogne to 'invade' Paris Plage, Le Touquet's fashionable beach. Halder noticed that the landing craft made slow headway – more than an afternoon would be required to grasp what Churchill called 'the mysteries of tides and currents'.

After nearly a month of action on the Channel coast, III JG 26's *Kommandeur*, Major Adolf Galland found things 'not too rosy' for the *Jagdgeschwader*. Its job of escorting bombers and striking at British fighters was not working out. First, there was the Me. 109's limited range. Next there were problems with the Ju. 87 *Stukas* which had swept all before them in Poland and France – yet they were now suffering catastrophic losses. 'They attracted Hurricanes and Spitfires as honey attracts flies,' said Galland. And the stronger escorts ordered by Goering did not solve the basic problem: the *Stuka* was too slow for the Me. 109 to stick with it. But Goering would not hear of such excuses: the *Jäger* were to blame.

It was no better with the level bombers which needed close escort. It gave them confidence to see Me. 109s buzzing round them. But the *Jäger* objected: close escort shackled them, deprived them of the initiative. As Galland said, 'The fighter must seek battle in the air.' Twenty years earlier Manfred von Richthofen had said the same thing: 'Fighter pilots have to rove ... in any way they like and when they spot the enemy, they attack ...; anything else is rubbish.'

Ex-fighter ace Goering, Richthofen's successor as *Kommandeur* of the 'Circus' ignored the Red Knight's precepts. He ordered the *Jagdgeschwader* to stick close to the bombers, and in the same breath reproached them for lack of aggressive spirit. He was grossly unjust. The *Jäger* preferred the *frei-jagd* (free chase) offensive sweep as prescribed by ace Manfred. But this had not worked out either; it took bombers to make the British fighters rise. So the *Jagdgeschwader* tried other ways: 'extended protection', where they roved within sight of the bombers, free to pursue enemy fighters. And another plan: 'fighter reception', where they swarmed above the English coast to shepherd the bombers home. But bomber losses still mounted. So did Goering's wrath. 'The reproaches from higher quarters became more unbearable,' complained Galland.

This, and considerable losses were demoralizing for the *Jäger*. Adolf used to talk things over with his younger brother Wilhelm, who served in a *Flak* regiment on the Channel coast. Things could not go on much longer as they were, he told him. 'You could count on your fingers when your turn would come.' The fighter pilots grew despondent. 'We saw one comrade after the other . . . vanish from our ranks. Not a day passed w..thout an empty place remaining at the mess table.' They felt bitter, too. 'We complained of the leadership, the bombers, the *Stukas*, and were dissatisfied with ourselves.' In this frame of mind Adolf Galland landed at Berlin-Staaken on Sunday 18 August.

A staff car took him to Carinhall where Goering had called commanders of *Fliegerkorps* and *Geschwader* engaged on the *Luftkrieg gegen England* to a conference for the next day. Adolf Galland watched the contented crowds downing their *Steins* of beer in the cafés and strolling on the Kurfurstendamm, and felt angered at the 'I-could-not-care-less attitude . . . and the general lack of interest in the war.' To him 'the colossus of this Second World War seemed to be like a pyramid turned upside down, balancing on its apex, not knowing which way to lean . . . the whole burden of the war rested on a few hundred German fighter pilots on the Channel coast.'

As it did on a few hundred RAF pilots on the other side. A few hundred British and German boys, evenly matched in skill and bravery and sharing a single passion for flying, were locked in a life-and-death struggle upon which depended the future of civilization. It was the contrast between that small band of determined warriors and the idle, unheeding crowds that so depressed Adolf Galland. 'I had come straight out of a battle for life and death . . . the battle we were fighting on the Channel was of decisive importance . . . to the final outcome of the struggle.'

Far away over the Channel the battle had again flared up. *KG* 76, which had stopped short at West Malling the other morning, was airborne from Vermeille-en-Vexin and at 1.00 p.m. heading directly for the vital sector stations Biggin Hill and nearby Kenley. Nine Dorniers flying at tree-top height, spearheaded the assault on each airfield. Their arrival was planned to coincide with a high-altitude strike by 50 Dorniers on Kenley, 50 Ju. 88s on Biggin Hill.

The low-flying Dorniers slipped through the radar screen unnoticed; they were only picked up inland by the Observer Corps, who flashed a warning to Biggin and Kenley. The Kenley controller (Squadron Leader Anthony Norman) scented danger. Without waiting for orders from 11

Group he 'scrambled' 64 and 615 from Kenley and III from Croydon. At Biggin the station commander (Group Captain Grice) had the same reflex – '32 and 610, Scramble!' A moment later Group's orders came through. 'You're too bloody late,' Grice told them.

His and Norman's quick thinking saved the squadrons from disaster. Minutes later the Dornier spearheads came streaking in across the airfields at zero feet. A few pushed on and bombed Croydon. At Kenley they were so low behind the trees that the AA could not fire until the last second. That saved them – they only lost two – but it meant that some bombs fell flat and failed to explode. The low and high strikes had synchronized perfectly. *KG* 76 hit Kenley hard: ten hangars, several aircraft and a bull's-eye on the Ops. Room.

At Biggin Hill things did not work out so well. The high strike Ju. 88s arrived late and the nine low Dorniers caught a packet. Their leader (*Oberleutnant* Lamberty) became entangled in a weird device, the PAC (Parachute and Cable) – rockets trailing one thousand feet of cable which were shot up in the path of the bombers and descended on parachutes. Chasing a Dornier, Tommy Thompson was nearly caught by one himself.

Lamberty crash-landed his blazing Dornier. As he struggled out, Home Guards covered him with their rifles. Then, as he staggered towards them they recoiled in horror: Lamberty's skin, scorched off his body, hung down in tattered shreds. The Home Guards came quickly to their senses. At Lamberty's request they took out of one of his pockets a packet of cigarettes – twenty Players bought in Jersey. Lamberty apologized for his appearance. 'I'm sorry to say it may be some time before I am allowed to fly again.'

Of his *Staffel* only two Dorniers returned to Vermeille-en-Vexin. One of them was piloted by a flight mechanic. His pilot had been shot through the heart over Biggin Hill.

Biggin escaped serious damage, although Grice warned his staff, 'Don't think because we've escaped this time we're safe.'

At Kenley smoke and flame belched from the hangars and craters pocked the airfield. Beppo Schmid read the pilots' reports, took a blue pencil and crossed Kenley off the map. He did not know the Ops. Room had been hit and had not even suspected its existence. Vital buildings, he reasoned, must be buried underground. Nor did he know that Kenley Ops. had moved immediately to temporary premises in a butcher's shop in Caterham High Street, while GPO engineers worked feverishly to reconnect the maze of wires which tied Kenley into the Fighter Command network. There were many things which Beppo Schmid did not know. But he was able to report one thing to Goering truthfully: it had cost *KG* 76 ten bombers to 'wipe out' Kenley. And Goering decided, 'No more low-level raids.' In a quick decision Goering himself eliminated what the RAF feared the most.

Hot on the Kenley-Biggin raid came four Ju. 87 *Gruppen* heading for Gosport, Thorney and Ford – South Coast airfields covered by Tangmere sector. Eighteen Ju. 87s peeled off above Poling radar station, near Ford.

It was 1.00 p.m. when WAAF Corporal Avis Hearn took a last look at the sky above Poling, a perfect blue, before entering the new Receiver block to take over the watch with C crew. A few minutes later the cathode tube showed a mass of aircraft off the coast of France. Hostile! Filter Room, Stanmore, confirmed and then Avis saw on the plotting map that they were heading straight for Poling. Some minutes later the telephone rang. As Corporal Avis picked it up, the duty sergeant yelled 'Duck!' 'I can't leave,' Avis heard herself protesting weakly, 'Stanmore needs all this information.' The sergeant never heard her. He had run for it.

'I could hear the deafening roar of aircraft, and then Stanmore said, "Poling, that plot I have just given you is right overhead." '

'You don't say!' Avis shouted back, 'the bombs are dropping on my head.' Her voice was drowned in a terrific explosion. 'The noise was tremendous, the scream of diving planes, machine-guns crackling, bombs bursting.'

'Are you all right?' the Stanmore plotter kept asking.

'Yes, keep listening for my plot.' the gallant Corporal Avis shouted back, proving how wrong the Air Ministry had been when they objected: 'Women might be emotionally unstable under the strain of operations.'

Avis stuck to her post until the line went dead, cut by bombs. 'It seemed suddenly quiet as death, and I put my hands to my head and wept.' For what seemed like 'hours of unbearable stillness', Avis remained there 'in a dazed, uncomprehending state of terror. I seemed to be engulfed in a jelly of silence.' Then suddenly she came to her senses as the door fell in almost on top of her, and an officer entered and led her away. Outside 'everything was a heap of rubble, our transport lorry ablaze, all our bicycles twisted into shapeless lumps of metal'. Poling was so badly damaged that, as with Ventnor, a mobile unit had to cover the gap.

Above, the *Stukas* were being mauled by 43 and 152 Squadrons. Flight Lieutenant Frank Carey led 43 head-on into the Ju. 87s near Selsey Bill.

'I fired at one – it stood straight up on its nose with flames coming out of it.' Sergeant Hallowes 'caught up with five Ju. 87s in line astern, opened fire . . . two people baled out of No. 5 aircraft and a further two from No. 4.' Two birds with one stone. Then Hallowes pounced on a *Stuka* as it pulled out of its dive over Thorney. 'I gave it three short bursts . . . it broke in two, just in front of the tail fin and fell in the Solent.'

To the west over Gosport *Oberleutnant* Rudolf Braun was in trouble. He dived straight through the balloon barrage and sent his bombs down with deadly accuracy. Climbing up again through the balloons was nerve-racking. Worse, fighters were waiting for him and as soon as he got clear they attacked. His air brakes jammed, he limped out to sea, and then an amazing thing happened. 'I saw fighters all around me, who knew I was winged. They passed me to right and left and above me. Incredibly, they did not shoot, but only waved.'

That was to be Rudolf's last attack on England. 'I had a better guardian angel than most,' he said. Better certainly than those 12 *Stukas* of I *St G.* 77 which had been mercilessly cut down by 43 and 152 Squadrons. Of them their general, Wolfram Richthofen wrote in his diary that evening, 'A *Stuka Gruppe* has had its feathers well and truly plucked.'

In 85 Squadron at Debden we waited with growing impatience as the battle in the south heated up. At 5.00 p.m. on Sunday evening the dispersal telephone rang. '85, patrol Canterbury, Angels 20.' In a few minutes twelve of us (or so I thought) were roaring off the ground and climbing south-east.

So far I had met the enemy only in single combat, except for that lonely skirmish with twenty Me. 110s of *Erprobungs Gruppe* 210. Now I must admit I had qualms about leading my little band into the midst of a vast horde of the enemy. For this is how we fought – independently in squadrons of twelve aircraft. We had often discussed among ourselves how to go about it; our job was to go for the bombers. It was the Spitfires' job to look after the enemy fighter escort. Only if they barred the way would we mix with them. I led 85 in four sections of three, each section in line astern, my own in the centre, one on each side, one behind, and each at a comfortable distance. The squadron had a narrow front and was easy to manoeuvre. Each pilot was able to search.

The Germans laughed at our serried formations. Their real weakness lay in the section of three, which was later abandoned for the German *Rotte* of two. With their eyes riveted on the leader, pilots in close 'vics' of three could not keep a proper look-out. But it was not as if we were on a *Frei-jagd*. 'Vectored' here and there under controllers' orders, our squadrons needed to keep a reasonably compact formation for mutual protection, for contact in bad visibility, and above all for concentration in the attack. The formation we used in 85 gave us manoeuvrability, concentration, yet freedom to search.

We would attack by sections, with aircraft extended in echelon for a clear field of fire. I would lead my section in first followed by the right hand, then the left hand and finally the stern section. We had it all worked out; it would need quick thinking, good flying, and above all blind faith in the section leaders. I knew I could count on every pilot in 85.

One other problem confronted us: the Me. 109. It had the legs of the Hurricane and, thanks to fuel-injection could jump straight into a dive without the engine cutting, as did our carburettor-fed Merlins. But we had one great advantage: we were more nimble in a turn. So everyone knew what to do: 'If the Me. 109s interfere and it's each one for himself – never climb, never dive. Just turn. Since you haven't got eyes in the back of your head, keep weaving and bear in mind: you're always in danger. Attack from the sun if possible, but never forget to "beware of the Hun in the sun".'

'And remember,' I told the pilots, 'our job is to seek out and destroy the enemy. If you believe you have shot one down, never follow it. You may get "jumped" on the way. Leave it and look for another. The aim is to destroy the enemy, not to mark up a personal score.'

The squadron was flying well together as we entered cloud at ten thousand feet, heading straight towards 'a hundred plus'. We emerged from clouds somewhere over the Thames Estuary and there advancing towards us was a massive column about a mile and a half high, stepped up wave upon wave. At the base were Ju. 87s, above them Heinkels, then Dorniers and Ju. 88s, then a layer of Me. 110s, and above, at about twenty thousand feet, a swarm of Me. 109s.

Somewhere in that lot was Werner Borner. When they saw the British fighters KG 2 closed in tight. This gave them a formidable concentration of fire especially now that they had an extra MG15 on each side (or six guns per aircraft). Guns after all were better than some of the other gadgets with which they had tried to fox the British fighters: hand grenades, confetti, and even rolls of lavatory paper.

As we closed in on the bombers, the Ju. 87s and Heinkels turned away seawards. A dozen Me. 110s cut across us and immediately formed a defensive circle. 'In we go,' I called over the R/T, and a moment later a

M

Me. 110 had banked clumsily across my bows. In its vain attempt to escape, the machine I was bent on destroying suddenly looked pathetically human. It was an easy shot – too easy.

For a few more seconds we milled around with the Me. 110s. Then down came a little shower of Me. 109s. Out of the corner of my eye I saw one diving for me, pumping shells. A quick turn toward it shook it off, and it slid by below, then reared up in a wide left hand turn in front of me. It was a fatal move. My Hurricane climbed round easily inside its turn. When I fired the Me. 109 flicked over and a sudden spurt of white vapour from its belly turned into flame. Down came another. Again a steep turn and I was on its tail. He seemed to know I was there, but he did the wrong thing. He kept on turning. When I fired, bits flew off, the hood came away and then the pilot baled out. He looked incongruous, hanging there a wingless body in the midst of this duel of winged machines.

I chased more Me. 109s diving coastwards. But with 'everything pushed and pulled' my Hurricane could not catch them. I gave one a long-range burst for good measure. Then with a *psst* of compressed air, my guns went silent. No more ammunition. Thirty miles out to sea off Margate I closed in on another Hurricane. It was Dicky Lee, just ahead, with the Me. 109s still visible ahead of him. 'Come back, Dicky,' I called but he was drawing away. Again and again I called, but he kept on. It was useless to chase Huns out to sea; they would be back again the next day. Something had got into Dicky and there was no stopping him. We were both low in fuel and I was out of ammunition. There was only one thing to do: turn back. On the way I spotted a yellow dinghy with four Germans in it. I would not have fired on them, even if I had been able to. But judging by their expressions as I skimmed over their heads, they thought their last moment had come.

When I landed at Debden most of 85's aircraft were already down. Only Paddy Hemingway and Dicky Lee had not shown up. We waited anxiously. One more Hurricane came taxiing in, its starboard wing tip missing. As the pilot climbed out I recognized the tall, lean figure of Nigger Marshall. 'What the devil do you mean by taking off without orders?' I asked him. 'I'm sorry,' he said, 'but when I saw you all going off it was just too much, so I followed. I'm terribly sorry about the wing, but I was out of ammunition and had to ram a Heinkel. I'm sure you will agree it was worth it?'

So we had been thirteen. News came of Paddy; he had been picked up by a lightship east of Clacton. But as we waited on for Dicky, hope faded to tragic certainty.

18 August was a day of violent, intensive fighting which cost Fighter Command a vital sector airfield, a radar station and twenty-seven fighters. But in the air it was even more disastrous for the *Luftwaffe*, with 71 planes shot down, 28 of them *Stukas*. 'It was a black day for the *Stukas*,' wrote Richthofen's Chief of Staff, *Oberst* Hans Seidermann. Their death knell had sounded.

It had been a great day for 85. Everyone had fired their guns and we had put it across to the enemy. The young ones had fought well and were all safely home. That evening while we let off steam in the mess, two signals were handed to me. The first one read: 'From the Chief of the Air Staff. Well done 85 Squadron in all your hard fighting. This is the right spirit for dealing with the enemy.' The other ordered 85 Squadron to Croydon at dawn next morning.

Croydon was Kenley's satellite a few miles to the north. The air was deliciously scented and Tommy Thompson (there to meet us) explained: On 15 August *Erprobungs Gruppe* 210 had not only missed their main target (Kenley) but hit the Bourjois Soap factory. For days the flowery scent persisted.

Tommy was to take 111 back to Debden for a 'rest' – which would never materialize. We had left our ground crews there. At Croydon those of 111 would look after us magnificently. Tommy and his pilots gave us 'the form'. Fighting had been hard, losses high. One day two new sergeant pilots arrived. Tommy met them. 'Sorry,' he told them, 'we are desperately short of pilots. You will both be on the next sortie.' They left their car outside the crew room, their baggage inside. One of them never recovered his. He was killed on that sortie and his friend seriously wounded.

85 Squadron was now in the forefront of the battle, which was about to enter its most crucial phase. Of the eighteen pilots I had led to Croydon fourteen were to be shot down (two twice) within the next two weeks.

In the luxurious atmosphere of Carinhall, Goering opened his conference at noon sharp. He was not handing out any bouquets. Glaring at his air commanders he told them, 'I'm not at all pleased with the way the battle's going. It should have been decided in a few days. But serious mistakes have led to unnecessary losses.' The heaviest were among the *Stukas* and Goering ordered the 220 Ju. 87s of *Fliegerkorps* VIII to be withdrawn from the battle. Inspector General Milch was present and he said, 'Goering was very angry. In his opinion it was the fighters' fault.' But in a heated dispute with Goering, Milch stood up for the fighters. 'I told him it was the fault of the High Command. They gave the wrong orders.'

Goering summarized: 'We have entered the decisive phase of the Battle of Britain. Everything depends on our beating the RAF. First of all we have to smash the RAF fighter force. If they refuse to come into the air to do battle with us we will attack them on the ground or force them into the air by bombing targets within the range of our fighters.' In Goering's opinion, that was the way to defeat Fighter Command: leave it to the Me. 109s. He believed the main point was to force the British fighters into the air (the *Luftwaffe*'s appalling losses should have told him there was no need). The Me. 109s would then hew them down.

Relying on Beppo Schmid's faulty intelligence, Goering made a crucial error. For Fighter Command was more vulnerable on the ground than in the air. But wild claims of the *Luftwaffe* aircrews beguiled High Command into thinking that the RAF's fighters were being annihilated. On 18 August they claimed 134 against a real loss of twenty-seven. Certainly, one way to defeat Fighter Command was by attack *in* the air. But by far the surest way was by attack *from* the air. Flatten the radar stations and the Sector Ops. Rooms, cut their vital communications and no matter how many fighters it still possessed, Fighter Command was finished. But Goering and his men were obsessed with the desire to massacre the British fighters. Was it that ex-fighter ace Goering wanted to fight the Circus's battles all over again from an armchair? Perhaps. But the main reason was that he never understood the value and vulnerability of Fighter Command's radar and sector stations, of their power cables and telephone lines – the umbilical cords which tied them to Command and Group headquarters, and enabled them to function.

Getting down to details, Goering allotted the main burden of day attacks to *Luftflotte* 2; *Luftflotte* 3 was to prepare for a night attack on Liverpool, *Luftflotte* 5 on Glasgow. 'There can no longer be any restrictions on the choice of target,' which meant that the British public was then going to have a taste of total air warfare. 'Only I personally reserve the right to order attacks on Liverpool and London.' This was treading on the Fuehrer's toes – and the Fuehrer took note. As Wolfram von Richthofen summed up the conference, 'The campaign against England is to proceed energetically, but differently.'

Goering had not finished – not with his *Jäger* pilots. He drew Galland and Moelders aside after the conference, softened each of them up with the coveted jewelled Gold Pilot Medal, and then lambasted them. 'The *Reichsmarschall* let us know quite plainly,' said Galland, 'that he was not satisfied ... with ... the fighter force, particularly with the execution of fighter protection, and energetically called for greater efforts.'

The *Kampfgeschwader* crews too demanded an escort system which really worked. They wanted a forward sweep, top cover, and low cover, with fighters accompanying the Ju. 88s as they dive-bombed. Fine! But where were all those fighters to come from?

Goering had his own ideas on how to remedy the 'lack of aggressiveness' among the *Jäger*. He made a shuffle in the eagle's eyrie. The process had begun at the end of July when that brave old eagle Theo Osterkamp gave way to top ace Werner Moelders as *Kommodore* of JG 51. Moelders was wounded the next day, but it was only a month's respite for Uncle Theo, who became *Jagdfliegerführer* (Fighter Leader).

The road to stardom naturally depended on a high killing rate. Moelders held the lead, Adolf Galland, Helmut Wick and Walter Oesau followed. The faster they killed, the faster they got promoted. But it did not stop there. They had to maintain their leads in kills, or lose the *Reichsmarschall*'s favour. To stay in business they had to take the same road as the ace of aces Manfred von Richthofen, whose triumph turned to nightmare until death closed his eyes.

So Goering made twenty-eight-year-old Galland *Kommodore* of JG 26 in place of Handrick, four years his senior; a born leader, Hannes Trautloft (also twenty-eight) took over JG 54 from thirty-seven year-old Major Mettig. Youth was the key-note. Some of these young aces were later to prove unequal to their responsibilities. 'Although good flyers, they were unable to cope with problems of over-all planning and ... broader strategic aspects,' said Focke-Wulf designer Dr Kurt Tank. But for the present they acted as a shot in the arm to the *Jagdgeschwader*.

Far from the luxurious trappings of Carinhall, Air Vice Marshal Keith Park, in his office at 11 Group HQ, Uxbridge, was also reviewing the situation that day, and in a rather more airmanlike manner. On him, more than any other group commander, depended the salvation of Britain. During periods of intense fighting, there was no time for C-in-C Dowding and Park, to consult. Park acted from day to day on his own initiative and won high praise from his C-in-C for the way he adjusted his tactics to meet new developments.

To counter attacks on airfields, Park ordered his controllers to dispatch fighters only against enemy formations overland and within gliding distance of the coast. 'We cannot afford to lose pilots ... in the sea.'

Against these mass attacks 'dispatch a minimum of squadrons to engage enemy fighters. Our main objective is to engage enemy bombers.' Park had no intention of his fighters dancing to Goering's tune.

It had happened and could very well happen again – all 11 Group Squadrons might be engaged at once. In this case, 'ask 12 Group or Command controller to provide squadrons to patrol ... Debden, North Weald, Hornchurch,' 11 Group's northern airfields. This instruction was based on an order by Dowding. In it lay the seeds of dispute.

At Fighter Command Dowding took stock: in the previous ten days, six of his main radar stations had been attacked; two were out of use, covered by mobile sets. Three sector stations had been heavily hit. Here the enemy could strike a mortal blow at Fighter Command. It was a miracle he had not already done so.

Since 8 August, Fighter Command had lost 175 aircraft (the *Luftwaffe* claimed three times more), but Dowding still had ample reserves. His friend Lord Beaverbrook had seen to that. The Beaver had cut through red tape, reduced bottle-necks, given priority to fighter types. His 'Spitfire funds' and his appeal for aluminium pots and pans had fired the public's imagination. The industry had buckled to; constant threat of enemy bombs made night joint labourer with the day. Through sheer exhaustion some workers had collapsed on the job. But fighter production had soared to nearly five hundred a month.

Fighter aircraft were not of immediate concern to Dowding, but ninety-four pilots killed and sixty wounded in ten days' fighting were more than a worry. He had never lost a sensitivity about casualties which twenty-five years before had embroiled him with Trenchard. He grieved over the loss of these well-trained men. Volunteers and fledglings from the training schools, however brave, simply did not have the necessary experience.

But the need for more pilots was urgent. Volunteers were released from light bomber squadrons and from Army Co-operation Command. After a week's conversion course fifty more pilots joined Fighter Command.

In this grave hour, Londoners, whoever they were, remained as incorrigible as ever. 'To hear Alice [Keppel] talk about her escape from France,' joked Mrs Greville, 'one would think she had swum the Channel with her maid between her teeth.'

Goering's captains had left Carinhall. The next day he ordered them to 'continue the fight against the British Air Force ... with the aim of weakening British fighter strength. The enemy is to be forced ... to bring his fighter formations into operation.'

In London, Churchill addressed Parliament: 'The enemy is of course far more numerous than we are. But ... our bomber and fighter strengths now, after all this fighting, are larger than they have ever been, we believe we should be able to continue the struggle indefinitely ... and the longer it continues the more rapid will be our approach ... into that superiority in the air upon which in large measure the decision of the war depends.'

Churchill gave no hint of depending on Russia, as Hitler believed. 'The American production is only just beginning to flow in ...' he said, and he counted eventually on his half-mother-country (Churchill's mother was American). But meanwhile he believed that if only the RAF could hold out Britain could turn the tide of battle alone.

Twenty-three years had passed since Churchill had criticized Britain's air defences: 'Never had the situation been more serious,' he had protested in April 1917 after eighteen months of German air raids. Now before Parliament, in the phrase which had been on his mind he voiced his feelings toward the 'few thousand airmen' upon whom the eyes of the world were fixed: 'Never in the field of human conflict has so much been owed by so many to so few.'

Chips Channon, MP, was in the House. 'Winston made a great speech, Archie Sinclair (Air Minister) ... made the almost incredibly magnificent exploits of our airmen sound dull and trite.'

On the day of Churchill's speech young Charles Ingold, condemned to death by the Vichy Government for joining those few, borrowed the beautiful words of his compatriot A.M. de Gibergues to write his last will and testament: 'If one day my wings are broken in the blue sky and I fall to earth on my way back to God, may these lines bring to my mother and my father the last thoughts, the desires and the fondest dreams of their beloved son.

'When my machine is mortally hit and refuses to answer, when I can no longer do my duty and my task is finished, when I fall I shall know an infinite, longed-for peace and shall sing with all my heart: Gloria in excelsis Deo.

'Think of those few moments before the final anguish, before I die, moments which strike such terror in people's minds that they shrink from them as if they were abominable. Bless them with me! They are a gift of the Almighty Judge.'

Chapter 25

With our arrival at Croydon came five days of bad weather. It was as if a referee had blown the whistle for half time. The respite was needed. Squadrons like 54 had been in combat almost daily since Dunkirk with hardly any rest, or blasted on the ground at Manston, or wrestling with the high-flying Me. 109s. Many of Al Deere's best friends were dead; three times he had been shot down, three times saved by a miracle. From then on, he said, 'Our efficiency gradually deteriorated as we grew more and more tired.'

Although 85 Squadron had been north of London in the more quiet Debden sector, two months of convoy patrols (day in, day out, dawn to dusk) had worn us down more than we cared to admit – especially the half dozen of us who flew the night patrols as well. We too had had our triumphs and our tragedies.

A letter dated 21 August came from Air Marshal Trenchard asking for news of 'that great boy, Dick Lee, who is my godson . . . Is there anything you can tell me?' I could only tell him the worst. Like all great men, Boom Trenchard knew the meaning of humility. I was at nursery school when he began his lonely battle to save the RAF from extinction. Because of him, we were there then with the fate of England in our hands. To the young squadron commander that I was, Boom saw fit to write, 'I am proud ever to have been connected with a Force that is doing what it is today. It far exceeds even what I have always thought about the air, that is, that it is the weapon which is peculiarly suited to us and one that will save the Empire.'

The greater issues were beyond us. We sat in a tiny cockpit, throttle lever in one hand, stick in the other. At the end of our right thumb was the firing button and in each wing were four guns. We aimed through an optical gunsight, a red bead in the middle of a red ring. Our one concern was to boot out the enemy.

Goering paid a special visit on 21 August to Kesselring's *Luftflotte* 2 advanced HQ at Cap Blanc Nez. Through special high-power binoculars Goering closely scrutinized Dover radar station. It happened that the Fuehrer's favourite weapon (long-range coastal batteries) were blasting off at Dover town. If the *Reichsmarschall* was spotting through the binoculars for hits he was out of luck. *The Times'* headline commented the following day, 'Better Aim Likely With Practice.'

Action and more action was the only antidote against the deadly, crushing fatigue creeping up on us. While rain clouds hung low over southern England, we were kept limbering up with frequent but fruitless searching for elusive raiders. One, a Dornier 17 of *KG* 2, crept through the grey clouds up the Thames Estuary at 6.30 a.m. on 23 August. Werner Borner radioed back to base: visibility nil, ceiling nil, and the Dornier hurried back to Arras St Leger. The bad weather had given Werner and his friends a chance to relax.

Later that morning they forsook their Dornier for the pleasures of driving. Flight Mechanic Lohrer, the only 'country bumpkin' among them, took the reins. The horse immediately bolted and, for the second time, the crew of *Gustav Marie* belly-landed heavily in a field. Only this time it hurt more.

Our dispersal point, with ground crews and pilots' rest rooms, was in a row of villas on the airfield's western boundary. Invariably I slept there half-clothed to be on the spot if anything happened. In the small hours of 24 August it did. The shrill scream and the deafening crash of bombs shattered my sleep. In the doorway young Worrall, a new arrival, was yelling something and waving his arms. Normally as frightened as anyone, not even bombs could move me then. I placed my pillow reverently over my head and waited for the rest. Worrall still had the energy to be frightened. I was past caring. It was a bad sign; I was more exhausted than I realized.

Two of our Hurricanes were blazing while the German bomber circled above in the pitch dark. How did he land a direct hit on our dispersed aircraft? Some of the men reported that when the bomber arrived over-head they had seen the door of a lighted room opening and shutting, as if signalling. The police investigated; meanwhile more weighty issues now had to be faced. The weather was clearing.

I stuck my toothbrush in my left breast pocket, took my spongebag, and made for the bathroom. The Duke of Kent, brother of the King, was expected at 10.00 a.m. Halfway to the bathroom, the alarm went. 85 Squadron, Scramble! A few minutes later I was climbing away from Croydon at the head of six Hurricanes. '100 plus' from *Fliegerkorps* II were heading for Dover. By the time we arrived they were on their way home. Sergeant Sam Allard, our finest pilot, sent a stray Me. 109 into the sea. James Lockhart, one of our young ones, was slightly wounded by Dover AA. That had to be accepted as an occupational risk.

Back at Croydon, Tim Moloney (adjutant of 85 – its friend, father and managing director) told me to hurry. The Duke was waiting. 'Get the pilots lined up, he wants to meet them,' Tim told me.

'Flight Lieutenant Hamilton from Canada,' I introduced Hammy, who to my consternation seemed to be squinting at me and doing his best not to laugh. I retreated a pace and glanced down at the front of my tunic. On my left breast, beside my wings and a solitary DFC ribbon a gleaming white toothbrush stuck out of my pocket. I had taken it into battle with me.

'Force them into the air by bombing targets within range of our fighters,' Goering had told his air commanders on 19 August. He talked a lot about bombing aircraft factories and aluminium plants, but never made any precise mention of sector airfields. To Intelligence Chief Beppo Schmid it was still inconceivable that the control centres of Britain's air defence should be located above ground at airfields within reach of escorted German bombers. For Beppo an airfield meant a lair where British fighters lurked, reluctant to do battle with the German *Jäger*, but waiting for bigger game – bombers.

The *Luftwaffe* plan was to smoke out British fighters from the airfields round London, where they were thickest. Destroy them on the ground by all means, but above all make them rise, then leave it to the Me. 109s to knock them down – that was the way to smash Fighter Command. Forget about all that nonsense of radar stations and ops. rooms hidden away somewhere underground.

The *Luftwaffe* was now advancing on London. They had finished with forward airfields like Manston, or nearly. On 24 August they savaged Manston for the last time. Philip Hunter, dark, soft-voiced CO of 264 Squadron had at dawn led his 2-seater Defiants forward from Hornchurch sector airfield to Manston. Once I had talked with Philip at Martlesham; he was the 'gentle, parfit knight', a man of quiet and selfless courage.

Manston, and the battle raging above it, was no place for Defiants. A month before 141 Squadron had been cut to pieces there by Trautloft's III JG 51. Like the Ju. 87, Defiants were helpless against single-seater fighters, as they had no forward-firing guns, only a four-gun turret at the rear. Out of the Me. 109s reach, they had proved themselves as bomber-destroyers. Jim Bailey, barely twenty and the green-horn of 264, had dared the previous evening at Hornchurch to broach the question that worried everyone to his CO. What was the sense in sending Defiants forward to Manston? Slow and clumsy as they were, they should be the last, not the first, to meet the enemy. And Philip had answered quietly, 'We are in the place of honour, and we must accept it.'

On Saturday 24 August, Philip Hunter had led his Squadron to Manston for a farewell flight before handing over command. When Ju. 88s dived out of the sun at 1.00 p.m. they caught seven Defiants on the ground refuelling. Somehow, the Defiants got off despite the falling bombs. With desperate courage Philip Hunter and his squadron charged after the enemy. But Me. 109s trapped him and two others against the sea and killed them. So Philip handed on his squadron and remained himself in 'the place of honour'.

The Ju. 88s left Manston a shambles of wrecked and burning hangars, a wilderness strewn with bomb craters and unexploded bombs. Another raid came three hours later. It was the *coup de grâce* which ended Manston's twelve-day martyrdom. Bombs severed 248's telephone circuits, cutting the airfield off from 11 Group HQ. Three GPO cable jointers moved in and, working a few feet from an unexploded bomb, restored the main circuits within two hours. But Group ordered Manston's evacuation. And while Chief Officer Albert Twyman and his men of the Margate Fire Brigade risked their lives to douse the raging fires, civilians looted tools and stores. To the last, Manston was the scene of the finest and the most abject in human nature. 600 Squadron, which had fought to the last with improvised anti-aircraft pieces, retired with its surviving Blenheims to Hornchurch. The survivors of 264 Squadron had already landed there, only to catch it once more from the *Luftwaffe*.

It was 3.45 p.m. The station commander, Group Captain 'Boy' Bouchier (a wiry, well-groomed, and electrifying personality) had warned some minutes earlier on the Tannoy broadcast system, 'They're boiling up over Calais.' Jim Bailey (the tyro of 264) 'being left on the ground as usual,' scanned the sky. There they were, a formation of Dorniers, 'tiny specks glinting lethally in the sunlight, approaching us on the bomber run'. Men started crowding into the bomb-bays. South African Derrick Smythe found a carthorse wandering and tried to wedge it in. (Jim, millionaire Abe Bailey's son, himself had hostages to fortune in South Africa.) 'The long stick of bombs began to burst, running up towards us ... Panic scythed the crowd and all lay as one man ... the stick killed six civilians and three cows.'

Escorted by Me. 110s fifty Dorniers and Heinkels pushed on to North Weald sector airfield. 11 Group's squadrons were fully engaged, so following Park's recent instruction they asked 12 Group to put a patrol over North Weald. 11 Group controller John Willoughby de Broke said, 'We got on like a house on fire with 12 Group controllers.' But something went wrong that afternoon. As the bombers sent down fifty tons of bombs on the station there was no sign of the 12 Group patrol over North Weald. Had 11 Group called too late for help? Had the 12 Group Squadrons been too slow in taking off? No one would say. All that was certain was that North Weald had been badly hit, its power-house half-wrecked, and several airmen killed. Others had fled the bombs into nearby Epping Forest.

For the citizens of Portsmouth there was no such escape. While Joachim Poetter and his *Kameraden* of *KG* 51 droned above in a clear blue sky, the bomb-aimers were lining up on His Majesty's Dockyard. A single fighter squadron climbed – but too late – to reach the Ju. 88s at fifteen thousand feet. Then the AA opened up, punching holes in several of the bombers and breaking open the formation. Some *Bombardieren* lost their nerve and released their bombs haphazard. In the streets of Portsmouth a hundred civilians paid with their lives to save the dockyard.

'Hammer at the enemy day and night to break his nerve,' Goering had recently urged his leaders, adding that he alone would approve attacks on London and Liverpool. But an OKW order was signed by Keitel that day, 'Attacks against the London area and terror attacks are reserved for the Fuehrer's decision.' Whoever was running the show was losing his grip. Part of Greater London, Croydon had been bombed several times with heavy civilian losses. Only Rubensdorffer's death in action had saved him from court-martial. Liverpool had also been hit. And of 170 bombers ranging over Britain on the night of 24 August on the *Storangriffen* (harassing attacks) Goering's prescription for breaking British nerves, again some trespassed on forbidden territory. Bombs crashed down into the heart of London. *KG* 1 had been briefed for targets at Rochester and Thameshaven. Someone had blundered, and Goering wanted to know who.

Early next morning Major Josef Knobel, Ops. officer of *KG* 1, received a signal from the C-in-C: 'Report forthwith which crews bombed in London prohibited zone. The Supreme Commander (Hitler) reserves punishment of commanders concerned by transferring to infantry.' But the damage was done. Not even a firing squad could reverse the fatal train of events which had been triggered off.

Another man with an account to settle was Group Captain Victor Beamish, North Weald's station commander. With his gleaming eyes and square, jutting jaw, Victor was not a man to cross, though his heart was as soft as his Irish brogue. But his men had panicked under the enemy's fire. He went around to every flight to do some straight talking. Those on the ground, he told them, must risk their lives as the air crews do in the air. Then without losing its charm the voice hardened: 'If any man on duty leaves the camp, I shall personally shoot him.' Victor was known to be a man of his word.

Bombs had dropped on central London. The War Cabinet was 'much in the mood to hit back; to raise the stakes, and to defy the enemy'. Churchill felt sure they were right. 'Nothing . . . disturbed Hitler so much as his realization of British wrath and will-power.' In fact, the RAF had been hitting back night after night, hard enough for Goering to put Bomber Command airfields on his black list.

British bombers had been concentrating on industrial targets in the Ruhr, not that it helped much in the defence of Britain. But their hour would soon come. Berlin had remained undisturbed; five hundred miles away, the bombers could only reach the capital with a reduced load. But reach it they would. On the night of 25 August eighty-one bombers set course for Berlin.

As Adolf Galland had said, Berliners hardly noticed the war. True, the *Luftschatzwarten* (air raid wardens) had recently called to tell householders to fill bath tubs and every other receptacle with water each evening. 'They will come tonight,' they said, but no one took them seriously. The Germans after all had won. Country after country had come *'heim ins Reich'*, home to the Reich. There was only England, as good as finished:

Else Wendel wrote, 'Everything was fine in Germany ... we waited feverishly for the invasion ... at the time we did not hate the English; we were rather sorry for them when we thought of the thrashing they were going to get.'

The German public could listen on two radio networks: *Volksempfaenger* and the *Grossdeutsche Rundfunk*, which signed on with the Preludes of Liszt, one of the few approved composers. Shops sold only Reich-standard goods; lipstick was taboo and notices warned, 'The German woman does not smoke.' Not only that, but she had to adopt a compulsory hair-do, the 'gretchen' plait. Soon the word went round, 'Friends, do enjoy the war – peace will be dreadful.'

No one had forgotten Goering's pre-war 'call me Meier' boast. And now, on the night of 25 August, the Berlin sirens were howling. It couldn't be serious. 'Let's get on with dinner'; 'Don't let it spoil this hand'; 'Nothing's going to get me out of my bath', was how people reacted, wherever they were. Those who did move went up to the attic rather than down to the cellar. It was exciting to see the 'tiny birds' caught in the searchlight beams.

One British bomber crashed in Dahlem, a Berlin suburb. The pilot's body was hanging in a tree. Some cows from the big farm which supplied the district with milk were killed. A school was hit. What were the British aiming at? Dahlem was strictly residential.

The British of course were aiming at military targets, but in thick cloud few found them, let alone hit them. Damage was negligible. But, as William Shirer noted in his diary, 'Berliners are stunned. They did not think it could ever happen ...' It would continue to happen until Hitler could stand the affront no longer.

Bomber Command crews were sleeping soundly at their bases when Fighter Command squadrons rose to meet the *Luftwaffe*'s first attack of the morning on 26 August. The main effort, directed at Biggin Hill and Kenley, was repulsed. Back came more serried columns (*KG* 2's and *KG* 3's Dorniers) with Me. 109s weaving round them, bearing down on Hornchurch, North Weald and Debden. Ten squadrons of 11 Group fighters fought them all the way in. But they failed to pierce the fighter screen of the bombers advancing on Debden. Once again, 11 Group called hastily to 12 Group for reinforcements. 'Put a squadron up over Debden!' But the squadron sent from Duxford, only ten miles away, arrived too late. Debden was hit by one hundred bombs. Whose fault was it this time?

The enemy held the initiative: they could choose the targets and the time to attack, and they varied their tactics cleverly, spreading our defences with feints and diversions. At 2.50 p.m. I led 85 Squadron away from Croydon climbing eastwards to meet a diversionary attack coming in towards Kent. Thirty minutes later a dozen Dorniers came sailing majestically towards us – an impeccable phalanx in vics of three, stepped up in line astern. 7 *KG* 3 had good reason for packing in tight. They carried no bombs, but were just acting as *lock-vogel* (decoys) to draw us into combat with the Me. 109s of von Lutzow's *JG* 3 and Hannes Trautloft's *JG* 54 swarming above.

There was one way to get at the bombers without getting mixed up with the fighter escort. 'Stand by for head-on attack and watch out for those little fellows above,' I called. Then I brought the squadron round steadily in a wide turn, moving it into echelon as we levelled out about two miles ahead on a collision course. Ease the throttle to reduce the closing speed – which anyway allowed only a few seconds' fire. Get a bead on them right away, hold it, and never mind the streams of tracer darting overhead. Just keep on pressing on the button until you think you're going to collide – then stick hard forward. Under the shock of 'negative *G*' your stomach jumps into your mouth, dust and muck fly up from the cockpit floor into your eyes and your head cracks on the roof as you break away below.

The Dorniers swept by overhead, their underbellies painted a pale blue except for one which was black – out the night before, no doubt. Trailing smoke the three leading bombers were going down to crash-land, while the rest of the *Staffel* immediately turned and made out to sea. One more Dornier failed to make its base at Melville, France.

The *Kampfgeschwader* crews were not enthusiastic about *Lock-vogel* flights. The cost was too high. 7 *KG* 3 was officially the 'decoy' *Staffel*, but they became known as the 'plucked' *Staffel*. This time it had cost them four Dorniers against one of 85 Squadron's Hurricanes: tempted to have a go at the Me. 109s, Paddy Hemingway finished up in Pitsea Marshes. It was his second 'brolly-hop'!

11 Group had been fighting furiously all day to defend its centre and its northern flank, where the defences at Debden had been breached. Then in the middle of the afternoon a massed assault came in the west – 150 aircraft from *Luftflotte* 3 were advancing on Portsmouth, with diversions to draw off the British fighters.

Park called on 10 Group for help. He had often done so before and South African Air Vice Marshal Quintin Brand had never failed him. If only he could get the same co-operation from Trafford Leigh-Mallory's 12 Group on his north flank! It would not take long to defeat the *Luftwaffe* then.

Up rose three 10 Group squadrons to join five more from 11 Group. The RAF fighters would make amends for the massacre in Portsmouth two days before. They caught *KG 55*'s Heinkels out to sea and sailed into them. Hard pressed in their loaded machines, the Heinkel captains yelled down the intercom to the bomb-aimers, 'Jettison, jettison!' And down went their bombs into the sea. Portsmouth and its dockyard were saved.

Luftflotte 3 was now pulled out of the day battle. For the next few weeks its *Kampfgeschwader* were switched to night attacks. Its *Jagdgeschwader* would shortly move to the Pas de Calais for the coming invasion. *Fliegerkorps* VIII, the *Stuka* specialists, set up an advanced HQ at Tourcoing under *Hauptmann* von Heinemann to liaise with General Busch's 16th Army. *Oberst* Seidemann, chief of staff, turned energetically to direct the massive preparations for the *Stukas'* participation in 'Sea Lion'. The air front was now reduced to fill the narrow-front invasion crossing. Kesselring's *Luftflotte* 2 and Keith Park's 11 Group faced each other in a titanic struggle for mastery of the skies over south-east England.

We were now well into the crucial phase of the Battle of Britain. For the next two weeks *Luftflotte* 2's bombers were to hammer at 11 Group's air-fields; its Me. 109s would attempt to overrun the defending Hurricanes and Spitfires and cut them down. In Air Vice Marshal Keith Park General Albert Kesselring had a formidable adversary. Kesselring was a soldier and had learnt to fly only five years before. Park had fought the Germans in the air twenty-five years past. He knew them as 'good, natural warriors, brave, well-disciplined. I also learnt they were slow to adapt themselves when a set plan was thrown out of gear by weather or . . . surprise action.' The very essence of Park's defence was flexibility. It had to be, with so small a force of fighters.

Park had 21 single-seater squadrons – a fighting force of 250 fighters had to hold south-east England, including London, against four times their number. Behind the 250 in the air, he was backed by a superlative organization under Beaverbrook which produced and repaired his replacement aircraft. 'He used to ring up every night and get the score . . .' And the Beaver's staff would see that the gaps were filled by the next morning. 'It was heartening. I was never grounded by lack of aircraft,' said Park.

Pilots were another matter. Since the *Luftwaffe* had returned to the assault British fighter losses were mounting at an alarming rate: sixty-nine killed and as many wounded in the last three days. Losses were beginning to exceed replacements – brave but inexperienced warriors straight from the training schools. At this rate Fighter Command could not last long. Perhaps the *Luftwaffe*'s 'slaughter them in the air' policy would work out after all. Fighter Command had its back to the wall.

No amount of criticism could make Dowding increase 11 Group's fighting force of 250. He knew too well that the airfields and control system could not stand more. On the other hand, he had given clear orders that when Park's squadrons were fully engaged, 10 and 12 Groups should send reinforcements as requested. It had worked out perfectly with Brand's 10 Group. But Leigh-Mallory's 12 Group squadrons had failed to prevent heavy damage to two of Park's sector airfields. On 27 August Park, dismayed and furious, brought matters to a head in his instruction No. 7:

'Thanks to the friendly co-operation afforded by 10 Group they are always prepared to detail two to four squadrons to engage from the West mass attacks . . .

'Up to date 12 Group . . . have not shown the same desire to co-operate by dispatching their squadrons to the places requested . . . When 12 Group offered assistance and were requested by us to patrol our aerodromes, their squadrons did not in fact patrol over our aerodromes . . .'

Result. North Weald and Debden were heavily bombed.

'As . . . direct offers of assistance from 12 Group have not resulted in their squadrons being placed where we have requested, Controllers are from now onwards . . . to put their requests to Fighter Command . . .' – but only when mass attacks of 160 or more appear to be too much for 11 Group squadrons.

It was only too natural that 12 Group squadrons should be straining at the leash. Commanding 242, Douglas Bader 'sulked and stormed in the dispersal hut at Coltishall (one hundred miles north-east of London) where he and the pilots sat . . . waiting for the telephone call that never came. Ops. ignored them . . .' But when 12 Group, crying out to join the battle, was told: patrol North Weald or Debden, it did not turn up.

10 Group always made it; 12 Group missed. Not for the first time, Park was furious with Leigh-Mallory. 'L-M' was an outsider to Fighter

Command. In the First World War he had been an Army Co-operation man. He still was when I met him in 1929. Never a fighter-boy born and bred like Keith Park, L-M (reputedly ambitious and stubborn) only joined Fighter Command just before the war. One day in March 1940 when Park was Dowding's senior air staff officer, Leigh-Mallory had called at his office after an interview with C-in-C Dowding. 'Leigh-Mallory was very angry and said he would move heaven and earth to get Dowding sacked.' Park, who had loyally backed his chief during those difficult times of Fighter Command's early development, was 'greatly annoyed', and gave L-M a piece of his mind. Thereafter, his 'peacetime friendship for Leigh-Mallory drained very rapidly'.

Douglas Bader was very close to Leigh-Mallory and well aware of the rift between the two men. 'It stuck out a mile,' he said, but he never heard Mallory criticize Park. Yet the fact remained that with the bombing of North Weald and Debden a dispute had broken out in the high command of the British air defences at the very moment that they were in danger of being overrun by the enemy.

Dowding, who professed to be 'very fond' of Park, later said, 'The only thing I have blamed Park for was because he did not come and tell me about this trouble before it came to a head. Then I would have intervened.' Park stated, 'I reported the matter to the Commander-in-Chief.' Dowding did not, Park adds, ever visit him at 11 Group HQ during the battle (Park went to Dowding's HQ or telephoned him).

Dowding recalled later that he thought, 'I must not go interfering with the group commanders, who are responsible people.' He did not discover until afterward that 'the conduct of the number 12 Group Commander (Leigh-Mallory) was a challenge to my orders'.

Had he known of the controversy, 'my decision would have been . . . "I have got you two fellows together so we could talk this over . . . I want you to know what I wish you to do and if you won't fall in with my wishes I shall have to do something else." ' It was not until mid-October when the battle was won that 'I decided I would have to do something . . . and get rid of Leigh-Mallory.'

By then it was too late.

The behind the scenes battle warmed up but there was a noticeable slump at the operational level. All day, reconnaissance planes were busy photographing damage of the day before. One was caught by Innes Westmacott and his Flight Commander 'Jumbo' Gracie. The crew baled out over the

Channel, where an E-boat was waiting for them. Their luck did not stop there. With his burning hatred for the Germans, Jumbo never gave any quarter. He would have gunned the E-boat and everyone in it. But he and Innes were out of ammunition.

85 was not ordered off that day. We sat around at dispersal talking of trivial things, waiting. Sam Allard said he preferred metal propellers to wooden, because they would chop through the trees better when flying low. Little Sergeant Ellis told us, 'If I go, it will be in the sea; my second name is Mortimer, Mort-i-mer.' But we never thought it would happen. Ceaselessly the gramophone churned out some well-known tune: *Tuxedo Junction, I'm in the mood for love, Don't you ever cry.* They were the favourites.

> 'Don't you ever cry, don't ever shed a tear
> Don't you ever cry after I'm gone . . .'

There seemed nothing melancholy in those lilting words and the catchy little tune seemed suited to our mood. Some of us would die within the next few days. That was inevitable. But you did not believe it would be you. Death was always present, and we knew it for what it was. If we had to die we would be alone, smashed to pieces, burnt alive, or drowned. Some strange, protecting veil kept the nightmare thought from our minds, as it did the loss of our friends. Their disappearance struck us as less a solid blow than a dark shadow which chilled our hearts and passed on. We seemed already to be living in another world, separate and exalted, where the gulf between life and death had closed and was no longer forbidding.

We were afraid, though, some more than others. Sidney Bazly of James McComb's 611 Squadron was haunted by fear. Even when he drove his Lagonda his knuckles were white on the steering wheel. Shot down in flames, he confessed to James, 'I've hated every minute of it.'

'Why not take a rest?'

'Because,' said Bazly, 'the country has paid for me to be a fighter pilot. As long as I have two eyes, two arms and two legs I shall go on being one.' Sidney Bazly was one of the unknown heroes. Perhaps they were the bravest of all.

Tom Gleave thought the more intelligent a man was, the more he had to fear. It's possible. But intelligence could defeat fear. Innes Westmacott's greatest fear was fire. So he took intelligent measures. He covered as much of his flesh as possible – with goggles, gauntlet gloves, and boots. He locked his hood back before going into action 'and put up with the draught'.

I was for being lightly clad, and usually wore only a blue jersey next to my skin, with the sleeves rolled up – with a 50-gallon petrol tank just in front and no fire-proof bulkhead in between! But some sixth sense convinced me I had nothing to fear from fire.

Tom Gleave took no precautions either. 'I never worried about fire,' he said. On 28 August Tom was enjoying forty-eight hours' leave from 253 Squadron at Prestwick, Scotland, with his wife Beryl. The next time they met she would not recognize him.

With *Luftwaffe* 3 withdrawn from the day battle and concentrating on night attacks, the *Storangriffen* against British industry and aerial mining of ports and harbours were greatly on the increase. Fighter Command's night defences were pitifully weak: half a dozen Blenheim squadrons fitted with rudimentary air interception radar ('AI') formed the nucleus. Despite Dowding's intense preoccupation with the day battle, he often would go off alone to the night-fighter stations, returning wearily in the early hours. One night his personal aide, Flying Officer Robert Wright, offered to go along to help with note-taking, but Dowding brushed him aside kindly. 'No, I don't think so, somebody's got to be in the office first thing in the morning.' Dowding preferred to be alone with his problems, not the least of which were the night battles.

That very night the crash of bombs disturbed Dowding, who was working late at Bentley Priory. 'Did you hear that?' he asked his Senior Air Staff Officer, Air Vice Marshal Strath Evill. 'I did, sir,' Evill replied. 'Tell them to stop it,' said Dowding. 'Of course, sir, I'll write to Fighter Command about it.' Dowding smiled at the crack. But he realized all too painfully that Fighter Command, practically impotent against the night bomber, had to confide security of base to the toughness and grit of the unarmed citizens of Britain. Sperrle, whose original 'act of force' had killed hundreds at Guernica, had plenty more in store for the British.

In each of the day fighter squadrons was a handful of 'night-operational' pilots. We were often sent off on a patrol to work with the searchlights, which hindered as much as helped us. Day combats were exhausting enough; night patrols pushed us to the limits of our resistance. Landing at 3.00 a.m. on the morning of the 28th after two hours on patrol, I had a short 'kip'. Just after dawn I led the squadron off on the first of four sorties that day.

Jim Bailey's turn to fight came at last. 'I had a great deal more confidence in my ability than my ability warranted.' He might have had even less, had he known that ace Adolf Galland was climbing away from Audembert leading the Me. 109s of *JG* 26 to confront 264 Squadron. The Defiants were at seventeen thousand feet when a 'flock of Heinkels' came in over Folkestone. Far above, like 'black dots in the empyrean' the top cover of Messerschmitts was already fighting back against the high-flying Spitfires.

The Defiants climbed up beneath the enemy bombers. 'The Heinkels looked as big as elephants,' said Jim. Hardie, his air gunner, was firing into the belly of one of them which then fell out with an engine on fire. If only the British fighters could have fought off the Me. 109s the Defiants might have routed the Heinkels before they bombed Eastchurch.

But Galland's Me. 109s were diving and pulling up under the unwary Defiants. Jim heard strikes on his aircraft and a voice, 'I'm wounded.' Flicking over he went for the ground in a steep spiral. It was most likely his Defiant that Galland came diving at, but overshot. Jim's luck still held as he glided beneath some high tension cables and crashed through a hedge. Hardie was out in a flash. 'I thought you said you were wounded?' said Jim, squinting down a cut nose. 'No, I said turn to starboard,' replied Hardie.

Three more Defiants were lost, five aircrew dead. Squadron Leader John Garvin had been shot to pieces by Galland, who wondered, 'How can they put such planes into the sky?' Garvin jumped. He was flown back to Hornchurch in a transport plane with one other passenger – Al Deere, who had been shot down by a Spitfire!

This was the end for 264. With only two aircraft fit for the air, they were withdrawn from the battle. 'We were hushed all the next day, quietly subdued in the mess,' wrote Jim Bailey. In four days they had lost 11 aircraft, 14 air crew.

Four times that day I led 85 Squadron up from Croydon. At 4.25 p.m. we were searching at eighteen thousand feet somewhere over Dungeness – Hamilton's Red section on my right, Allard's on my left, Patrick Woods-Scawen's Green under my tail. Then, I could hardly believe it: 'Me. 109s below, two o'clock,' I called. A dozen of them were skating along above a layer of broken cloud. Our orders were to attack bombers and avoid fighters. But this was too good to miss. 'Come in Red and Yellow.' As I put my finger to my oxygen mask as if to say 'Sh!' I could see that Hammy was grinning. The sun was at our backs. Everything was set to 'jump' those Me. 109s before they saw us.

'Down we go! Pick your own,' and we tore in among them. It was as if we had flushed a covey of partridges. One pulled across me in a steep left hand turn, giving me a perfect shot. It rolled over belching white smoke – a hit in the cooling system. The pilot was taken prisoner. I fastened on to another Me. 109, but it dived away and even with the 'plug' pulled (full boost) I was lagging. Then it zoomed, giving me a long shot from below. No result. Whipping all that I could out of my Hurricane I followed, hoping to slow up the Me. 109 by firing short bursts. But in the heat of the chase I forgot the basic rules, until suddenly, *wham!* a bullet splintered in the cockpit. Never did I get out of anybody's way so fast. Stick forward, bottom rudder, engine cuts, clouds of black smoke – and it must have looked to the Me. 109 pilot behind: *Ein Englander Kaput.*

Meanwhile 85 was laying into the Me. 109s. Sam Allard sent one flaming into the sea three miles off Folkestone. 'Honk' English saw it. Sam chased another half-way back to France and left it smoking. Confirmed destroyed next day.

'Ace' Hodgson got in a blow for New Zealand, shooting most of the rudder off a Me. 109 in a dive from fifteen thousand to twenty feet above sea level, near Cap Gris Nez. Confirmed next day. The Me. 109 attacked by Sergeant Walker-Smith exploded on hitting the sea. And Patrick Woods-Scawen sent down a sixth Me. 109 streaming black smoke and petrol. The Observer Corps reported that it crashed in the sea off Dymchurch.

The *Jäger* of the *Luftwaffe* did not think the Hurricane was much good. This may have been partly because they often mistook Hurricanes for Spitfires. Both Kesselring and Osterkamp fell into the trap. Uncle Theo 'saw' Spitfires on the ground in the Battle of France; Kesselring said, 'Only the Spitfires worried us.' Both were wrong. There were no Spitfires in France and in the Battle of Britain they shot down, in the aggregate, fewer than the Hurricanes.

We ourselves thought the Hurricane was great, and we proved it. The Air Ministry was later to confirm: 'The total number of enemy aircraft brought down by the single-seater fighters was in the proportion of three by Hurricanes to two by Spitfires.' There were more Hurricanes engaged. 'The average proportion ... serviceable each morning was approximately sixty-three per cent Hurricanes and thirty-seven per cent Spitfires. *In proportion* ... Spitfires brought down about six per cent more than the Hurricanes.' This was no reason for the Hurricanes to blush, considering they were slower than the Me. 109 and Spitfire.

Fighter Command lost more fighters than the *Luftwaffe*, not that this gave any indication of their relative merits, nor of the battle's progress. The RAF fighters' battle was against both the German fighters and bombers, mainly the latter. But on 28 August something must have got into us. In all, we destroyed nineteen German fighters, losing twenty ourselves. But we captured twelve bombers as well.

As we fought the Me. 109s that afternoon a man watched from below, his shoulders slightly hunched, a cigar clenched between his teeth. Touring coastal defences, Winston Churchill needed more than faith to believe that the woeful lack of weapons and the pathetic, improvised road blocks could ever stop the invader. He pinned his faith on the RAF, and the combat overhead must have heartened him. But in the morning, surveying the chaos and the unfilled craters at Manston, he was led 'to protest emphatically against this feeble method of repairing damage'. The whole process was 'disproportionate to the value of this fighting vantage ground'. Which may give the answer to those like Al Deere who had been bombed to blazes there, and asked: 'Who made the decision to retain Manston for so long?' . . . Was it the Prime Minister?

It had been fifteen days since Eagle Day. According to the OKW Directive of 1 August the time was up for Hitler to 'decide if the invasion would take place or not . . .' The decision, said the directive, would depend on the air offensive. The Supreme Commander had been relaxing for the past ten days in the cool heights of the Berghof, where, despite no signs of victory in the air, Ciano found him 'firmly optimistic on the future course of events . . .'

But the Army was driven to despair by the *Kriegsmarine*'s reluctance. On 23 August Halder had noted, 'an attack has no chance of success this year'. Three days later Brauchitsch insisted on seeing Hitler, who told him the Army had to knuckle under to the *Kriegsmarine* and its narrow-front crossing.

In fact neither Hitler nor Brauchitsch were cooling off, but they saw the invasion as the *coup de grâce* for a vanquished enemy. Even Halder felt better. 'Interest in this operation seems to have increased,' he wrote in his diary.

Everyone from Hitler downwards was watching the air war. Britain was still safe as a base, which enabled RAF bombers again to sally forth against Berlin, this time hitting the Goerlitzer station and killing ten civilians. Top Nazis were outraged and the *Voelkischer Beobachter* screamed, 'Dastardly English attacks . . .' forgetting the Germans had started the ball rolling by bombing London twenty-five years ago.

At the Chancellery in Berlin Hitler told Ciano the next day that 'persistent bad weather' had foiled the *Luftwaffe*. 'If the weather is more favourable . . . two weeks are sufficient to gain mastery of the air over Britain, which is indispensable to neutralize British naval superiority and carry out a landing.' Weather permitting, the RAF should therefore be *kaput* by about 12 September.

Chapter 26

Tom Gleave had said goodbye to Beryl and their little boy John and returned to Prestwick the evening before. The mess was empty. 'The chaps must be out on safari,' thought Tom and ordered himself a beer. The telephone rang. It was 'Johnny', one of the sector controllers at Turnhouse. 'The squadron's to go south tomorrow,' he told Tom, 'but you're to report to Turnhouse.' Tom pleaded, 'For Christ's sake, do something to save me.' Johnny was a good friend and Tom heard no more.

Starr and the others must have been at the Orchard Blossom, so Tom rang through. When Starr heard the news he slammed down the telephone and within a few minutes Tom heard the screech of brakes outside the mess. 'You're coming too?' asked Bill Cambridge, a flight commander, and Tom said he was 'wanted' by Turnhouse. 'Get going before they grab you, sir,' advised Bill. Would Starr mind? 'No, of course not, you must certainly come,' he told Tom. 'You take half the squadron and push off when you like tomorrow.' Someone fetched the NCOs over. The ante-room was cleared and an old cushion bound with string. Then a rugger match started: Officers v. Sergeants, with several breaks for beer. The 'magnificent' Dredge scored a try for the Sergeants. Then a session of all-in wrestling, a final drink, and bed. 'I was decidedly bruised,' said Tom, 'but it was the best party I can remember.' It would be his last, too, for some time.

The two Joachims, Poetter and Helbig, were out on another kind of party night. They were among 160 aircraft of Sperrle's *Luftflotte* 3 sent against Liverpool. Most of their bombs went wide; in fact, the Liverpudlian defences did not realize they were the main target.

253 had no sooner landed and refuelled at Kenley on 29 August when,

at 4.00 p.m., Tom was ordered to patrol with his half of the squadron. Kenley control had already ordered 85 off from Croydon and at that moment we were embroiled at great disadvantage with the enemy. I had sighted eighteen Heinkels coming in over Beachy Head several thousand feet above us. As we climbed, hanging on our propellers, the blue above glinted with little silver flashes. Me. 109s! As I watched, they grew in number until there were myriads of them – we thought some two hundred in all. That afternoon the *Luftwaffe's* massive fighter sweeps totalled seven hundred fighters and destroyers, out to slaughter our fighters as they went after the *Lock-vogel*.

Labouring up painfully beneath the Heinkels, our twelve Hurricanes were sitting ducks, but there were bombers to get so I kept on – telling Sammy and Patrick to keep a sharp look-out and shout when menaced.

It was grotesque, Air Vice Marshal Leigh-Mallory protested (with the support of the Deputy Chief of the Air Staff Sholto Douglas – a fighter pilot to the bone – and certain armchair tacticians) to send 12 Hurricanes after such a host of the enemy. And as we closed on them it did seem to us that we were twelve against two hundred, for we never saw a single other British fighter. Yet a dozen other squadrons were bearing down from all directions on the enemy '*Mahalla*'* as it penetrated deeper into the English sky. This was the essence of Park's tactics: flexibility and speed. They were perfectly suited to 11 Group's battleground.

The enemy was on top of Park's squadrons only a few minutes after leaving France, but he had to wait until then to see how the attack would develop. To succeed with his 'forward interception' tactics – engaging the enemy before he reached target – flexibility and speed were essential. For this he had to manoeuvre his defence in squadrons of 12; wings of 3 or more squadrons would have been too slow, too cumbersome, and would have cost him the battle.

We were still climbing, trying to reach the bombers. Keep well away from those fighters! Not easy, though, with them sitting on top of us, able to strike as they pleased. Better move out towards the sun. But a dozen Me. 110s now pinned us down. Every time they dived out of their defensive circle, I called, 'Leave them alone,' and wheeled the squadron towards them to shake them off our tails.

Then the inevitable – down came the Me. 109s and it was each one for himself. When my Me. 109 came, firing, I whipped round and caught him doing that fatal turn across my sights. Tighten the turn, nose up a little, and I had him. The Me. 109 staggered, like a pheasant shot on the

*According to Hans Ring, from Arabic 'a crowd'.

wing. A big piece flew off, maybe the hood. A plume of white smoke trailed. I had a split-second impression of the pilot, seemingly inert during those last dramatic moments. Then the aircraft stalled and dived to earth near Hastings.

This time I had the feeling I had killed a man, but there was no time for remorse. If it was him this time, it could be me the next. In the mounting frenzy of battle, our hearts beat faster and our efforts became more frantic. But within, fatigue was deadening feeling, numbing the spirit. Both life and death had lost their importance. Desire sharpened to a single, savage purpose – to grab the enemy and claw him down from the sky.

Not as wary as the rest, two of our young pilots were caught in that rush of Me. 109s. Sergeant Ellis baled out of his blazing machine none the worse. Hit in the foot, Sergeant Walker-Smith parachuted safely out of the raging battle into the placid little Kentish town of Hawkhurst. But Hammy had slipped in behind one of those Me. 109s and sent it down flaming into the sea. It would only be a matter of hours before Hammy was himself caught in the murderous process.

Return to Croydon, taxi in. Ground crews waiting anxiously: has my pilot fired? They scanned from afar to see if the fabric covering had been blasted from the gun ports. Now a man holds each wing tip. Swing her round, switch off. The fitter is up, leaning into the cockpit. 'Any joy?' Briefly you tell what happened.

Quick re-arm and refuel. Men are on the wings. Men with spanners, with bands of belted ammunition. Cowlings are 'unpinned', the 'Bowser's' nozzle rammed into the tank, right wing, fuselage, left wing – three tanks full up. Oil checked. Radio checked, re-tuned. Oxygen bottle changed. Windscreen cleaned. Five minutes, and the Hurricane is ready to go again.

A close bond linked us with the ground crews – skilled, loyal, enthusiastic youngsters working under the eagle eye of their NCOs (themselves seasoned by experience, dry of humour). Between them, they held our lives in their hands. The public encouraged from the stands, but our brave and loyal 'ground troops' cheered right from the touch-line. Solitary individualists as we were in our tiny cockpits, they gave us heart to go back again and again into the battle.

85 scramble! For the fourth time (at 6.16 p.m.) we were climbing away from Croydon. Patrol Dungeness. At eighteen thousand feet a lone Spitfire joined us. It was a foolish, almost criminal act. Our wave-lengths were different and thus we could not communicate. And, end-on, a Spit.

could be taken for a Me. 109. 'Watch him very closely,' I called to our tailguard, our 'arse-end Charlies'.

The controller's voice was faint. A blood-red, sinking sun stained the blue-grey haze. With the thin voice of the controller calling, 'Bandits in your vicinity', we turned aimlessly here and there and craned our necks, searching uneasily in the treacherous light.

One evening at the end of August (he doesn't say when), a pilot of 603 Squadron had a 'most amusing though painful experience . . . acting as "arse-end Charlie" to a squadron of Hurricanes'. His name was Richard Hillary. He 'found a squadron of Hurricanes flying round the sky . . . so I joined on . . . I was peering earnestly into my mirror when bullets started appearing along my port wing.'

It was the 'Ace' who noticed the Spitfire had changed into a Me. 109. 'Look out, Messerschmitts!' he yelled, and each of our sections slammed into a left hand turn, but not before the square wing tip of a Me. 109 flashed by just above my head. Straightening out, my heart sank. To starboard, Hammy's Hurricane was heeling slowly over, wreathed in flame and smoke. Then it tipped downwards into a five-mile plunge to earth. Only Nigger Marshall got in a shot at the Me. 109. It dived abruptly into the haze, but its destruction was never confirmed.

Was Richard Hillary in that Spitfire? The height and position agree. It was only after he 'managed to pull himself together and go into a spin' that he thought of warning the Hurricanes – impossible anyway on his wave-length even had his radio not been shot away. Hillary crash-landed 'in the back garden of a Brigade cocktail party'. The timing agrees, too.

Whoever it was, we felt bitter about the Spitfire. Had it kept on the flank where we could see it, Hammy might never have died. 'If this Spitfire pilot can be identified, I would like these facts brought home to him, because his . . . action contributed to the loss of one of my flight commanders,' I wrote in my combat report.

Ill luck and control problems had placed us at the mercy of the Me. 109s, to which we had lost a fine leader and three aircraft without firing a shot at the bombers. Other squadrons had rightly avoided the German *Jäger*. As OKL remarked that evening: 'The British fighters could not be tempted . . .' Park's clever tactics had cheated the German fighters of their prey and kept our losses to half of theirs. The situation was to change abruptly in the next few days.

For the third night running enemy bombers were over Liverpool – nearly two hundred of them.

Friday morning, 30 August, saw the beginning of the fiercest forty-eight hours' fighting of the whole battle. A supreme effort by the *Luftwaffe* to destroy sector airfields and the fighters themselves was met by more desperate and costly fighter resistance than ever before.

The day dawned with a layer of cloud lying over south-east England at seven thousand feet – frustrating for the Observer Corps. But from where 85 Squadron circled over Dungeness at eighteen thousand feet I could see the enemy circling at Cap Gris Nez like a swarm of gnats. Then they formed up in columns: '*wir fliegen gegen England*'. We waited up-sun in the English sky – eleven Hurricanes ready to pounce. I gave their course, numbers, and height to the controller – a drill standardized a few days previously to overcome the Observers' plotting problems. Escorted by scores of Me. 109s and Me. 110s, a score of Heinkels advanced further towards the English coast. 'Stand by for head-on attack!' I took my little band of Hurricanes down in a shallow dive, slipped them into echelon and turned in well ahead of the Heinkels, heading straight at them. Our attack, I wrote later in my combat report, 'had the desired effect'. The Heinkels were thrown into confusion. 'They did not stand up to the head-on attack at all well . . .'

More waves were advancing. Park had at all costs to save Biggin Hill and Kenley. He threw in fifteen more squadrons and called on 12 Group. His tactics were perfect but again things went wrong with the 12 Group squadron, ordered to guard Biggin Hill. It flew around aimlessly while Heinkels showered bombs on the airfield.

At Kenley, Tom Gleave was on his way to snatch a quick lunch when the loud-speakers blared, '253 Squadron, patrol base.' With his section, Tom had reached seventeen thousand feet over Maidstone when he saw 'a fantastic sight: stretching as far as the eye could see were rows of Me.109s riding above the haze'. The 'Yellow bellies' – silver Me. 109s with yellow underside and wing-tips – were travelling at a leisurely pace, as Tom led his three Hurricanes into their flank. 'I turned with the tide and took a bead on the nearest Me. 109.' With that, he began a short-lived but sensational career at Kenley. The Me. 109 rolled over gently. 'I saw sunlit pieces of his shattered hood . . . he slewed and dived out of sight.' Then a Me. 109 crossed ahead 'as though completely ignoring the fracas going on behind'. A short burst, and it slowed up, trailing black smoke.

Tom nearly hit it but instead pulled up and all but collided with another at which he fired point blank. It towered like a wounded bird and then fell out of the sky. Amazing, Tom thought, to be swimming about this shoal of Me. 109s snapping at every one that gets in the way. Not too good for the health either. 'Tracers passed above and below, curving downwards . . . as if I were flying in a gigantic cage of gilt wire.' He looked around in vain for Brown and young Francis, his wing men. 'The amount of lead flying about could hardly have been for my sole benefit.' But 'jumped' at the start, Brown had had to pull out. To his grief, Tom never saw Francis (the youngest in the squadron) again. 'To charge into that hell, a mere boy, stamped him as a lion-hearted hero.'

Tom had not finished. A fourth Messerschmitt passed just above, and firing again at point blank range Tom saw the German roll slowly over and go down, 'full bore'. Back at Kenley, squadron intelligence officer Henry told Tom, 'Unless you saw them break up, catch fire, or crash, we can not count them destroyed.' But Tom thought, 'Those Me. 109 pilots will not be needing any more rations.'

Badly damaged, Biggin Hill was still in action when the *Luftwaffe* returned to the attack. This time Park put up eight squadrons, including 85. The attack was repulsed. Six miles west, Tom Gleave watched from Kenley 'the glistening shapes of friend and foe twisting and turning to the accompaniment of machine-gun fire. Tracer streaks and vapour trails wove fantastic patterns . . . the shriek and whine of diving aircraft added sound . . .'

Over at Northolt, on the western fringe of London, Zdzislaw Krasnodebski relaxed in a deck chair. The year before, almost to the day, the Germans had invaded Poland, his country. Determined that the German bombing and machine-gunning of Polish towns and villages should not go unpunished, Krasnodebski and his friends had fought desperately in their slower machines. When the end came he left his wife to fight the hated foe on French soil. That chapter ended, he came to England to fight on for freedom, 'yours and ours'.

Many Poles had followed him – among them burly, deep-voiced Jan Zumbach, Miric Feric, Witor Urbanowicz and young Ludwig Paszkiewicz ('Paszko'). Since arriving in England their biggest fight had been with the language; they were still too shaky in English (said their station commander Group Captain Vincent) for 303 Polish Squadron to join the battle.

Zdzislaw lay back in his his deck chair and thought of his wife. Occasionally he received a cryptic note, 'Am well, in good health . . .' In truth she was only just holding out on terrible food – roots, bones, and the like. Some days she did not eat at all. But she had seen how the Germans massacred sick women in hospitals – that drove her on to work with all her might in secret against the invaders. Zdzislaw and his comrades would keep faith with her and her friends of the Resistance.

But 303 still had to get operational. That afternoon they took off from Northolt at 4.15 p.m. and flew off to rendezvous for practice attacks near St. Albans with six Blenheims. But above the little cathedral town 303 ran into a *Mahalla* of sixty bombers escorted by Me. 109s, heading for the Vauxhall Motor Works at Luton. Young Paszko first warned his British squadron leader, Ronald Kellett. Then without orders Paszko peeled off and careered straight at a Dornier. He kept firing until it burst into flames. In that moment 303 became operational. Dowding confirmed it: he was only too thankful to have an extra squadron.

As 303 was landing at Northolt just before 5.00 p.m., Tom Gleave led nine Hurricanes of 253 off from Kenley. Over Kent they were caught up in 'a wheeling mixture of Me. 109s and Hurricanes, each one firing at the chap in front . . .' He saw a Me. 109 blasting bits off the tail of a Hurricane. 'My blood boiled; no darned Hun would get away with that.' They were in Indian file, Tom firing at the Me. 109 which was shooting at the Hurricane in front. Then the Me. 109 pulled out, mortally hit. Tom could not believe that the Hurricane had survived.

But upon landing at Kenley he saw it on the tarmac: flaps, undercarriage, elevators, rudder, 'which now consisted of a few tubes and thin air', still worked. The pilot, 'Colonel' Bill Wedgewood, surrounded by a knot of pilots, 'was giving vent to his feelings on the Huns in general, particularly the one who had written his name on that Hurricane . . . roars of laughter assured him of full agreement'.

Tom 'had sworn to get at least one Hun before I bought it myself'. His Me. 109 was confirmed down in the sea off Dungeness. But Tom's feeling of accomplishment was marred by news of Sergeant Dickinson. He had been shot dead by a Me. 109 while coming down by parachute. By the rules of war it was justifiable to kill a pilot who could fight again. But few of us could bring ourselves to shoot a helpless man in cold blood. Tom was bitter. Starr just thought . . . 'What a cruel way to die . . .'

At Duxford in 12 Group, Douglas Bader's prayers were at long last answered. 'Scramble 242 Squadron! Vector 190 degrees,' called the Duxford controller. But Douglas steered thirty degrees further west to get up-sun. Then he saw fifty Dorniers, escorted by Me. 110s, bearing down on North Weald. 'Bastards, flying over here – it's *our* sky,' he thought and dived from above. He led 242 right into the midst of the bombers, splitting their formation wide open. This time 12 Group had saved North Weald.

Bader was elated. Back at Coltishall he was told the AOC was on the telephone. 'Douglas, congratulations on your splendid success,' said Leigh-Mallory and Bader replied, 'Well sir, if we had had thirty-six aircraft we could have shot down thirty-six Germans instead of twelve.' Conceived long ago in Leigh-Mallory's mind, the 'Wing' was born that evening. (85 had done a wing practice with 66 Squadron, Duxford, on 21 June.)

The defence was standing up well. Biggin Hill still held out. Then the unexpected happened. Fate did the job which Goering had seen 'no point' in continuing. In one blow a mains failure put all the south-east radar stations out of action. For Fighter Command, thereby blinded, it was disastrous. Eight Dornier 17s of III *KG* 76 (the low-attack specialists) escorted by Hannes Trautloft's *JG* 54, came streaking up the Estuary unseen in the evening haze. Suddenly they turned southwards and a few minutes later took Biggin Hill completely by surprise. Their daring attack killed and wounded sixty-five, including several girls of the WAAF. Hangars burned; technical buildings were smashed. Bombs severed the main telephone cable and Biggin Hill, lynch-pin of the fighter defences, was cut off. Its squadrons had to be transferred to Hornchurch control. Luckily, the GPO Maintenance Officer, himself badly shaken by a near miss, was able to get an SOS through to Maintenance Control at Tunbridge Wells.

Dusk was falling when 56 Squadron returned to North Weald after its seventh sortie that day. Innes Westmacott had been in some terrific battles, once hitting a Me. 110 from so close that the oil from its engines spurted all over his windscreen. Exhausted, he pushed his goggles up on his forehead to concentrate better on landing. But when he slid back the hood the slipstream caught the goggles, smashing them against the armour plating behind his head.

Fighter Command's frenzied efforts to fight off the enemy – over a thousand sorties – had only partially succeeded. Biggin Hill was temporarily out of action, the Vauxhall Motor Works at Luton badly hit (with fifty civilians killed) and twenty-five fighters were down. Despite losses of thirty-six planes, the *Luftwaffe* was pressing Fighter Command hard – much harder than it thought.

When he saw Jodl that afternoon, Hitler told him that he did not 'consider the pre-requisites for "Sea Lion" yet fulfilled, judging from the progress of the air war against England'. He therefore postponed his decision on 'Sea Lion' until 10 September. But if something were not done to ginger up the air war and settle with the RAF, it would be too late. Moreover, these attacks on Berlin were if not all that damaging at least highly embarrassing. Hitler had the answer. He told Jodl, 'I now give permission for large-scale reprisal attacks on London.' The veto applied at the outbreak of war was lifted. The consequences would be far-reaching.

That night the Fuehrer heard bombs crashing down on the Siemens electrical works. It was the RAF's third attack on Berlin. A *Luftwaffe* force twice as strong was attacking Liverpool for the third night in succession. There could now be no stopping the bombing-war and its resulting massacre of civilian populations.

The air war did not look rosy to Hitler because Goering – not knowing himself – was unable to tell him that the *Luftwaffe's* blows on sector stations were doing mortal harm. Hitler judged by results, and the RAF was still in action. Goering and his staff were mesmerized by the 'score'. Army Liaison Officer at *Luftwaffe* HQ, General Major Stapf, reported 'official' OKL figures to General Halder. Since 8 August, he said, the RAF had lost 791 fighters (the real figure was 261). The *Luftwaffe* had lost 353 bombers and fighters (the Quarter-Master General's figure was nearly 500). Was OKL cooking the books for Army consumption? Quite possibly, for they inflated the effective bomber and fighter forces by nearly fifty per cent. A few days later Major von Falkstein (OKW's man at *Luftwaffe* HQ) was to come out with some staggering figures: 'Since 8 August, the RAF losses were 1,115 fighters and bombers; the *Luftwaffe's*, 464. Eighteen British airfields were destroyed, twenty-six damaged etc. Conclusion: the British fighter defence is severely crippled.'

First on the scene at Biggin Hill on 31 August was the GPO working party, led by Inspector 'Jock' Thomson and his foreman, Amos (Mossy)

Adams. After a nightmare journey in the pitch dark they had reached Biggin Hill at 10.00 p.m. the previous evening and spent the rest of the night playing cribbage in a draughty, rat-infested shelter. Only when dawn broke did they discover that one end of it had been blown off. From the bottom of a bomb crater alongside the Met. Office – twenty-six yards across, ten yards deep – came the hiss of escaping gas, and floating in the muddy water were a trilby hat and one or two RAF cans – pathetic relics of the Met. staff.

Thomson and his men got down to work on the severed main cable – seventy-four pairs of wires – in the crater near the officers' mess. 'Take no notice of air raid sirens to the north or south,' the station commander (Group Captain Grice) told them. 'Just listen for the bugler. Then you must run like hell.' But for the moment it was the gas escaping from the bottom of the crater that worried the GPO men most. A half hour was all they could stick before clambering out, nauseated, to gulp fresh air. Patiently the jointers worked on to put Biggin Hill back in the circuit.

Like 85 Squadron, 56 was given thirty minutes' notice on the morning of 31 August. Innes Westmacott allowed himself the luxury of a bath. Then, he decided, he would go to Stores and draw another pair of goggles. Man proposes . . . In the middle of his bath, 56 was called to readiness. Innes did not even have time to pull on his flying boots. Lowering himself into the cockpit he felt naked – no goggles, no boots. Then he was off, climbing eastwards. Over the Blackwater Estuary, 56 tore into a formation of Dorniers. Innes's bullets struck home. A Dornier was going down. Then he glanced over his shoulder at the Me. 110 escort then closing in. 'Just time for another Dornier,' he thought, but a second later, crash! His instrument panel shattered into fragments and a searing blast of flame smothered him. 'This is it,' he thought and felt resigned to die. Then – quite deliberately – he changed his mind. With the hood already open, he was out in a second, his clothes still burning. So he fell until everything went cold, and then pulled the rip-cord. But the furnace heat had glued his eyelids together, blinding him. Desperately he tried to pull them apart. He could see nothing and only hear the unmistakable sound of a diving Me. 109. 'He's going to shoot me,' thought Innes, who had never felt more frightened and helpless. But the shots he heard were not from the Messerschmitt; they came from the Brownings of Sergeant Robinson's Hurricane, diving to the rescue.

At last Innes managed to force his eyelids open. 'I did not like what I saw.' His trousers had been burned down to a pair of singed blue pants and his legs were flayed and terribly hurt. He was falling straight towards a thick wood – already it hurt to think of his raw flesh smashing through all those branches.

Innes fell in a tiny clearing and missed the trees completely. He was too dazed to stand, even to undo his parachute harness. Men were crashing through the woods; trigger-happy Home Guards, he thought. So he called out, and heard an answering shout: 'All right mate, we're coming.' The mellow country voice was reassuring. This part of Essex was Innes's own country. He had been born and bred here. People he had known all his life had watched him floating down. At Chelmsford Hospital friends began arriving before the doctors had tidied him up.

In that raid, North Weald got off lightly. Duxford was saved by Tommy Thompson's 111 Squadron from Debden. But Debden got a pasting. Wing Commander Larry Fullergood (who had been so good to 85) was in the bathroom lathering his face when Ops. rang. A few minutes later he panted into the Ops. Room, the lather still clinging to him. Bombs had flattened the WAAF's quarters and Larry Fullergood threw his own house open to sixty homeless girls.

Further north, Air Vice Marshal Leigh-Mallory landed at Coltishall and talked Wings to Douglas Bader between two patrols. Douglas would lead the Wing with 242, 310 (Hurricanes) and 19 (Spitfires) would make up the permanent basis of the Wing. The Hurricanes (242 and 310) would work out of Duxford, 19 Squadron's Spitfires from its satellite, Fowlmere. 'Get going as from tomorrow,' Leigh-Mallory said.

Standing by with the Emergency Section, Tom Gleave watched the squadron taxi in at Kenley. Some were shot up, one was missing – Starr. At that moment the good Starr's body lay in a Kentish church. One bullet had pierced his heart. But not until he had jumped from his disabled machine. Starr had died in the very way he thought so cruel – shot in cold blood on the end of his parachute by a German fighter. A wave of anger and disgust ran through the squadron. 'I have never seen such collective temper,' said Tom, who for the second time found himself commanding 253 Squadron.

It was noon; the Biggin Hill bugler had blown three times during the morning, but at last Jock Thomson and his men had finished. Biggin was back in business.

Over at Arras, Dorniers of *Oberst* Fink's *KG* 2 had taken off and were heading for Dungeness. There they split into two columns, one heading for Hornchurch, the other for Biggin Hill.

Tom left 'Colonel' Bill Wedgewood on guard with two sections while he and the rest went to snatch some lunch. But once again the controller caught him. '253 scramble!' came the stentorian broadcast command. Tom ran, as he had when, as a boy, he had tried to catch the aircraft before they took off. His fitter had already started up and a moment later Tom had slipped into the lead, the Colonel and two sections following. Again the controller called, 'Look out for bandits approaching from the south-east.' The western column of *KG* 2 was advancing on Biggin Hill.

KG 2's other column was already running up on Hornchurch. 54 Squadron had taxied out but was recalled. Back at dispersal, they had hardly switched off when a wildly gesticulating orderly signalled to the pilots to start up again. Some of them, who had over-doped their warm engines, were having starting trouble when the controller called, 'Hornet aircraft get airborne, enemy in the vicinity.' To Al Deere the controller sounded 'nearly hysterical'. Strolling across the airfield to 603 Squadron dispersal, Richard Hillary heard the 'emotionless voice' of the controller, 'Enemy formation approaching . . .' He looked up and saw 'a dozen slugs, shining in the bright sun and coming straight on'.

Nine Spitfires were hauling up their undercarriages when Al Deere (leading Red Section, the last off) swung into wind. He opened the throttle and careered down the runway, followed by Sergeant Davies (Red 2) and Pilot Officer Eric Edsall (Red 3). At that instant Richard Hillary heard 'the rising scream of the first bomb – out of the corner of my eye I saw three Spitfires. One moment they were about twenty feet up . . . the next catapulted apart as though on elastic; the leader went over on his back . . .; No. 2 put a wing in . . . while the plane on the left was blasted wingless into the next field.' Hillary thought to himself, 'That's the shortest flight he's ever taken.'

A tremendous blast of air, followed by showers of earth struck Al in the face. Vaguely he realized he was ploughing along the airfield upside down. Stones and dirt flew into his eyes and his helmet was torn by the stony ground. Miraculously he was alive; so, too, were Edsall and Davies.

85 Squadron narrowly missed the same treatment at Croydon. Before coming to readiness at 1.00 p.m., we had just started lunch when I was called to the telephone. It was the Kenley controller. 'Please be on your toes. We may need you in a hurry.' 'Come on boys!' I felt as if I were a Western sheriff with his posse. Within a few minutes we were climbing into our Hurricanes, their engines already running. Impatiently I called Kenley control: 'For God's sake let us go.' 'Wait a bit, old boy,' came the impassive voice. Then I glanced back at my squadron, which had formed up behind me. They looked superb, all those Hurricanes – straining against the brakes with their long, eager noses tilted skywards and the sun glinting on their whirling propellers. Every pilot was watching me, waiting for the signal. At last it came: 'Off you go,' called Kenley, and we were racing forward with a bellow of twelve thousand horsepower. It was the last time I led my squadron into battle by day.

The bombs were already on their way down. I had just moved the lever to raise the undercarriage, when my engine faltered, faded, and picked up again. Blast had struck the motor like a punch in the wind. Turning in the cockpit, I saw the rest of the squadron emerging from a vast eruption of smoke and debris. Then I looked up: thousands of feet above, Me. 110s were wheeling in the blue, with Me.109s swarming above. I thought the Me. 110s had bombed. Yet some say a dozen Dorniers had attacked from lower down. If so, I never saw them. I was mad with rage at the Me. 110s. 'After them, but look out for the 109s,' I called and the furious chase began.

Somewhere above us, Tom Gleave and his seven Hurricanes were engaged with the Dorniers of *KG* 2. Like us, they had been sent off too late. Attacking from below, Tom heard a metallic click from the right wing. A long spout of flame shot out viciously, lapped over the cockpit and engulfed him. The cockpit was like the centre of a giant blow-lamp. He groped in the mass of flame to disconnect his radio lead and oxygen tube, but in vain. The skin was rising in hideous white bubbles off his hands and wrists. His clothes were alight, the flesh of his legs bared to the flames. Tom was being burnt alive, yet he felt no great pain. Like Mick Mannock, the First World War ace, he carried a revolver for just such an occasion and at that moment he thought of using it. But first, another titanic effort. He undid his harness and tried to fight his way out but still the oxygen tube and radio lead held him. Somehow he wrenched off his helmet and dragged back the hood. There was a blinding flash and Tom was shot from the cockpit like a projectile. Turning over and over, his blistered hand travelled to the rip-cord and he pulled.

He hit the ground hard, sat up, and surveyed his mutilated body. His skin had lifted and draped his legs like outsize plus fours; the skin from his wrists and hands hung down like paper bags. He felt like a 'Michelin Man' and could only see through slits of swollen flesh. Staggering to his feet, he somehow hobbled to the end of the field where a cowhand helped him to Mace Farm. There Mrs Wilson laid him on a bed of spotless linen. He protested, 'I shall spoil it.' Mrs Wilson would not listen but packed her son Alec off to the air raid shelter. Tom was not a fit sight for a nine-year-old boy.

Climbing away from Croydon at full boost, I saw ugly black mushrooms of smoke burgeoning to the south. Biggin Hill had bought it again, the Ops. Room demolished, all the toil and travail of Jock Thomson and his men brought to nothing. When the bombs fell, they decamped to the woods. Wriggling under a barbed wire fence, Jock left part of his trousers behind. People followed Mossy Adams, who was supposed to be lucky. Crouching round a stout tree heads down, they heard WAAFs singing bravely as the bombs crashed. To jointer Sid Sharvill 'it was like hell on earth'.

I had flogged my Hurricane mercilessly during that climb and was then closing in fast on the Me. 110s. The squadron were somewhere behind; that was enough. I did not give them a further thought. Only 'get those ill-mannered bastards' who had disturbed our lunch, smashed our airfield, invaded our sky. When they saw us coming, they went into a defensive circle. No matter, I thought, keep straight on into the middle of them. I had pushed my hood back to watch the Me. 109s better. Down they came, and a violent cut-and-thrust combat followed, which I vaguely felt must end badly for me. Streams of tracer, turn this way; more tracer, turn that way. Then a Me. 109 passed below and turned left, climbing. My favourite shot. Belching black and white smoke, he staggered, slowed up, and rolled over. No time to see more.

More Me. 109s were coming, but by then I had marked out a Me. 110 for execution. But first shoot that Me. 109 out of the way. I fired, it disappeared, that was all. Then another came just below – so close I could see the pilot. An intimate shot – but beyond was a Me. 110, guns winking. So intent was I aiming at the Me. 109 sitting just below, I never realized the Me. 110 was aiming at me.

My thumb was on the firing button, but I never fired. A blast of shot suddenly splattered my Hurricane, my left foot was kicked off the rudder-bar, petrol gushed into the cockpit. The shock was so terrific that for a few instants I lost control and went into a steep dive. 'Christ . . .' I heard myself say quite softly, as if I'd spilt some tea on the drawing-room carpet. Over to the right a Hurricane was going down vertically, etching a black line of smoke across the sky.

Then I straightened out. By some miracle, my Hurricane had not burst into flames. Sitting there in my blue jersey, sleeves rolled up, I had escaped the agony of Tom Gleave, lying on Mrs Wilson's spotless linen, burnt beyond recognition. My windscreen was starred with bullets – how lucky that Dowding had insisted that we be at least as well protected as the gangsters of Chicago.

But I still had to land, and did not fancy the densely wooded country below. So I baled out and watched my poor Hurricane dive into the trees and blow up. A house appeared below and at the back-door two girls were looking up at me. Swinging in my parachute a few hundred feet above their heads, I called to them rather stupidly, 'I say, would you mind giving me a hand when I get down?' For I was rather shaken, there was something in my foot, and I still had to fall into the trees.

I had the same luck as Innes Westmacott. Missing a wood of old oaks by a few yards, I fell with a thump among supple young fir trees. After that mortal combat I felt idiotic sitting on my backside in a wood with a large hole in my shoe. My foot was in a mess, so I lit a cigarette and waited. A man burst from a thicket and levelled his rifle at my head. A policeman ran up. 'Name and address, please,' he asked as if he had caught me speeding. Speeding had yet to come. During the break-neck drive with Mr Sauter through the Kentish lanes to Hawkhurst I spent my most frightening moments since leaving Croydon.

Mr Sauter delivered his prize to Hawkhurst Cottage Hospital, where the doctor looked at my foot: 'I could sew it up, but there might be something in it.' Of that I was convinced; it was beginning to hurt like hell. I was dying of hunger, too, since those Me. 110s had done me out of lunch. A beautiful plate of scrambled eggs was brought. Then they made me lie down and Admiral Harper (a hero of Jutland) came in and soon convinced me that his battle was much more dangerous than mine. 'Just a superficial wound,' he said glancing at my foot, but this didn't stop the throbbing pain.

Tradition required that I be conducted to the Royal Oak. We raised our tankards to the damnation of our enemies. Pyers Worrall came in; he had been shot up from behind and collected some splinters in his thigh. In came a chubby little Australian, in his dark blue RAF uniform. 'Bill Millington,' he said, and a pint was thrust into his hand. He had left his home in Sydney a year before especially to fight this battle. To his sister Eileen he described 31 August as 'a rather epic day. Morale is very high and our tails definitely up.' That morning Bill had been shot down, crash-landing near Folkestone. A police car had delivered him at Biggin Hill by noon, just in time to take off again and get one of *KG* 2's Dorniers before he was once more shot down.

A Bedford truck was waiting to drive us back. Handing me my parachute a policeman told me, 'Hope you don't mind, we put it on show for the Spitfire Fund. Collected a few quid, it did.' A little crowd pressed round our lorry, lovely people, good and warm and solid. They asked for autographs, and it made us feel like champions of the home team. A fragile, old-fashioned lady thrust her grey fabric glove at me, 'I've no paper, but please sign this for my grandson.'

Then the driver let out the clutch and we moved away with a cheer, 'Go it, RAF.' It was their war every bit as much as ours.

The driver was deathly pale and wore a ginger wig. Pyers, Bill, and myself lay on the floor of the lorry wrapped up in our parachutes, shivering as the pain of our wounds became more insistent. Through the glass panel behind the driver's head I watched the ginger wig bobbing up and down.

At 10.00 p.m. I lay in the operating theatre at Croydon General Hospital. The house surgeon, Mr Brayn-Nicholls, bent over me. 'We'll try to save the toe,' he said gravely. A mask was clapped over my face and the wailing air raid siren faded into oblivion. For me the battle was over.

The squadron held out for a few more days. With its two flight commanders and me out of action, Patrick Woods-Scawen took over. That evening he led nine Hurricanes out of the setting sun on to a group of Me. 109s, sending down four.

Led by *Hauptmann* Keller, I *JG* 3 was heading west up the Thames Estuary. When they had come to standby (*Sitsbereitschaft*) that afternoon they could only muster seventeen Me. 109s instead of the normal forty.

Hauptmann Helmut Rau's 1 *Staffel* could contribute only four. He was furious – the *Gruppe* was heading straight into the low sun and he could not see anything. Rau's wing man *Oberleutnant* Loidolt was there, but the other two, *Leutnant* Binder and *Feldwebel* Vollmer, had disappeared in the haze.

Suddenly Keller yelled, '*Achtung*! we're being attacked from the sun.' The next second Helmut Rau was caught up in a dogfight. Loidolt was going down in flames, when Helmut received some 'very noisy hits'. One word leapt to his mind – a word that Goering had forbidden – *verreisen* (home James!). When he pulled his Me. 109 out of a five hundred m.p.h. dive the engine did not answer. Too low to bale, he glided toward the shore of the Estuary. It was low water; Helmut just managed to lift his Me. 109 over a jetty, so close that he could read a notice, 'No trespassing.' Then the Me. 109 dropped 'like a piano from a four storey building' into the mud. The Home Guard was waiting for Helmut.

Not far away after setting a Me. 109 on fire, Ace Hodgson was hit by another's cannon shells. He was half out of the cockpit when Thameshaven oil tanks loomed below. So he climbed back again and just scraped in between a mass of anti-invasion obstacles to land in an Essex meadow.

Both the RAF and the *Luftwaffe* were stretched to the limit of their endurance. 'There were only a few of us,' wrote *Oberleutnant* von Hahn – illness had prevented him from leading I *JG* 3 that day – 'who had not yet had to ditch in the Channel.' And *Leutnant* Helmuth Ostermann said, 'Utter exhaustion from the English operations had set in.' But with the combined weight of its bombers and fighters, the *Luftwaffe* was gradually overpowering Fighter Command.

Eighteen days had elapsed since Eagle Day, but the battle had intensified from those extravagant mass attacks on a broad front to incessant, concentrated assaults at the very approaches to London held by 11 Group.

During the forty-eight hours of 15 and 16 August the *Luftwaffe*'s massive onslaught of 3,500 sorties between the Tyne and Portland was repulsed by 1,750 RAF fighter sorties. The *Luftwaffe* suffered its heaviest losses: 120 against 55 British fighters. 18 August had been a day of bitter fighting; only 950 *Luftwaffe* sorties against 760 of Fighter Command, but it had cost the Germans 71 planes with only 29 fighters down on the British side.

During 30 and 31 August the *Luftwaffe* launched a supreme effort against the sector airfields guarding London, storming them with nearly 2,800 sorties. Never during the whole battle did Fighter Command hurl so many of its fighters against the enemy as in those two white-hot days. And never at greater cost: 2,020 sorties, 65 fighters down. 31 August, when we lost 39 fighters, was the blackest day of all.

Casualties (115 pilots killed and wounded a week) were catastrophic – nearly double the output of the training schools. And the situation was worse than it looked; experienced pilots, killed and wounded, had to be replaced by new men without battle experience. Fighter Command's situation was becoming highly precarious, and the onslaught continued unabated.

Our strength was even sapped from within. On the morning of 1 September, Sergeant Geoff Goodman of 85, with only four guns working, shot down a Me. 109; the air lines to the other four guns had been blocked with matchsticks, sabotaged by some German sympathizer at the depot.

Just before 2.00 p.m. Patrick Woods-Scawen led his last patrol. Disaster overtook 85. Sergeant Booth (a tall quiet youth) jumped with his parachute on fire – to endure months of agony before dying. Ellis (the 'cock-sparrow') was never found. He had joked about his name – Mortimer, 'dead in the sea' – but perhaps he knew in the depths of his young heart that he was going to die like that. The irrepressible Gus Gowers, to whom life was a huge joke, was wounded and badly burnt; they took him in at Caterham Mental Hospital. Despite his agony the thought tickled him: he never expected to finish up in a luny-bin.

Little Patrick, who smiled with his eyes, was the first of the Woods-Scawens to die. A day later it was the turn of his brother, 'Wombat', who was so blind that he apologized to Flight Sergeant Parker for being shot up so often by saying 'I can hardly see anything. But don't breathe a word, or they might whip me off Ops.'

The battle went badly for Fighter Command on 1 September. Two raids hit Biggin Hill. Sergeant Helen Turner and Corporal Elspeth Henderson stuck to their switchboards while around them the Ops. room was reduced to a shambles. In the darkness another WAAF groped among the debris for her knitting; Group Captain Grice refused to leave until he had found his pipe. That day Fighter Command lost 15 planes, the *Luftwaffe* only 14. On 2 September (the day that 'Wombat' died) the *Luftwaffe*, though losing 35 planes was still gaining: 31 British fighters down (the Germans thought 88) and Biggin Hill, North Weald and Debden badly hit.

Detling and Eastchurch were pulverized, but that was effort wasted. They belonged to Coastal Command.

On the morning of 2 September, 85 left for Debden; still sorely depleted of pilots, 111 Squadron returned to take its place at Croydon. Dowding reported: 'Our losses became so heavy that newly arriving squadrons were run down more quickly than resting squadrons could take their place.' On the German side it seemed the British fighters were collapsing. 'There is no longer anything going on over there,' reported Major Walter Grabmann, *Kommandeur* of ZG 76's Me. 110s. And *Jafu* 2 (Theo Oster-kamp) believed that 'unlimited fighter superiority' was already achieved.

Not that the *Luftwaffe* bomber *Geschwader* agreed. Their losses were alarming but they kept on hammering undaunted at London's screen of airfields. On 3 September North Weald was badly knocked about; despite close packing of the escort, other raids were broken up. In the furious fighter-to-fighter combats, 310 Czech Squadron saved Duxford. Sixteen planes were lost on each side. The margin had narrowed to nothing.

The German High Command agreed that the invasion was to be the *coup de grâce*. But the *Luftwaffe* had first to beat Britain to her knees, and quickly. The *Kriegsmarine* was already moving. On 24 August the crucial order had been given for invasion shipping to begin assembling as from 1 September. 16th Army noted the first '*Prahms*' (barges) at Ghent on 27 August. On the 31st, Wing Commander Geoffrey Tuttle's Photographic Reconnaissance Unit reported signs of the gathering. High-flying PRU Spitfires painted pale blue and stripped of guns and other encumbrances had photographed 18 *Prahms* at Ostende. On 1 September photos showed great numbers of them moving to the sea in Belgium's South Beveland and Terneuzen-Ghent canals. The next day, the number at Ostende had risen to 70.

The *Kriegsmarine* early on confirmed its worst fears: 'The enemy's continuous fighting defence of the coast, his concentration of bombers on 'Sea Lion' embarkation ports, his coastal reconnaissance activities, indicate he is now expecting an immediate landing . . . the English bombers . . . are still at full operational strength.' At last, after months of pin-prick raids on the Ruhr, Bomber Command was to weigh directly in the defence of Britain. While Fighter Command secured the base, bombers would sally forth to harass the invaders.

On 3 September (with 1,910 barges, 1,600 escort vessels, 419 tugs and

168 transports requisitioned) OKW directed: 'The earliest date for the invasion fleet's departure has been fixed for 20 September; landing on 21 September. Orders for launching the attack will be given on D-day minus 10, probably 11 September.'

There was no time to lose. The *Luftwaffe* had to hot things up. Goering held a palaver with his chieftains at The Hague. Beppo Schmid was present too. Things had become grim since Goering had told them, exactly a month before, 'The Fuehrer has ordered me to crush Britain with my *Luftwaffe*.' Goering had counted then on a four-day war. Now after four weeks, Britain refused to be crushed. The last hope was to bomb London. Goering was all for it. Deichmann of *Fliegerkorps* II had advised it right from the beginning. The British were sure to throw in all their fighters in defence of the capital, the Me. 109s would round them up and polish them off. Then the bomber *Geschwader* would be able to roam freely without escort.

Deichmann did not reckon with Dowding, who refused to concentrate his fighters around London and leave the rest of the country unprotected. In any case, Hitler's ban on bombing London had scotched the plan. But when it was lifted Kesselring pressed for an all-out attack on the capital. Apart from its value as a target the chances were good that London's morale might crack. So thought Smiling Albert, and he had bombed Warsaw and Rotterdam into submission.

The burning question was: could the Bomber force attack London without too much risk? No problem, maintained Kesselring – the British fighters were practically *kaput*. Sperrle disagreed; the British must still have 1,000 fighters (it was nearer 750, deployed over Britain). Keep hammering at the fighter airfields, insisted Sperrle.

'We'll never destroy their fighters on the ground,' Kesselring argued. Had Beppo Schmid been a better Intelligence Officer he could have told the General, 'It's the control system which counts, and there we've nearly got them.' But Beppo was ignorant of the shattered telephone wires, power cables and Ops. rooms, which had thrown Fighter Command into such disarray. His chiefs knew no better. 'Besides,' said Kesselring, 'if we destroy their airfields south of London they can withdraw to the north, out of range of our escorted bombers.'

Here again the Germans did not reckon with Dowding. 'It was right in the back of my mind,' he said later, 'but I had a kind of blind faith that we could hold on in the south . . . if I had had to withdraw squadrons north of London it would have been difficult to operate them successfully without radar warning over the Channel. There would also have been problems with fighter endurance (fifty-five minutes at full throttle) and ground control.' Kesselring simply did not appreciate the situation. He was a soldier, not a professional airman.

Sperrle suggested: airfields by day, London docks by night. But Kesselring would not listen, and he won the day. The new target was to be London.

That morning the Margate lifeboat picked up a young British pilot, terribly burned, delirious with pain: Richard Hillary. His ancestor Sir William Hillary had founded the Lifeboat Service 110 years before.

With plans for *Zielwechsel* (target switch) in full swing, the Fuehrer had only to put it across. This he did on the afternoon of 4 September at the opening of the *Winterhilfe* (Winter Relief campaign) in the Berlin Sportspalast before a crowd of hysterical matrons. The sarcasm was heavy, the technique well tried: blame the British, incite the Germans to revenge (but already during August the *Luftwaffe* had killed over one thousand British civilians). After the usual jibes at Churchill, Hitler turned to the questions everyone was asking: when will England be invaded? 'England will collapse ... I know no other end than this ... and if people in England today ... are asking: "Why doesn't he come?" I reply: "Don't worry, he is coming." '

What could be done about the RAF raids? 'We are now answering, night for night, and in growing strength ... we will eradicate their cities.' Frenzied applause from the matrons. Hitler concluded, 'The hour will come when one of us will go under, and it will not be National Socialist Germany.'

Listening in to Hitler in Rome, Ciano thought, 'He's getting nervous.'

The next day Hitler ordered 'attacks on the inhabitants and air defences of British cities, including London'. In Germany they waited hourly for news of the invasion. At 43 Dohlerstrasse, Rheydt, Karl Missy was expected home soon. And Karl, in a hospital at Woolwich about ten miles from where I lay, thought, as he heard the bombs falling closer, 'There go my *lieber Kameraden.*' Wounded *Luftwaffe* men who kept arriving always told the same story, 'We shan't be here for long. Invasion's around the corner.'

Chapter 27

By 5 September, damage to 11 Group's airfields was so bad that Park reported it 'greatly reduced the defensive power of our fighter squadrons. The destruction of numerous telephone lines, . . . using emergency sector Ops. Rooms . . . and an almost complete disorganization of the defence system made the control of our fighter squadrons extremely difficult . . . had the enemy continued his heavy attacks against Biggin Hill and the adjacent sectors . . . the fighter defences of London would have been in a perilous state.' Later, Park would accuse bitterly: 'By persistently declining to give fighter cover to my sector aerodromes . . . in late August and early September, No. 12 Group jeopardized our victory in this critical battle.'

On 4 September, a dozen low-flying Ju. 88s had devastated the Vickers factory at Brooklands, killing a hundred civilians and stopping production of Wellington bombers. On 5 September, Park immediately issued a new instruction: 'As the enemy bombing attacks on our fighter aerodromes during the past three weeks have not *outwardly* [author's italics] reduced the fighter defence, he is now directing some of his main attacks against aircraft factories.' Intuitively Park felt the target switch coming, but could not yet guess its full extent.

He ordered special patrols for the three Hawker Hurricane factories, just west of London, and the Supermarine factories at Southampton. 'The Southampton factories are of vital importance to the RAF.' They were the home of the Spitfire.

The main attack, Park reminded his controllers, 'Must be met in maximum strength between the coast and our line of sector aerodromes. Whenever time permits, squadrons are to be put into the battle in pairs,' Spitfires to go for enemy fighters, Hurricanes for the bombers.

'Whenever time permits.' Park had to make the best of what he had got: a score of single-seater squadrons, and a ring of sector (control) airfields closely surrounding London, with numerous subsidiary airfields. Time was his great problem. Rarely was it possible to discern the enemy's intentions until his formations reached the coast – only twenty minutes' flight from the heart of London. And it took all that time for the British fighters to reach twenty thousand feet. Park's squadrons had to be off in a flash, instantly obedient to ground control. He had no choice but to manoeuvre in small units: A squadron or two at the most. 'My overall plan,' he said, 'was to concentrate my fighters in time and space.'

Yet in principle Park entirely agreed with Dowding, who was 'personally in favour of using Fighter formations in the greatest strength tactically desirable'. He had used four squadron 'Wings' at Dunkirk, but then they had time to build up *en route* before meeting the enemy. Now, in Dowding's opinion, there was neither the time nor the means. Dowding and Park were both men with twenty-five years' experience in operating fighters. They knew what they were talking about.

Leigh-Mallory, a new-comer to fighters, had other ideas. And behind them was the tempestuous energy of Douglas Bader. Douglas was certainly inspired by the First World War aces; Leigh-Mallory perhaps by his experience as an Army Co-operation pilot who instinctively had an unholy fear of enemy fighters. Backstage, Leigh-Mallory had a redoubtable supporter in the Deputy Chief of Air Staff, Sholto Douglas. The First War commander of 43 Squadron was a full-blooded fighter pilot. But Sholto believed 'it does not matter where the enemy is shot down as long as he is shot down in large numbers', and later he would confirm that he had 'never been very much in favour . . . of trying to interpose fighter squadrons between enemy bombers and their objectives'. From the commanding height of the Air Ministry, Sholto was able to see both sides. But mentally he was an 'offensive' fighter, like Leigh-Mallory and Douglas Bader.

Dowding and Park were past-masters of defensive fighting, and Sholto's ideas ran slap against their principle of 'forward interception'. In Dowding's words, 'If . . . big Wings had been used at this time, many more bombers would have reached their objectives without opposition.' But Park was even more explicit. 'Had I tried to adopt Bader's theories of the big Wing I would have lost the Battle of Britain.'

Sholto Douglas thought it 'ideal' if Park's squadrons could attack the in-coming bombers, with Leigh-Mallory's Wings harrying them as they retreated. Douglas Bader's idea was exactly the opposite: operating only from 12 Group or the flanks of 11 Group, Wings should take off and gain height as the enemy was 'building up' over France, and then advance in mass to attack them as they crossed the coast. Meanwhile, 11 Group squadrons climbing from forward airfields beneath the fray would tear into the retreating enemy. Bader never thought Wings could operate from 11 Group's forward airfields.

Douglas Bader's theory went further: he wanted control by Fighter Command, by Dowding himself in the last resort. But as Commander-in-Chief, Dowding was far too preoccupied with strategic problems to follow the battle blow by blow. He left that to his Group Commanders. 'Bader's suggestion beats the band,' was Park's comment. 'It would have been impossible for one controller to handle fifty squadrons.'

Keith Park had 'the greatest admiration for Douglas Bader's gallantry'. Dowding also, for Douglas's 'courage and other qualities'. ' . . . Just imagine,' he said, 'to lose both legs and go on flying and fighting in the thick of it and being so damned good at it.' But to neither did Bader's Wing theories appear sound. Dowding was not worried about their originality, but because 'with his qualities of courage and impetuosity' he had persuaded Leigh-Mallory to accept them.

Admittedly, Leigh-Mallory's 12 Group airfields were further back, beyond the range of escorted bombers; he had time to get his Wings off. But Dowding had given clear orders for 12 Group to reinforce 11 Group when called upon, and the stark fact remained that by 31 August 12 Group had three times failed to prevent damaging attacks on 11 Group sector airfields. What was the trouble? The 12 Group Wing was not implicated; it was not yet in existence. Was 11 Group asking for help too late? Douglas Bader had often begged the controller, 'For God's sake, send us off now,' but the reply was always the same, 'Sorry old boy, 11 Group haven't asked for you yet.'

Was 11 Group 'hogging' the battle? Why should they? They had repeatedly asked Brand's 10 Group for help and Brand had never once failed. 10 Group's intervention saved hundreds of casualties in Portsmouth and Southampton. Why had 12 Group not co-operated in the same way? It looked as if Leigh-Mallory was using his squadrons as he himself thought fit, disregarding his C-in-C's orders. 'I can never find it in my heart to blame Bader,' said Dowding later, 'but I did consider him to be an absolute curse in this respect. He got on like a house on fire with Leigh-Mallory and gave him a lot of help and encouragement with his Wing plan.'

Only six months earlier Leigh-Mallory had said to Park that he would 'raise heaven and earth to get Dowding sacked'. He had the ear of Sholto Douglas, hence the Chief of Air Staff and the Air Minister. The conflagration was bound to spread their way.

Meanwhile, by 5 September, the Wing theories had not yet been tried. Douglas Bader had been practising with the Duxford Wing since 1 September. He claimed to have reduced take-off time down to three minutes – the same as a squadron. The rendezvous in the air was reduced to its simplest: he would climb 242 Squadron on a straight course; 310 and 19 Squadrons had only to follow.

Bloody fighting continued above the sector airfields during 5 and 6 September. Back from a rest, Werner Borner was with II *KG* 2 when, at about 10.30 a.m., Biggin Hill was 'thoroughly plastered with *Deutsche Bomben*'. Very heavy AA, he noted, but enemy fighters scarcer. Losses were about even, but bad news came for *Generalfeldmarschall* Milch. That evening *Oberst* Max Ibel (*Kommodore* of *JG* 27) called to say 'Your son-in-law is missing.' *Hauptmann* Joachim Schlichting had baled out of his flaming Me. 109 over the Thames Estuary.

The wheel was about to turn full circle. The accidental bombing of London by *KG* 1 twelve days before had sent RAF bombers speeding to Berlin. That was too much for Hitler. Off came the Fuehrer's ban; London was now fair game. But first, a little softening up: that night picked crews from four *Geschwader* flew up the Estuary to unload sixty tons of bombs on London's docks. With an attack – which failed – the next day on the Hurricane works at Brooklands, the signs were growing: the *Luftwaffe* was easing up on the sector airfields and creeping closer to London.

On 6 September Fighter Command was in a sorry state: six out of 11 Group's seven sector airfields and five of its advanced airfields were seriously damaged. Fighter losses in the previous two weeks exceeded production by nearly two hundred. Reserves were at an all-time low of 127. During August, three hundred pilots had been killed or wounded. The output of new, raw pilots lagged by forty behind the losses. The little company of about a thousand fighter pilots had dwindled by one quarter. But the unarmed citizens of Britain were bearing the brunt of the slaughter: 1,075 during August, among them 355 women and 113 children. Other countries had paid heavily for the monstrous crimes committed in the name of Adolf Hitler, but in vain. A higher price was needed to redeem the liberty of Europe. Britain alone was left in the bidding, and it was bound to cost her dearly. For the second time in twenty-five years the Germans were out to subdue the British with their own Teutonic invention, murder from the sky.

The British remained calm and thought of more homely things. There were complaints that horses, terrified by the bombs, had broken loose, endangering life; there was an urgent need for more iron rings to tie them up. Ardent bird-watchers noticed odd tendencies: pheasants would give their alarm call when the sirens went, but swallows were less affected. They had been seen turning and twittering unconcernedly round a burning aircraft, while four parachutes floated down.

The St Mellons Golf Club amended its rules: 'A ball moved by enemy action may be replaced ... a ball lying in a crater may be dropped ... A player whose stroke is affected by the simultaneous explosion of a bomb ... or by machine gun fire, may play another ball ... penalty one stroke.'

In London itself people swam and boated in Hyde Park's Serpentine. 'What's the score today?' they would ask of the bloody, desperate battle overhead as if it had been a Test match. Within hours the reek of blood and burning would be in their nostrils.

At the Chancellery in Berlin, Admiral Raeder made his final report on the *Kriegsmarine*'s preparations. Everything was going according to plan; mines had been laid in the Hoofden area east of Dover Straits, though mine-sweeping was behind schedule owing to the weather. 'But if air supremacy is increasingly established,' Raeder told the Fuehrer, 'we can be ready.' The crossing, he thought, would be 'very difficult' but possible as long as the *Luftwaffe* could master the air. The Fuehrer was sure they would. 'He is firmly convinced that the defeat of England will be achieved, even without invasion,' the *Grosse-Admiral* noted. And who but the Admiral's favourite enemy could perform such a feat? That evening the train *Asia* puffed to a standstill in the Pas de Calais. Hermann Goering had arrived to take personal command.

That day the PRU Spitfires' photographs revealed the gathering of the invasion fleet: 205 barges at Ostend, 120 at Flushing, an increase of 34 at Dunkirk, 53 at Calais within the previous 48 hours. *Kampfgeschwader* 26 and 30 had joined *Luftflotte* 2 from Norway and von Richthofen's *Stukas* were massed in the Pas de Calais.

Four spies caught after landing at Romney Marshes a few days before confessed their mission: to report information to invasion units. Instead, they went to the gallows. Moon and tide were right for a landing between

8–10 August. All these were threatening signs which led the Chiefs of Staff to signal units: 'Invasion probable within three days.'

That night, while Blenheim bombers assaulted the armada lurking cross Channel, the skies over England were ominously quiet.

There had been a time when the entire *Luftwaffe* swore by Hermann Goering, hero of the First World War. And *unser* Hermann loved to be with his men, who playfully called him *der Dicke* (Fatty). But with the *Grosseinsatz* stumbling badly, Hermann was now on the verge of nervous exhaustion. Even Hitler jibed, 'You have apparently shot down more aircraft than the British ever possessed.' And Goering's arch enemy Goebbels had to help the *Luftwaffe* with propaganda victories, or simply by vilifying the RAF. The little Doctor was behind Hitler's 'We'll eradicate their cities' speech which, said a staff report, 'eased the task of the *Luftwaffe*; it cleared the way for night attacks in every respect'.

Goering was back to his bad old habits, living on drugs. His 'needle-woman' (Christa Gormanns), constantly at his side, had been supplemented by a *Luftwaffe* doctor, Ondarza. Goering felt listless; only the Fuehrer's telephone calls could shake him out of his lethargy. 'We knew when he was talking to Hitler,' said an officer. 'He acted as if the Fuehrer was standing in front of him.' Goering would bow and cringe to the harsh voice from the other end of the line.

But when the attack on London – code-named *Loge* after the god who forged Siegfried's sword – was all lined up, Goering felt better. The clamps were off London; at last the way was clear for Hermann to 'force this enemy to his knees', as he had promised over a month before. The *Luftwaffe* had never failed at the job. Guernica had been the 'testing ground'. (A pity, but there was nowhere else, said Hermann.) Vienna and Prague had succumbed to the mere threat. The vicious attacks on Warsaw and Rotterdam had produced immediate surrender. Paris never had any stomach for Nazi bombs.

And now the *Luftwaffe* was bombed up for London – with more than five times the bomb load which tore the heart out of Rotterdam. If they had failed to settle with the British at Dunkirk, it was because, dispersed on the beach, soldiers were difficult targets and disciplined under fire. But there was the East End of London: plenty of the bombs aimed at the docks would fall on Londoners themselves. Civilians – women and children – would never stand up under the hundreds of tons of bombs that Hermann Goering had in store for them. He cheered up at the idea.

The *Luftwaffe* would lay waste to the greatest city in the world and bring the British to heel. With *Loge*'s shining sword, Siegfried would win the war single-handed.

On 7 September, Goering felt more optimistic than he had for weeks, even if certain people were making cheap jokes behind his back. *Der Dicke* – he liked that; but 'the Pasha', 'Nero' were not so kind. Those two unruly airmen Junck and Osterkamp were a bore, too. They openly made fun of his orders to set up their command posts as far forward as possible. He overheard Junck, 'Well, Osterkamp, what about your advanced HQ? You can always try to beat mine. It's so advanced that at low tide I'm up to my knees in water; at high tide I'm up to my eyes, but still facing the enemy!' On the door of Osterkamp's HQ at Cap Blanc Nez was the legend, 'We should only give orders to others when we mean to lose the war.' 'Osterkamp,' said Hermann sternly, 'that must come down.'

Until then, Adolf Galland had been as disillusioned as those two old eagles; he was utterly fed up with Goering's attitude towards the *Jäger*. During a visit on about 2 September, Goering had 'nothing but reproaches . . . he expressed his dissatisfaction in the harshest terms'. Goering took the bombers' side and demanded 'close and rigid protection'. Galland remonstrated, 'The Me. 109 . . . is not so suitable for purely defensive purposes as the Spitfire.' But Goering continued to rail. Then as the time came to leave, he grew more amiable. What could he do to help matters? Moelders asked for more powerful engines. 'And you?' Goering turned to Galland, who did not hesitate. 'I should like an outfit of Spitfires for my *Jagdgeschwader*.' Goering was speechless. 'He stamped off, growling as he went.'

After that stormy meeting at The Hague with the *Luftflotten* commanders, Goering was back (apparently in good form) and *Loge* was ready to go. Two *Fliegerkorps* (I and II) formed the attacking force. *Fliegerkorps* I's commander, General *Oberst* Ulrich Grauert a few weeks earlier had produced a four-page paper, *Thoughts on a War Against England*. Among other things, Grauert had recommended 'strangling' England by destroying harbours, and 'ruthless terror attacks as reprisals against big cities'. The actual attack would be a judicious mixture of the two.*

Fliegerkorps I's operations order detailed three waves to be over the target at (British Time) 5.00 p.m., 5.40 p.m., and 5.45 p.m. (Many thought morning the best time, to make use of the sun, but the fire of evening attack would provide guiding beacons for the night bombers.) The purpose of the initial wave was to get the British fighters up, so

---

*Grauert was shot down and killed in May 1941.

that by the time the two last waves came in they would be out of petrol. (This showed a naïve understanding of the way Dowding and Park ran their end of the business.)

Each bomber *Geschwader* would have one *Jagdgeschwader* as escort (it was a bit thin; they would have liked more).

The three waves were to cross the coast between Cap Gris Nez and Boulogne to the south. (Annoying for Goering, watching from Cap Gris Nez with the sun in his eyes.)

'It is essential that direct courses be flown.' (No fooling around on the way – that had too often ended with the wretched Me. 109s having to ditch in the Channel.)

'It is essential that units fly as a highly concentrated force'; bombers would thus fly at staggered heights between fifteen and twenty thousand feet.

Galland felt better, now that the *Mahallas* were assembling over the Channel coast. 'When . . . this air force, never before seen in such strength, set course for London, each of the participants felt the importance of the hour.' 378 bombers, 645 fighters – over 1,000 aircraft. Had not Goering sworn to Felmy two years before that 'The sky will darken over London.'

Nearly 500 tons of bombs! And curiously enough, it was exactly twenty-five years before (less one day) that the Germans first raided London. The resolute *Kapitänleutnant* Heinrich Mathy in Zeppelin L13, had then delivered half a ton of bombs, which caused 'widespread damage'. Since then, the Germans had come a long way.

The creator of this means of mass slaughter was at that moment rubber-necking at Cap Gris Nez surrounded by Kesselring, Loerzer and other top brass. He cut a grotesque figure, in his pale blue uniform, festooned with medals, pinkish top-boots and spurs. By then recovered from his wounds, Hans-Heinrich Brustellin (who had served with the cavalry during Black *Luftwaffe* days) raised his eyebrows when the *Reichsmarschall* waddled past, sucking the end of his jewel-studded baton.

As the *Mahallas* thundered northwards to London, Goering was jubilant. This was his hour of triumph; '*wir fliegen gegen England!*' exulted the German radio, with running commentaries from its on-the-spot reporters. And the German people caught the mood. Little did they dream what a terrible whirlwind they would reap.

Considering Hitler's blood-curdling threat against British cities, it was extraordinary that no special measures had been taken to protect London. Park sensed that the *Luftwaffe*, evidently unaware that the assault against

sector airfields had brought 11 Group to the verge of collapse, was beginning to strike at new targets – aircraft factories and London docks. But he
dared not lower his guard; those airfields must be defended at all costs, or
the game was up.

That morning Park remarked tartly in a new instruction that the heights
given by the Group Controller were being increased 1,000 or 2,000 feet,
first by the Sector Controller 'in his superior knowledge', then by the
Squadron leader 'in the vain hope that they will not have any enemy
fighters above them'. Result: many enemy bomber raids had slipped in
unnoticed below.

No one in Goering's vast armada ever thought he would slip by
unnoticed. But the incredible happened. 11 Group waited as usual for the
mass of plots to split into separate raids on crossing the coast, but they
didn't. They kept on solidly, inexorably. *KG* 30 checked position over
Sevenoaks and began its run up to the target. Its object was 'to force the
British fighters into the air', but there wasn't a fighter in sight. *KG* 1
followed, running up from Riverhead. Then *KG* 76 from Westerham,
challenged only by stray fighters as they steered straight for the familiar
U-bend in the Thames, the heart of Dockland.

'Keith Park was adept at sensing the Germans' most likely methods of
attacking and directing his controllers,' said one of them, Wing Commander Willoughby de Broke. 'He would leave it to us to "set the stage,
then review the situation and make the necessary changes".' But that
evening, the Commander of 11 Group was not in his Ops. Room to
manoeuvre his squadrons. He was in conference with his C-in-C at
Fighter Command.

Park had laid plans carefully to protect his battered sector airfields, and
that evening in readiness for a new assault his squadrons were patrolling
well back from the south coast. Advancing from the south, *Fliegerkorps* I
found the road to London clear. Their orders were to steer directly to
London, no feints, no diversions. Without either, they had completely
outflanked the enemy. Bombs were deluging on the Millwall and
Commercial Docks, on Silvertown, Tilbury and Thameshaven before
11 Group recovered from its surprise and counter-attacked. From Northolt
a 'pair' (1 and 303 [Polish] Squadrons) had climbed straight to 24,000 feet.
To 12 Group came a call for help; Douglas Bader led 242 Squadron away
from Duxford followed by 19 and 310 (Czech) squadrons, both of the
Duxford Wing. And 43 Squadron, due to stand down that afternoon, was
ordered off from Tangmere in a desperate attempt to catch the bombers
before they reached London.

The *Kampfgeschwader* of *Fliegerkorps* II did not have such a quiet ride. *KG* 2 was one of them, and for Werner Borner it was one of the most eventful days of the Battle of Britain. *KG* 2 was to attack the Victoria and the Albert Docks, east of the U-bend. From the French coast Werner could see the enormous black cloud of smoke which had been pouring from Thameshaven oil tanks since the day before and now rose three miles into the sky. *Nach London!* Navigation was superfluous. And Borner and his *kamaraden* felt good with all those Me. 109s wheeling around them.

In the distance over London white smudges of AA fire and contrails furrowing the sky told of wild air battles. Now *KG* 2's own escort was repulsing the British fighters and Werner saw them drawing further and further away. AA began to rock the *Gruppe* formation – first the Medway guns, then the batteries of the London inner artillery zone. The bombers' rule was always 'open up for AA, close in for fighters'. Now that there were both the Dorniers dared not spread too much nor get too close. Aircraft were going down all around; some of *KG* 2's own Dorniers dropped behind, certain prey for enemy fighters. And a fighter which came within range of the formation 'was welcomed with all the bullets we could fire'. It was impossible to tell friend from foe. Werner saw below a chaos of fires, smoke, and bomb explosions. At 15,000 feet they were flying through the black smoke cloud. At last the Albert Dock and the Victoria Dock beyond. *KG* 2's bombs went down, 'on the exact spot'. Then the Dorniers wheeled right and turned back for France. The Me. 109 escort had disappeared, no doubt short of fuel and ammunition. It was to be a rough ride home.

Led by Caesar Hull, nine Hurricanes of 43 Squadron closed in on the Heinkels of *KG* 1 as they ran up to bomb Dockland. Since taking command a week before, Caesar had not even managed to have the 'scraper ring' sewn on to his tunic. 43 had been fighting ceaselessly and that afternoon it was its turn to stand down. But the weary pilots did not think of that; the Heinkels appeared and leading the rear section Flight Lieutenant John Kilmartin heard Caesar's husky voice, 'Killy, do what you can to upset the fighters.' Three Hurricanes against a *Jagdgeschwader* (Hannes Trautloft's *JG* 54). The remaining six fought against one of *KG* 1's 3 *Gruppen*. Then Killy 'heard his chuckle as he told us to sail in and smash 'em'. No more was ever heard from the gay and gallant Caesar, symbol of 43's invincibility.

303 Squadron's Hurricanes were diving in one line, all guns blazing.

'We gave them all we'd got,' said their British squadron leader, Ronald Kellett, 'only breaking away when we could see the enemy completely filling the gunsight.' Ten Dorniers succumbed to the Poles' avenging fury. But their leader, Krasnodebski, was not there. Shot down the day before, he lay that moment between life and death, his body flayed by fire.

'Hello, Douglas,' came the calm voice of Group Captain Woodhall, Duxford station commander. 'Seventy plus crossing the Thames east of London.' Ordered to patrol at 10,000 feet, Douglas Bader had done the forbidden – added another 5,000 feet. Even then, 242 was still well below the Dorniers and Me. 110s – probably *Zerstörer Gruppe* 76, ordered to 'clear the air' over London (hardly the job for cumbersome Me. 110s).

Bader looked round for the rest of the Duxford Wing. But 19 and 310 Squadrons were straggling below and behind. Lieutenant Dickie Cork, Royal Navy, was the only 19 Squadron pilot anywhere near. The mariner must have clapped on all available sail, for normally the Spitfire had not the climb of a Hurricane. So there was Douglas with no Wing and no height. His Wing tactics – the hard hitting, mass dive into the midst of the enemy – were not for that day. The rest of his Wing never caught up, but aided by the redoubtable sailor, Bader's own squadron hit the Germans hard. A good day for 242, but not a brilliant début for the Duxford Wing.

'If only we could get off earlier,' Bader pleaded with Leigh-Mallory. 'It's 11 Group's decision,' replied Leigh-Mallory. 'They feel they should wait until the Germans start moving in. That doesn't give them much chance to scramble big formations.' Leigh-Mallory understood 11 Group's problems; the root of all the trouble was his stubborn insistence (against Dowding's wishes) on using the Wing; a Wing was bound to get off more slowly than a squadron.

In Whitehall, the Chiefs of Staff had begun their meeting at 5.20 p.m. Less than half an hour later they were startled by the crash of bombs from down-river. More than three months earlier, as the Dunkirk evacuation started, they had advised the Prime Minister, 'While our Air Force is in being, our Navy and Air Force should be able to prevent Germany carrying out a serious seaborne invasion . . . The crux of the matter is air superiority.'

Air superiority. Well, we still held it – just. But a mass attack on London itself – coming on top of all the other signs – this could very well be judged a prelude to invasion. The Chiefs of Staff decided to order a state of 'immediate action' for the Army's Eastern and Southern commands.

Having made for Northolt after his conference at Fighter Command, Keith Park climbed away over London in his Hurricane. He looked down on the conflagration. 'Now London is taking it,' he thought, 'we shall be saved.' As long as the great city drew the enemy's fire, Fighter Command would have a chance to repair its shattered communications and restore its ruined Ops. Rooms.

Mr J. J. Cotterell of the Auxiliary Fire Service was enjoying his first day of annual leave in his garden near Forest Hill Fire Station. When the sirens went he took no notice. Then came a bedlam of bombs and machine-gun fire, and huge columns of smoke on the north side of the river. Not even his wife's pleas, 'Don't go, you're on leave,' could hold Cotterell. He jumped on his bike and set off for the fire station. His crew was dispatched immediately with a taxi-towed trailer pump to the Siemens Works at Woolwich. Pasted in Berlin by the RAF and in London by the *Luftwaffe* Siemens was out of luck. Scores of other pumps were there and at first the men ducked or lay flat on their faces as the bombs whistled down. But soon they ignored them and worked on steadily.

Then Cotterell and his crew were moved to the Surrey Docks. 'That was really something, whacking great stacks of timber, a real go, that was,' he said. And though he did not yet know it, they would be toiling there all night.

Constable Ernest Hooper of Catford Police Station said, 'We just carried on as usual, only there was more to do. We got used to it.' For Constable Hooper incidents were either 'routine' or 'bad'. The worst he would ever see was the school at Ardgowan Road, Hither Green – a direct hit which brought the building down in flames. Fifty children were inside it. 'The carnage was indescribable. There were children lying all over the playground, some dismembered, some partially buried, some simply blown to pieces' – children just a little older than Hermann Goering's pretty little Edda. Hooper noticed that 'one little girl was crying all the time because she had blood in her eyes and couldn't see. She had nothing left to see with.'

At Cap Gris Nez, Goering was called to the telephone. Frau Emmy was on the line. 'You've heard already, Emmy? Yes, it has been a wonderful day, Emmy. I've sent my bombers to London; London's in flames.'

Goering was beside himself and Kesselring felt embarrassed when he seized the microphone from a radio reporter and blurted out to German listeners, '*es um historischen Augenblick geht*' (this is a historical moment). After all the attacks on Berlin these last nights, the Fuehrer decided to order *einen gewaltigen Vergeltungschlag*, a monster reprisal against the capital of the British Empire.

'I personally have taken command of the attack . . . and have heard the roar of victorious German squadrons, which have for the first time struck the enemy right to the heart.' Goering was convinced that the attack succeeded in achieving its purpose. Events would soon prove how wrong he was.

On 6 September victory was within the *Luftwaffe*'s grasp. The previous two weeks' offensive on airfields had cost Fighter Command 295 fighters (daily average 21) and 103 pilots killed (over 7 daily), with 170 fighters badly damaged, 128 pilots wounded. During the following three weeks' offensive (to 27 September) on London and air factories, RAF losses dropped off sharply: 199 fighters (9·5 daily) and 95 pilots killed (4·5 daily).

During those two desperate, bloody weeks of the airfields offensive the *Luftwaffe* was never nearer to defeating Fighter Command even though Dowding's squadrons themselves were making unprecedented slaughter among the *Luftwaffe*: 378 aircraft, 27 daily. But British fighter and pilot losses were not the whole story; the appalling damage to Ops. Rooms and communications nearly paralysed the control system. Had the *Luftwaffe* airfields offensive continued, Park said, 'the fighter defence of London would have been in a perilous state'. And for General Theo Osterkamp (*Jafu* 2) 'It was with tears of rage and dismay that, on the very point of victory, I saw the decisive battle against the British fighters stopped for the benefit of attacking London.'

Goering had made another blunder: first he had ceased bombing the radar stations, then believing he could crush the spirit of London, he had turned from the sector airfields.

Throughout that night 247 bombers kept up the attack, hurling their loads into the raging fires – no need to bother much about aiming. *Hauptmann* Hajo Hermann was over London in his Ju. 88: 'A very clear night . . . everywhere the German bombers were swarming in . . . Everything was lit up by fires, like a huge torch in the night.' Until 7

September orders were very strict not to bomb indiscriminately. 'But now, for the first time, we were allowed to bomb regardless.'

The *Voelkischer Beobachter* of 8 September blared: 'Last night the enemy again attacked the Reich capital ... therefore the *Luftwaffe* has started to attack the city of London with strong forces.' Goering's men killed about a thousand Londoners, about twice as many as the RAF pilots killed during the whole Battle of Britain. As a disciple of Douhet, Goering could congratulate himself on his improvement of *Kapitänleutnant* Mathy's old fashioned methods.

But beating hell out of the civil population was not going to win air superiority. 'Goering should certainly have persevered against the airfields on whose organization and combination the whole fighting power of our air force at this moment depended. By departing from the classical principles of war, as well as from the hitherto accepted dictates of humanity, he made a foolish mistake.' That was the opinion of Prime Minister Winston Churchill.

But Goering believed he was doing fine, and OKL boosted his optimism with a report of 98 British aircraft down. 25 was the real figure, while the *Luftwaffe* Quarter-Master General wrote off 41 German planes and wondered how with production slipping badly he was ever going to replace such losses. Even Goebbels's news bulletin admitted 'heavy sacrifices'.

Goering was not unduly worried – London had to go under, like Rotterdam and Warsaw. The Japanese military attaché in London reported 'the good effect of the German air attacks', and splendid news was on the way from the Reich's own military attaché in Washington, General Friedrich von Boettischer: 'The morale of the British population is strongly affected. Signs of great weariness. Optimism has disappeared. Effect in the heart of London like an earthquake. Great damage to public utility services.' Even Hitler seriously believed a revolution would break out in England.

Goering warmed to his task of destruction. He had carved London up into two sections: 'A' section being the East End and the docks, 'B' section West London. The *Luftwaffe* had so successfully plastered the East End that now he ordered the treatment to be extended to the West End, with its railway termini and power stations. For this type of wholesale destruction bigger bombs and four-engined bombers were needed – but Goering had cancelled the four-engine bomber programme in 1937 ...

Chapter 28

Dowding heaved a sigh of relief when he saw the *Luftwaffe* veer away from sector airfields on 7 September. That day he lost nineteen pilots out of twenty-eight shot down. It seems an infinitesimal loss compared with the thousand Londoners who died in that fearful massacre, but by then Dowding's squadrons in the battle zone were being decimated at such a rate that he could not even maintain standing patrols over convoys.

On 8 September, as Goering separated London into sections A and B, Dowding too decided to label his squadrons A, B and C in a 'stabilization scheme'. Category A squadrons were to remain in 11 Group and on its flanks; B formed a small operational reserve; C squadrons, based away from the main battle, were the 'nursery' which provided pilots for the front. Some felt it was a slight on the C squadron, of which 85 became one, which were considered unfit to do battle at the front. But we did not feel insulted; we were in excellent company with 43, 54, 111 and many other of the most doughty fighting units. Like them, we had been in the South for three months or more and fought through the most murderous phase of the Battle at heavy loss. Our morale was high, and we knew that much more would soon be expected of us. We were not sensitive about being in Category C.

Only Dowding's immense strength of purpose enabled him to keep such a firm control of the battle at this moment. His fighter force had stared defeat in the face. By a miracle it now seemed the situation could be retrieved. But the salvation of Britain still rested precariously in his hands. The battle was not yet won; the fighting of it demanded all his energy and time. And more, a terrible inner struggle to vindicate himself before the hostile forces conspiring against him. Patiently, stubbornly he refused to bow to them. This was his battle and he meant to run it his way.

The *Luftwaffe* C-in-C's enthusiasm for personal command was apparently short-lived. That day, 8 September, Goering went picnicking with Jeschonnek at Dunkirk, while fifteen of his aircraft were shot down in fruitless attacks on south-east England. And the strain eased on Fighter Command – only two fighters were lost.

But London again suffered grievously during the night. An OKL report spoke of an attack which started fifteen to twenty fires in the West part of the city. 'Centre of effort: Kensington, Buckingham Palace, West Ham.' This hardly tied up with the *Voelkischer Beobachter* of 9 September: 'The attacks of our *Luftwaffe* against important military and economic targets were continued with strong forces and the heaviest bombs . . .' The Germans killed 412 of London's citizens that night.

When the *Luftwaffe* returned to the assault on London in the late afternoon of 9 September, nine of Park's squadrons were ready for them. 'The sky was full of roundels,' said *JG* 54's *Kommodore*, Hannes Trautloft. 'For the first time we had the feeling we were outnumbered.' And the bombers, surprised by a defence they thought was moribund, blamed their fighter escort. The first bomber raid was repulsed over Canterbury; but another was forging inland from Beachy Head. From 10 Group Park called for reinforcements to cover the Hawker and Vickers aircraft factories and more from 12 Group to patrol sector airfields north of London.

'Hello, Douglas' – it was Woodhall calling Bader, leading the Duxford Wing. 'Will you patrol between North Weald and Hornchurch, Angels 20?' (20,000.) But Douglas thought of the sun. He 'forgot' North Weald–Hornchurch and climbed to twenty-two thousand feet. Then distant glints in the sky grew into two great swarms of bombers. He called to 19 Squadron to climb higher; their Spitfires must cover the Hurricanes of 242 and 310 Squadrons. Then to the Hurricanes, 'Line astern, we're going through the middle,' and down they went.

Split wide-open short of their targets, the enemy bombers showered a hundred tons of bombs far and wide over the southern suburbs. This time the Wing had brought it off, although their claim of twenty destroyed looked a bit optimistic: the *Luftwaffe* lost twenty-eight all told, which left only eight to the other nine fighter squadrons engaged.

When Douglas first sighted the bombers he thought, 'Just as well I ignored controller's orders to patrol North Weald–Hornchurch.' No one could argue with the result. But to Dowding and Park it was rank disobedience. Now Douglas wanted to do better. To Leigh-Mallory he said, 'If we'd only had more fighters we could have hacked the Huns down in scores.' Leigh-Mallory promised him two more squadrons - a wing of 60 fighters.

'London witnesses a morning of terror after 9½ hours of air raid,' announced the *Voelkischer Beobachter* on the morning of 10 September. The night before, the *Luftwaffe* had slain 370 Londoners and injured 1,400. For the third night, total casualties exceeded 1,700.

Fighter Command's impotence against the night bomber left London wide open to attack. But for all the slaughter, *Kriegsmarine* saw the bare truth: their diarist noted on 10 September: 'No sign of defeat of the enemy's air force.' In spite of 'considerable German fighter superiority' the *Luftwaffe* 'have not yet attained ... operational conditions ... essential to the enterprise (invasion) – undisputed air supremacy in the Channel area and elimination of enemy air activity in assembly area of German naval forces'. It would help 'Sea Lion' 'if the *Luftwaffe* now concentrated less on London, more on Portsmouth, Dover and other naval ports'.

But, added the naval scribe sanctimoniously (considering the sailors' real feelings about Goering's 'absolute air war'), 'the Naval Staff do not consider this a suitable moment to approach the *Luftwaffe* ... as the Fuehrer thinks the major attack on London may be decisive, and ... render "Sea Lion" superfluous.'

The Fuehrer was in two minds. On the one hand, like Raeder he accepted the cold facts: the RAF had given the *Luftwaffe* a hard time of it yesterday; and RAF bombers and minelayers were actively hindering the assembly of the invasion fleet. On the other hand, if Goering's enthusiastic accounts could be believed, London looked like cracking. The *Luftwaffe* might do it alone. It was Hitler's as much as Raeder's fervent hope. He hesitated at the decision on 'Sea Lion' as much as Raeder funked the actual job. And now the day for decision was at hand. It was supposed to be for tomorrow, 11 September. As Raeder needed ten days' notice, invasion could start on 21 September. But moon and tide made 24 September a better day. All things considered, Hitler put back the fatal decision to 14 September. Let the *Luftwaffe* keep trying; everything depended on them.

Winston Churchill 'never thought of the struggle in terms of the defence of London or any other place, but only who won in the air'. On 11 September he told the British, 'This effort of the Germans to secure daylight mastery of the air over England is, or course, the crux of the whole war.'

Churchill had fewer qualms over invasion than the Fuehrer. 'For him to try and invade this country without having secured mastery of the air,' Churchill continued, 'would be a very hazardous undertaking. Nevertheless, all his preparations for invasion on a great scale are going forward . . . there are now considerable gatherings of shipping in the . . . harbours – all the way from Hamburg to Brest. Behind . . . there stand large numbers of German troops awaiting the order to . . . set out on their very dangerous and uncertain voyage . . . no one should blind himself to the fact that a heavy full-scale invasion of this island is being prepared with all the German thoroughness.

'It does not seem it can be long delayed . . . we must regard this week as a very important period of our history. It ranks with the days when the Spanish Armada was approaching . . . or when Nelson stood between us and Napoleon's Grand Army at Boulogne.'

The German High Command were surprised that the RAF were still holding out, considering all the optimistic reports being put out by OKL and its Chief. But the air battle that day reassured them. A hundred bombers got through to London; the Supermarine factory at Southampton was hit, with heavy loss of life, and the RAF were outfought. Although OKL believed they had destroyed fifty-six RAF fighters the real number, twenty-nine, was still four more than the *Luftwaffe*'s loss.

Hope rose again in Berlin, but not on the banks of the River Spree, at *Kriegsmarine* HQ. The sailors got in a crack at the *Luftwaffe* behind the Fuehrer's back. A couple of days before, when he was intent on London, they went along with him. But now on 12 September, they complained that, 'the air war is being conducted as an absolute air war without regard to the present requirements of naval war and outside the framework of "Sea Lion". In its present form the air war cannot assist preparations for "Sea Lion".' That sounded pretty hollow, considering *Kreigsmarine*'s lack of enthusiasm for invasion. But they had a genuine cause for anxiety at the *Luftwaffe*'s neglect to attack units of the British Fleet, 'which are now able to operate almost unmolested in the Channel . . .' That day, in fact, HQ Naval Group West at Paris had reported, 'Interference caused by the enemy air force, long-range artillery and light naval forces have, for the first time, assumed capital importance.' Ostend, Dunkirk, Calais and Boulogne were completely unsafe as night anchorages.

At the back of Britain's spirited resistance was the fact that London still held firm. Fortunately, bad weather brought Londoners a much needed respite during the day and night of 12 September.

No one appreciated it more than *Unteroffizier* Karl Missy who, in his hospital bed at Woolwich, was a helpless target for the bombs of his *lieber Kameraden*. They hit Woolwich Arsenal close by, and bombs rained down on the docks across the river.

When the sirens went, each prisoner was given three cigarettes. They smoked one at every warning, but lately they were always short of cigarettes. The sirens went all day and above the din of the bombardment they could hear aircraft diving to destruction. Bomber, fighter, Me. 109 or Spitfire – they could tell by the screaming engine note.

Still more prisoners kept arriving. Missy met up with some friends of his old unit, *KG 26*, heavily hit the day before. The idea of bombing the Port of London, they said, was to block it with sunken ships and make it useless. And as always, invasion was for any moment now; Hitler would soon be in London, then they would be free.

'Lying in bed with the risk of being killed by our own bombs was not pleasant,' said Karl Missy. 'I knew how effective German bombs could be; if they hit us there would not be much left.' During the lulls Karl and his friends would ask, with forced grim humour, 'Why aren't they coming? Surely there must still be some left.' And as time went on Karl Missy got used to being afraid.

Not so the hospital guard. At the first wailing of the sirens, about fifty soldiers entered the ward; one man stood at the end of each prisoner's bed. As the bombs crashed closer, some of the guards would dive under the bed. Karl would then lean over and ask, 'How are you, there below?' and a string of oaths would come up from under the bed. Meanwhile the orderlies had disappeared into the cellars below. Only the nurses remained.

It was the same at Croydon General Hospital, where I lay, ten miles away from Karl Missy. The bombs did not fall so thickly there, but we had our share. Stuck in bed, unable to walk, I was terrified. The nurses, always superbly calm, would pull our beds away from the windows – just as well, for some were shattered by bomb splinters. And these girls came and held

o

our hands and told us not to be afraid – us, who were supposed to be the aces and the heroes. The roles were reversed in hospital.

Pyers Worrall, Bill Millington and I whiled away our time alone in a big ward. Bill wrote to his sister Eileen in Sydney, 'I can recommend the hospital . . . the nurses are terrific. Most of the splinters in my thigh were removed. The rest will eventually work out.' Bill's letter would not reach his sister until he had left the hospital, climbing back into his Spitfire, never to return. There came another letter too, written back in June:

My dear Parents,

I have asked Miss Macdonald of the Isles, who has been a particularly good friend to me, to forward this short note . . . the possibility of a hasty departure from this life is ever present . . . I go forth into battle light of heart and determined to do my bit for the noble cause for which my country is fighting. Having studied the subject from all angles I am certain that freedom and democracy will eventually prove victorious.

Being British I am proud of my country and its peoples, proud to serve under the Union Jack and regard it as an Englishman's privilege to fight for all those things that make life worth living – freedom, honour and fair play.

For any sorrow or suffering I may have caused I sincerely apologize, but please do not grieve over my passing . . . Flying has meant more than a means of livelihood . . . the companionship of men and boys with similar interests, the intoxication of speed, the rush of air, and the pulsating beat of the motor awakes some answering cord deep down, which is indescribable.

Farewell,

Your loving son,
Bill

Chapter 29

Before lunch, on 13 September, the Fuehrer was closeted in the Chancellery's sombrely lit *Arbeitszimmer* with *Reichsmarschall* Goering. Hitler was in a spot; time was running out and he had to make a decision on invasion. The entire nation was waiting for it. Goebbels had publicly fixed a date for victory day, and the radio, blaring at all hours of the day, *'wir fliegen gegen England'* and *'Bomben auf En-ge-land'* had put the public in a fever of expectancy. The C-in-C, Brauchitsch, touring Army invasion units on 10 September, found his soldiers rearing to go; sailors of the *Kreigsmarine* stood by, ready to sail. Yet Hitler waited. Not for anybody would he risk failure; that would be fatal to Germany's prestige. He longed for deliverance from his awful quandary: to invade? or not to invade?

Now Goering spoke. The Fuehrer could leave everything to him. The RAF had only about fifty Spitfires left. England was obviously badly hurt. The bombing of London had produced a terrific effect. The proof was there; all the AA was concentrated in the city. British nerves were at cracking point. The weather as usual had fouled things up, but four or five more days, and the *Luftwaffe* would do it.

Had Goering given more time to the 'personal command' he had so proudly assumed, and less to picnicking in Dunkirk and shopping in Paris, he would not have told such rosy tales. As it was, he revived the Fuehrer's spirits and bolstered up his hopes of a rapid British collapse. Hitler and Goering were in great heart when they went into lunch, which was being given in honour of the new *Generalobersten*. Twenty of them sat down at the round table in the great red-carpeted dining-room, with its red marble pillars and white walls.

To this august assembly, dominated by a huge painting of Aurora in the clouds, Adolf Hitler, according to Halder, 'expressed himself most optimistically ... in the present favourable [air] situation he would not think of taking such a great risk as to land in England'. Jodl had the impression that the Fuehrer had decided to abandon 'Sea Lion' altogether.

Everything, then, was up to Goering. But the *Luftwaffe* eagle only pecked at England that day, with attacks by single raiders on targets like Buckingham Palace, Downing Street and Chelsea Hospital – not that this could do anything but harden British resistance. In the air, losses on both sides were negligible. But that night, while shipping at Ostend, Boulogne, Dunkirk and Calais was being shelled by the Royal Navy, the RAF bomber force lashed out at full strength and sank eighty barges at Ostend.

That evening, Douglas Bader celebrated. Leigh-Mallory had telephoned to congratulate him on winning the Distinguished Service Order and added, 'two more squadrons, 302 and 661, will be joining your Wing tomorrow'. That meant more to Bader than the medal.

If Goering knew how to calm his Fuehrer, Raeder, with his contempt for the *Luftwaffe* Chief and his healthy respect for the British Navy, had the opposite effect. Raeder was absent from the luncheon on 13 September when Hitler had cast 'Sea Lion' overboard in an effusion of high spirits about the air war. Now, the admiral was about to break the spell that Goering had cast on his bemused Fuehrer.

At 3.00 p.m. on 14 September, Hitler met Raeder, Brauchitsch and Jeschonnek (Goering had escaped back to the Pas de Calais). Just before the meeting Raeder slipped a memorandum under the Fuehrer's nose. It started, 'The present air situation does not allow the undertaking of Operation "Sea Lion".' That implied that the *Luftwaffe* were not doing as well as Goering's rosy tales had suggested. 'Meanwhile,' continued the Admiral, 'it is indispensable that "Sea Lion" should not be abandoned.'

The Fuehrer was once again in a dilemma. The invasion he had so cheerfully dropped the day before now reappeared. Halder noted the Fuehrer's words: 'A successful landing followed by occupation would end the war.' There was apparently no need to rush things, but 'a long war is not desirable'. In other words, Britain must be completely overwhelmed – and the chances had improved. 'The hopes Britain placed on Russian support had not materialized; American rearmament will not be fully effective until 1945.'

By all appearances Britain was a sitting duck. Hitler continued: 'The quickest answer would be to land in England. The *Kreigsmarine* is ready (this must have sent a chill down Raeder's spine); coastal artillery is in position; the *Luftwaffe*'s performance is above all praise. Four or five days of clear weather . . . and we have a good chance of forcing England to her knees. The effect so far is terrific, but total victory needs those four or five days of fine weather. All AA defences are massed in London. The enemy is badly hurt.' Thus the Fuehrer parroted Goering's homily.

But there was one horrible snag. 'The enemy keeps on coming back. Enemy fighters are not yet eliminated; our own reports of success do not give an entirely reliable picture.' With this sly dig at Goering, the Fuehrer summed up: 'The prerequisites for "Sea Lion" have not yet been completely realized.'

Not that everyone at the top had lost hope. Army Group A Order No. 1 for the execution of 'Sea Lion' was signed that day – not by General von Runstedt, its commander, who thought 'Sea Lion' a lot of rubbish, but by General Busch, whose 16th Army had the toughest task – forming a beach-head from Folkestone to Worthing. This Order was also signed by Admiral Lutjens, Fleet Commander at Boulogne.

Hitler was still hoping: 'Even if victory in the air can only be won in ten to twelve days, the English might meanwhile succumb to mass hysteria.' The idea gripped Jeschonnek; but he begged to disagree with his Fuehrer: 'Material success exceeds our expectations,' he said, 'but there has as yet been no mass panic, because residential areas have not yet been attacked and destroyed.' The thousands of dead and injured in a week's bombing of London was not enough for this bloodthirsty wretch. He 'wants a free hand in attacking residential areas', noted Halder.

Even Raeder, who passed for an upright, God-fearing sailor, warmly approved the idea. *Gott mit uns.* Blow defenceless women and children to bits any day, rather than risk the necks of his paid hands in that crazy adventure 'Sea Lion'. But Hitler hesitated, sensitive to what the neutrals might think of *der Deutsche Kultur*. 'All right,' he half agreed with Jeschonnek, 'but strategic targets must have first priority. The horrible threat of bombing population centres must be our last trump.' Meanwhile one could count on the 'shorts' and the 'overs' to take a good toll of British civilians.

Yet for all the Germans' talk of mass hysteria and forcing England to her knees, Englishmen saw things differently: 'The attacks were for us a breathing space, of which we had the utmost need,' wrote Winston Churchill of the *Luftwaffe*'s London offensive, which drew the fire away from Fighter Command's bases.

The result of all that animated talk in the Chancellery that day was an order from the Fuehrer to the *Luftwaffe* to keep attacking. 'The air attacks on London are to be continued, the target area to be expanded.' Raeder, sceptical as ever, pointed out that as the air situation would not change before 17 September the date limit for invasion, 27 September, could be pushed back to 8 October. Brauchitsch suggested landing under heavy smoke screens if the *Luftwaffe* could not give support. But Hitler, now that the Admiral had aroused his enthusiasm about the invasion, was not to be put off. That day, 14 September, the RAF defence had been scrappy. Score: 14 – all. Four or five more days, at least four. 'A new order will follow on the 17th. All preparations to continue,' the Fuehrer commanded. Invasion was still on. Let Hermann meanwhile do his damnedest. The *Luftwaffe* were all set for a supreme effort on the morrow.

Kriegsmarine were less hopeful; that night they had to put up with violent RAF attacks from Antwerp to Boulogne. 'At Antwerp, heavy damage . . .'

Since 1.00 p.m. that afternoon the C-in-C of Fighter Command had been visiting his day and night fighter squadrons. Dowding knew better than anyone in England, including Churchill, what England's chances were of survival, for they depended first and foremost on him and his 'fighter-boys'. Dowding was the strategist. He fought the battle well ahead of its day-to-day actions, leaving them entirely in the hands of his group commanders. Not before midday on 15 September did he return to his headquarters at Stanmore.

Air Vice Marshal Keith Park would remember the 15 September as 'one of those days of autumn when the countryside is at its loveliest'. It was his wife's birthday too, but – he apologized at breakfast – he had been so pushed lately he had forgotten to buy her a present. Mrs Park was a cipher officer on her husband's staff; the atmosphere of domesticity was ever present in this life and death struggle for Britain's survival.

Mrs Winston Churchill accompanied the Prime Minister when he dropped in on Park at 11 Group HQ, Uxbridge, at 10.30 a.m. that morning. He sensed the weather was right for the enemy. He was about to witness, in the shuffling of discs on the Ops. Room table and the flashing of coloured bulbs, one of the decisive battles of the war. Like the Battle of Waterloo it was on a Sunday. Park led his visitors down into the Hole, 11 Group's underground Ops. Room. 'All his arrangements and apparatus had been brought to the highest perfection . . . fused together into a most elaborate instrument of war, the like of which existed nowhere in the world.'

On the other side of the Channel the battle was controlled by Kesselring at Cap Blanc Nez and Sperrle at Deauville, with Goering in 'personal command' in his train, *Asia*, at Boulogne. 'The pilots and crews felt repeatedly that victory was almost within their grasp,' wrote *Oberst* Werner Kreipe, of Sperrle's staff. And never more than on that sunny morning. For Goering this day was to be the crowning glory; with London crumbling in ruins and the British on the verge of mass hysteria, and only a handful of British fighters left, today's might be the final assault.

It was 11.00 a.m., and the radar stations were coming alive. Corporal Daphne Griffiths reported from Rye, 'Hullo Stanmore, hostile 6 is now at 15 miles. Height 15,000.' 'How many, Rye?' 'Fifty plus. Plot coming up. Read,' came Daphne's steady voice over the wire to the Fighter Command plotter. Now she could hear the *Mahalla* overhead, a throbbing roar that filled the whole sky. Corporal Syd Hempson, who had been outside to get a 'visual', burst in. 'That was the finest sight I've ever seen yet – our fighters came down from above and simply went right through the lot.' The massed *Kampfgeschwader*, flanked by Me. 110 *Zerstörer*, and rising in columns towards the *Jagdgeschwader* of Galland, Moelders and Trautloft swarming up to two miles above, had to fight for their lives from the moment they crossed the coast.

In 11 Group Ops. Room Churchill watched in silence as the controller, Wing Commander Eric Douglas-Jones, put up twelve squadrons; while these fought the enemy all the way into London, he kept another dozen in reserve and called on 12 Group for reinforcements. Seventeen squadrons, two hundred British fighters.

Bader's 5-squadron wing met the bombers, already in disarray, on the city's southern fringe. 'The finest shambles I've ever been in,' Douglas called it. Caught in this turmoil, it was imposssible for the enemy to achieve accuracy or concentration. Their bombs were scattered for miles across London's southern boroughs, from Tooting to Lambeth, from Lewisham to Kensington. People coming out of church ran for cover. Five miles above Hannes Trautloft wondered, 'Who'd know it was Sunday if it hadn't been announced on the radio?'

A heavy bomb hit Buckingham Palace, another fell on the lawn. Above,

Sergeant Holmes, of 504 Squadron, fired at a Dornier which exploded, sending his Hurricane into a spin. While the Dornier crashed through the roof of Victoria Station its crew were parachuting down on to Kennington Oval Cricket Ground. Holmes's parachute delivered him, less gracefully, in a dustbin in Chelsea; he was extricated by the daughters of the house, who fell on his neck and embraced him.

For Red Tobin, of 609, 'it was the toughest day we had . . . a terrific battle over London'. Red shot at a Me. 109, 'One of the yellow-nosed boys'; then, after sending a Dornier down south of the city, he saw 'a Spitfire . . . spinning down on fire. I sure hope it wasn't Jeff (Gaunt, one of his best friends), and if it was – well – from now on he'll be flying in clearer sky.' In this, as in all battles, the tragic and the comic went hand in hand: while Jeff (for it was he) was crashing to his death, part of a shattered Dornier, noted 609's diarist, 'reached the ground just outside a Pimlico public house, to the great comfort and joy of the patrons'.

A few miles south of Pimlico, I was at that moment preparing to leave the hospital. Adjutant Tim Moloney had said to me, 'Hurry up and get well. If you're not back in three weeks, they'll give us a new squadron commander.' Three weeks would be up on 21 September. I had graduated from crutches, and with a stick and one leg could get around well.

It was seven years to the day that my instructor, Poyntz Roberts had said, 'Off you go,' and I had flown away alone from earth for the first time. My passion had been all for flying. Never did I dream it would lead me into this charnel house where most of my friends had now become burnt and mutilated corpses. Yet transcending all the hideous slaughter was the eternal, immaculate purity of the blue heavens and the notion, which these few days on the ground had sharpened, that we were dying for a country we loved which had nourished us and breathed its formidable, unconquerable spirit into our souls.

Using the clutch with the heel-end, the good end, of my left foot, I drove away from Croydon as the sirens wailed for the second time that day. Through Surrey and over the Hog's Back into the Sussex Weald. In those few hours it became plain to me why this old country would never yield. It had been there too long; it vast ancient wealth lay thickly stored in those clustering villages, those tended fields and orchards, and ancient, steepled churches. Five centuries had passed since Geoffrey Chaucer sang of those joyous, ribald pilgrims who trooped along the Hog's Back to Canterbury; more since the martyr Becket died there defying his tyrannous king; and even more since the rude, warlike Saxons had settled peacefully in Sussex. And nearly nine hundred years since William, the last conqueror. For reasons which Englishmen knew in their souls, but could not explain, there could never be another.

Nine hundred years after William and a stone's throw from where he landed, a girl in pale blue uniform looked into a tube of dancing light and realized more clearly than words could tell how the invader was now being routed. She was Daphne Griffiths: 'First we saw the big formations as wide, deep, steadily beating echoes moving slowly from right to left across the trace, almost majestically . . . The raids making landfall to the east and north of us would slowly decrease in strength until they finally faded, but those approaching Dungeness increased until the echoes were beating to a depth of three to four inches below the trace . . . The tube became saturated for at least ten miles and stayed that way while our fighters broke up the formation, destroyed many of them and sent the rest straggling back home.

'Out of the ground ray would emerge a single echo, then another; a three plus, a two, another one . . . The height readings on many of them would drop fast and we watched, fascinated, as the echo got weaker and weaker until it finally faded – into the drink we hoped!' It was quite another story from the Battle of Hastings.

An hour later the enemy was back in even greater numbers. This time Daphne looked up into the sky, shielding her eyes against the glare, 'It was a sight I shall remember . . . a dense swarm of black insects was advancing on me, each trailing miles of white ribbon . . . I could not take my eyes off those wonderful condensation trails.'

To meet the second, heavier assault 11 Group put up 23 squadrons, calling on 10 Group for three more – about 310 fighters. Winston Churchill realized, 'There was not one squadron in reserve. At this moment Park spoke to Dowding at Stanmore, asking for three squadrons to be put at his disposal . . .' A moment later there were something like 370 British fighters airborne. Somewhere over London *JG* 27, escorting the Dorniers of *KG* 76, ran into a whole mass of them. *Oberleutnant* Ludwig Franzisket could not resist. 'Here they come, boys, the last fifty Spitfires'; for this, according to official sources, was all the RAF had left.

The Dorniers that Bader's sixty-strong 12 Group Wing intercepted were well above. Although his two Spitfire squadrons reached them, Bader and his three Hurricane squadrons were jumped by Me. 109s and dispersed. Douglas was sick with rage. 'Once again off too late.'

In one sense he was right. But the unwieldiness of the Wing was also to blame. Bob Tuck led an 11 Group Wing of only three squadrons off from Debden that afternoon. Thirty-two aircraft. But when he closed on the bombers a meagre little posse of eight fighters were all that he had with him. The rest were straggling below. It was inevitable; scores of fighters took longer to get airborne and collected than a simple, compact dozen. Even a 'pair' was appreciably slower. Time was the deciding factor; and so often in this battle the issue hung on a few fleeting minutes.

While Park walked up and down on the controller's dais, 'watching with a vigilant eye, every move in the game', Churchill's attention was drawn by a 'youngish officer' who sat beside him and continued to relay the orders of his Group Commander in a 'calm, low monotone'. It was John Willoughby de Broke; John, who had forsaken the mastership of the Warwickshire Hounds for the command of an Auxiliary Squadron, was now in the forefront of one of the world's crucial battles. He found his job like a 'glorified game of chess, only infinitely more exciting and responsible, considering that an error of judgment could mean an irreparable loss of life in pilots, and at the docks, airfields and factories, or in the streets of our cities'. John had been on duty when the Prime Minister arrived one day with his secretary. 'This is just what the PM will love,' she told him. 'I've spent week-ends with him reconstructing the Battle of Blenheim with toy soldiers on the library carpet.'

The discs on the operations table were the same idea. So were the coloured lights; the red bulbs showed that nearly all 11 Group squadrons were engaged. Churchill, who had not uttered a word, now noticed Park's anxiety and asked, 'What other reserves have we?' 'There are none,' replied Park tersely. Exactly four months earlier, at the Quai d'Orsay in Paris, Churchill had posed the same question to the French Generalissimo Gamelin, and received the same answer. England could thank its lucky stars that Park had a better grip on things than the pusillanimous French general.

At Boulogne, in his train, *Asia*, Goering waited nervously for progress reports. Christa Gormanns came and went with pills and potions to still his feverish anxiety. At the very moment that the red lamps in 11 Group Ops. Room showed almost all Park's squadrons engaged, Goering's aide, Hauptmann Bernd von Brauchitsch remarked, 'They must be reaching the limit of their resources. Today's assault should complete the operation.'

Brauchitsch was half right. But red lamps were also glowing at that moment in the cockpits of the German Me. 109s. Fuel was running low; there was nothing for it but to turn and run for home. Me. 109 pilots were haunted by that little red lamp; Galland had already lost 12 of his *Jagdgeschwader* in one sortie through ditching and forced-landing short of fuel. Johannes Janke lost nearly his entire *Gruppe* IV *JG* 51. Sticking loyally to their bombers above cloud they only just made the French coast, where forty of the Me. 109s had to crash-land on the beach and in neighbouring fields.

With dogged courage the *Luftwaffe Geschwader* kept flying on in the face of the British fighters and a storm of AA fire. They hurled their bombs down on London's long-suffering East End, but, as in the morning, accuracy and concentration were impossible in the face of such resistance.

Only two units got by relatively unscathed: *KG* 55, whose Heinkels slipped in during the tumult over London and bombed – ineffectively – Portland naval dockyard; and *Erprobungs Gruppe* 210, who, diving to attack the Supermarine works at Southampton, had their aim deflected by AA fire.

By now General Albert Kesselring, appalled by the reports coming in to his Cap Blanc Nez HQ, telephoned to *Asia* and told Goering, 'We cannot keep it up like this; we are falling below the standard of safety.'

Churchill, exhausted on returning to Chequers by the 'drama of 11 Group', did not awake from his afternoon nap until 8 p.m. His chief private secretary, John Martin, came with the news budget. 'It was repellent . . .' – errors, delays, unsatisfactory answers, bad sinkings in the Atlantic. 'However,' said Martin, 'everything is retrieved by the air. We have shot down 183 for a loss of under 40.'

The RAF's own losses were 26, but its claim was a fantastic exaggeration, a phenomenon always most marked in heavy, widespread fighting. 12 Group Wing, for example, claimed 52 destroyed – only 4 short of the total loss of 56 inflicted on the *Luftwaffe* by over thirty squadrons. Fortunately for the British, such exaggerations served as an almighty boost to public morale. But *The Times* for one was not being carried away so easily. 'The figures . . . give grounds for sober satisfaction,' it announced. And Dowding never let the 'score' influence him – only the cold, hard facts. That day they spoke for themselves. Winston Churchill called 15 September 'the culminating date'.

The *Luftwaffe* had to face the bitter truth. Hitler and Goering had had great hopes that day, but in a mighty assault of over 1,300 sorties the

Luftwaffe had been routed by an air force they believed practically *kaput*; losses were higher than they had been for four weeks.

The unhappy *Jäger* were blamed as usual. Bomber crews complained bitterly at having been deserted by their escort and left to the mercy of British fighters, which according to all reports, had ceased to exist. *Luftwaffe*'s Major von Falkenstein at OKW reported 'large air battles and great losses ... due to lack of fighter protection'. OKL reported 'the heavy losses ... are due to British fighters attacking bombers returning in small groups without fighter escort'. The day's operations had been 'unusually disadvantageous'.

That night, RAF bombers were out in force: 'Powerful enemy air attacks along the entire coastal zone between Le Havre and Antwerp,' noted *Kriegsmarine* and sent an SOS for more AA guns.

Beside himself with rage and disappointment, the *Luftwaffe*'s C-in-C summoned his *Luftflotten* and *Fliegerkorps* chiefs to Boulogne on 16 September. 'Our fighters have let us down,' bellowed the purple-faced Goering at the unfortunate *Jäger*. Uncle Theo Osterkamp stood firm: 'While we are chained like dogs to the bombers, the British fighters attack us in ever-increasing numbers.' 'Just what we want,' fumed Goering, still living with the past glories of the Circus, 'we can shoot down all the more.' Uncle Theo knew it was useless to argue.

The object of Goering's London offensive since 7 September was to force up and destroy the last remaining British fighters. But the *Luftwaffe* had had by far the worst of it, losing 190 planes against the British loss of 120 fighters. Fighter Command's situation had improved, but Goering simply could not see it. First he blamed the bad weather; then he maintained, wrongly, that 'all available fighter and AA defence had been assembled in the London area'; that if the enemy failed to defend London, 'so much the better for us, ... we can destroy his capital ... it follows that we should keep at him with all our means, as with four to five more days with heavy losses he ought to be finished off.'

All this was exactly the line he had taken with the Fuehrer before the luncheon on 13 September. The Fuehrer had accepted it, and trotted it out at his next day's meeting. After the *Luftwaffe*'s performance on 15 September he was to be more doubtful about Goering's promises in future ...

In the evening of 16 September I hobbled aboard the destroyer HMS *Viscount* at Southampton. Having made an effort to look presentable in clean uniform, I felt rather stupid when I saw her captain, my brother Michael, standing on the bridge garbed in a white sweater, grey flannel bags and a pair of gym-shoes. 'It's easier to swim like this,' he explained, and I saw his point, having been in the drink myself. We were to join three other destroyers, one of them Polish, in an all-night Channel patrol. As we cast off Michael said, 'If we sink it will be in the next fifteen minutes – they were mining Southampton harbour last night.' All night our little flotilla scoured the Channel, silently, stealthily, in the bright moonlight, searching for signs of the invader. We need not have worried.

Hitler had fixed 17 September for a final decision on 'Sea Lion'. It came in the early hours from OKW in a teleprint message: *Wird Bis Auf Weiteres Verschoben* (postponed until further notice).

Whatever Goering might think, those five words spelled defeat for the *Luftwaffe*. Whether in its original form of a *gewaltsamer Flussue bergang* (a mighty river crossing) or in its pocket edition, a narrow front crossing of the Dover Straits to administer the *coup de grâce* to a bomb-shattered, demoralized enemy, 'Sea Lion' depended, as the Fuehrer had never ceased to repeat, on one essential condition – a *Luftwaffe* victory over the RAF. Once achieved, he could launch 'Sea Lion' in whatever form he chose.

Hitler, for all his havering and quavering, kept invasion preparations going right up to the date limit imposed by moon, tides and general weather conditions, and the ten-day notice required by his navy. That date was 17 September; until then he waited expectantly for Goering to win the vital air battle which, said the *Luftwaffe* chief, would take from four to five days. Thirty-three had already elapsed since *Adlertag*. No doubt Hitler's most fervent hope was that air victory would make an opposed invasion unnecessary; it would simply remain to occupy the country. But according to Ribbentrop, his Foreign Minister, 'the Fuehrer was resolved to conquer England on her own territory . . . he would also carry out that intention'.

Detailed plans were already laid for the Nazi 'New Order' for England. Oddly enough, that very day 'Butcher' Reinhardt Heydrich, deputy to the Gestapo's dreaded chief, Heinrich Himmler, whom Goering so detested, drafted a letter to SS *Oberst* Professor Franz Six, 'By virtue of *Herr Reichsmarschall* Goering's authority I appoint you Representative of the *Sicherheitsdienst* (Security Police) in Great Britain. Your task is to combat all anti-German organizations . . . I designate the capital London as . . . your headquarters.'

Professor Six, an intellectual who specialized in refined, scientific torture and killing, never, of course, got the job. But later he made a name for himself in Russia grilling high officials for the *Einsatzgruppen* SS, the mass murder specialists.

Hitler, acutely embarrassed by Goering's failure to subdue England, summoned the *Luftwaffe's* C-in-C to Berchtesgaden. And Goering, according to his old friend and aide Bodenschatz, was a much chastened man when on 17 September he puffed off in *Asia* to report to his Fuehrer.

The all-conquering *Grosse Feldherr* had suffered a reverse, the first he had ever known in six years of conquest and plunder in Europe. For the first time in history, a tyrant had been frustrated by a decisive battle in the air. Hitler missed out on invasion – and England. He would prevaricate, of course: 'Germany 'had already achieved air superiority . . . absolute mastery of the air was indisputable . . . the resistance of British fighters would grow weaker,' Ribbentropp would tell Mussolini a couple of days later, not forgetting the 'gigantic preparations' which had been made to invade England. Ciano was convinced Hitler meant business, but he did not share his optimism. 'This may be a long war,' he noted.

That problem stemmed from Hitler's failure to attain the very plausible aim defined in his original Invasion Directive No. 16 which was 'to eliminate the English homeland as a base for the prosecution of the war against Germany . . .' The starkest fact in Hitler's life at present was that the English homeland had not been eliminated. But Hitler's vision was clouded by his enthusiasm for exterminating the Russians. When a week later Raeder tried to convince the self-styled military genius that the war was getting 'on the wrong track', that England was always the main danger, Hitler argued him round. Yet if anyone understood the English it was that wary salthorse – certainly not the ex-corporal who disliked getting his feet wet.

So England, far from being eliminated, would remain intact as the one thing Hitler feared, 'a base for the continued prosecution of the war', a base from which to send convoys to Russia, a base for fighting the Germans in North Africa, a base for RAF and American bombers to blast Germany into ruins, a base from which to invade Europe and liberate it from Nazi domination – a base, in short, which would be a perpetual thorn in Hitler's side and cause his ruin.

The British Prime Minister told Parliament on 17 September, 'Sunday's (15 September) action was the most brilliant and fruitful of any fought . . . by the fighters of the Royal Air Force . . .' Churchill saw the future clearly: 'We may await the decision of this long air battle with sober but increasing confidence.'

Hermann Goering did not agree. He never had much faith in 'Sea Lion', but he still believed he could eliminate England his own way. It would take a little longer to disillusion him. While Hermann was trying to make amends with his Fuehrer on 18 September, seventeen RAF fighter squadrons were battling with 190 *Luftwaffe* planes at the approaches to London. The British actually outnumbered the enemy and when Douglas Bader's 12 Group Wing had finished with a formation of forty bombers, enemy parachutes were floating down everywhere. They had never seen so many. But once again, in the whirling confusion of sixty fighters, claims became doubled and trebled. The Wing claimed thirty destroyed, but only nineteen enemy aircraft were lost that day. But, most important, the enemy had again been routed.

The *Kriegsmarine*, rejoicing on the postponement decision of the day before, raised another cheer when the order was issued: 'Stop further assembly of transport units of every kind.' Next day yet another order hastened the scuttling of 'Sea Lion': 'Shipping to be dispersed.' That day there were over one thousand barges in Channel ports (not to speak of some 3,000 other vessels); by the end of September there would be less than seven hundred. Barges and motor boats were withdrawn into canals, and rivers, steamers and tugs spread around to neighbouring ports.

I reached Church Fenton, Yorkshire, on 21 September and made for 85 Squadron's dispersal point. The wound in my foot prevented my walking, but I could still fly. It only remained to prove it by putting a Hurricane through its paces. That day the station doctor cleared me as fully fit to resume command of 85 Squadron.

After his *tête-à-tête* with the Fuehrer, Goering returned to Paris for a conference at Sperrle's HQ in the Palais Luxembourg on 20 September. *Der Dicke* still maintained his *Luftwaffe* would defeat the RAF, but his generals found him subdued and unconvincing. When *Asia* steamed out of the Gare du Nord, both he and they were quite frankly glad to see the last of each other. Goering was tired of being a *Reichsmarschall*, but he held another office which could offer him more rewarding pleasures, that of *Reichsjägermeister*. Next day *Asia* brought him to Rominten in East Prussia, to his hunting lodge, the *Reichsjaegerhof*, a log cabin with a thatched roof jutting out over the eaves. It would be infinitely more restful to follow the war from there.

Adolf Galland, No. 2 fighter ace after Moelders, and Knight of the Iron Cross, was ordered to Berlin on 25 September to receive the *Eichenlaub*, Oak Leaves, or *Blumenkohl*, Cauliflower, as they were irreverently called. He found himself alone with Adolf Hitler and in a lengthy talk expressed his 'greatest admiration for the enemy across the water'. He was embittered by the false commentaries by the press and radio which reviled the RAF. Galland, always outspoken, expected a rebuff from the Fuehrer. But not a bit of it. Hitler agreed with every word; his great respect for the Anglo-Saxon race had made it all the harder for him to enter this life and death struggle with England, which must end in the destruction of one of them. If it was to be Britain, that would leave a void impossible to fill. Hitler spoke passionately of his sympathy for the English race, of his admiration for their leaders. 'The English are a hundred years ahead of us'; their inherent virtues were now, in this critical moment of their history, showing up. Hitler's great regret was that he had not been able to bring the English and the Germans together.

Hitler's sympathy for the English did not prevent his bombers that day from killing and wounding 250 men and women workers in the Bristol Aeroplane factory at Filton. Nor from sending 200 bombers to attack London that night. Werner Borner's Dornier was one; it was hit by AA fire and limped back on one engine towards France. Before they reached the coast Werner and his comrades were in trouble.

Bale out! came the order; the flight engineer jumped first. Werner was next – but there was the sea below – and he quickly changed his mind. Werner's luck never failed for at that moment the engine picked up again and they managed to make Arras St Leger safely. Meanwhile the flight engineer, blown inland by a strong west wind, was celebrating his birthday with his rescuers near Abbeville.

The bomber crews felt the *Jäger* were showered with medals while they were forgotten. So in *KG* 2 they invented their own order of chivalry. A straw boater for 80 flights over enemy territory; for 100, a grey bowler; for 120, a grey top hat; over 120, a grey topper with *Eichenlaub* (oak leaves), though not quite the same as Galland had received from Hitler that day.

The incessant night raids on London brought no joy to Karl Missy. Since 15 September fewer wounded prisoners had been arriving at the hospital in Woolwich. Those that came told of the invasion fleet dispersing. The sound of the day bombing was fading into the distance and the special air raid guard, the ones who dived under the bed, did not come any more. And now with the days shortening no one believed in the invasion which they hoped would free them. Gradually, sadly, Karl Missy gave up all hope of an early return to Kohlerstrasse.

No thoughts of *bomben auf England* disturbed Adolf Galland that 26 September. His mind was on a promised shooting holiday. 'He would hunt anything from a man to a sparrow,' said Hans-Heinrich Brustellin of Galland. And when he ran low in aircraft he would shoot a few partridges and send them to Goering, asking for Me. 109s in return. Now he came as Goering's guest to the *Reichsjaegerhof*.

The *Luftwaffe* chief was in his element, hundreds of miles from the anxieties of personal command, from the battle which was costing the *Luftwaffe* so dearly in young lives and precious aircraft.

As Galland arrived Goering came out of the house 'wearing a green suede hunting jacket over a silk blouse with long, puffed sleeves, high hunting boots, and in his belt a hunting knife. He was in the best of humour . . . his worries about the *Luftwaffe* in the Battle of Britain seemed to have been spirited away.'

It was rutting time; the stags were roaring in the forest, and Goering had a special treat for Adolf Galland: a *Reichsjägermeister* stag, a royal beast. They talked hunting and shooting late into the night. Although that evening *Luftflotte* 3 made a devastating raid on the Spitfire works at Southampton, 'no mention was made of the war in general or the Battle of Britain in particular'.

Galland was up early on the morning of 27 September but not as early as the *Jäger* in the Pas de Calais. By 8 a.m. they were already streaming in over Dungeness with a *Gruppe* of Me. 110 *Jagd-bomber*. The *Jäger* fought hard all the way to London and stayed on over the target to clear the air for two more bomber waves – which never made it, so violent was the British fighters' resistance.

The *Jagd* over London was more arduous, less rewarding than the one in the Rominterheide. By the time the Me. 109s were back, dejectedly counting their losses, *Jäger* Galland had shot his stag, a 'stag of a lifetime'. His one thought then was to get back to his beloved *Jagdgeschwader* 26. But Goering would not have it; the daily reports from *Luftflotten* 2 and 3 would be in by the evening and they would examine them together. So Galland stayed to a 'perfect lunch'; his host was in cracking form and afterwards sent him off to walk around the lake while he himself got down to some paperwork.

Two hours later, an orderly showed Galland into the *Reichsmarschall*'s office. He was amazed at the change in Goering, who had joked and laughed so freely at lunch and now seemed completely shattered. With a weary gesture he pointed at the reports which had just come in. 'I glanced through them,' said Galland. 'The news was indeed catastrophic; in this latest attack on London we had suffered greater losses than at the start of the battle . . .'

The *Luftwaffe* had suffered a defeat nearly as grievous as that of 15 September – 55 planes, 34 of them fighters. 28 RAF fighters were lost. The RAF Spitfires and Hurricanes had broken up and routed most of the bomber *Geschwader* before they reached London; and more, they had overwhelmed the strong German fighter escorts.

'Goering was very shaken,' said Galland. 'He could not understand why our losses kept on increasing.' He asked Galland to give him the true story. 'Don't keep anything back,' he said. So Galland told his C-in-C what he had told his Fuehrer a couple of days before: despite the large numbers of British fighters destroyed, the enemy showed no decrease in strength, nor any lowering of morale. On the contrary, the RAF was giving it back to the *Luftwaffe* blow for blow.

It was after that disastrous day which had so shaken Goering that Dowding at last felt sure his fighters were winning; for the Germans changed their tactics, attacking with formations of only 30 bombers, escorted by 200 to 300 fighters. The *Luftwaffe* had a last attempt on London on the 30th and lost 47 more planes.

In the airy spaces of the *Rominterheide* Goering pondered on Galland's words, and the stark truth already acknowledged by his subordinates at last dawned on him: the *Luftwaffe*'s efforts to secure control of the air over Britain had failed. Well might he order a change in tactics, promise 'with four or five days of heavy losses' the RAF fighters would be finished off. But it was the *Luftwaffe*'s losses which had more than doubled the RAF's since that humiliating reverse on 15 September.

With things going from bad to worse, the mass daylight raids were called off. Kesselring gave the reason: 'Because our losses were too high; because we didn't have enough fighters to escort the bombers.' Uncle Theo Osterkamp confirmed, 'Our fighters were practically annihilated' – yet at the outset he had insisted 'never let the loss ratio exceed 1 to 5 in our favour'.

Sperrle had always warned, 'There are more British fighters than you think.' His Chief of Operations, *Oberst* Werner Kreipe, said 'The *Luftwaffe* was bled almost to death, and suffered losses which would never again be made good throughout the course of the war.'

Goering had a last·card up his sleeve. Since the *Jäger* had failed to protect the bombers, let them do the bombing themselves. He ordered a third of each *Jagdgeschwader* to be converted to *Jagd-bombers*, '*jabo*', to carry a 500-pound bomb. The Me. 109s, *Jäger* and *jabo* now took over the offensive – again, the significance was not lost on Dowding: the *jabo* could have no more than a nuisance value.

The *Jäger* were crestfallen. Galland himself felt 'impotent with rage'. Goering's continual reproaches had already caused deep resentment among the *Jäger*, lowered their morale. Now they bitterly criticized him and the High Command in general. With the bomber force out of the day battle, the fighter force, already woefully short of aircraft, were further weakened by this thankless bombing role.

That astute old veteran General Theo Osterkamp boiled with indignation at this 'senseless order'. As *Jafu* 2, chief of *Luftflotte* 2's fighters, no one knew more than he about the fighter arm. In despair he asked Jeschonnek the reason for such a stupid decision. The *Luftwaffe* Chief of Staff could do nothing; it was a personal order of the Fuehrer's. 'We have very reliable information,' he said, 'that the English are completely demoralized. The next bomb might well be the one which will make them crack.'

'I then realized,' said Uncle Theo, 'that we had finally lost the Battle of Britain.'

Dowding, with a sigh of relief, had come to the same conclusion.

Epilogue

During October, the curtain gradually fell on the daylight phase of the Battle of Britain. With the days shortening and the autumn weather closing in, it was now too late for the *Luftwaffe* to retrieve the situation. By day, Dowding's fighters remained the undisputed masters of Britain's skies.

Dowding had all along been the architect of victory, labouring for over four years in the conviction that it could only be won 'by science thoughtfully applied to operational requirements'. His principal commander, Park, was the master tactician; with a greatly outnumbered fighting force he had outwitted and repulsed a courageous, determined enemy.

If the Battle's full significance was not yet realized, it was clear enough that Dowding and Park had gained a unique, decisive victory. Britain was saved from a peril against which her ancient, trusted shield, the Navy, was impotent.

But the victorious air marshals, at whose hands Hitler had suffered his first defeat, were not acclaimed. Dowding, it is true, was raised on 30 September, to the dignity of Knight Grand Commander of the Bath. Soon afterwards he was replaced by Sholto Douglas as Commander-in-Chief, Fighter Command. Park was also replaced – by Leigh Mallory – and relegated, one might say, to Training Command.

The two victors thus realized the sad truth: that men are seldom grateful for their saviours. But in this case the British people, themselves under heavy fire from the enemy, could be forgiven for not knowing that they owed their salvation to Dowding and Park, especially as both men remained in the background throughout the Battle.

Shortly before being removed from their posts, both were summoned to appear before the Air Council, not to be thanked, but to answer for their conduct of operations. They had vanquished the foe but not, apparently, in the approved fashion.

Keith Park relates, 'One evening at the end of October, Dowding told me that the Air Ministry wished me to accompany him to a conference there the following morning. Imagine my surprise to find those in attendance included Sir Archibald Sinclair (Air Minister), Chief of Air Staff Newall and his successor, Sir Marshal Portal. Sitting in an honoured place at the table was Air Vice Marshal Leigh-Mallory, supported by Squadron Leader Douglas Bader.' The Deputy Chief of Air Staff Sholto Douglas took the chair.

How things had changed since that night at Wertangles in 1917 when, at Park's invitation, Sholto Douglas had attended the film show in 48 Squadron's hangar, and dived under the piano when the bombs started falling. Now, as Park said, Sholto 'was the public prosecutor. He asked why I had not, throughout the Battle of Britain, adopted the big wing formations which had been used so successfully by Leigh-Mallory.'

Only a few weeks earlier, on 15 September, the Prime Minister had stood beside Park, watching in admiration as he manoeuvred his squadrons to win 'the most brilliant and fruitful' action up to date. Now the victorious commander of 11 Group felt he was on trial, accused of mishandling his forces. 'I explained to the august gathering that it was a time and distance problem ... The short warning I received of the approach of the enemy formations was not time enough for me to despatch, assemble, climb and manoeuvre wings of three, let alone five squadrons, before [the enemy] had unloaded their bombs on vital targets. I explained that I should have lost the Battle of Britain had I allowed uninterrupted bombing of fighter aerodromes, aircraft factories – and London ... Further, my clumsy fighter wings would themselves have been attacked by the enemy fighters who had the advantage of height and sun.'

Leigh-Mallory then spoke. According to Douglas Bader, he said that the 12 Group Wing had proved that big formations paid handsomely as long as they could be organized from airfields in the rear. The 12 Group Wing should have taken off first to meet the enemy, and the 11 Group squadrons, 'which had taken off later', would pursue the retreating bombers. Considering Park's airfields had been blown to bits, sometimes under the very noses of 12 Group's fighters, Park was not very enthusiastic about keeping his squadrons waiting about on the ground, while 12 Group charged the enemy. 'Leigh-Mallory floundered a bit,' relates Park, 'then called on Squadron Leader Bader.'

The core of Bader's argument was 'it is much more economical to put up a hundred aircraft against a hundred than twelve against a hundred', and no one could dispute the principle. But, as the Battle on the 15th showed, Park sometimes had as many as 250 of his fighters in the air at once – in compact, flexible units of twelve or twenty-four.

Park knew he had the full support of his C-in-C. Moreover he felt that the inquisition amounted to a personal attack directed at Dowding and himself, especially as Brand, the 10 Group commander, who had supported Park so well, was not present.

To Park it seemed that the Air Minister and Chief of Air Staff 'appeared not only interested but pleased with the Air Council meeting at which Dowding and I were condemned — that is the only word. The Wings controversy was used as a pretext for dismissing Dowding. I was also sacked.'

The Battle of Britain was over; it would prove to be one of the most crucial battles in history. A few weeks later the victors retired into the shade. Twenty-eight years later Dowding told an American journalist: 'I felt a bit sorry at having to retire in the middle of the war. But they had every justification in putting somebody else in instead.' For well over four years he had been C-in-C Fighter Command, a post whose normal tenure was three years. Park was more trenchant. He said: 'To my dying day I shall feel bitter at the base intrigue which was used to remove Dowding and myself as soon as we had won the Battle of Britain.'

'The Reichsmarschall never forgave us for not conquering England,' said *Oberst* Keller, later to become his Chief or Staff. Furious and frustrated, Goering brooded in his Rominten retreat. The British had baulked him from the start, made a fool of him when he tried to gatecrash the 1937 Coronation, turned up their noses at his furtive efforts to save the peace, and now humiliated him by repulsing his invincible *Luftwaffe*. But he had not finished with them, not by a long chalk.

In the autumnal peace of the Rominterheide he was dreaming up more tortures for the recalcitrant British. On 7 October he defined the *Luftwaffe's* new aims: 'Progressive and complete annihilation of London'; the 'paralysing' of Britain's war potential and civil life; and, through terror and privation, the 'demoralization of the civil population of London and its provinces'. These congenial tasks he allotted almost exclusively to his night bombers whom he would exhort with the words, 'Your indefatigable, courageous attacks . . . have reduced British plutocracy to fear and terror. The losses you have inflicted on the much-vaunted Royal Air Force are irreplaceable . . . ' Once again his 'windy wordiness' (the expression was Churchill's) concealed the truth: Fighter Command, on the verge of defeat a month ago, now had more pilots and machines than when the Battle started.

On 20 October Goering called a halt to day bomber attacks; the night offensive against Britain's cities was well under way. That day Dowding declared Fighter Command would never rest until 'we can locate, pursue and shoot down the enemy by day and by night'. The following day I received a signal from Fighter Command H.Q.: '85 Squadron will in future operate as a night fighter squadron.' A grim task lay ahead. While the enemy laid waste our cities, we would grope for him in the night skies until he turned away seven months later to unleash his invading hordes on Russia.

Visiting Berlin on 12 November, Russian Foreign Commissar Molotov was whisked off to the Wilhelmstrasse air raid shelter when the RAF bombers appeared overhead. Even then, Ribbentrop kept up his refrain, 'England is defeated, the war is won . . .' 'Then whose are those bombers overhead,' asked the Russian icily, 'and what are we doing in this shelter?' Neither Molotov nor Ribbentrop could yet tell, but Germany's doom was sealed.

It was not until nearly three years after the Battle of Britain ended that Karl Missy was repatriated and returned to 43 Dohlerstrasse. It was here, in his tidy little house, that I called on him one day in the summer of 1968, here where he was born and where his father started him off in the plumbing trade. The old man had brought Karl up to be honest and hard-working like himself, and a first class tradesman. It was from this house, where I now sat talking to Karl Missy, that he had set out on the road which would lead him into a gun battle with me.

He reminded me of what I had said (his pilot, Hermann Wilms had interpreted) when I saw him in Whitby Hospital next day, 'Sorry for having shot you down. English and German airmen should only try to compete with each other in peacetime.'

Looking at him now and listening to his story, I realized how futile it was to have tried to kill a man like Missy – a good, solid type, the kind the world needs. It was a pity that he had to leave his plumbing and go off to fight for Adolf Hitler. But now that affair is settled, Karl Missy and I can look each other straight in the face, despite the harm I have done to him. That is a small victory at least for humanity.

The last time Werner Borner had seen me was in 1940 when he looked down the barrel of his machine gun, trying desperately to shoot me. Now he greeted me in his home at Münster as if I had been a long-lost friend. He told me, 'It felt great when I shot you down, but it's better still to see you here today.' Could I bear any grudge against Missy, Borner and their comrades? On our side, we felt we were fighting for a just cause. And they?

I did not ask Karl or Werner what they were fighting for; probably they did not give the question much thought. I hope not, in view of the verdict that civilization has passed on their leaders. One of them, as he stood before the gallows confessed, 'A thousand years may pass, but still the guilt of Germany will not be wiped out.'

Appendix

Diagrams and essential features of the main British and German aeroplanes used in the Battle of Britain.

RAF
Fighters

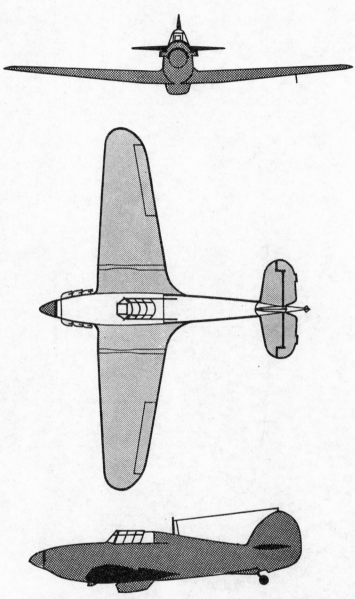

HURRICANE Single-seater monoplane. One Rolls-Royce Merlin engine (1,030 h.p.). Dimensions: wingspan 44·8 feet; length 33·8 feet; height 16·2 feet. Weight (empty) 2·3 tons, (loaded) 3·2 tons. Weapons: eight ·303 in. Browning machine-guns. Maximum speed: 320–330 m.p.h. Initial rate of climb: 2,616 feet per minute. Range: 560–620 miles. Built by Hawker.

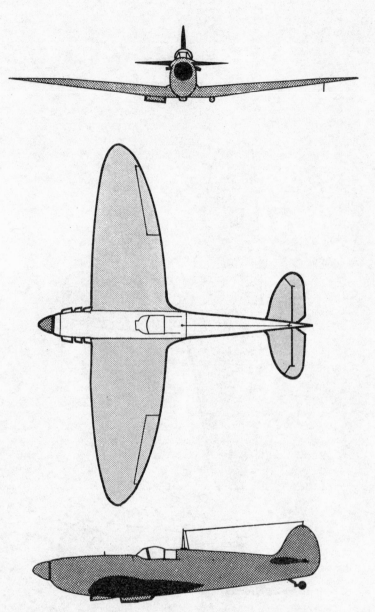

SPITFIRE Single-seater monoplane. One Rolls-Royce Merlin engine (1,030 h.p.). Dimensions: wingspan 39 feet; length 32 feet; height 13 feet. Weight (empty) 2·5 tons, (loaded) 3·1 tons. Weapons: eight ·303 in. Browning machine-guns. Maximum speed 353 m.p.h. Initial rate of climb 2,780 feet per minute. Range: 370 miles. Built by Supermarine (Vickers-Armstrong).

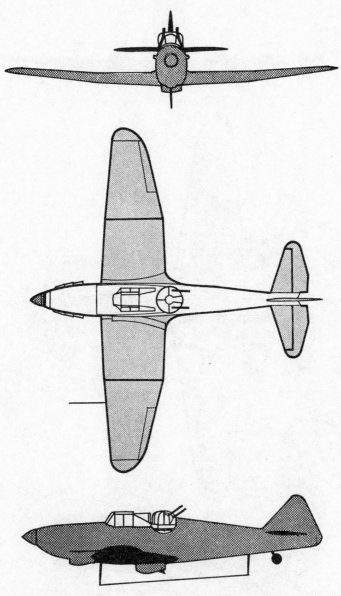

Defiant Two-seater monoplane. One Rolls-Royce Merlin engine (1,030 h.p.). Dimensions: wingspan 42 feet; length 38 feet; height 13 feet. Weight (empty) 3·1 tons, (loaded) 3·55 tons. Weapons: hydraulic tower with four Browning machine-guns, fire power towards the rear.

Maximum speed 298 m.p.h. Initial rate of climb: 2,224 feet per minute. Range: 590 miles. Built by Boulton Paul Aircraft.

BLENHEIM Two-seater monoplane. Two Mercury engines (840 h.p. each). Dimensions: wingspan 60 feet; length 43 feet; height 11 feet. Weight (empty) 4 tons, (loaded) 6.2 tons. Weapons: five machine-guns at front, one at rear (later two). Maximum speed 260 m.p.h. Initial rate of climb: 1,635 feet per minute. Range: 1,074 miles. Built by Bristol Aeroplane Co.

Luftwaffe
Bombers
and
Fighters

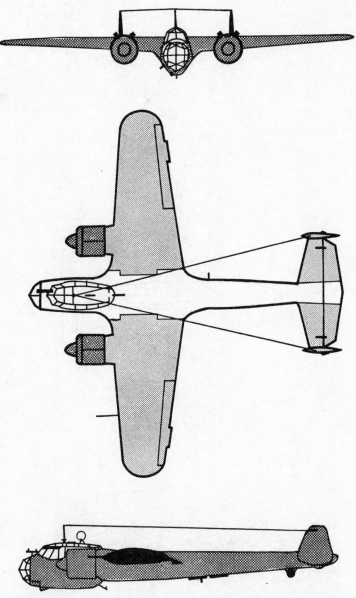

DORNIER 17 Monoplane for crew of four. Bomber (originally planned for the *Lufthansa*). Two Bramo engines (1,000 h.p. each). Dimensions: wingspan 62 feet; length 57 feet; height 17 feet. Weight (empty) 5·9 tons, (loaded) 9–10 tons (1,100–2,200 lb. of bombs). Weapons: six 7·9 mm. machine-guns (two fore, one dorsal, one ventral, two laterals). For the Battle of Britain two machine-guns and one 20 mm. cannon were added. Maximum speed: 263 m.p.h. Range: 680–1,740 miles. Built by Dornier.

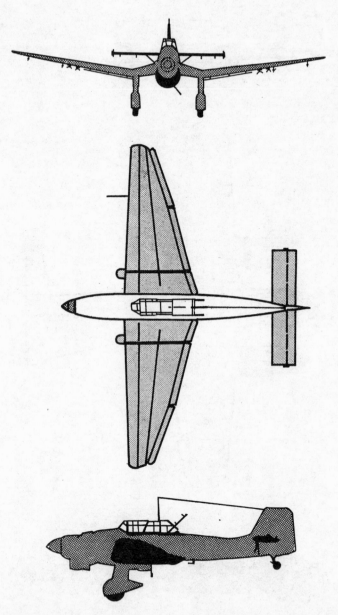

JUNKERS 87 B STUKA Two-seater monoplane. Dive bomber. One Jumo engine (1,150 h.p.). Dimensions: wingspan 49 feet; length 39 feet; height 14 feet. Weight (empty) 3 tons, (loaded) 4·8 tons (one 1,100-lb. bomb under under the fuselage or a 550-lb. bomb in the same place plus four 110-lb. bombs under the wings). Weapons: three machine-guns. Maximum speed 230 m.p.h. Range: 500–800 miles. Made by Junkers.

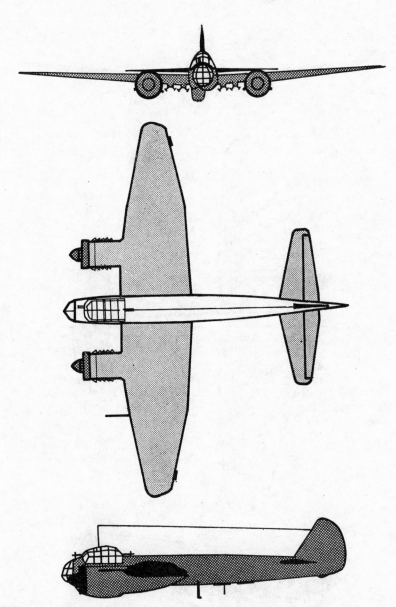

JUNKERS 88 Monoplane for crew of four. Medium and dive bomber with speed of a
fighter. Two Jumo engines (1,220 h.p. each). Dimensions: wingspan 62 feet; length 51
feet; height 16 feet. Weight (loaded) 13·5 tons (4,400–5,500 lb. of bombs). Weapons:
three machine-guns. Maximum speed 280 m.p.h. Range: 1,426 miles. Built by Junkers.

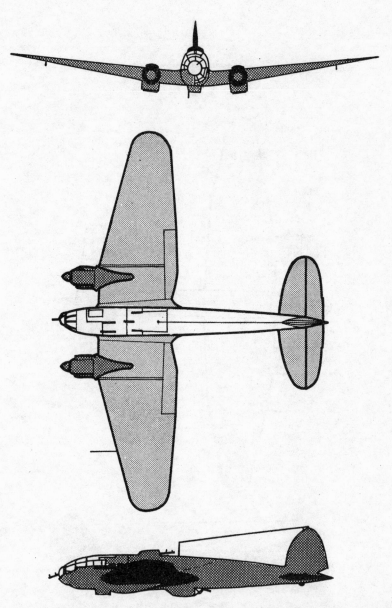

HEINKEL 111 Monoplane for crew of five or six. Bomber (particularly effective at night). Two Jumo engines (1,200 h.p. each). Dimensions: wingspan 77 feet; length 59 feet; height 15 feet. Weight (empty) 7 tons, (loaded) 12·5–13·2 tons (2,200–4,400 lb. of bombs). Weapons: five 7·9 mm. machine-guns and one 20 mm. cannon. Maximum speed: 254 m.p.h. Range: 680–1,420 miles. Built by Heinkel.

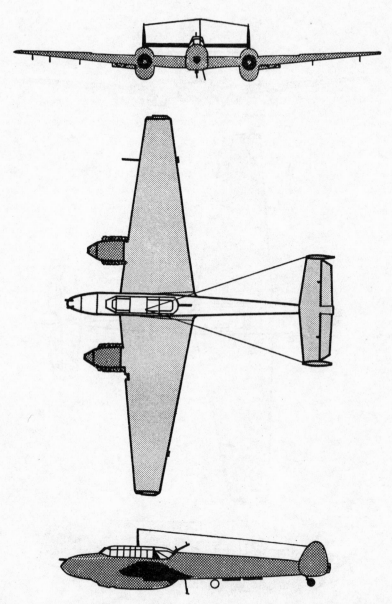

MESSERSCHMITT 110 ZERSTÖRER (DESTROYER) Two-seater monoplane. Long-range escort plane. Two Daimler-Benz engines (1,100 h.p. each). Dimensions: wingspan 56 feet; length 42 feet; height 13 feet. Weight (loaded) 7·5 tons. Weapons: five machine-guns and two 20 mm. cannons. Maximum speed: 335 m.p.h. Rate of climb: 2,000 feet per minute. Range: 600–745 miles. Built by Messerschmitt.

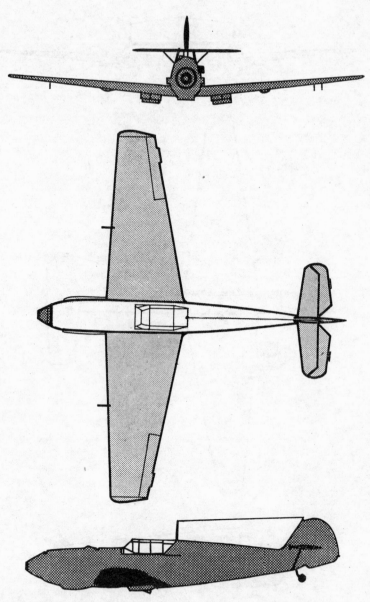

MESSERSCHMITT 109 E–3 Single-seater monoplane. Fighter. One Daimler–Benz engine
(1,150 h.p.). Dimensions: wingspan 34 feet; length 28 feet; height 9 feet. Weight (empty)
1·2 tons, (loaded) 2·75 tons. Weapons: two machine-guns and two 20 mm. cannons.
Maximum speed: 350 m.p.h. Initial rate of climb: 3,270 feet per minute. Range: 400
miles. Built by Messerschmitt.

Index

441

Q

R

Index